CW00740460

THE

REFORMERS

BEFORE THE REFORMATION.

The Fifteenth Century.

JOHN HUSS AND THE COUNCIL OF CONSTANCE.

BY EMILE DE BONNECHOSE,

LIBRARIAN TO THE KING OF FRANCE.

AUTHOR OF "HISTOIRE DE FRANCE" "HISTOIRE SACRÉE," &c.

"In ea tempora natus es quibus firmare animum expediat constantibus exemplis."
Tacitus, lib. xvi.

L'homme n'est un homme et ne demeure libre et vrai qu'à condition de rester au pouvoir de sa conscience, ce qui est la vraie liberté."
Vinet.

Translated from the French,

BY CAMPBELL MACKENZIE, B. A.,

TRIN. COL., DUBLIN.

COMPLETE IN ONE VOLUME.

NEW YORK:
HARPER AND BROTHERS.
1844.

CONTENTS.

HISTORICAL INTRODUCTION.—I. Origin of the Great Schism of the West.—Division of Europe.—II. Continuance of the Schism—Its disastrous effects.—The Courts of Avignon and of Rome. III. Efforts of France to bring about the Union. IV. Council of Pisa.—Continuance of the Schism.—Manifestation of the Public Mind.—V. Wycliffe and Gerson............................Page 9

BOOK I.

CHAP. I. The Early Life of John Huss—His Doctrines—Discussions in the University.. 29

CHAP. II. First Disturbances at Prague.—Election of John XXIII.—The first Exile of Huss—His internal Conflicts............................ 32

CHAP. III. State of Parties in Bohemia.—Jerome of Prague.—Bulls of the Pope against Ladislaus.—Refutation of them by John Huss.—Fresh Troubles at Prague 36

CHAP. IV. Progress of the Hussites.—Controversies.—Second Retirement of Huss.—Convocation of a General Council at Constance..................... 42

BOOK II.

CHAP. I. Departure and Presentiments of John Huss—His Journey—Arrival at Constance............................ 49

CHAP. II. Composition of the Council of Constance.—Subjects and Order of the Deliberations.—Canonization of St. Bridget..................... 53

CHAP. III. Arrest of John Huss.—Arrival of the Emperor..................... 56

CHAP. IV. Struggle between the Pope and the Emperor.—Huss in Prison.—Flight of John XXIII............................. 58

CHAP. V. Proceedings of the Emperor and the Council against the Pope.—Speech delivered by Gerson, and conclusions of the University of Paris.—Intrigues of John XXIII.—Measures of the Emperor.—Second flight of John XXIII.—Decrees of the Fifth Session.—Fresh flight of John XXIII. 63

CHAP. VI. Judgment and Condemnation of Wycliffe and his Works..................... 69

CHAP. VII. Arrest of Jerome of Prague—His first Examination—His Imprisonment... 72

CHAP. VIII. Submission of Frederick of Austria.—Condemnation and Deposition of John XXIII—His Removal to Gotleben..................... 75

BOOK III.

CHAP. I. The Cup............................. 80

CHAP. II. Abdication of Gregory XII............................. 83

CHAP. III. John Huss before his Trial............................. 85

CHAP. IV. Trial of John Huss.—First and Second Audiences..................... 89

Page

Chap. V. Continuation of the Trial of John Huss.—Third and Last Audience........ 93
Chap. VI. Firmness of John Huss.—Last Interview................................... 96
Chap. VII. John Huss takes leave of his Friends—His Condemnation—His Death..... 100
Chap. VIII. The Affair of John Petit.—Gerson accused of Heresy...................... 106
Chap. IX. Journey of the Emperor.—Benedict XIII.—Capitulation of Narbonne....... 111
Chap. X. Bohemia, after John Huss's Death.. 115
Chap. XI. Jerome of Prague.. 117
Chap. XII. Sentence and Execution of Jerome.. 121

BOOK IV.

Chap. I. Disputes concerning the Reformation of the Church and the Election of the
    Pope.. 126
Chap. II. Decrees relative to the Reformation of the Church and the Election of the
    Pope.—The Conclave.—Election and Coronation of Martin V........... 130
Chap. III. The Reforms.. 134
Chap. IV. Affair of the Poles and the Monk Falkenberg.—Decrees and Bulls of Mar-
    tin V.—Close of the Council... 139
Chap. V. General Considerations on the Council of Constance.—Results of the Council
    and of the Schism, relating to the Gallican Church and the Reformation 145

BOOK V.

Chap. I. Continuation and End of the Schism....................................... 149
Chap. II. France and Gerson... 151
Chap. III. Bohemia and the Hussites to the Death of Ziska........................... 156
Chap. IV. The Hussites after Ziska... 165
Chap. V. The Moravians, or the United Brethren of Bohemia......................... 173
Conclusion.. 177

NOTES.. 181

PREFACE.

AFTER the accomplishment of great events, the most useful work is, perhaps, to perpetuate their remembrance; and it is doing good service to humanity to hold up to its admiration such noble actions as redound to its honour. We love the men who dispute with time the memory of those whom they revere, like that Puritan of the olden-day, whose indefatigable hand restored on the monumental stone the half-defaced inscriptions of his people.* That was also a Christian work*which the famous Bollandists performed, when they consecrated their lives to the task of collecting the marvellous legends of the Saints in the Catholic church;† and similar was the conduct of John Fox, who wore out his existence in seeking out the acts of the martyrs who perished in the primitive church, and in the early days of Protestantism.‡ The object of these pious labours was to arouse the faith, to stimulate men's minds by great examples, and to show, in the midst of the struggles carried on against human powers, the irresistible power of divine grace operating in the heart of the Christian.

And yet, something has been wanting in such works; for they have not been marked by a character of universality. It is too clearly felt that the authors of them lived in an age when each person was so penetrated with reverence for his own religious tenets, that he did not feel sufficient respect for those of others; and considered none worthy of esteem, who were to be found outside the pale of his own church. The sentiments which we desire to inspire our readers with, are respect for all convictions that are truly Christian—for all instances of disinterested devotedness, under whatever banner they are displayed—and gratitude towards every one who, during eighteen centuries,

* Robert Patterson—*Old Mortality*—(Scott.)
† *Acta Sanctorum.*
‡ Fox's *Acts and Monuments of Martyrs.*

has contributed a stone to the Christian edifice. Such are the sentiments which, above all, it is important to diffuse at the approach of the religious movement which, at present, gives indications of its coming.

It is with this object, that it is useful in the present day to call attention to a man whom no church in particular is entitled to lay claim to, as belonging to it alone, but who appertains to all which repose on the double foundation of faith in the gospel, and respect for the rights of conscience. That man is JOHN HUSS. None, better than he, has taught by his life and by his death, that without sincerity of heart, without obedience to the convictions of the mind, and without courage to declare them, there is neither true religion nor solid piety.

Do we find this courage in France? Is liberty of conscience written in our hearts as it is in our laws? In fine, has the conscience, up to the present day, possessed a sufficient share in the religious movement of the epoch? It may be permitted to doubt it. Society, in fact, presents a strange phenomenon; and two orders of facts are seen to take place together, which might be supposed quite incompatible. Much noise is made about a Christian awakening; and yet nothing is heard but bitter complaints about the moral condition of the age. The spiritual wants of mankind are intellectually an object of the most serious attention; and notwithstanding, vile gratifications are eagerly sought after in works of imagination. The chambers, the press, the drawing-room, resound with religious interests; but how many persons are there who feel seriously concerned in religion for its own sake alone? Men call themselves Christians, and boast of the evangelical word; but how many have opened the gospel? They declare themselves to be Catholics; but what do they understand by Catholicism? One beholds in it the

1

ancient traditions; another, the logical connection of certain principles; this person regards its external pomp, its happy alliance with the arts; that other, the imposing hierarchy of its power, the powerful institution of the theocratical government, the masterpiece of time and of the genius of man. But are there many who behold Catholicism in what really constitutes the church—its doctrines? Are there many who examine what relations exist between these doctrines and the nature of God and of man, with the ideas which they themselves entertain of the other world; or with the state of society in the present one? The greater number imagine that they believe, because they admire: and without reflection they repeat the common saying, "Our worship is that of our fathers;" never considering that if their fathers had said the same, they would have remained stupidly cowering down before some idol, and that human blood would still flow on the altars of the Druids. In all this may be perceived the effect of habit, or of a blind compliance, but no sign of faith.

The name of the Redeemer, it is true, is met with at each page of some boasted productions, but the Saviour whom they extol is not he who instructed mankind in prayer, resignation, and devotedness; the canvas and the marble reproduce, everywhere, the figure of Christ, but where is the imaginary form found to represent the sublime beauty of the immortal type? And how many accusing works, rapidly thrown off, bear testimony against those who have been in such haste to produce them? Is the artist or the poet aware that life can be imparted only to those thoughts, of which the flame has long smouldered in their breasts; and that in order to affect their contemporaries they must think of posterity. And will they speak of God and of immortality who do not believe in the morrow? *

In other points, however, it is impossible not to perceive, from striking signs, the approach of a religious awakening. None, however, is worthy of the name, but that which moves the soul in its very depths; at present, the surface is more agitated than the parts below—the head more touched than the conscience; there is in men's minds a want to believe, rather

* It is unnecessary to observe that we make honourable exceptions. France reckons with pride some men of genius, and every one would name them as we do.

than the belief itself; and such will continue to be the case, until such time as the men in a position to comprehend the importance of a religious conviction, shall have seriously interrogated themselves from a sincere desire to possess one, and a firm determination to manifest it. It is to them that it is fitting to declare that the great principles appealed to and defended in the sixteenth century had been recognised from the very beginning, and proclaimed, by courageous voices, long before the Reformation had assured their triumph.

The object of this work is not to convert believers—to engage in proselytism at the expense of any church—to draw away the living members of one communion to the bosom of another. No creed will be presented here as the only creed; no particular formula will be advanced as the sole real expression of the truth, out of which there is nothing but error and falsehood; for we believe, that it is, before all things, important to serve the universal Church; and there is one religion in our eyes higher than all particular forms of worship—above Roman Catholicism as above Protestantism; and that religion is CHRISTIANITY.

Christians have too often acted as if they were persuaded of the contrary; they have clung to details rather than to the whole; to particular parts more than to the general bearing; and they have unfortunately assigned less importance to what is positive and clear in the sacred text, than to what is figurative and obscure. They appear in this to have run counter to the wishes of God himself; the divine, wisdom having undoubtedly intended, that what was a matter of absolute necessity for each to comprehend, should also be most clearly evident. But the commands the most general and the most frequently repeated, are, above all, addressed to the heart, whilst the others offer some occupation to the intelligence. It will always be easier to exercise the latter than to change the former; and there will constantly be found in man a disastrous inclination to make up, before God, for the absence of strength of will, by an effort of the mental powers. For our parts, judging of the tree by its fruit, as is recommended in scripture, wherever we shall behold an active faith manifested by its good fruits, we shall recognise Christian convictions—we shall pay respect to the true spirit of Christianity.

Faithful to our duty as an historian, if we have to signalize the errors of a church, the particular vices of any fraction whatever of the Christian family, we shall not hesitate to do so; but contemporary testimonies shall speak by our pen, much more than we ourselves. Struck by the spectacle presented in the fourteenth and fifteenth centuries by the catholic world, and anxious to establish, by the strongest proofs, the necessity of the double reform attempted at that period in France and some other countries of Europe, we proposed to ourselves to place before the reader, in support of the description of those deplorable times, some authentic documents; and amongst others, the celebrated treaty of Clemangis on the *Corruption of the Church;* but we recoiled from the too deep colouring, and the unmeasured virulence of expression, which we found employed; we were apprehensive that our intentions might be misunderstood, and that we might be supposed anxious to apply to the present time, what could only be true in an age not yet emerged from barbarism. They who extol the middle ages, merely prove that they are not well acquainted with them; we believe the clergy of our days to be far superior to those of the times that are so much regretted; we respect them in spite of their errors, for these are not sufficient to efface their virtues.

We shall not discuss in this work the peculiar doctrines of Catholicism, but we shall strongly contest two principles, common to that religion with all others throughout the universe, which are governed by sacerdotal authority, and which no defender of religious liberty can admit; principles, in virtue of which an order or college of priests, on the one hand, consider themselves *infallible;* and on the other, *close heaven against every one that does not recognise in them a power to open it.* The error and the danger of such a doctrine will be pointed out, for no other has led men more astray, or been attended with more baneful consequences. The gospel has said, "Judge not;" but in all ages and in all countries the spiritual power, which has deemed itself infallible, has sanctioned very different maxims; it has judged, condemned, and cursed. It is difficult for men not to hate those whom they have cursed, and not to smite those whom they hate. What, besides, are temporal interests in comparison with those of eternity? The

law gives leave to punish the man who attempts to deprive us of a perishable existence, but it will be meritorious to kill the unbeliever who places our eternal existence in peril. It is necessary for the public good to destroy the haunt of robbers who lay waste a country; but it will be requisite to take up arms for heaven, to employ fire and sword against other brigands still more dangerous—those who destroy men's souls—and swords blessed by the church will be drawn by brother against brother, and the stake will always be held in readiness to avenge God.[*] The spiritual power that is reputed infallible, will behold only an obstacle or an instrument in the temporal power; and the latter, what it may desire or do, will always be either its enemy or its accomplice.[†]

If such are the results of sacerdotal infallibility in politics, what are they in human knowledge? Knowledge develops, in the mind of man, in very different degrees, faculties which before remained unknown; and will thereby endanger the uniformity of beliefs: perhaps even it may throw light on the errors of the infallible body: from that moment this latter power will treat knowledge as their enemy. They had diffused it as long as they considered themselves its master, and whilst it was an instrument in their hands; but they will extinguish or proscribe it when they find that it escapes from their

---

[*] There is a remarkable analogy between the effects produced by sacerdotal infallibility in all religions. Wherever it has been admitted throughout the world, the following maxims have been adopted: "The human species is on the earth only to accomplish the will of the gods; all the actions of individuals have a connection, more or less direct, with that will; the priests are acquainted with it, and make it known; and, therefore, it belongs to them to judge and punish disobedience ———." See also the terrible and similar consequences of the excommunication pronounced by the Druids, the Magi, the Brahmins, and the Egyptian priests.—(Benj. Constant, *De la Religion,* book iii. chap. x.)

[†] The reign which has best established this truth is, perhaps, that of Louis XIV. No prince ever purchased, at a dearer rate, peace with the sacerdotal authority. He obtained it by the sacrifice of a million of protestant subjects, by the destruction of Port Royal, and by the withdrawal of the celebrated declaration of 1682, which established the liberties of the Gallican church, and which had always been considered as one of his titles to glory. He caused Europe to tremble, and he was not at liberty to choose a confessor!—(See *Mem. de St. Simon.*)

jurisdiction; ignorance will then possess their sympathies, as being compatible with the uniformity of beliefs which are confounded together like colours in darkness; and in order to reign, they will endeavour to establish mental night. If a lively faith and severe morals could not be preserved but at the price of the evils inseparable from sacerdotal infallibility, perhaps it would be necessary to pay even that price for them; for a people which should deny God, the immortal soul, and the sacred rule of duty—which should reject the gospel after having received it—would soon sink to the lowest rank of nations, and would cease to be a people. Let us hasten to show that this is not necessary.

In the rude infancy of nations, a religion may be successfully imposed. Mankind, incapable of reflection, will accept the creeds already prepared, as they spare them the trouble of thinking for themselves; but at a more advanced, a more intellectual period, the uniformity insisted on in the name of infallibility, far from imparting life to religious beliefs, most frequently extinguishes and destroys them. If, at this period, many men still demand a religion ready prepared to their hand, for many others the maintenance of the faith will depend, above all, on the strength of their convictions; and conviction always involves the idea of examination; but the latter is with reason considered as proscribed, from the moment that whoever examines is forbidden to depart from the object previously aimed at.

What, however, will become of those who shall have departed from it? Some will avow that they have done so, and will affront the peril that may await them; but, for one determined mind that will speak, how many weak ones will keep silence! The great majority, however, will not dare either to reflect or to examine, but, turning away from noble thoughts and sublime questions of speculation, will give themselves wholly up to gross and temporal interests, and placing their intelligence at the service of their passions, they will remain completely passive. And yet, when the occasion requires it, all these men will still adhere with their lips to a doctrine which says nothing to their hearts; fear, habit, social proprieties, will weigh on them as so many obligations; they will be heard now and then to stammer forth in public certain forms of doctrine, the sense of which they will not run the risk of discovering, or

which they have rejected in secret. The predominating church, whatever its name may be, will in this way preserve a sort of external empire over society; but it will have in great part lost its moral authority: it will then lavish its favours on those thus apparently retained, and will be terrible to the small number who, in separating from it, will have placed their convictions above their interests. "What a triumph! What a conquest!" exclaims, on this subject an eloquent writer, "to pick and choose mankind, in order to make sure of the refuse! to attach to one's self the mercenary legions, and proscribe the sacred battalion which defends the truth as it would its native land!"* This church, which in the beginning reckoned its believers by souls, will perhaps still boast of its immense flock—will reckon up its children with pride, rejoicing in the millions that it contains within its fold; but *souls* will be for the most part absent, and its believers will be mere inert bodies.

Some persons, and amongst them Catholics—priests, even—justly honoured —have contested the strict and necessary connection between the principle, *The Church is infallible*, and this other, *Out of the Church there is no salvation;*† but their private opinions on this point are not confirmed by any general authority having the force of law. The doctrines of a church declaring itself to be infallible, are not drawn up or established, but by those who are entitled to represent them; and catholicism consists for us altogether in the decisions of *the popes* and *the councils*. There we everywhere find consecrated, and, as it were, enchained together, the two principles of which we point out the danger; and in no instance, perhaps, have the abuses of them been more clearly manifested than in the œcumenical Council of Constance. To relate the history of that illustrious assembly will be to adduce an unanswerable testimony against these same abuses. It will be perceived, in carefully examining its proceedings, that there are general truths applicable to all men, and that there is never greater danger of erring, than when infallibility is laid claim to.

But it is objected, if no church is infallible, if the voice of none is the voice of

---

* Vinet, *Mém. en faveur de la liberté des Cultes.*
† See the conferences of the Abbé Fraysinous.

God himself, the truth will be nowhere evident, and the world will be divided into innumerable sects, without root and without authority. This is what is repeated over and over again by those who acknowledge no veritable worship without a uniformity of rites, and no religious law without a visible authority alone invested with the right to draw up creeds, and to impose them. But because no one should happen to possess the exclusive privilege of interpreting the eternal word, does it follow that this word has not been made manifest? Because no particular church should have a monopoly of the gospel, must the gospel, on that account, not have been given to the universal Church? Before pretending that the truth cannot be, where uniformity does not exist, it would be necessary to ascertain if this uniformity be possible—if it really exist anywhere.

How can any one be certain that in this church, reputed infallible, an apparent uniformity of practice does not conceal an infinite variety of sentiments and opinions; and, on the contrary, that in the churches separated from it there is not to be found a grand principle of unity of doctrine under unimportant or purely external differences. How can any one be sure, that in the very heart of the Roman religion, the ignorant worshipper, prostrated before his patron saint, or the gloomy fanatic who fancies he is pleasing God when he lacerates his flesh with his hand dripping with blood, is not at an incomparably greater distance from a disciple of Fenelon, than are from each other the members of the most opposite communions? that, in fine, notwithstanding the common name of Catholics, the Ultramontane does not differ more in his doctrines from the Gallican, the Jesuit from the Jansenist, an Innocent III. from a Vincent de Paule, than the Quaker from the Lutheran, the Presbyterian from the Independent, or a Penn from a Wilberforce?

Before condemning the free interpretation of the gospel, it would be necessary to inquire, if, from that liberty, even when carried to excess, there have arisen more evils than from the principle of blind obedience to a power which declares itself to be oppressed if it does not oppress; and which never stops until it has either subjugated or crushed every thing; it would, in fine, be requisite to ascertain if, for nations, several creeds are not preferable to a single one—if, in a religious point of view, England, Scotland,* Holland, and the United States,† have in any respect to envy Italy, Spain, or Portugal. Who would dare to assert it? Who is there that does not know that a single river, whether it run dry or overflow its banks, must endanger a soil which several canals fertilize?

The word of the Divine Master, as the most eminent men of the Catholic church of France in the fifteenth century used to declare, is the true foundation—*the rock on which the faith rests* ;‡ it is also the only possible bond of unity amongst his disciples; it is already better comprehended, and particularly by a greater number, than was the case in Europe some centuries back; new advancements in the truth are predicted to humanity; but as to the truth, one, complete, and absolute, it does not enter into the category of this world's goods; and mankind would have spared themselves grand mistakes and frightful misfortunes, had they been more mindful of the saying of the apostle: "For we know in part, and we

---

* See in the *Archives of Christianity*, 1843 and 1844, the account given of the religious movement which has just taken place in Scotland, where a population limited in number, but strong in faith, has in less than a year subscribed the enormous sum of £400,000 for the construction of churches, the keeping up of schools, and for the support of five hundred free-church clergymen. The eloquent Dr. Chalmers has thus remarked on this subject: "This renunciation, on the part of five hundred ministers, of all that is precious in the eyes of the flesh, has produced, in favour of the cause which we defend, the same impression as the martyrdom of the early Christians produced in favour of Christianity."

† In a remarkable work just published by the Rev. Robert Baird, on *Religion in America*, he successfully refutes certain allegations brought forward by M. de Tocqueville; to whom, however, he renders otherwise the justice which he merits. "The Americans," says this last named writer, "having admitted without examination the main dogmas of the Christian religion, are obliged, in like manner, to receive a great number of truths flowing from, and having relation to it." On this, Mr. Baird thus remarks: "Hardly any assertion concerning his country could surprise a well informed American more than this. It is impossible to find a country in which the people demand reasons for every thing more frequently or more universally; nowhere are the preachers of the gospel more called upon to set forth, in all their force, the arguments by which the Divine revelation of Christianity is established."—(*Religion in America*, book i. chap. x.)

‡ See p. 160.

A 2

prophesy in part. But when that which is perfect is come, then that which is in part shall be done away. For now we see through a glass, darkly, but then face to face."[*]

: The more the gospel is studied, the better it will be seen, that, notwithstanding a variety of interpretations on secondary points, the unity of the spirit can subsist amongst Christians, and be maintained by one common faith in the doctrines which are truly essential; this unity is the only one that God has enjoined; and if men still hope to really establish another on earth, they deceive themselves. These assertions will be better understood in this age than in any that has preceded it. The lowering of moral barriers between nations, the disappearance of a crowd of prejudices which separated them, and the extension of the general ideas which draw them together, are so many peculiar signs of the times in which we live. It is better known in the present day that all mankind are but one family; that it is not the names which they bear, that really separate men; that the veritable distinctions between them depend on the possession or the absence of faculties which do them honour, and on the several degrees of these faculties in all; it is felt, that there is something which establishes between Christians a more lively sympathy, a stricter union, than the same corner of the world which chance shall have made their birthplace, than the registry of the same church where their names shall be inscribed; it is felt, that when men's hearts are touched by a living faith, they are closer in the eyes of God to all the true creeds of all Christian churches, than to the frivolous or indifferent persons whom we meet in our own; it is, in fact, very nearly acknowledged, that the men who have walked by the light of the gospel, taking as their model him who gave it, are fellow-citizens and children of the same heavenly country. In travelling over the sanguinary annals of religious history, sympathy is accorded to all the noble victims, whether they be called John Huss, or Barnevelt, or Coligny, or Wishart, or More; they who immolated them are detested; and Tertullian's saying may be well applied to them, "Those scaffolds of infamy to which you bind them, the branches with which you burn them, are the instruments of their triumph—their car of victory."[*]

It is thus that men's hearts and thoughts strive to rise above the distinctions of country and sect; and that nations advance by intelligence and liberty towards the spiritual unity which is so immeasurably superior to that external and factitious kind, in which ignorance and servitude so long retained them.

Such a work is grand and novel; enlightened nations could assist in it; and, in the first rank, that one in which the sympathetic bond is the strongest—where liberty causes every heart to throb—wherein invincible repugnance to the sacerdotal yoke is united to an ardent desire for unity; we allude to France. But France does not know herself; and many profit by her ignorance of herself, to lead her away, without her being aware of it, in a direction contrary to her tendencies, her wants, and her wishes; whilst others, very dissimilar to those just spoken of, aid, without their knowing it, in the same object. They may be recognised by an indelible sign—by the contempt which they affect, by the implacable laughter with which they pursue whoever attempts to raise towards God the face of a great people bent towards the earth; they have rejected the ancient faith and they will not have another; they hate that church, now grown old, in which they were born, and they await its fall—for a hundred years have they awaited it—and, seeing it still upstanding, they are lost in astonishment; they do not know that, in the order of ideas, nothing is destroyed that is not replaced, and that one religion is only replaced by another. If a blind and enjoined faith can suffice for an enslaved people, a free nation has need of conviction; without it, liberty of conscience is a nullity, and no nation wants it more than France, particularly when the horizon is becoming sombre.

The signs of the times may prove deceitful; we cannot say if the tempest will follow the lightning's flash; but, whatever comes to pass, it is not they who raise their voice the loudest, who appear to us the most to be dreaded; it is not the apostles of the League, or the seids of the Inquisition, who would bring back its days amongst us, if they could again revive. Religious liberty has enemies who remain silent, dissemble, and contradict

---

[*] 1 Corinthians xiii. 9, 10, 12.

[*] Tertullian, *Apolog. Christ.*

themselves; these are to be feared. It also reckons partisans who do not all come forward, or only do it by halves. And still there are noble lists into which it is not permitted to enter but with the brow uncovered; it is in the full light of the sun that truth should be combatted for. It is not war, but peace, that is the object of our ardent wishes; and if each man, before the struggle, dared to be sincere and declare himself, all contest would be impossible. France has gained religious liberty, and she dares not make use of it; she would avail herself better of it, perhaps, were she aware of what it cost; a single day was sufficient for her to write down the victory in her laws; but the combat was going on for three centuries. Let us venture to declare, that France is not sufficiently proud of her martyrs; all did not perish under the lion's claw in the arena; many others have said, *To leave Christ or to die—I prefer death*; they died, and France forgets them! She honours her children who have fallen on the field of battle, when serving the princes of the earth, and she neglects or disdains her no less heroic sons, who have expired by the hand of the executioner, confessing the King of heaven! The example which they have shown to their country, John Huss gave, three hundred years before them, to the whole of Europe assembled at Constance. In narrating the life of this man, we shall not conceal our sympathies, but we shall make allowances for the prejudices and passions of the time; we shall brand with reprobation the sentence passed on him, but we shall do full justice to the virtues of several of those who passed it. We live in an age when, whilst we pay the tribute of our admiration to a John Huss, who died a martyr, we are at liberty to render homage to the sincerity—to the great mind, of a person who was so unfortunate as to be his judge.

This work, in an historical point of view, is intended to make known and appreciated the great religious movement which took place a century before the Reformation in Europe. It embraces a period of seventy years, which elapsed from the beginning of the GREAT SCHISM of the WEST, in 1378, to the end of the war of the HUSSITES, towards the middle of the following century. The principal doctrines which divided Europe during that memorable period are exposed to view in it; and the illustrious men who originated or defended them are carefully depicted.

We shall describe the famous quarrels of the Schism; the struggles of the popes with each other; that of the emperor, the kings, and the councils against the pontiffs; the proceedings of the Gallican church and of the University of Paris; the persevering, and, for a time, victorious efforts of the men who represented both one and the other against the partisans of the papal omnipotence; and the scenes for ever to be deplored, in which the great doctors of Bohemia perished.

Theological differences were then accompanied by the flames of funeral piles and the shock of arms. A place is reserved in this work for these gloomy pictures; the reader will there find the combats of the word to be succeeded by those of the sword; and men of learning and piety, the Husses, D'Aillys and Gersons, to be followed by men of blood and war, the Ziskas and Procopiuses.

The furious deeds of mankind bring with them their lessons; in beholding the disasters caused by the excesses of all the powers, the time in which they are kept within salutary bounds is the better appreciated; and in reading the account of the dreadful battles in which the Hussites only too well avenged their master, it will be acknowledged that though men abuse the noblest principles, yet that great ideas do not perish with human bodies in the ashes of the stake. After so many terrible scenes, a few pages will be appropriated to the establishment of the Moravian church, or the United Brethren of Bohemia, who were also the disciples of Huss, and who have shown how God knows how to extract good from evil, and to produce enlightenment and life from darkness and destruction. The author of this work has constantly endeavoured to be actuated by a religious feeling in writing it, and if he has succeeded according to his wishes, he will not have laboured altogether in vain for the Christian cause. But a useful object and conscientious researches do not suffice to protect a book against those who behold only error and falsehood in every work that does not respond to their own ideas —does not satisfy their ardent passions.

As the historian of John Huss, we are well aware that whilst we gain for his name the admiration of many, we also expose it to outrage. But to whatever person should meditate insulting his memory, we would say, "John Huss was condemned because he refused to believe that a man, for any motive whatever, ought to stifle the voice of his conscience and to act contrary to his internal persuasion. What he did not believe, do you believe? Examine his life, peruse his letters—his touching letters, where the most candid soul is laid open, and the most holy fervour manifested. See what a love of good, what a horror of evil, what devotedness to truth, are there displayed! Consider how he lived and how he died. Having done this, place your hand on your heart and say, 'I am a better Christian than this man!'——Then insult him!"

EMILE DE BONNECHOSE.

REFORMERS

A CENTURY

BEFORE THE REFORMATION.

HISTORICAL INTRODUCTION.

I.

ORIGIN OF THE GREAT SCHISM OF THE WEST.—DIVISION OF EUROPE.

THE history of Christianity presents few periods more worthy of our attention than the close of the fourteenth and the commencement of the fifteenth centuries. The monarchical constitution of the Roman Church, in which the popedom had obtained predominance over the other powers, exposed to view all its vices, without exhibiting any of those redeeming qualities which had belonged to it at an anterior period, when it had been necessary to complete the conquest of Pagan Europe, and force back Islamism to the East.

Could experience have moderated the ambition of the sovereign pontiffs, they would long before have acknowledged how striking was the wisdom and foresight of Him whose place they considered they held, when he declared, "My kingdom is not of this world." This pontifical authority, which laid claim to infallibility, and asserted its right to dispose not only of all churches, but even of all kingdoms,[*] could not have remained in such hands; and, in order to escape from the violence which was unceasingly called forth by its unbounded pretences, it ought to have been as inviolable in reality as it claimed to be in right.

But this was far from being the case. The enterprises of some of the popes had drawn on them the indignation of the temporal sovereigns; and their real power was so little in accordance with their imaginary rights, that they who assumed to themselves dominion over the whole habitable globe, were rarely independent in any one part of it.

A twofold danger to the popes arose from

this contrast between the authority which they arrogated to themselves and their real weakness. On the one side, the princes whom they menaced or attacked, contested the validity of rights which encroached upon their own power, and responded to the fulminations of the popes by actual war. Whilst, on the other side, the sovereigns who considered themselves in a condition to turn those censures of the papal see against their own enemies, were strongly tempted to use them to their own advantage. The struggle was to decide who should take possession of that invisible sword whose point turned in every direction—who should wrest the envied weapon from the feeble hand that grasped it. Thus, therefore, this pretended absolute power over temporal affairs, which the popes had employed as a perpetual menace against all, became the cause of a double and permanent peril to themselves. They found that they were inevitably condemned to have recourse to all the grievous extremes of the position which they had created: they required large armies to fight with kings, and abundance of gold to pay them; and the gold thus destined for profane uses they could only obtain by the most infamous means. Hildebrand's[*] grand aim was forgotten; for, far

[*] See the celebrated Maxims of Pope Gregory VII., in note A at the end of the volume.

[*] Hildebrand, better known by the name of Gregory VII., the son of a carpenter of Soano, in Tuscany, was born in 1013, and elected pope in 1073, after the death of Alexander II. He formed vast projects for the aggrandisement of the temporal power of the popes, and sought to lord it over the kings of Europe. He excommunicated the Emperor Henry IV. in 1076, and supported the election of Rodolphe Duke of Suabia against him. He had some idea of reforming various abuses in the Church, but died in 1085, before he could carry his plans into effect. Under him the papal power was at his apogee.—*Note of the Translator.*

from relying on their temporal power to enforce respect for their spiritual authority, it was the latter that several popes employed most scandalously to maintain their terrestrial grandeur. Men then beheld criminal wars carried on by means of frightful simony : piety and charity faded away in proportion as indulgences and sacrilegious pardons were multiplied; and corruption flowed forth in a copious stream from the very source from which should have issued all moral truth and purity.

After two centuries of success, mingled with striking reverses, the popes beheld the failure of their gigantic undertaking. Innocent III. was perhaps the only pope who, at a favourable period, and by dint of boldness and genius, ran his career, an object of dread to all, and perfectly independent.

From the time of Clement IV., who gave the final blow to the house of Suabia, the power of the pontiffs was no longer unlimited but in their own imagination ; and during their long residence at Avignon, they found themselves, with respect to the crown of France, in a state of dependence very nearly as grievous as that which had degraded the tiara beneath the Imperial sceptre.

However, the papal authority, as a spiritual and infallible power, was as yet but slightly shaken in the opinion of the people—the scandalous scenes which the world had witnessed, and the torrents of blood that were shed, had not destroyed its influence. But Heaven at length permitted the great resources of this power to be employed by itself for its own destruction, so that the nations that were subject to the pope, and bent the knee before this new divinity, at last knew not where to find their idol.

It was this that caused THE GREAT SCHISM OF THE WEST, which commenced in 1378, just after Gregory XI. had re-established the Holy See at Rome, and which lasted half a century.

Several causes had contributed to recall Gregory XI. to Italy. Rome had become exasperated at the absence of her bishop—she was torn by factions; and the presence of the sovereign pontiff alone could repress the acts of sedition and depredation that were going on. On the other hand, the influence of the King of France, as we have just stated, was far too powerful at Avignon: the popes no longer found there a sufficiently safe asylum: they had seen the lances of the adventurers, under Duguesclin's command, glittering in the neighbourhood ; and they could even remember the day when those ferocious men had levied from them a tribute of golden marks, and forced benedictions. To these causes were added certain religious motives, which were strengthened by the visions of two women venerated in the Church. St. Catharine of Sienna and St. Bridget announced, that they had received revelations from on high, which enjoined the pope, as an act of duty, to return to his bishopric.

Determined, therefore, by these circumstances, he returned to Rome, where he died in the second year after his arrival. He uttered in his last moments expressions of deep regret at the calamities which he foresaw were about to occur. "Gregory XI.," says the illustrious Gerson,[*] "being on his death-bed, and having in his hands the sacred body of Jesus Christ, exhorted all around him to beware of certain persons, whether men or women, who, under the pretext of religion, published visions, which only proceeded from their own brain. He added, that, misled by such persons, he had acted contrary to the counsels of his friends, and that his conduct, he feared, would generate a schism after his death, unless the Lord stretched forth his hand to prevent it."[†]

What he had predicted soon took place. Out of sixteen cardinals who were at Rome with Gregory, only four were Italians; amongst the rest were eleven Frenchmen and one Spaniard.[‡] Had the choice of the cardinals been free, they would in all probability have elected a French pope, but the people of Rome were determined to have an Italian. A furious crowd besieged the entrance to the conclave, and uttered menaces of death, crying out, "Reflect, be wise, Lord Cardinals, and hand us out a Roman pope, that will remain amongst us; if you do not comply, we will make your skulls redder than your hats."[§] An Italian was elected—the suffrages having unanimously fallen on the Archbishop of Bari, who assumed the name of Urban VI.

"This prelate," says Thierry de Niem, who was his secretary, "before his elevation to the pontifical throne, was a pious, humble, and disinterested man; vigilant and laborious, the enemy of simony and its abettors, fond of the society of learned and upright men, regular in his life, austere in morals, and exceedingly zealous for the proper exercise of justice;[||] but he exhibited to the world a striking and melancholy example of the change which high advancement often produces in the best dispo-

---

[*] The Chancellor of the University of Paris. He was a pupil of Peter d'Ailly, and took a prominent part in all the religious disputes of his time. He strongly maintained the supremacy of councils over the pope, and examined the question at length in his well-known treatise De Auferibilitate Popæ. —Note of the Translator.

[†] Gers. Oper., De Examinatione Doctrinarum, v. i., p. 16.

[‡] The Spanish cardinal was the celebrated Peter de Luna.

[§] Froissart.

[||] Theod. Niem, De Schism, lib. i. c. 1, No. 2.

sitions. Raised to the highest pinnacle of human greatness, his brain grew dizzy—his heart swelled with pride—and the modest and humble priest became an intractable and ferocious despot."

He had preserved a praiseworthy zeal for the reformation of the morals of the clergy, but he evinced so rash an eagerness in his attempts to carry out his views, that, in three months after his elevation to the popedom, the very persons that had chosen him protested against his election. The eleven French cardinals and the Spanish one first left Rome, and repairing under different pretexts to Agnani, and from thence to Fondi, addressed to all the powers and universities of Europe the following letter:—

"We have apprized you of the horrible fury, cruel tyranny, and audacious and sacrilegious proceedings of the people of Rome and their governors, against our personal safety and property, when we were engaged in the election of a pope, with a view to force us to choose one according to their phantasy. It is owing to this unbridled wickedness, that the see of St. Peter is now occupied by an apostate, who propagates erroneous dogmas and tramples under foot all truth. He is not our pope by canonical election; for, neither was he impelled by the Holy Ghost to present himself, nor was he fixed on the pontifical throne by unanimous consent—he was placed there by the most barbarous fury on the one hand, and by mortal terror on the other. Wherefore, we are obliged to make a public protest against this intruder, (whom ambition has delivered up to the guidance of his evil imagination,) as we greatly fear that believers may be seduced by his artifices."[*]

The warning thus given by the cardinals, in order to be useful and meritorious, ought to have been less tardy ; the date of their letter, and the violence of the style, rendered the purity of the motives, by which it was dictated, doubly suspicious.

The three Italian cardinals[†] had remained with Urban, but their French colleagues planned an unworthy artifice to gain them over. They wrote to each separately, and, under the seal of profound secrecy, promised him the sovereign pontificate. The temptation was too powerful—the Italians hurried to Fondi, and, with the others, proceeded to a new election. But their expectations were disappointed. For a Frenchman, the Cardinal of Geneva, was elected pope; and under the name of Clement VII., he took up his residence at Naples.

* Lenfant, Hist. du Conc. de Pise, t. i. p. 25.
† The fourth, the Cardinal de St. Pierre, was dead.

It was a difficult matter to choose, according to the principles of right, between the two pontiffs; and, in consequence, Europe was divided according to the interests of the various sovereigns. The kingdoms of the north, England, Germany, Hungary, Bohemia, Holland, and almost the whole of Italy, remained obedient to Urban; whilst France, Spain, Scotland, Savoy, and Lorraine, embraced the side of Clement. The world thus beheld the commencement of a frightful struggle, which no crowned head in Europe was then in a position to bring to an end. The reins of government vacillated, as chance directed, in the hands of the degraded, indolent, and cruel Wenceslaus, King of Bohemia—Richard II. in England, and Charles VI. in France, were entering on their disastrous reigns—in Spain, Italy, and Hungary, feeble or ferocious despots alternately rose and fell. On no throne was there seated a man capable of applying a remedy to the schism, or of giving a salutary impulse to Europe. One could almost have said that an open field had been left to the papal power, only that it might inflict on itself the most terrible wounds—as if it were of so indestructible a nature, that its ruin could only proceed from itself.

II.

CONTINUANCE OF THE SCHISM.—ITS DISASTROUS EFFECTS.—THE COURTS OF AVIGNON AND OF ROME.

From the very commencement of this long schism, the position of the Church appeared desperate. The temporal monarchs perceived, that then, more than on any previous occasion, a rich treasure was to be reaped from the double authority which the popedom, at its last extremity, arrogated to itself—they beheld arms likely to serve their ambition in the pardons and ecclesiastical censures which the rival pontiffs still disposed of. The latter dared not refuse any thing to the sovereigns whose support they solicited; they paid in spiritual gifts the temporal succours that were afforded them, and they trembled before those who called themselves their humble and submissive sons. In this deplorable conflict—in the calamitous uncertainty in which the Christian world lived—it was the kings who were called on to point out to the people the true vicar of the King of heaven, and he had no choice but to be their slave or their victim.

The first interest of the two competitors was to get their authority recognised in the powerful state nearest to Rome—the kingdom of Naples. There, for many years, had reigned a queen of sad celebrity in history, Joan, granddaughter* of Robert of Anjou, accused, though not convicted, of complicity in the death of Andrew of Hungary, her husband, assassinated five-and-thirty years before. Joan had named as her successor Charles de Duras, the last scion of the elder branch of Anjou, and who had also a prospect of possessing the inheritance of the royal family of Hungary. His restless and fiery ambition was already prompting him to extreme measures against her, when Joan precipitated her fate by declaring herself in favour of Clement VII., whom she received at Naples, and acknowledged as sovereign pontiff.

This conduct drew down on Joan the anathemas of Urban VI. He excommunicated her—released her subjects from the oath of obedience—invited Charles de Duras into Italy—crowned him King of Naples—and let him loose on the prey which he was already so anxious to seize. Clement VII. abandoned a capital which was distracted by factions, and found a safer refuge at Avignon, whilst Joan sought support and vengeance in the royal family of France. She applied to Louis Duke of Anjou, brother of Charles V., to lend her his assistance, offering to constitute him her heir. This prince, who was the head of the younger branch of the house of Anjou, raised an army, received from Clement VII. the investiture of the kingdom of Naples, and marched on Italy. Such was the origin of the sanguinary war between the partisans of the two houses of Anjou—a war, iniquitous on both sides, and yet proclaimed holy by two hostile priests, each laying claim to infallibility!

We find in the works of their secretaries very precise details relative to this sad period of the lives of the two pontiffs. Thierry de Niem represents Urban, his master, as a prey to the poignant grief of an ungovernable ambition: he describes him as irritated almost to madness by the conviction of his weakness—writhing in despair under the hand of that same Charles whom he had made king†—

issuing against him a sentence of excommunication and malediction, after having given him the papal blessing—casting into loathsome dungeons the cardinals who had revolted against his tyranny—torturing and then strangling them—and at last dying himself of impotence and rage.*

The historian of the court of Avignon, the celebrated Clemangis, has handed us down a very different, though not less deplorable, picture of Pope Clement VII., under the yoke of the princes of France, whom he had just enriched with a new crown.

"What was there ever more wretched," says he, "than our Clement, up to the day of his death? He had so completely rendered himself the *servant* of the *servants* of the royal family of France, that scarcely would a lowly slave have suffered the indignities which he daily endured from the courtiers. He bent to circumstances, yielded pliantly to the importunity of suitors—he feigned and dissembled, promising largely, for the purpose of gaining time, giving benefices to some and deceitful words to others. He paid court to flatterers and buffoons, in order, through them, to obtain favour with the princes and nobles. He gave away bishoprics, and the principal dignities of the church, to gay young sparks, whose company he loved—he distributed valuable presents to maintain and augment his credit amongst them, and granted them all the exactions over the clergy that they pleased to demand. Thereby, he placed the whole of the clergy so entirely under subjection to the secular magistrates, that there was not one of them that was not as much pope as he."

In this way, the sovereigns turned to their own profit the superstition of the public, and also employed, as an arm against their enemies, the violence of one of the pontiffs and the weakness of the other. What respect for the popedom, therefore, could there still exist in men's minds, when the two competitors—between whom the soundest judgment would find it a difficult matter to pronounce—turned their ecclesiastical thunderbolts against each other. How was it still possible to place any faith in the infallibility of the pope, when there were neither churches, nor thrones, nor armies, but were, on the one hand, rich in indulgences, and, on the other, overwhelmed with anathemas? On both sides was apparent an equal abuse of spiritual gifts for the gratification of the vilest passions. It was necessary to degrade the tiara in order to retain possession of it—to procure creatures at any price, or cease to be pope; and the powers which the two priests smothered between two mattresses, by orders of this prince.

* Th. de Niem, *De Schism.*

---

* Joan of Naples, daughter of Charles of Sicily, and granddaughter of Robert of Anjou, King of Naples, born in 1326, was barely seventeen when she succeeded her grandfather in the kingdom of Naples and the Comté of Provence. She was already married to Prince Andrew of Hungary, her cousin, who was assassinated by the queen's friends, and, it was surmised, by her connivance, because he aimed at making himself master of the authority which she insisted on reserving to herself. He was only nineteen at the time, 1345. She immediately married her cousin, Louis of Tarento, but did not remain in quiet possession of her throne, as Louis, King of Hungary, and brother to Andrew, marched against her, and forced her to take refuge with her husband in Provence. It was then that she sold Avignon to the Pope for 80,000 golden florins.—*Note of the Translator.*

† When her capital was taken, Queen Joan was

arrogated to themselves over heaven and over hell, for the desolation of the world, constituted at once their greatness and their servitude.

The schism survived its principal authors; and it was in vain that hopes were entertained that when one of the two rivals should chance to die, the cardinals who had been submissive to his authority would unite with the others who were in favour of the surviving pontiff. This was to suppose that the public good and the welfare of the Church would have more weight with them than private interest;—and this supposition was a grand mistake. In the opinion of the greater number of them, the public good and welfare of the Church consisted above all in the maintenance of their own privileges, the preservation of their honours, and the security of their wealth; but to refrain from naming a successor to the deceased pontiff, would be to abnegate what constituted their own strength. They were aware that scarcely should they have ceased to excite apprehension, ere their former opposition would be far more remembered than their sacrifice appreciated;—they also knew, that if they desired to negociate with safety, they must do so on equal terms; and that if they wanted the chances to be even between the two electing colleges, there must be two popes. Therefore, although they protested strongly against the schism, their first care was to fill up the vacant see on which their fortune was dependent. The deputies of the states, and the ambassadors of the princes, who, at each vacancy, came to implore the cardinals to restore union and peace to the Church, by coalescing with the rival college, always arrived too late; and a natural fear induced the cardinals to hurry on the election before time was afforded to hear the reasons that were likely to prevent it.

Another apprehension, however, balanced in the mind of the cardinals that which has just been mentioned. They felt that the schism, by agitating men's minds, and substituting the necessity of examination for a habit of implicit obedience, was endangering both the authority of the Church and their own. If, on the one hand, a present interest impelled them to keep up the schism, on the other, a more distant, though not less important one, urged them to adopt every means to bring it to a close; and, therefore, were they continually taking fresh precautions to attain this object, but always in vain. Each readily pledged himself, that, in case of being elected, he would do every thing to bring about the union of the Church—even, were it found necessary, to sacrifice to this grand object the pontifical dignity itself. Each took an oath to this effect

previously to the election; but the moment the choice was made, the newly appointed pope hastened to forget his solemn promise. Thus, all who endeavoured to put an end to the schism moved in a vicious circle, as was forcibly observed by the celebrated French preacher, Pierre-aux-Bœufs. After having described the luminous circle called a *halo*, which is occasionally observed round some of the planets, he added, in his quaint old style, "To this circle do I liken the schism, from the great similitude which I perceive between them. Alas! doth not the present schism the form of a circle show, in which can be found neither end nor outlet. Several others have been, but they were only semicircles, whereof the end could be found, and the issue arrived at. But in the schism presently existent, we find neither bottom nor shore."[*]

During a period of forty years, five popes or anti-popes exhibited to Europe such a scandal as we have just described. Urban VI. died in 1389, and the Italian cardinals appointed as his successor Peter de Thomacelli, who assumed the name of Boniface IX. A contemporary author has made the following remarks on his election: "The second epoch of this schism commenced under Boniface; but this second was more depraved and flagitious than the first—in fact, in every way worse. It was under his pontificate that simony waxed strong and flourished, and that other evils still more grievous gained new strength."[†] No man, in fact, knew better than this pope how to turn every thing into money. It is said that it was he who first made the *annats* perpetual;[‡] and Niem, who was a personal witness, informs us that nothing was seen throughout Italy but couriers of the pope, going about inquiring whether any holder of a rich benefice might not be ill, in order that it might be made matter of traffic at Rome.[§] Sins of every description had their tariff; and it was in that capital that absolution was promised for them. In order to participate in the spiritual advantages attached to the journey, it was sufficient to feel a readiness to undertake it; and to obtain a dispensation for not going, all that was required was to pay the price of it. The public paid, and came in crowds to receive their pardons from one who had none to expect for himself—so powerful does an idea become when it has taken root in the heart of man, and makes common cause with his most important interests. And what in fact was more im-

* *Preuves de la Nouvelle Hist. du Conc. de Const.* By Bourgeois du Chastenet.
† Vrie, lib. iii. ap. Von der Hardt, v. i.
‡ By '*annat* is meant the revenues of a year, which were paid to the apostolic chamber by each person that obtained a benefice.
§ Theod. Niem, *De Schism.* lib. ii. c. 8.
B

portant to the immense majority of men, than the privilege of redeeming their sins by payment of some sums of money—of measuring, as it were, the right to err by the avidity of him who pardoned.

Boniface, however, wrote to Charles VI. a letter, in which he manifested an ardent zeal for the peace and union of the Church: he deplored the wretched condition to which the schism had reduced it, and urged the king, his very dear son, to employ all his means for its extinction; promising, on his part, to sacrifice his own interests to the welfare of Christianity. Clement VII., on the other hand, was playing his part with equal cleverness at Avignon. He ordered daily processions for the acquisition of peace—he composed a new form of divine service to that effect, with orders to have it chanted in his pontifical palace*—and he preached sermons in favour of the union. To all appearance his intentions were good; but, as an old author remarks, " He was too agreeably habituated to the honours of the world, to feel any taste for the means of obtaining this union, or to submit to the necessary sacrifices." He accorded great indulgences to all persons that attended the new form of service; but at the same time he granted others far more extensive, accompanied with considerable presents, to a fiery preacher of Paris, named John Goulain, to advocate war. The two pontiffs undoubtedly wished for peace and union; but in the minds of each these words signified his own triumph, and the ruin of his rival.

Several temporal princes, who might have united their efforts for the extinction of the schism, thought, with a view to their own benefit, less of bringing it to a close, than of maintaining it. The two first competitors for the throne of Naples, Louis of Anjou and Charles de Duras, were dead;† but their quarrel was transmitted to their posterity. The sons whom they had left behind, Louis II. of Anjou, and Ladislaus of Hungary, inherited the fury and rival pretensions of their fathers. Clement VII. supported the claims of the former, whilst Boniface declared himself in favour of Ladislaus—and Europe was again in flames.

III.

EFFORTS OF FRANCE TO BRING ABOUT THE
UNION.

The King of France, more easily than any other sovereign, could have extirpated the

canker which was eating into the Church; but the unfortunate Charles was perhaps the only person of his family and his court, that would have preferred the general interests of Christianity to the private advantage which the crown of France derived from possessing the pope at Avignon—and it may be truly declared of him, that the power to do good failed him, rather than the desire. His unfortunate insanity again placed him under the fatal yoke of the princes of the blood; and one of them, the Duke of Anjou, whose creature Clement was, frustrated every effort to produce union— he served at the same time Clement's cause, and made an instrument of him for his own purposes.*

But what the court could not effect was undertaken by a celebrated body. Amidst the profound darkness in which Europe was plunged, the Universities alone shed abroad some lustre; and none was then more renowned than that of Paris, which D'Ailly and Gerson rendered illustrious; and which, at the period when the humiliation of France was the greatest, had retained a glorious pre-eminence in public opinion.

This great body, and particularly that part of it called the Sorbonne,† at that period took an immense share in public affairs, sometimes usefully, and sometimes with disastrous effect:—a strange position, which it would be difficult to comprehend, did not the circumstances of the time afford the explanation. In an age when theology was almost the only science, and when the great majority of questions of law received a theological solution, theologians necessarily enjoyed great credit, and every party endeavoured to secure the concurrence of so puissant a tribunal as the Sorbonne. Its importance was doubly increased, when the grand affair of the age—the great problem for solution—was the extinction of the schism. All other questions were subordinate to or connected with this, which was itself within the domain of the great doctors of the period, the Cramauds, the D'Aillys, the Gersons. The schism affected every thing, and therefore the University took part in all that was done in endeavouring to extinguish it. It thus accustomed itself to interfere in the affairs of the Church, in politics, and in government; and when the principal powers

---

* Relig. de Saint Denis, liv. xii.
† The Duke of Anjou died in 1384, it is said, of grief, at not being able to prevail against Charles de Duras. The latter had ascended the throne of Hungary, and was assassinated there in 1386, by

the order of Elizabeth, mother of Maria his queen. —*Note of the Translator.*
* See in *La Chron. du Relig. de Saint Denis,* book xi. c. 11, the list of the exactions of Clement VII. and his cardinals, as well as the incredible acts of violence by which the Duke of Anjou, the regent, forced the clergy of France and the University of Paris to submission.
† The *Sorbonne* was the Faculty of Theology of the University of Paris.

of the State perished or were eclipsed, it assumed the chief place. It certainly could not maintain itself there independently; for, in departing from its own attributes, it departed also from that moderation of which it ought to have set the example:—it was too frequently the dupe of those who applied to it for support:—but, every thing considered, the part which it performed did it honour; for it endeavoured to effect the predominance of ideas of rectitude in the midst of the most brutal violence. Its conduct was no doubt illegal; but at that time the laws were mute; and if this conduct was a proof of the extreme anarchy into which France had fallen, it attested also the eminent rank to which the University of Paris had risen in the estimation of Europe.

In 1394 the University held a solemn sitting to deliberate on the means of putting an end to the schism, and came to the conclusion that this must be effected by one of these three means: the voluntary resignation of the two competitors—an arbitration agreed to by both parties—or, finally, a general council.

Clemangis laid before the king in writing the result of this deliberation. Charles VI., in a lucid moment, greeted it favourably; but a fresh attack of his malady restored the advantage to the Prince's party, and the University was formally forbidden to intermeddle in the affair of the schism. It persisted, however, in spite of this injunction, and announced that the lectures should be closed and the public lessons cease, until such time as a favourable answer was given to its demands. It wrote, at the same time, a strong letter to Clement VII., calling on him to choose between the three modes of arrangement. "This letter is pernicious and poisonous," was the observation of Clement VII.; and the fury which he felt at it was such, that it was said to have been fatal to his life; for a few days after he had received it, he expired.

Kings, Princes, the Church, and the Universities, were now unanimous in their endeavours to prevent the cardinals of Avignon from effecting a new election; but the secret desires of the latter to keep up the schism were more powerful than all the efforts made to extinguish it. Each of the eighteen cardinals took an oath, that, in case of being elected, he would employ every means—even including the resignation of the pontificate—to bring about the union of the Church, adding, however, this clause, "*Provided the present, or any future cardinals, or the majority of them, deem it expedient for the well-being of the Church.*" The late legate of Clement VII., Peter de Luna, took the oath like the rest, and on him the election fell.

The restrictive clause of the oath rendered it illusive; for was not the newly elected pope perfectly at liberty to appoint additional cardinals disposed to look on the maintenance of the pontificate as more beneficial to the Church than a resignation? Could he not make it a matter of conscience with himself not to lay down the ring of St. Peter, after having received it? In fact, this was the very thing that took place; for Peter de Luna, known as pope by the name of Benedict XIII., after having employed the most consummate artifice to ascend the throne, maintained himself in it with the most insuperable obstinacy.

This pontiff, who belonged to the illustrious house of Luna, one of the first families in the kingdom of Arragon, was now about sixty years of age, of small stature, slight, and feeble in appearance, though in reality enjoying robust health. He possessed a mind remarkable for its shrewdness, subtlety, and penetration; he was much given to study, and of great acquirements, particularly in canon law. To these qualities he joined the defect of an ambition which no scruple could restrain; he was deceitful, treacherous, and utterly regardless of sworn faith, provided he could save appearances; and, lastly, as Maimbourg says, "he was furiously obstinate, beyond all that might be expected even from an Arragonese." [*] Gregory XI., who nominated him cardinal, saw into his character, and observed, as he handed him the hat, "Take care, my son, that your moon[†] be not one day eclipsed."

No person had evinced a more ardent zeal than Benedict for the extinction of the schism; it was to it that he owed his elevation; and he had recourse to the same means to strengthen himself on his seat. In notifying, through his legates, his election to the King of France, and to the University of Paris, he declared himself perfectly ready to make the desired resignation—they had only to speak. "Choose,"—was his language to them—"choose whatever course you deem best calculated to restore peace to the Church, and I shall subscribe to your wishes." In a letter which he wrote to John, King of Castile, he drew a frightful picture of the schism, and of the evils inflicted by it on Christendom: he declared that "he was unworthy of the pontificate—that he had carried his repugnance to accept it even unto tears—and that if he at last consented, it was with the sole design of effecting, without any further delay, the peace and union of the Church—it was to show forth the great glory of God, who had been pleased to employ for this work so humble an instrument as himself,

---

[*] Maimbourg, *Hist. du Grand Schisme d' Occid.* book iii. p. 236.

[†] An allusion to the name of Luna, which signifies "moon."

in order that his Divine wisdom might be the more transcendent." He made a great parade of these fine sentiments, and asserted that he would prefer shutting himself up in a cloister for the remainder of his life, to retaining the tiara at the expense of the repose of Christendom. One day, when conversing with the deputies of the University of Paris, he took off his cope, and throwing it on the table, assured them that he would quit the pontificate with the same facility, if the union of the Church required it. He blamed his predecessor in stringent terms: " Clement VII.," he said, "had shown too much apathy and procrastination in the accomplishment of this holy work."

Who would not have been deceived by this specious behaviour? Who could have believed that this man would in reality become the most uncompromising adversary of that peace and union, for which apparently his most ardent prayers were offered up? Yet nothing could bend his heart of iron—neither the withdrawal of France from her obedience to him, determined on for the first time in 1398, and which lasted five years—nor the annoyances attendant on a long siege—nor the desertion of his cardinals—nor the tears of Christendom—nor the cry of his own conscience. When informed of the withdrawal of France, he coolly observed, " What matters it? St. Peter did not reckon that kingdom amongst those that were obedient to his sway." When besieged by Boucicault he excommunicated him; and for five years replied to the attacks of the besiegers by the thunderbolts of the Church. During one hard winter, being in want of firing, he ordered one part of his palace to be pulled down to heat the other; yet still he appeared every day on the fortifications, holding in one hand a bell, and in the other a taper, and hurled forth his anathemas on the enemy.[*] At last he escaped in disguise: he again entered Avignon in triumph: France once more returned to her obedience; and the only result of all the efforts made to induce him to yield, was to confirm him in his inflexibility.

His competitors regulated their obstinacy by his own. Boniface IX. had been succeeded first by Innocent VII., and next by Angelo Corrario, Cardinal of St. Marc, known by the name of Gregory XII. They, too, before their elevation, were zealous partisans of the union of the Church, although they subsequently raised against it insuperable obstacles. Perhaps they acted thus according to their conscience;—for having acquired the right to

absolve mankind from their oaths, they made use of the same privilege to free themselves, and so committed perjury without remorse.

The time, however, arrived, when, seeing themselves on the point of being universally abandoned, the two popes were obliged to furnish some personal pledge in favour of the longed-for union. An interview was proposed and assented to; and they repeated on this occasion, towards each other, the same comedy that they had previously been playing in the presence of Europe. Never could either the time or the place of meeting be agreed on. Savona had first been appointed; and Benedict had proceeded thither, having previously received certain information that his competitor would not come. " Gregory," says a celebrated contemporary, " made a new proposal which was accepted—that Benedict should repair to Porto-Venera and Gregory to Lucca, in order to be more at hand to hold the conference. Gregory, in consequence, left Vienna in the month of January and proceeded to Lucca, where several fruitless embassies were commenced on both sides. Benedict declared that all places were perfectly indifferent to him for the meeting, provided it was near the sea, in order that he might be constantly within reach of his fleet; but Gregory, on the other hand, would only listen to an interview on *terra firma*. You would have imagined one to be an aquatic animal, that dreaded the dry land; and the other a terrestrial one, in fear of water. This conduct irritated men's minds the more, because everybody was convinced that these terrors were merely affected, as both popes would have been equally safe by land or by sea. The general dissatisfaction was loudly expressed: it was, indeed, impossible to see, without feelings of horror, two men upwards of seventy years of age, thus sacrificing the Church, the interests of religion, and their own conscience, to the ambition of reigning a few days longer."[*]

The Church of France, at this conjuncture, made use of bold language, which the circumstances justified. The parliament, at the king's demand, had, the preceding year, pronounced a second withdrawal of obedience from Benedict XIII. This withdrawal, though only a partial one—relating to tithes, annats, and the disposal of benefices, was condemned by influential persons, and the kingdom seemed divided in opinion. The sanction of the Church being deemed necessary, a general assembly of the clergy of France was convoked at Paris in December 1406, in presence of the king, the princes of the blood, and the parlia-

---

* Sismondi, *Histoire des Français*, vol. xii. p. 113.

* Letter written by Leonard Aretin, secretary of Gregory XII., to Petrello of Naples.

ment. "There were present," says Maimbourg,[*] "sixty-seven archbishops or bishops, about one hundred and forty abbots, and an infinite number of doctors and licentiates of the universities of the kingdom."

This was a theological tournament, as it were, between the University of Paris, on the one hand, demanding an absolute withdrawal, and the partisans of Benedict on the other. Amongst those entering the lists for the University, were the Franciscan friar, Pierre-aux-Bœufs, the famous Doctor John Petit, Simon Cramaud, patriarch of Alexandria, Archbishop of Rheims, and subsequently Cardinal. Pierre-aux-Bœufs spoke first, and it was then that he compared, as has been already stated, the schism to a circle called a halo. "This resemblance," remarked he, "does not exist merely as to the form, but also with respect to the origin of the two things. For, if one be formed from the vapours of the earth, the other takes its origin in the fumes of pride, of ambition and of cupidity—of ambition to rule, and eagerness to possess: it is the wind described in Job (ch. i. 19), whence proceed so many grievous tempests, perturbations of kingdoms, enmities between nations, revilings of our faith, doubts in our sacraments, and devourings of poor clerks."[†]

The speaker accused the two popes of being the authors of all these evils, and added: "As the planets have two motions—one attracting them towards the firmament, and the other peculiar to themselves, to moderate their rapidity ; so the cardinals, the patriarchs, and the prelates, who are the planets of the heaven of the Church, or of its chief, ought to allow themselves to be influenced by his will, when it is properly regulated: but when the pope, by his disorderly humours, keeps the Church in trouble, or compasses its ruin, no one can deny that the aforesaid planets, the above mentioned prelates, ought not to be anxious to come in conjunction with him." Pierre-aux-Bœufs, amongst other proofs, referred to the Council held at Rome in 963, where John XII. was deposed. He concluded his speech by loudly demanding acts, not words, in order to reduce Benedict XIII.

John Petit spoke next, and to the same purport: and after him came the patriarch of Alexandria, the celebrated Simon Cramaud, who had already been the president of several preceding meetings of the French clergy.[‡]

He endeavoured to throw new lustre on the university, by ascribing to it a strange origin, previously unsuspected. "When Julius Cæsar," said he, "had transferred this university from Athens to Rome, he gloried in what he had done, and willingly followed the counsels of its masters and doctors. The Emperor Charlemagne, also, who removed it from Rome to Paris, esteemed it one of the noblest jewels of his kingdom." The orator next depicted most vividly all the exactions of the Court of Rome. "As to dispensations," said he, "are they not mere profligacy? Would not a bishop or archbishop know better how to regulate them in his diocese, than a secretary could do at the Court of Rome? In what relates to Church property, Cramaud professed exceedingly bold opinions. "The pope and the prelates," observed he, "are not masters of the property of the Church, but merely its defenders and procurators—the temporal lords are its real masters." Next, recurring to Benedict, he forcibly contrasted his conduct antecedently to his election to the popedom, with that which he afterwards displayed—the disinterestedness which he had at first affected, with the ambition that had afterwards burst forth. He terminated by reminding his hearers of the opinion pronounced by the doctors, that "whoever should violate an oath, in order to retain the papacy, must be considered a heretic."

The conclusions come to by the university, conformably to this opinion, were, that a pope who had sworn to yield, for the union of the Church, when the college of cardinals, or the majority of them, should consider it necessary, was bound to give way;—that if he refused, and persisted in his refusal, he was guilty of perjury, was false to God and man, and should be declared a heretic by the assembly of prelates. The university added, that it then would become the duty of the assembly to prosecute him as a heretic, whilst it would be that of the secular princes to compel him to yield.[*]

The chief adherent of Benedict was William Filastre, Dean of Rheims. The presence of the king made no difference in his language. "Charles VI.," he said, "had rendered himself culpable by his behaviour towards Benedict, in pronouncing the withdrawal of obedience; he had in that resembled Uzziah encroaching on the rights of the priesthood, for which that king's face had been covered with leprosy."

---

* *Histoire du Grand Schisme d' Occid.* part i.
† See the text of the speeches delivered on this occasion, extracted from Saint Victor's manuscripts, in the proofs of the *Nouvelle Histoire du Concile de Constance,* by Bourgeois du Chastenet.
‡ This patriarch, reputed one of the luminaries of his age, was so great a personage, that, at the royal banquet offered at Rheims by the King of

France to the Emperor Wenceslaus, Cramaud occupied the first place, Wenceslaus the second, and the King of France the third.—See Froissart, ann. 1397, book iv. ch. lxii.
* Maimbourg, *Histoire du Schisme d' Occident.* part i.

Filastre, besides, did not consider the withdrawal as practicable. "Let me take," said he, "a familiar term of comparison. The citizens of Paris pretend that their provost is a man of immoral conduct,—a reproach now addressed to our Holy Father,—and for that reason the citizens refuse to obey him. He, however, seizes, tries, and hangs some of them, and hanged they are. In the same way, our Holy Father can excommunicate us; and we should be as truly excommunicated as the others were hanged; for we cannot take away from him the power of the keys."

But the real power was at this time neither at Rome nor at Avignon. . The Dean of Rheims had chosen an inauspicious moment to boast of the pope's greatness; his language was considered as an outrage against the king's majesty, and he was compelled to offer him his most humble apology. "Sire," said he, "I have spoken unadvisedly, but it was with the lips alone. I make this avowal not to exculpate myself, but to gain your clemency. I am a poor man, educated in the fields, and rude by nature; I have never lived with kings and princes, to acquire the proper style of speaking in their presence. I shall, for the future, be more careful and more faithful to your Majesty, if it please you to take pity on me."

Peter d'Ailly, Bishop of Cambray, next spoke. He opposed the withdrawal, and called for a general council, composed of the persons in obedience to both popes, to concert together for the union of the Church, and for the reformation of public morals.

The advocate-general, John Juvenal des Ursins, wound up the discussion, and showed more good will than erudition. He sharply rebuked the Dean of Rheims for having said that the pope was their sovereign in temporal as in spiritual matters. He made no difficulty about canon law or historical evidence. "It was not by the authority of the pope," said he, "that Pepin succeeded Childeric; it was because the latter, having no children, abdicated, and embraced a religious life." The right of assembling councils, in which it was purposed to bring popes to judgment, and pronounce on religious matters, belonged to kings; and he proved it by the examples of Constantine and of Theodosius, and by a decision of Nicholas. "This right," said he, "belongs to the crown; not to the person of Pepin or of Charles, but to the King of France. The Roman bishop was formerly elected by ecclesiastics and by laymen, in the same manner as the other bishops who are his fellows." And as regarded what was alleged respecting the right of St. Peter, he added, that the apostolic seat had been first of all at Jerusalem, next at Antioch, and then at Rome; "and if it could be replaced at Jerusalem, where it was at first, I believe," added he, "it would be for the best."

The council, representing the Gallican Church, issued a decree which re-established the withdrawal of obedience, as in 1398, and it was confirmed by the king. Benedict replied to this by a bull of great violence, in which he excommunicated the authors of the decree of withdrawal, whoever they might be, whether cardinals, archbishops, princes, kings, or emperors.

This bull reached Paris at a moment when the greatest horror was excited in the public mind by the perpetration of an atrocious crime. The Duke de Orleans and Jean-sans-Peur, Duke of Burgundy, who had long been at enmity, met before the altar, were reconciled, and received the communion together; three days afterwards, on the night of the 23d Nov., 1407, Jean-sans-Peur caused the Duke of Orleans to be murdered. This deed found a barefaced apologist in the celebrated Dr. John Petit, and the king pardoned his brother's murderer. There was now no longer in France either civil or religious authority; the kingdom was a prey to the triple plague of foreign, civil, and religious war; from one extremity of the country to the other, nothing was heard but the clash of arms, the shouts of the combatants, and the groans of an agonized people; whilst loud over all were the voices of the two high priests cursing the king, the clergy, and the nation, and thundering their maledictions at each other.

IV.

COUNCIL OF PISA—CONTINUANCE OF THE SCHISM.—MANIFESTATION OF THE PUBLIC MIND.

The University of Paris did not lose its courage amidst the general desolation, but redoubled its efforts for the extinction of the schism. After having uselessly deputed to the two popes its most illustrious doctors, it addressed itself to the cardinals of both parties, and its exhortations were at last listened to. Ambition, and the pride of power, might support the two pontiffs in danger, fatigue, and privations of every kind; but such sufferings had become at length insupportable to the men who followed their fortunes. The cardinals who were condemned, through the schism, to lead a wretched wandering life, began most sincerely to wish for repose; it only remained to discover how such an end might be attained, without compromising themselves or being subjected to the discretion of the opposite party. The voluntary and simultaneous resignation of the two competitors being no longer to be hoped for, the only means left was to depose them both by a council. The cardinals of the two courts had recourse to this plan: they met together, and convoked for this purpose a general council.

This celebrated meeting opened at Pisa in the year 1409. There were present twenty-four cardinals; upwards of two hundred arch-bishops and bishops, either in person or represented by procurators; three hundred abbots; forty-one priors; the heads and grand-masters of almost all the orders; the deputies of the principal universities of Europe; those of the chapters of more than a hundred metropolitan churches and cathedrals; the ambassadors of the kings of France, England, Bohemia, Poland, Portugal, Sicily, and Cyprus: several great princes, to whom were soon added those of the courts of the north and of the King of Hungary; and, finally, upwards of three hundred doctors in theology and canon law. Never had such an imposing assembly been seen in Europe, and never had any, from the number and quality of its members, been so justly entitled to claim the name of an œcumenical council.

Convoked for the double purpose of reforming and uniting the Church, the council turned all its efforts towards extinguishing the schism which now overran Europe. It deposed both popes, declaring them its defenders and promoters, and, as such, backsliders from the faith, heretical,* and perjured.†

For these causes the council deposed them, and declared both incapable of ever presenting himself as a candidate for the papal throne;—pronounced the Roman see vacant;—and forbade all Christians, under pain of excommunication, to continue in obedience to either of the competitors. A few days afterwards, Peter de Candia, Cardinal of Milan, of the order of Minor Brothers, was unanimously elected pope by the cardinals, and took the name of Alexander V. When sovereign pontiff, he retained all the narrow views and petty passions of the monk; and was much more preoccupied as to the means of advancing the triumph of his own order, than by the general interests of Christendom. After a few regulations of small importance, he dissolved the assembly, postponing all reforms to the next council.

Alexander V. possessed none of the remarkable qualities which were necessary to overcome the difficulties of the time :—before the meeting of the council these difficulties had

been immense; after the meeting they were still greater.

The deposed popes, Gregory and Benedict, protested against these proceedings, and each convoked another council, the one at Civitat de Frioul, the other at Perpignan. With much difficulty they succeeded in assembling each a few prelates devoted to their cause; yet they, nevertheless, bestowed upon these assemblies the name of œcumenical councils, which they had refused to give to that of Pisa. It is certain, said they, that the Church is the pope; and it suffices that the pope be present in any place for the Church to be there also; and where the pope is not in body or in mind, no Church is. According to these principles, the Council of Pisa, to which indeed had flocked the representatives of all Christian Europe, but which the pope neither convoked nor presided over, was not a universal council, but a conventicle. Many ecclesiastics shared this opinion, as well as several sovereigns; and among others, the Emperor Robert. This prince, who had been nominated King of the Romans by the electors, who had deposed his predecessor Wenceslaus, was not considered the legitimate emperor by a part of the members of the Council of Pisa: his authorization had not been demanded for the convocation of the assembly; and he revenged himself in refusing to acknowledge, during the lifetime of Gregory, either the rights of the council, or the validity of the election of Alexander.

Thus, after so many efforts, the only result had been a new cause of trouble and discord, and a new danger for Christendom ; for, instead of two popes, there were now three.*

The great object of the council—the termination of the schism—had failed ; the next—that effecting the reforms, which had become urgent—had failed also, though a point of vast importance. The corruption prevailing in the Church and in society was the great evil of the times; and but little idea can be formed, in the present day, to what an extent it had been carried.

The proof of the great disorder of the clergy is not in the invectives of their enemies; we find it in the writings of the most illustrious of their own order; of those, who, from their character and situation, had every interest to see their Church pure and uncontaminated. It is not to the poets and chroniclers alone, that we owe the picture of its corruption. Prelates, cardinals, and doctors, as celebrated as they were respected, laid open, with an un-

---

* It is a principle in canon law, that continuance in schism degenerates into heresy.

† Niem, *De Schism.* lib. iii. chap. xliv.

* Only a few of the towns of Italy and Germany had remained obedient to Gregory XII. Benedict still kept possession of Spain, Portugal, Scotland, and the counties of Foix and Armagnac.

shrinking hand, the vices which were preying upon it, as a skilful physician unhesitatingly probes the wounds he wants to cure.

The terrible treatise of Clemangis on the corruption of the Church is well known. He describes, in the most indignant language, the usurpations of the Roman Court; he shows, in the shameful simony of the popes, the fatal consequences of their unbounded pretensions. "To maintain their rank, which they affirm to be superior to that of kings or emperors, they were forced," said he, "after having dissipated the patrimony of St. Peter, to lay hands on other parts of the fold, and take from the flock their food, milk, and fleece. It was thus that they arrogated to themselves the disposal of all the churches, the right of election and patronage, that they might draw into the gulf of the apostolic chamber all the gold of Christendom. The benefices, of which they disposed a first time as present favours, they sold a second time as matters of reversion; and they were thus disposed of, neither to the best, nor to the most learned, but to the most wealthy." Clemangis goes on to trace a hideous picture of the excessive ignorance and degradation into which the clergy had fallen; he describes them as gadding from house to house, gambling, drinking, and giving themselves up to all kinds of excess. Passing from the corruptions of the secular clergy to that of the monasteries,—"Now," says he, "when a maiden takes the veil she may be looked upon as dishonoured."[*]

It has been said by modern writers, that the famous work of Clemangis was exaggerated.[†] We do not, however, find that it was contradicted by any contemporary: no voice was raised to refute these overwhelming accusations; they were, on the contrary, confirmed by all. If we turn to the Cardinal of Cambray, Peter D'Ailly, the master and friend of Gerson, we read in one of his treatises: "The corruption of the Church is so great, that it is said proverbially to be only fit to be governed by reprobates."[‡]

Gerson himself declares, "The Court of Rome has invented a thousand Church services to make money, but few, indeed, have been made for the sake of virtue only. We hear much from morning to night in that court, of armies, and lands, and towns, and money, but we seldom or ever hear of chastity, charity, justice, fidelity, and morality; so that that court, which was formerly spiritual, has now become worldly, devilish, tyrannical, and worse than any secular one. . . . The secular powers ought not to suffer the spouse of Jesus Christ to be thus profaned."[*] Gerson protests against the rules of the chancellor's court, which permitted churches, prebendaries, and other benefices, to be conferred on persons of the meanest condition, such as cooks, grooms, muleteers, and even upon assassins, whilst the ablest and the best were neglected.[†]

If such were then the clergy, what must have been the state of the laity educated entirely by them, and who, receiving such melancholy examples, never thought of the simple and affecting precepts of our Saviour, but sought for instruction and direction in the subtle lessons of casuists and theologians? What pure and sound morality could be expected from those who were taught to consider an error in doctrine more offensive to God than a crime—that money would buy the pardon of sin—that none were bound to keep their word when given to a heretic—and that to betray or destroy such was a work of piety?

These principles produced their fruits; never in Europe, and above all in France, even in times of the most violent political convulsions, had there been so few great characters; so many men guilty, and so few just; so great a number of evils, and fewer remedies.

The consolations of Heaven were wanting to the wretched; and the promises of a future life possessed no balm for present misery, among those who turned a look more of fear than hope towards another world. The confidence of the people in the pardons of the Church had been shaken, when they beheld one pope excommunicated by another, and found that an error of judgment might change blessings into maledictions. Among the many evils of the schism, this certainly was the greatest, although the least spoken of by the historians; and it drew from the despairing multitude long stifled cries of rage—they turned with fury against those who prolonged the scourge, to which they attributed all their woes—its extinction had become their only thought—they firmly believed, that the day which saw the end of the schism, would also behold the term of all their sufferings.

Although this was the opinion of the mass, those who added to a real desire of good some degree of intellectual illumination, whether priests or laymen, saw farther, and demanded

---

[*] The expressions Clemangis uses are far more energetic than those we can employ here.
[†] Michelet, *Histoire de France*, t. iv.
[‡] Petr. de Alliac, *Can. Reform. ap. Von der Hardt*, v. i. p. 424.

[*] Gers. *De Mod. Uniend. et Reform. Eccles.*
[†] Cum illi qui sunt familiares cardinalium, aliquando homicidæ, illiterati, seu irregulares, coqui stabularii, mulaterii, per hujusmodi regulas cancellariæ possint in ecclesiis cathedralibus habere dignitates, canonicatus; sed illi qui sunt magistri in artibus vel medicinis, baccalaurii in jure canonico vel civili, nequaquam possint tali gratia gaudere. (Gers. *Ibid.* v. ii. p. 194.)

more; they awoke as out of a protracted slumber; and from having long suffered through the ambition of the popes, they ventured, at length, to judge of the rights of the papacy.

It was now possible to look upon that sun which, dimmed and divided, no longer dazzled the eye of investigation—spots were discovered, which had hitherto been unknown—the title to all this power was sought for, and the book, in which such title was said to be consigned, was opened; that which had not been attempted for ages was now undertaken—the Scripture was searched to find the model of the primitive Church, and the surprise, on discovering what was sought, was great in the extreme. Formidable and important questions then arose in the hearts of men; and the world was pregnant with those fruitful ideas which can arrive at maturity only amidst the tempest. There were many who looked upon the disorders of the Church as mere external vices—as infractions made by the clergy to the laws of morality; they were for preserving intact the doctrines of the Church and its hierarchical organisation; they considered that a better balancing of its power would suffice to render its action less liable to misuse; and that, to purify the edifice, it was enough to cleanse the outside to restore it to its former beauty: those reckoned in their numbers many well-meaning persons, but who, held down by the double trammels of habit and prejudice, dreaded above all things the novelties or aberrations of individual judgment.

Others, less timid, thought that it was the edifice itself which must be renewed—that it was not merely degraded outwardly, but that it was decayed at its foundation, and that human hands had meddled with that basis which had been laid by a hand divine. They considered that the clergy who had so far wandered from the truth on points so clearly defined as all moral questions are in the Scripture, had, no doubt, wandered still farther on obscure and dogmatical points, which are subject to so many different interpretations; they asked, whether the surest sign of a false doctrine was not, as in the time of the apostles, its immorality; and if that Church, from which had proceeded so many maledictions against heretics, were not itself tainted with heresy.

Once entered upon this bold path, they no longer paused, but applied this rule of appreciation with rigorous precision and unswerving logic to the doctrines of popery; many of those doctrines appeared to them false, dangerous, and culpable; they looked upon them as so many heresies, and branded as such the right which the popes assumed of making use of excommunication to serve their temporal interests—of setting at variance the nations whom they called to arms—of trafficking in the pardon of sins—of releasing from oaths taken—and of proclaiming themselves to be holy, infallible, and sovereigns of the world. In none of these claims or pretences could they discover the good Shepherd who gives his life for the sheep, nor the servant of the servants of God.

Finally, considering that the lamentable anarchy into which the Church had fallen was the consequence of such reprehensible doctrines, they felt assured that the errors which might arise from liberty of conscience could never become more fatal to the world than had been the abuse of the principle of authority.

This twofold manner of viewing the evil of the Church gave birth to two important opinions as to the means of curing it—one was to act with the clergy, and by the clergy; the other without the clergy, and against it, should such an extreme become necessary. The first opinion hoped every thing from the synods, and acknowledged the œcumenical councils as the only infallible authority; the second attributed infallibility to the Divine word alone, as it is revealed in the Holy Scriptures; and left to reason and conscience the care of its interpretation. The first of these opinions was that of the Universities, and of the greater number of the prelates who were not Italians; and its most illustrious advocate was, at the time of the schism, John Charlier Gerson, Chancellor of the University of Paris. The second opinion had been for ages that of all those who had separated from the Roman Church, on seeing it, under its ambitious pontiffs, wander so far from the narrow road traced by its Divine Founder. Towards the end of the fourteenth century, at the commencement of the schism, this opinion was that of Wycliffe, who had for disciples, in the fifteenth century, John Huss, and in the sixteenth, Luther.

V.

WYCLIFFE AND GERSON.

The men who have become celebrated in the struggles of their time, by their character or their genius, are better understood, in proportion as we are more intimately acquainted with the guides whom they selected, or the adversaries with whom they had to contend.

Under this twofold aspect the grand and melancholy features of John Huss are inseparable in history from those of Wycliffe and of Gerson; to mention these is almost to speak of Huss—one was his master, the other his accuser and judge.

Both, besides, hold an immense place in the period of which we are now retracing the history—Gerson, by his life, his zeal in resisting the pope and heretics, in defending the Gallican doctrines, and the principles of morality, and in establishing the Church upon the authority of councils—Wycliffe, by the remembrance he has left behind, and by his writings, which inspired John Huss, and were the objects of emulation and admiration to the Reformers, and of anger and alarm to the Roman clergy.

These two great characters, which appear even in our day in such opposite ranks, offer, nevertheless, in their dispositions, as well as in their conduct, many more points of resemblance than of contrast.

In the one, as in the other, active and fervent piety was united to superior intelligence; in both, the great cause of religion was inseparable from reason and morality; both were equally enemies of that scholastic divinity which would substitute the discourses and writings of theologians, and the vain cavils of logic, for the inspirations of a clear-headed reason, and a liberal mind; both sought for that living knowledge which could reach the heart, instead of the idle system of dialectics, of which Bacon has said that it was the art of splitting a hair in four, and which Gerson compares to a spider's web, the slender thread of which can be of no use to the truth.[*] Both were animated with an equal indignation against the guilty conduct of a clergy who had forsaken the worship in spirit, for a religion merely ceremonial, and who neglected or disdained to awaken the soul by oral instruction, and the preaching of the Gospel.[†]

Finally, Wycliffe and Gerson endeavoured, each, to arrest, by the temporal arm, the encroachments of the priesthood; they possessed the confidence of the kings whom they represented in circumstances of much difficulty; and subsequently, when such countenance was withdrawn from them, they did not hesitate to sacrifice their interests to their principles, and after having wasted their lives in thus heroically resisting the intolerable oppressions of papacy, they died—the one censured and suspended by the Church, and disgraced by the king; the other in the rigour and seclusion of a voluntary exile. Both had been accused of heresy by the implacable and bitter enemies whom each had raised up against himself amongst his own order; and it would, in fact, be difficult to tell which of the two, when he brings to light the abuse made of riches and power, and the fatal consequences of the ambition of the Court of Rome, and stamps with infamy the corruption of the clergy, regular or secular, assumes a loftier tone, and employs more energetic and stringent language. This will be seen by the following examples.

In defining the Church, and limiting the spiritual power of the pope, Wycliffe thus expresses himself:—"When men speak of holy church, anon they understand prelates and priests, with monks, and canons, and friars, and all men who have tonsures, though they live accursedly. . . . . Nevertheless, all who shall be saved in the bliss of heaven, are members of holy church, and no more. Many, on the contrary, who are called such are the enemies thereof, and the synagogue of Satan.[*] Prelates, also, make many new points of belief, and say it is not enough to believe in Jesus Christ, and to be baptized—as Christ saith in the gospel by St. Mark—except a man also believe that the Bishop of Rome is the head of holy church. But certainly no apostle of Jesus Christ ever constrained any man to believe this of himself. And yet they were certain of their salvation in heaven. How, then, should any sinful wretch constrain men to believe that he is head of holy church, while he knows not whether he shall be saved or lost? Certainly, when the Bishop of Rome is one who shall be condemned for his sin, it is a devil of hell that they would compel men to regard as the head of holy church!"[†]

The opinion of Gerson on this capital point is not less precise:—

"The universal church," said he, "is an assemblage of all Christians, Greeks, and Barbarians, men and women, nobles and peasants, rich and poor. It is that church which, according to tradition, can neither err nor fail;

---

[*] Vitandæ sunt araneæ, quæ ipsi Minervæ (quam sapientiæ Deam fingunt) ideo invisæ ac odiosæ feruntur, quod in subtilissimorum, sed fragilium filorum contextione se ipsas eviscerant. Debent enim solida esse et fortia sapientiæ documenta, nec tam cassæ soliditatis quam planæ veritati deservientia.—Gers. *Sermo in die Septuag.* an. 1388, vol. iii. p. 1029.

[†] Christ preached the Gospel, and has ordered all his apostles and his disciples to go and preach the Gospel to all men. . . O Lord! since Jesus and John, pressed by charity, left their solitude and preached to the people, what heretics are those who dare to say, that it is better to rest in retirement, and practise pretended ordinances, than to preach the Gospel of Christ?—*Wycliffe MS. Of a Feigned Contemplative Life.*

Gerson writes from Bruges to Peter d'Ailly, in his Fourth Letter on Theological Reform:—"I speak from experience. I declare, that in our cathedral churches, and almost everywhere, there are absurd rites celebrated, which are the remains of the sacrilegious ceremonies of pagans and idolaters. . . The word of God, which is indeed the great balm for all spiritual malady, the preaching of which is the principal duty of prelates, is given up as useless and beneath their grandeur."—*Gers. Oper.* b. i. p. 121.

[*] Wycliffe. On Eight Things by which Simple Men are destroyed.—Vaughan, vol. ii. p. 279.

[†] Manuscript of Prelates.—Vaughan, vol. ii. p. 273.

its chief is Jesus Christ alone; pope, cardinals, prelates, clergy, kings, and people, are, all members of it, though in different degrees. There is another church nominated apostolic, which is particular, and contained in the universal church—namely, the pope and the clergy; it is that body which is called the Roman Church; which has the pope as head, and the other ecclesiastics as members. That church can both err and fail—it may deceive or be deceived—it may fall into schism and heresy—it is merely the organ or the instrument of the universal church, and has no authority, except as far as the universal church allows it, for the exercise of that power which belongs to it alone. . . . . The church has the right of deposing popes who render themselves unworthy or incapable of exercising their office; for if a king, who holds the kingdom from his ancestors, may be deposed when the public good requires it, how much more may a pope, who owes his dignity only to the election of the cardinals, and whose father or grandfather may never have had even *his fill of beans?* Is it not intolerable that *the son of a Venetian fisherman** should pretend to the possession of the pontificate as if it were his inheritance, to the great discomfort of the church, and notwithstanding the opposition of kings, princes, and prelates?

"It is not the authority which falls to the pope that can render him holy, as that authority may devolve upon good or bad men; it is not even the papal seat, for it is the man who should sanctify the place, and not the place which sanctifies the man. . . . . What folly to allow that a poor mortal, a child of perdition, a miser, a liar, a fornicator, a wicked profligate, should assert that what he binds on earth is bound in heaven!"†

Speaking of the temporal and respective authority of popes and kings, Wycliffe not only disputes the rights of the pope over kingdoms and church possessions, but exposes the great abuse of decretals, and establishes, as a principle, that priests should be subjected to the civil law, and to the magistrates, in whatever regards either their property or their personal conduct.‡

Let us now turn to Gerson on the same subject, in his famous treatise already quoted, on the means of uniting and reforming the Church. He gives it to be understood that the books which had caused so much prejudice to the rights of the bishops and emperors, entitled, *The Sexte, The Clementines,* and *The Decretals,* owed their appearance entirely to the arrogance and pride of the Roman pontiffs. "And yet," says he, "the popes required that they should be received as gospel.* . . . . And as to the maxim that the pope may be judged by none, it is their own invention, and is contrary both to natural and divine right, which require, that as the pope is a man, and consequently subject to error and sin, he should be judged like any other man for every fault, and even more severely than another, as his elevation renders his faults so much more dangerous. . . . The pope is not greater than Jesus Christ or St. Peter, who were subject to the secular powers, and ordered all men to be subject to them, in like manner. Jesus Christ, more particularly, declared that his kingdom was not of this world, and fled when the multitude would have made him a king. Can we, then, suffer that a guilty pope should be exempted from subjection to that authority which was submitted to by Him who knew no sin? . . . In times of schism," continues Gerson, "it is the part of the emperor, as advocate and defender of the Church, to assemble the councils, with the concurrence of the kings and princes of Christendom; it is their part, as well as that of all other nobles, to employ their authority, and even to sacrifice their life, for the good of the Church, of which they are the fathers, the physicians, and even the surgeons, who have the right to cut or pluck away all gangrened parts, from head to foot."†

The analogy between the words of Wycliffe and those of Gerson, when speaking of discipline and morals, may also be found on some dogmatical points, particularly on that which

---

* Gregory XII.

† Ridiculum enim est dicere, quod unus homo mortalis dicat se potestatem habere in coelo et in terra ligandi et solvendi a peccatis, et quod ille sit filius perditionis, simoniacus, averus, mendax, fornicator, superbus, et pejor quam diabolus.—Gers. 211, p. 168.

‡ "Christ and his apostles were most obedient to kings and lords, and taught all men to be subject to them, and to serve them truly and cheerfully. The wise king Solomon, also, put down a high bishop, who was unfaithful to him and his kingdom, and exiled him and ordered a good priest in his room; and Jesus Christ paid tribute to the emperor.

. . . Our Saviour meekly suffered a painful death under Pilate, not excusing himself from that jurisdiction by virtue of his office; . . . and Paul appealed to the heathen emperor from the priests of the Jews. . . . Lord, who hath made our worldly clergy exempt from the king's jurisdiction and chastening, since God hath given kings this office over all misdoers? . . . and this seems well, according to their new law of decretals, where proud clerks have ordained that our clergy shall pay no subsidy nor tax, nor any thing for the keeping of our king and our realm, without assent from the worldly priest of Rome; and yet many times this proud worldly priest is an enemy of our Lord, and secretly maintaining our enemies in war against us with our own gold. Thus, an alien priest, and the proudest of all priests, they make the chief lord over the greater part of our country."—(MS. Sentence of the Court expounded.)

* Gerson, *ubi supra,* p. 166.

† Ibid. p. 180, 187.

treats of the power of the priest in the tribunal of penitence.

Nothing, assuredly, is more worthy of remark, in all the doctrine of Gerson, than that; and on no subject has he ventured so far on the extreme limits which divide the catholic and dissenting communions. "The pope," he says, " does not possess the power he supposes, either on earth or in heaven. He has no other power than that of declaring that absolution exists in the spiritual domain. . . . . The pope cannot forgive sins, but God alone, who cleanses from all iniquity; the pope absolves, that is, shows the sinner how he may be absolved. It must be confessed that the pope does not trouble himself much about setting forth this doctrine, which is, however, conformable to both truth and reason. Let us admit that he says,—All power is given to me in heaven and on earth, in purgatory and in paradise : of the plenitude of my own power I can do all things; and none may say to me, What doest thou ? But then the pope ought not to lie in his letters, and call himself the servant of servants. He ought rather to say, I am the master of the masters of the world."[*]

Wycliffe scarcely went farther, and on this very important subject he thus gives his opinion : " Worldly prelates blaspheme against God, the Father of heaven, by taking to themselves a power which is especially and only his, that is, a power of absolving from sin, and of giving a full remission of them; and they induce the people to believe this of them, when, in truth, they have only absolved as vicars or messengers, witnessing to the people that, on their contrition, God absolveth them. Without the sinner be contrite, that is, fully have sorrow for his sins, neither angel, nor man, nor God himself, absolveth him."[†]

The difference, upon this point, between Wycliffe and Gerson, is rather in the conclusions they draw from their principles, than in the principles themselves; it is a difference in the spirit, not in the letter. Gerson removes still farther from the dogma of the Church of Rome, and agrees with St. Augustin and Wycliffe upon the doctrines of election and justification by faith without works; and perhaps on this subject he speaks even more clearly and more absolutely than the reformer of England. " Man," says Gerson, "can do nothing of himself to recover from the fall ; he merits nothing by his own works; Jesus Christ is the only Saviour, and he saves those only who have been predestined from all eternity."[*]

Gerson, no doubt, felt how short, in the appreciation of the clergy, was the distance which separated him from the heretics; at the price of his blood he would gladly have widened the space which he himself felt to be so narrow. He was anxiously advancing in what he considered the way of salvation, and he shuddered to think that one step beyond was an abyss into which, according to his catholic ideas, the Church might sink and disappear. Hence his excess of severity against those who overstepped this limit; the narrower it appeared to him, the greater were the obstacles which he conceived himself bound to raise against it, and for this end he called to his aid both terror and punishment. His mind, in that respect, led away his heart : he thought he should save the Church by the violence of the means made use of against those whom he considered as infected with heresy. The manner in which he persecuted Wycliffe, then dead, in his disciples and in his memory, shows sufficiently how little he would have spared him if living, and the affinity which we have discovered between that great man and himself would have been, in his opinion, a mortal outrage.

Several causes explain the very different ends at which Gerson and Wycliffe arrived, though they set out from principles which were quite analogous; and among the chief must be reckoned the great difference which existed in the religious establishment of the two countries.

In France, the glorious reminiscences of the episcopacy were linked, from the fall of the Roman empire, with all the great national traditions; they recalled ideas of protection, independence, and patriotism. In that country the greatest abuses of the Roman court had been repelled by the kings acting with their clergy ; the Church of France had preserved some liberties and several precious privileges. For these causes, those who, in France, called for a reform, were inclined to put their trust in the bishops, and to expect every thing from them. In England the case was different; the

---

[*] Ergo ipsi Papæ non est attributa potestas illa quam ipsi Papæ credunt in cœlo et in terra; sed solum est ei data potestas spiritualium denunciatoria ac absolutoria . . . nam Papa non remittit peccata, sed solus Deus est ille qui delet iniquitates. Sed bene absolvit, hoc est absolutum ostendit. . . Sed ponamus quod Papa non curet de ista expositione, quæ tamen verissima est, et rationis secutiva; sed dicat: certe potestatem habeo in cœlo et in terra, in purgatorio, in paradiso, et de plenitudine potestatis meæ possum facere quod mihi libet, et nullus debet esse qui dicat, Cur hoc facis? Revera tunc Papa non deberet mentiri in litteris suis, dicendo *servus servorum Dei*, sed Dominus dominorum mundi.—Gers. *ubi sup.* t. vi. p. 198.

[†] MS. *of Prelates*, c. xliii.—Vaughan's *Life and Opinions of Wycliffe*, vol. ii. p. 264.

[*] Neque confugiendum est ad illorum merita vel opera quos ab æterno prædestinat Deus: quia si ex operibus, jam non ex gratia.—Gers. *De Consol. Theol.* vol. i. p. 137, and the fol.—Compare this treatise of Gerson's with that of Wycliffe, entitled *De Veritate*, Script. Exposit.

remembrance of the Norman Conquest was not yet effaced; the inhabitants of Saxon origin, who composed the immense majority of the population, had not forgotten that the holy see had made over England to William, and that the bishops of their own race had been deposed to make way for the conquerors. It was the Norman prelates who had subjected Saxon England to the exactions of the Roman court; and the episcopacy, to the great mass of the nation, recalled only recollections of oppression and plunder. They, therefore, who demanded a reform, expected from the bishops neither aid nor sympathy.

This twofold fact, therefore, explains to a certain degree the very different object to which Wycliffe and Gerson tended, amidst circumstances which in so many respects were similar. Gerson, a member of that illustrious body which itself formed a part of the Gallican Church, placed his hope in the episcopacy, the universities, the bishops, and the doctors. Wycliffe, who looked upon the bishops of his country as foreigners and masters rather than pastors, placed his hope elsewhere; he did not acknowledge the ecclesiastical hierarchy, and sought for strength in the Holy Scriptures, which he declared to be the only infallible guide.

Once entered upon this path, each pursued it with the ardour which was natural to him. Influenced, however, by his situation and character, Gerson, a statesman and a man of action, formed from his youth to great affairs, attached a vast importance to ideas of order and authority, and sought to conciliate the institutions of the Church with sound morality, without weakening either. Wycliffe, leading a more retired and contemplative life, found that there were more motives for condemnation in the Church, than necessity for forbearance; he thought less of outward discipline, than of inward purification—of means of temporal coercion, than of the regeneration in spirit and in truth—of the priest, than of the Christian —of conformity to the traditions of the Church, than of the precepts of the Gospel.

Gerson said, " The papal see hath been filled by heretics and murderers; infallible authority is not, therefore, in the pope; it is in general councils which represent the Universal Church."

Wycliffe had said before him, " God alone can never err nor be deceived."

They both acknowledged that no man was really absolved or excommunicated, if he were not so by God himself. Gerson did not, however, conclude from this, that the word of the priest was unnecessary to declare and confirm the Divine sentence; but in the sight of

Wycliffe, the judgment given by God in heaven needed no ratification on earth by man.[*]

Gerson wished that the disposal of ecclesiastical property should be subjected to certain rules, which should insure its appropriation to the benefit and edification of Christendom. Wycliffe, who was convinced that the clergy would never be very rich, without being very corrupt, desired that the priesthood should return to the poverty of the apostles; he affirmed that the clergy possessed nothing in its own right; that, in the New Testament, the tithes were simply given as alms; and that if the priests did not employ such riches according to the intentions of the givers, they ought to be deprived of them.

Gerson, who always rendered his bold views subordinate to ideas of external order and religious and spiritual authority, invariably considered the priest as a man endowed with power from the Holy Ghost; Wycliffe thought, on the contrary, that inward regeneration, in the hope of eternal salvation—that union with God through faith in His Divine Son—and a life in conformity with that of Jesus Christ, were the sole end of religion, the sum-total of Christianity. He thought that God endowed with spiritual power those only who were in a state to receive it; and he did not believe that a word of excommunication or absolution, pronounced by a priest, stained himself with iniquity, could open or shut the gates of either heaven or hell on any. He drew the logical conclusion, that it is for man, aided by Divine grace, to work out his own salvation; and he laid down unhesitatingly the following propositions, subversive of ecclesiastical power, such as it had till then been attributed to churchmen:—At the hour of death it is in vain that the wicked man be furnished with bulls of indulgences and pardons, and enriched with innumerable masses said by monks and priests—the prayer of a wicked priest is of no value in the sight of God—none are truly priests or bishops who do not conform their lives to the law of Christ; for it is by that law alone that any power is given to them.[†]

Lastly, Gerson admitted the greater part of the convictions generally received in the catholic world in his times; Wycliffe rejected, among other dogmas, that which had been imposed on the faith of England after the Norman Conquest; he rejected the doctrine of transubstantiation.[‡] It may be seen, from what has been already said, that Wycliffe's doctrines were followed up by him to their extremest.

---

* Vaughan's *Life of Wycliffe*, ch. v. and viii.
† Ibid. ch. v. and viii.
‡ He did not admit either the real presence.

consequences with unity and precision; whilst Gerson, less free and more divided, shrank from the deduction of the principles which he himself had laid down. His mind was in a state of perpetual and painful conflict; if, on the one hand, he yielded to the charm of these opening ideas, so well in harmony with the movements of his own soul, excited as he was by the indignation which the corruption of his Church called forth; on the other, he was kept back, restrained by his filial respect for that same Church, and by the very legitimate apprehension of the aberrations of individual judgment in the breast of a rude and ignorant population, in a country without a government, and nearly without law. Thus he not only stopped at those limits which, as we have seen, Wycliffe overstepped, but he was often inconsistent with himself. "We owe no obedience," said he, "to mistaken or criminal superiors."[*] He gave in his own person the example of invincible resistance to the orders of a pope whom he acknowledged as legitimate:[†] yet we see him devoting himself with indefatigable ardour, and composing several remarkable works,[‡] to effect the re-establishment of the hierarchical and ecclesiastical authority to which he had given so rude a shock. "The Universal Church alone is infallible," said Gerson; "it is composed of the clergy and of all believers." But in laying down democracy as a principle in the Church, he did not establish it as reality, or in deed; he sought security against the multitude as against the pope; and endeavoured to consti-

tute in the Church a representative power—a double aristocracy of rank and science, of prelates and of doctors; he wished that the people should be represented, but he did not admit that they should choose their representatives. The ecclesiastical authority thus rested on purely arbitrary bases; its decisions, supported by the civil power,' might regulate external and temporal things; but how could they bind the conscience, or govern the secret approach of man to God, and what connection was there between a certain rank in science, and sovereign authority in matters of faith? Gerson recommended, as the antidote to all great evils, the meditation of the Divine word; he wished that, like a torrent, it should flow into the heart of man; yet, at the same time, he forbade the reading of the Scriptures to the simple and unlearned, and condemned the translation of the Bible in the vulgar tongue.[*] In fine, he turned all his endeavours towards a moral reformation in the Church, and called upon those who lived by its abuses to aid him in effecting this object. This was his great delusion—the reformation of the clergy by the clergy themselves was the labour of his whole life. It was a noble and Christian aim, but a most unattainable one; and towards it he ever tended, with a courage and a constancy worthy of our admiration.

We shall follow him upon that grand theatre where he combatted, and where he so sadly erred, but where perhaps he alone escaped, such were his sincerity and devotedness, from the horror inspired by the guilty and barbarous scenes in which he was an actor:—the blood of the martyrs has left unstained his venerable head. We shall accompany him in his struggles, in his defeats, and in the ruin of his dearest hopes; and when, in the eyes of man, he is overcome, downcast, and vanquished, it is then that we shall find him truly great before God.

Finally, we may state that deceptions embittered and shortened the days of Gerson, whilst death itself was not sufficient to shield Wycliffe from the resentment of his enemies. The former was ill seconded in the noblest part of his undertaking, which was to reform the morals of the clergy; but in the struggle against the encroachments of the Roman Church, he was necessarily supported by the episcopacy, at whose expense the papal power had been increased. Wycliffe, on the contrary, as he not only attacked the morality, but also the power, of the priesthood, raised

---

[*] Sic ergo concludo quod superioribus sit obediendum in licitis et honestis; non autem compelli debemus ad eorum obedientiam, ubi opera eorum sunt notorie prava . . . Ubi pastores sunt tonsores; ubi non sunt agni sed lupi, ubi non sunt prælati ponentes animas suas pro ovibus suis, sed Pilati satisfacientes aliorum cupiditatibus et desideriis, et ubi non mittunt retia sua in capturam animarum, sed pecuniarum; ubi non Christi, sed mores gerunt Anti-Christi.—Gers. De Mod. un. et ref. Eccl. t. ii. p. 193.

[†] See especially the treatise De Anti-Christ. Pap., and the answer he gave, in the name of the University of Paris, to the bull of Pope Alexander V. in favour of the Mendicant Order of Monks. "A great trouble," said he, "has arisen in the Church, on account of a certain writing, under the form of an edict, which some of the four mendicant orders have obtained, or rather extorted by surprise from our Holy Father the pope; and it is certain that the Holy Father, who is a profound theologian, would never have granted it, had he taken time to examine it; but (as all the grave doctors of the University allow) it has been done without him, or at least without giving him time for previous judgment and deliberation; as it often happens to men much occupied to grant certain things to importunity, or by surprise, or by a yielding of conscience."—Gerson, Serm. Sup. Bull. Mend. vol. ii. p. 435.

[‡] Tract. de Eccles. Potest.—Tract. de Unit. Eccles.

[*] Rursus sequitur ex præmissis prohibendum esse vulgarem translationem librorum sacrorum nostræ Bibliæ, præsertim extra moralitates et historias. Gers. Secunda Lectio contra vanam Curiositatem, vol. i. p. 105.

up the whole body against him as his adversaries.

The doctrines of the Gallican Church were, if it may be so said, personified in Gerson. He was the soul and centre of the great assemblies in which they were discussed and acknowledged during the schism ; the doctrine of Wycliffe resumed the divers opinions of several great men who had preceded him, and, among others, of Claudius of Turin, Arnold of Brescia, Berenger, and Peter Valdo. Wycliffe united them in a more complete and scientific manner—he renewed and embodied them as it were : he grounded them, first, on the ruin of the ecclesiastical power, considered in a spiritual point of view as infallible, and in a temporal point of view as independent of the civil power ; and, secondly, on the authority of the Scriptures interpreted by the light of reason, and of which he gave the first translation in the English language.

Gerson was the great precursor of Bossuet. Wycliffe was the forerunner of Luther. By the boldness of his language and his genius,

and by the example of his whole life, he was the real parent of the great Reformation to which Luther gave his name. That glory was denied to Wycliffe, because the success of human opinions depends less upon their real value than upon the times and circumstances in which they are produced. To insure the triumph of the principles which Wycliffe, at one extremity of the Christian world, had laid down with so much logic and eloquence, it was necessary that those doctrines should be carried beyond the sea and take root, at a more suitable moment, in the heart of Europe ; it was necessary that men, whose intellect could only be equalled by their virtue, should spread these principles abroad, and afterwards seal them with their blood. This, in part, took place at the time of the great schism of the west ; it was the work of a Christian who offered his life in sacrifice to the cause of religious liberty—that Christian and martyr was JOHN HUSS.*

* See note B, relative to Wycliffe, at the end of the volume.

BOOK I.

CHAPTER I.

THE EARLY LIFE OF JOHN HUSS—HIS DOCTRINES—DISCUSSIONS IN
THE UNIVERSITY.

THE Emperor Charles IV. was reigning in Bohemia, when, in the year 1373, JOHN HUSS was born in that kingdom, in the small town of Hussinetz, from which he derives his name. This infant, destined to cause, both in his own country and in the whole of Germany, so profound a commotion, owed his existence, like Luther, to honest peasants, who spared no sacrifice to give him a good education;—kind, simple people, who had no other thought than to assure him a happy life, in getting him as well instructed as possible in sacred and profane learning, without once supposing that they were thus adorning, with all their care, a victim for the sacrifice.

Huss finished his studies at Praschalitz, a town not far from his birthplace; and afterwards his mother, who had become a widow, herself conveyed him to Prague, to take out his degrees in the celebrated university of that capital. Contemporary writers have handed us down a circumstance connected with this journey, which, though of but little importance in itself, yet depicts, in a simple manner, the artless and touching character of this estimable woman. Having taken with her a goose and a cake, as a present to the rector, it so happened that on the way the goose escaped. This untoward incident appeared to the poor mother of so disastrous an augury, that, falling on her knees, she prayed to God to pour a blessing on her dear infant's head, and then getting up, she continued her journey, affected alike with regret for the loss which she had sustained, and with uneasiness at such an omen.

History has preserved, respecting John Huss's youthful days, but few of these precious details in which we love to study the germs of a great character, and by which the man of mature age sometimes appears revealed in the child. We know, however, that at an early age he manifested marks of a fervent piety, and great leaning towards that enthusiasm which produces examples of sublime devotedness. One winter's evening, when reading by the fire the life of St. Laurence, his imagination kindled at the narration of the martyr's sufferings, and he thrust his own hand into the flames. Being suddenly prevented by one of his fellow-pupils from holding it there, and then questioned as to his design, he replied: "I was only trying what part of the tortures of this holy man I might be capable of enduring."

All persons have agreed in attributing to him an elevated mind, a persuasive facility of language, and an exemplary morality. "John Huss,"—says the Jesuit Balbinus, a writer who cannot by any means be considered as favourable to him,—"John Huss was even more remarkable for his acuteness than his eloquence; but the modesty and severity of his conduct, his austere and irreproachable life, his pale and melancholy features, his gentleness and affability to all, even the most humble, persuaded more than the greatest eloquence."[*]

Huss made a rapid progress in his new studies, and his talents soon shone forth with great lustre. He had taken orders, as was the custom then for the greater part of men of learning and education, and he distinguished himself not less in the Church than he had done in the schools. His reputation reached the court of King Wenceslaus, in 1400, who had succeeded his father, Charles IV., on the hereditary throne of Bohemia, and the imperial throne. This prince's second wife, Queen Sophia of Bavaria, selected Huss as her confessor; and he made himself numerous and powerful friends, as much by the favour of

* Subtilior tamen quam eloquentior semper est habitus Hussus; sed mores ad omnem servitutem conformati, vita horrida et sine deliciis, omnibus abrupta, quam nullus accusare posset, tristis et exhausta facies, languens corpus, et parata omnibus obvia, etiam vilissimo cuique, benevolentia, omni lingua facundius perorabant.—Balbinus, *Epit. Rer. Bohem.* p. 431.

this queen, as by his personal merit. His celebrity, however, only dates from the year 1404; and the chapel of Bethlehem, in which he officiated, was the veritable cradle of his renown.

The writings of Wycliffe were then known at Prague. The marriage of Richard II., King of England, with Anne, sister of the King of Bohemia, having drawn the two countries more closely together, a pretty constant intercourse had been established between them; and a young Bohemian, on his return from a journey to England, brought back with him from Oxford the works of the great heresiarch. John Huss read them; but such daring opinions then astonished, without convincing him; and even, if we are to believe Theobald, a writer that must be classed amongst the best informed, John Huss, at first, perused Wycliffe's writings with a pious horror.[*] He gave the young man the advice to burn them, or throw them into the Moldau.

Soon after, however, a considerable number of copies of Wycliffe's works were brought to Bohemia, and Huss formed a far more favourable opinion of his doctrines. The scandalous struggle between the two pontiffs, the luxury and arrogance of the cardinals, and the corruption of the clergy, had made on him a painful impression, which disturbed him even in his sleep.

But a religious revolution was still far removed from his thoughts, and most extraordinary events were required to lead him to it. If the scandals of the Church, torn as it was by schism, were revolting to his pious mind, all violent rupture was offensive to his gentle and modest character; and it must be declared in his praise, that the insurrection, of which he was one of the first to give an example, was not, on his part, a systematic and coolly premeditated opposition, but the effect of a zealous indignation; and that it was much less the rebellion of a disobedient feeling than the generous outbreak of an upright and Christian heart.

Various circumstances wonderfully favoured, in Bohemia, the free movement of men's minds. The celebrated University of Prague, founded by Charles IV., had rendered this city a great centre of information: men of intelligence, at once enlightened and determined, resorted thither from all parts of Germany; and if in no country was the corruption of the clergy greater than in this kingdom, so nowhere also were the writings which branded it with reprobation more widely spread abroad, and more learnedly commented on. There, the culpable priests, when defied by the multitude,

found in the government neither favour nor support. The king of Bohemia, Wenceslaus, had, on account of his vices, been stripped of the imperial dignity in 1400, by the diet of Frankfort; and, irritated at his dethronement, he harboured an angry feeling towards the pope, because he had approved of what had been done. Indifferent, in other respects, to an intellectual awakening, of which it was impossible for him to appreciate the cause, or anticipate the consequences, he tolerated the reactionary movement much less through predilection for the partisans of a reformation, than through hatred for their adversaries. Queen Sophia, with the utmost freedom, afforded her powerful protection to the former, and particularly to John Huss.

In proportion as the schism continued, Huss studied more seriously the writings of Wycliffe, and spoke of them with greater praise. He put himself forward, neither as the leader of a sect, nor as an innovator: he laid claim to no admiration, or submission, or eulogium, from others; he simply drew his force from the authority of the Divine word, which he preached in his chapel of Bethlehem with an indefatigable zeal, and which, it was asserted, the priests had disfigured or veiled to such a degree, that it seemed as if the Holy Word was then for the first time brought forward in Bohemia.

Less daring than Wycliffe, John Huss admitted in principle the greater part of the fundamental dogmas of the Roman Church, which the former rejected. In certain points, such as the efficacy of prayers for the dead, the worship of saints, auricular confession, and the power of the priests to give absolution and to excommunicate, he blamed the principle much less than the abuse. He appeared to agree perfectly with Wycliffe on three points only, but each of them of extreme importance: viz. the appeal to Scripture as the only infallible authority—the necessity of bringing back the clergy to discipline and moral conduct, either by depriving them of all intervention in temporal affairs, or in stripping them of the property of which they made so bad a use—and, lastly, the communication of spiritual powers to the priests by the Holy Ghost, on account of their internal purity, and only in such proportion as they should be fit to receive them, and worthy to employ them.

The first of these three principles quite contained in itself the seeds of a revolution;—the second raised up the clergy in a mass against John Huss, and rendered their resentment towards him implacable and deadly;—the third was never clearly explained or defined either by Wycliffe or Huss, and it is not certain that either of them, and in particular

---

[*] Theobald, Bell. Hussit. c. ii. p. 2.

THE EARLY LIFE OF JOHN HUSS.

the former, ever very well comprehended its immense scope and influence. Such a principle is really admissible only in those religious communions where all the acts necessary for the regeneration and salvation of the Christian can be accomplished in himself, independently of the powers of the priest;—where the virtue of the sacrament, when given, is considered as operating only according to the frame of mind of the person receiving it;—and where the believer, in fine, feels that there is no need of any other mediator between him and God, than Jesus Christ. . Otherwise, if the ministry of the clergy is regarded as endowed with a peculiar power and virtue, indispensable either to free the young child from original sin, to absolve believers, to legitimise marriages, or to perpetuate in the Church the apostolic succession, how can it be admitted that the vices of the man annul in the priest the spiritual virtue of his words and acts? This was the formidable problem which John Huss could not resolve; and in all probability it was also the hidden source from which emanated the numerous woes that were legible on his pale brow, and his many aspirations after the sacrifice which was to terminate his life, and give him eternal rest.

We can now comprehend all the conflicts that he had to sustain before he dared to declare himself openly; and he informs us himself how at last he came to form his determination. After having referred to the well-known passage in Ezekiel,[*] where God orders the prophet to dig into the wall of the temple, in order to behold the abominations which were there committed, he exclaims, "I, also I, have been raised up by God to *dig in the wall*, in order that the multiplied abominations of the holy place may be laid open. It has pleased the Lord to draw me forth from the place where I was, like a brand from the burning. Unhappy slave of my passions as I was, it was necessary that God himself should rescue me, like Lot from the burning of Sodom; and I have obeyed the voice which said to me, *Dig in the wall*. . . . . I next beheld a door, and that door was the Holy Scriptures, through which I contemplated the abominations of the monks and the priests, laid open before me and represented under divers emblems. Never did the Jews and Pagans commit such horrible sins in presence of Jesus Christ, as those bad Christians and hypocritical priests commit every day in the midst of the Church."[†] Therefore, from that period, he went every-

where, as he himself declares, preaching, writing, giving no repose to his soul, pressing on, in season and out of season, grappling with the whole body of the clergy, without sparing even the most powerful.

This opposition became public in 1407, the very year of the Council of Pisa. The archbishop of Prague at that period was the timid Sbinko, a man of little learning, but of great zeal for the privileges of his Church. His zeal, however, knew how to yield on proper occasions, for the prudence of the courtier modified in Sbinko the absolute principles of the ecclesiastical dignitary; and his course of action, with respect to the favourers of the heresy, was violent or moderate, according as they met with indifference or favour at court. Already, a few months before the opening of the council, John Huss having invited the people to join the cardinals, and to withdraw themselves from the authority of Gregory XII., the archbishop, one of that pontiff's creatures, had thundered against him, and laid him under an interdict. Soon after, however, Sbinko saw himself forced to recognise as pope, Alexander V., whom the council had elected; and a first reconciliation took place between the prelate and John Huss. This peace was not sincere; and about the same time there burst forth in the bosom of the University a grievous dispute, in which Huss took too great a share. He triumphed, it is true, but his victory became fatal to him; for it raised him up more enemies than a defeat would have left him.

The University of Prague had been founded by the Emperor Charles IV., on the model of the Universities of Paris and Bologna, and was divided into four nations—Bohemia, Bavaria, Poland, and Saxony—the three last being comprised under the general name of the German nation. Originally three votes were given to Bohemia, and only one to the three other nations united; but in the course of time the latter changed the order of the deliberations—the Germans usurping the three votes, and leaving only one to Bohemia. John Huss protested against this in the name of his countrymen: he pleaded for their privileges with more ardour than prudence; and, thanks to his credit, he gained his cause. Incensed at the loss of their suit and pretended privileges, the Germans abandoned Prague, and scattered themselves amongst the other Universities of the Continent. Bohemia and her capital suffered much from this desertion, which, however, carried Wycliffe's doctrines into circulation throughout the whole of Germany, and materially served the cause of the Reformation at a later period. John Huss, whose zeal for the privileges of his nation had drawn on him

---

[*] "And when I had digged in the wall, behold a door. And the Lord said unto me, Go in and behold the wicked abominations that they do here." Ezekiel viii. 8, 9.

[†] *Hist. et Monument. J. Hus.* p. 503.

so many new enemies, was then appointed rector of the University of Prague; but it may be truly asserted that Providence did not elevate him in dignity, but in order to invest his word with fresh authority, and to exhibit in a stronger light his Christian piety, by exposing him still more to the resentment of his persecutors.

CHAPTER II.

FIRST DISTURBANCES AT PRAGUE.—ELECTION OF JOHN XXIII.—THE FIRST EXILE OF HUSS.—HIS INTERNAL CONFLICTS.

THE tranquillity of John Huss was but of short duration, for, on December 20, 1409, Alexander V. published a bull against his doctrines, though without particularly designating himself. By this bull, it was forbidden to preach in private chapels, and to teach Wycliffe's doctrine in any place whatever; the archbishop was called on to proceed against all offenders as heretics, with the assistance of the secular authorities, and to suppress Wycliffe's books by every means in his power. To this Huss replied : "I appeal from Alexander ill-informed to Alexander better informed."

The archbishop, however, acted in obedience to the orders thus given, particularly as in doing so he followed his personal inclination. Already, the year before he had required all the holders of Wycliffe's books to deposit them at the episcopal palace: and now, emboldened by the pontiff's bull, he caused upwards of 200 volumes, beautifully written and richly ornamented, to be burned without any further proceedings,* which act gave birth to very formidable resentments. The price of books, which at that period were all manuscripts, was, before the invention of printing, elevated in proportion to their rarity, and their destruction almost always caused a serious loss to the possessors. A great number of the books burned by the archbishop belonged to members of the University of Prague. That dignitary had therefore violated their privileges, and John Huss undertook their defence, being doubly offended by this act of episcopal despotism, both in his authority as rector, and in his esteem for Wycliffe. He entered a protest against the sentence for its injustice, and the question was submitted to the University of Bologna.

But the archbishop went still farther, and summoned 'John Huss to appear before his tribunal, there to answer for his doctrine. When before him, amongst other causes of complaint, the archbishop charged him with

having denied the virtue of sepulture in consecrated ground, and with having asserted that the mortal remains of the dead could rest in fields and forests just as well as in cemeteries. "And yet, my dear son," added the archbishop, "you cannot be ignorant how many plagues from heaven formerly smote Bohemia on account of profane burials !" "If," replied John Huss, "any thing has fallen from me, either through error or forgetfulness, against the Christian faith, I shall amend it." The archbishop, in whose mind the orders of the pope and the influence of the court acted in contrary directions, dared not proceed farther, and dismissed John Huss. But the ensuing Sunday, the latter ascended the pulpit and said :—"It is a strange thing, my dear Bohemians, that a prohibition to teach manifest truths, and particularly those which obtain in England and other places, has been issued. Those private burials, those tapers and those bells, are of no other use than to fill the purses of covetous priests; and what they call order is nothing else but confusion. Believe me, that they want to enchain you by such commands, but you shall burst their bonds."

The University of Bologna gave judgment against the violent proceedings of the archbishop, and John Huss, strong in this decision, appealed to the pope. It is not unlikely that he might have obtained some respite from Alexander V., had not that dignitary merely remained for a moment on the pontifical throne. Allured to Bologna by Cardinal Balthazar Cossa, his legate in that city, and detained there for a short time, he died unexpectedly, in the beginning of the year 1410, and his death was imputed to the cardinal, both because he was deemed capable of having compassed it, and still more because he derived advantage from it. Balthazar, in fact, succeeded him ; he became pope, under the name of John XXIII., and never did the tiara chance to settle on a more unworthy brow.

Contemporary historians, though in other points differing much from each other, agree in speaking of this pontiff in very strong terms

* Supra ducenta volumina fuisse traduntur.— Æneas Sylvius, Hist. Boh. p. 69.

of reprehension. Thierry de Niem, who was his secretary, and who has written his life, represents him as a monster of avarice, ambition, lewdness, and cruelty,[*] and upbraids him in the bitterest terms with his simoniacal election—"You did not enter by the door," he observes, "but by the window. Of you it has been asserted, and with justice, that you broke through the threshold with a golden axe, and silenced the watch-dogs by cramming them with food, in order that they might not bark at you."[†]

Every man that recognised as true disciples and true ministers of Jesus Christ, only those who adopted him as their model, was sure to be looked on by John XXIII. as his mortal enemy; and consequently John Huss promptly became the object of his anger. The pontiff had him summoned before his court, and committed the affair to Cardinal Otho de Colonna, before whom he ordered him to appear at Bologna; but Huss, in risking the journey, would evidently place his life in jeopardy, and it then became apparent what prodigious influence he had been able to acquire. The King, the Queen, the University, and a great number of the principal barons of Bohemia and Moravia sent conjointly an embassy to the pope, to request him to dispense with John Huss's making the journey himself,—to receive his legal counsel,—and to send legates to Prague at the expense of the crown. Even the archbishop wrote in Huss's favour, declaring that they were reconciled, and that no heresy existed in Bohemia. All was useless; whether it was that the pope perceived that the position in which the archbishop was placed imparted but little value to his words,—or, as some authors assert, he never received his letter,—or, in fine, that Sbinko contradicted in secret what he affirmed in public, John XXIII. caused the proceedings that had been commenced to be pursued with vigour before new commissioners. Huss's legal defenders were not listened to, and had to undergo very unworthy treatment; and he himself, not making his appearance, was excommunicated. The pope confirmed the sentence, and laid Prague under an interdict. It was also forbidden to celebrate mass there, or to give baptism to children or burial to the dead, as long as John Huss remained there. This tremendous sentence threw the city into the wildest commotion, and was the cause of sedition and massacre.

Then John Huss's character shone forth in its true light, and it was perceived how completely his opposition was devoid of personal ambition. Although enjoying the protection of the court, with the people on his side, and

the indignation against the clergy general,—although he saw himself unjustly oppressed and borne down by a man who was an object of almost universal contempt, yet he did not profit by so many advantages to break irrevocably with an authority which he still respected even whilst he attacked it. In this conduct, too, was fully manifested the indecision of his feelings. He did not contest, in principle, the authority which he rejected in reality: he still beheld in the pope the successor of St. Peter, although debased and stripped of all spiritual power: he addressed the cardinals in humble and submissive terms, protesting his innocence, declaring that if it were necessary to prove it by suffering martyrdom, he would willingly do so; and concluded by praying that God might enlighten the pontiff who persecuted him. This Christian, so ardent and so strong when thundering forth against the scandals and abuses of the Church, was nothing but an humble, feeble, and unpretending man, when the question was to substitute the authority of his reason for that of his oppressors, and after having in vain appealed to men, he appealed to God. "Our Lord Jesus Christ," said he, "real God and real man, when encompassed by pontiffs, scribes, Pharisees, and priests, at once his judges and accusers, gave his disciples the admirable example of submitting their cause to the omniscient and omnipotent God. In pursuance of this holy example, I now appeal to God, seeing that I am oppressed by an unjust sentence, and by the pretended excommunication of the pontiff's scribes, Pharisees, and judges seated in the chair of Moses, —I, John Huss, present this my appeal to Jesus Christ, my Master and my Judge, who knows and protects the just cause of the humblest of men."

However, being surrounded with enemies, and beset with perils, he still hesitated,—torn as he was by a double fear, neither of which referred to his personal safety;—and in some affecting letters, written to his friends to ask their advice, he thus sets forth his hesitations and his struggles: "Our Saviour has said, 'You shall have tribulations in this world; but if the love of good is in ye, who shall injure ye?' Feeling, therefore, in myself," pursued John Huss, "the love of the heavenly word, and the zeal to disseminate it, my soul is sad, for I know not what to determine on. I have meditated on this word of our Saviour in the Scriptures: 'The good shepherd giveth his life for the sheep. But he that is a hireling and not the shepherd, seeing the wolf coming, leaveth the sheep and fleeth; and the wolf catcheth them and scattereth the sheep.' I have also reflected on this other text from St. Matthew: 'When they persecute you in one

* Ap. Von der Hardt. t. ii. part 14.
† Invectiv. in Job. xxiii. cap. vii.

5

city, flee ye to another.' Which of these two precepts must I follow ? Between these two contrary recommendations, which ought I to obey ? . . . . I cannot say."[*]

Huss at last determined on the latter course: he quitted his beloved chapel, and sought a refuge in his native village of Hussinetz, under the protection of the lord of the place. It was there that he wrote a little treatise, in which he proves, by the authority of the fathers, the popes, and the canons of the Church, as well as by reasoning, that *the books of heretics must be read, and not burned.*[†] From thence also he wrote to his disciples, to explain to them the cause of his retirement. "Learn, beloved," he says, "that if I have withdrawn from the midst of you, it is to follow the precept and example of Jesus Christ, in order not to give room to the ill-minded to draw on themselves eternal condemnation, and in order not to be to the pious a cause of affliction and persecution. I have retired also through an apprehension that impious priests might continue for a longer time to prohibit the preaching of the Word of God amongst you : but I have not quitted you to deny the divine truth, for which, with God's assistance, I am willing to die."[‡]

According to our Saviour's example, he went about preaching amongst the towns and villages, followed by an immense multitude, who listened to him with avidity, astonished that this man, so remarkable for modesty, gravity, and meekness, could be branded as a demon by the priests, and be rejected by the Church, when, without revolting against her spiritual authority, or against the principles from which she drew her strength, he merely attacked the abuses which placed her in peril.

His doctrines, however, had a more elevated meaning than that which he acknowledged to himself. He protested his attachment and respect for the Catholic Church : he declared his unwillingness to separate from it, and yet, unknown to himself, he was giving a sensible shock to its foundations, by maintaining that believers had the right to examine its decrees before they submitted to them. Who does not perceive that, on the one hand, obedience to a church which declares itself to be immutable and infallible, and, on the other, examination and appeal to an internal criterion—the conscience—are two things contrary to each other, and incompatible ? It would be a difficult thing to affirm that John Huss believed that he could reconcile them, or that he supposed that he had succeeded in the task. We cannot, indeed, comprehend how he could have

deceived himself on this point. Yet it is most certain that he attempted to effect an agreement between these two hostile principles, and that he thus carried in his bosom the germs of a violent struggle, at once irreconcileable and interminable. That was the formidable and insolvable problem, which agitated his life and hastened his end; and in a letter which he wrote from his retreat to his friend John Barbat, his internal combats, the reaction of a firm and upright heart against the influence of a preconceived idea, and of habit, are ingenuously displayed.[*]

"In order to be confirmed in the sweet peace of my spirit," said he, "I meditated within myself on the life and words of Christ and of his disciples. (Acts iv.) I called to mind in what manner Annas, the high priest, and Caiaphas, and John, and Alexander, and all the kindred of the priests, when addressing the apostles, forbade them to speak and teach in the name of Jesus. But Peter and John answered and said unto them, 'Judge ye yourselves, whether it be right in the sight of God, to hearken unto you more than to God.' . . . . And these same priests having again prohibited their preaching, they replied, (Acts v.) '*We ought to obey God rather than men.*' St. Jerome has said : 'If the master or bishop orders things which are not in contradiction to the faith or the Holy Scriptures, the servant is bound to obey; but should he command what is opposed to them, the Master of the spirit must be obeyed, rather than he of the body.' St. Augustine gives a similar opinion in his sermon on these words of our Lord : 'If an earthly power command that which you ought not to do, despise that power, and fear a higher one.' It is, therefore, our duty to resist the devil and men, when they suggest any thing against God ; and in doing so we do not really resist, but comply with, the orders of God himself. Gregory, in his moral instructions, also declares : 'Learn that obedience must never be paid, when evil would ensue from it.' St. Bernard, likewise, in one of his letters, says : 'To do evil by following the order of any person whatever, is not obedience, but disobedience.' " Such are the quotations which John Huss called to mind, in order to strengthen and encourage himself in preaching the word in spite of the prohibition of the priests. He betrays, however, in the same letter, the disquiet of his thoughts. "It is true," he remarks, "that the pagans, Jews, and heretics, all take their ground on the same precept of obedience due to God. Alas! it blinds those who are not Christians, but not the apostles and true disciples of Christ."

---

[*] *Hist. et Monum. Hus,* t. i. p. 117.
[†] Ibid. t. i. p. 127.   [‡] Ep. xi. p. 177.

[*] Ep. v. p. 119.

Who is there, that does not recognise in this language an ardent wish, rather than a serious conviction? Who does not perceive the cry of a heart upright and sure of itself, rather than the argument of a luminous and powerful reason?

Farther on, in the same letter, John Huss adduced this saying of St. Paul: "Though an angel from heaven preach any other gospel unto you than that which we have preached unto you, let him be accursed." Much more, argued he, ought it to be so with respect to those who are not angels, but carnal men, priests, bishops, or popes, and who not only teach a different gospel from that of Jesus, but even forbid others to inculcate and preach the latter.

The extraordinary contrast between the life of so many popes, cardinals, and priests, and the example of Jesus Christ and his apostles, was a source of poignant sorrow to Huss. The indignation which he felt, armed his language with sharp-edged and cutting shafts; and then, frequently, when too vehemently mastered by his eager emotion, he exhibited less of moderation than enthusiasm,—manifested rather the inconsiderate passion of a sectarian, than the cool moderation of an apostle. But those very faults were produced by a praiseworthy motive: those imperfections—the tribute which he paid to human weakness—were the abuse of a zeal too ardent in its nature, and forgetful alike of his own safety, of the passions of the world, and of the interests of the age he lived in. Each time that a reaction of his mind restored him to a state of calm,—whenever the question was to point out the path of salvation to others, or strengthen himself in it, he recovered a power of expression truly evangelical, and drew forth from his heart, as from an ardent and inexhaustible furnace of faith and love, glowing expressions of piety, charity, and self-devotedness to God and men. The humiliations, the voluntary sufferings, and comforting words of the Saviour, were always present to his mind; and in them he found consolation and strength.

"Beloved," said he, in one of his most admirable letters,* "do not allow yourselves to be cast down by terror, nor be frightened if the Lord should try some amongst you. God himself has said to his servant (Prov. ch. iii.): ' Be not afraid when the power of the wicked shall fall on thee, for I shall be on thy side;' and he has declared by the mouth of the prophet David, ' I will be with him in his trial: I will deliver him, I will glorify him.' . . . The Creator, the King, the sovereign Master of the world, without being constrained

to it by his Divine nature, humiliated himself, notwithstanding his perfection, to our humanity. He came to the aid of us miserable sinners, supporting hunger, thirst, cold, heat, watching, and fatigue; when giving us his Divine instructions, he suffered weighty sorrows and grave insults from the priests and scribes, to such a point that they called him a blasphemer, and declared that he had a devil; asserting that he, whom they had excommunicated as a heretic, and whom they had driven from their city and crucified as an accursed one, could not be God. If, then, Christ had to support such things,—he, who cured all kinds of diseases by his mere word, without any recompense on earth,—who drove out devils, raised the dead, and taught God's holy word,—who did no harm to any one, who committed no sin, and who suffered every indignity from the priests, simply because he laid open their wickedness,—why should we be astonished, in the present day, that the ministers of antichrist, who are far more covetous, more debauched, more cruel, and more cunning, than the Pharisees, should persecute the servants of God—overwhelm them with indignity, curse, excommunicate, imprison, and kill them? The same thing takes place in their case, as occurred to the Jewish priests:—they thought they could smother and put down the truth, which is always victorious,—ignorant that the very property and essence of truth is, that the more endeavours are made to darken it, the more brightly it shines forth; and the more it is attempted to be put down, the loftier it rises and the quicker it grows. The chief priest, the scribes, the Pharisees, the priests, Herod and Pilate, and the inhabitants of Jerusalem, formerly condemned the truth,—they crucified it—they buried it:—but it, rising from the tomb, was victor over them all."

John Huss, in several other letters, written at the same period, manifests a vague presentiment of martyrdom. It is thus, that, writing to the new rector of the University of Prague, he says: "I know well that, if I persevere in what is just, no evil, whatever it may be, will be able to turn me from the paths of truth. If I desire to live piously in Christ, it is necessary for me to suffer in his name. . . . What are to me the riches of the age! What the indignities, which, endured with humility, prove, purify, and illuminate, the children of God! What, in fact, is death, should I be torn from this wretched existence? He who loses it here below, triumphs over death itself, and finds the real life. As for me, I have no desire to live in this corrupt age:—I shall, I trust, affront death itself, if the mercy of the Lord comes to my aid." Huss goes on to draw an energetic picture of the licentiousness

* Epist. vi. p. 119.

of the clergy, in which body he sees antichrist; and then, giving free vent to his grief, he exclaims: "Wo, then, to me, if I do not preach against an abomination of the kind! Wo to me if I do not lament, if I do not write!... Already the great eagle* takes its flight, and cries, 'Wo! wo! to the inhabiters of the earth!'"†

This cry was, in a measure, prophetic for the unfortunate country in which John Huss uttered it; and for a long period of years Bohemia was the theatre of murder and carnage. The retirement of Huss had not calmed down men's minds, and what always occurs in such cases took place—when persecution cannot smother a doctrine, it gives it wings and strength. The multitude recalled their preacher with the language which is peculiar to them—with furious cries: blood flowed in Prague: the priests were insulted, and ran the utmost danger; and Sbinko, undecided, and without any power, between a besotted monarch and an exasperated populace, left the town, to implore the support of the new Emperor Sigismund, brother of Wenceslaus, and King of Hungary. Sbinko had become the declared adversary of John Huss's partisans, and therefore his departure was looked on by them as a triumph. But soon a sinister report got into circulation—that the archbishop had perished on the road, having come to his death by poison. The Hussites* were wrongfully accused of this crime; but the suspicion rapidly increased, although it was unjust—and perhaps, also, because it was so. This tragical event, which delivered Huss of a powerful enemy, raised up others against him not less inveterate, and rendered the animosity of all more ardent and more implacable.

CHAPTER III.

STATE OF PARTIES IN BOHEMIA.—JEROME OF PRAGUE.—BULLS OF THE POPE AGAINST LADISLAUS.—REFUTATION OF THEM BY JOHN HUSS.—FRESH TROUBLES AT PRAGUE.

THE historian‡ the least favourable to John Huss and his followers does not impute to the latter the death of the Archbishop Sbinko. But, at Prague, the question no longer was to clear up a fact which could be to one party a deep disgrace, and to the others a motive of vengeance: the hour of civil war were gathering at the bottom of men's hearts, and the rage of parties no longer required a real cause for bursting forth, but merely a pretext. It was impossible not to acknowledge the moral authority—the very serious ascendancy —which John Huss had acquired over men's minds; for no longer were the caprices of fashion, or an inconsiderate infatuation, sufficient to gain over partisans or disciples for his doctrines: the hour was approaching when his friendship would be attended with danger, and it was evident that each person would soon have to answer, with his life, for the esteem which he felt for the celebrated preacher of Bethlehem. Yet at this critical moment very few abandoned him: the queen, and a great portion of the people and of the nobility, remained faithful to him; and he also continued to receive the same manifestations of esteem from the students and men of letters. But amongst all those who conferred honour on themselves, by their constant and devoted friendship to him, the most illustrious was he whose name has been handed down to posterity, inseparable from his own—Jerome of Prague, doctor of theology.

A character bold even to rashness,—a vast intelligence,—a power of language reaching to the highest eloquence, but often borne away by passion,—such were the advantages and defects which met together in Jerome, one of the most eminent men of his time. He had studied at Oxford, and had defended most brilliant theses at Paris against Gerson, as well as the most celebrated universities of Europe. Even before his return to Bohemia, he had signalized himself by a strong opposition to the Church of Rome. He was thrown into prison at Vienna, as a favourer of Wycliffe; and, being set at liberty at the request of the University of Prague, he came to join John Huss in this city. In a short time, he guarded no measures with respect to the pope and the cardinals; and, amongst other problems, he openly proposed the following:—

---

*"And I beheld, and heard an angel flying through the midst of heaven, saying with a loud voice, Wo, wo, wo, to the inhabiters of the earth!" —Rev. viii. 13.
† Hist. et Mon. Hus. Epist. iv. t. i. p. 118.
‡ John Cochlœus, Hist. Hus. lib. i. p. 19.

* This was the name given to the disciples of John Huss.

Whether the pope possessed more power than another priest—and whether the bread in the Eucharist, or the body of Christ, possessed more virtue in the mass of the Roman pontiff, than in that of any other officiating ecclesiastic? One day, Jerome and some of his friends drew a sketch of Christ's disciples, on one side, following with naked feet their Master mounted on an ass; whilst on the other they represented the pope and the cardinals, in great state, on superb horses, and preceded, as usual, with drums and trumpets. Those pictures were exposed in public; and it is easy to conceive the effect that they ought to produce on an excitable and enthusiastic multitude. Another time, it is related, Jerome, when arguing with a monk, got irritated at being sharply opposed, and at last carried his violence so far as to fling his adversary into the Moldau. The monk reached the bank; "but," observes, very naïvely, the chronicler, "he found, when he touched the land, that he had lost the thread of his argument, and was unable to pursue the discussion." Such was Jerome of Prague, whom his contemporaries have recognised as superior in intellectual powers to John Huss; but the latter, by his manner of living, his character, and his piety, possessed so great an authority, that Jerome always felt its ascendancy. John Huss was the master, Jerome the disciple; and nothing does more honour to those two men than this voluntary humility of genius at the feet of virtue.

Jerome, besides, though far superior to the great part of his contemporaries by his eminent qualities, belonged by his defects to the age he lived in—an unfortunate period, when a spirit of boldness and violence agitated all classes of society, and produced in every direction sanguinary disorders. The different states of the Continent were so many theatres of war and rapine; and the clergy, instead of employing all their efforts to put an end to the evil, frequently excited it by their example. The schism afforded the ecclesiastics perpetual opportunities for insurrection: the bishops were men of war rather than churchmen; and one of them, when newly elected to Hildesheim, having requested to be shown the library of his predecessors, was led into an arsenal, in which all kinds of arms were piled up.—"Those," was the observation made to him, "are the books which they made use of to defend the Church: imitate their example." And how could it possibly not have been so, when three popes showed much more anxiety to destroy one another than ardour to gain over believers to God and Jesus Christ? Amongst them, the most warlike, as well as the most interested in exciting the martial

tendency of his partisans, was John XXIII., whose temporal power over Rome and her dependencies was as insecure as his spiritual authority was feeble over men's minds.

Italy was still torn asunder by the struggle between the two pretenders to the kingdom of Naples, Louis II. of Anjou, and Ladislaus of Hungary, of whom the former was supported by John XXIII., and the latter by Gregory XII. The interest of Ladislaus was evidently the prolongation of the schism, which united a pontiff to his cause: already, when at one time master of Rome, he had delivered it up to the wild excesses of the soldiery, and John XXIII. had no more formidable enemy.

At last, on September 9, 1411, the pope preached up a crusade against the prince, and fulminated a terrible bull, which, under pain of excommunication, *ipso facto*, enjoined all patriarchs, archbishops, and prelates, to declare, on Sundays and fast-days, with bells ringing, and tapers burning, and then suddenly extinguished and flung on the ground, that Ladislaus was excommunicated, perjured, a schismatic, a blasphemer, a relapsed heretic, and a supporter of heretics, guilty of lese-majesty, and the enemy of the pope and the Church. John XXIII., in the same manner, excommunicated Ladislaus's children to the third generation, as well as his adherents and well-wishers: he commanded, that if they happened to die, even with absolution, they should be deprived of ecclesiastical sepulture: he declared that, whosoever should afford burial to Ladislaus and his partisans should be excommunicated, and should not be absolved until he had disinterred their bodies with his own hands. The pope prayed all emperors, kings, princes, cardinals, and believers of both sexes, by the sprinkling of the blood of Jesus Christ, to save the Church, by persecuting without mercy and exterminating Ladislaus and his defenders. They who should enter on this crusade were to have the same indulgences as persons proceeding to the conquest of the Holy Land; and, in case they happened to die before the accomplishment of their aim, should enjoy all the same privileges as if they had died in accomplishing it.[*] A second bull, published at the same time, and in which Angelo Corrario (Gregory XII.) is termed " *the son of malediction*, a heretic and a schismatic," was addressed to the pontifical commissioners: it promises complete remission of sins to all persons preaching up the crusade, and to those collecting funds for this cause; it suspends or annuls the effect of all other indulgences accorded even by the apostolic see.

------

[*] *Hist. et Monum. Hus.* t. i. p. 212.

D

These two bulls, promulgated against a Christian prince, and for reasons purely temporal, show the extent of the rage which animated the see of Rome, and of the excesses into which it allowed itself to be drawn:—they set Bohemia in flames.

Nothing less than a double superiority of talent and virtue in the chief dignitary of the church of Prague could suffice to restrain and calm men's minds; but the successor of Sbinko, the Archbishop Albicus, formerly Sigismund's physician, was entirely unworthy of the title of shepherd of souls. "It was," observed a Catholic writer,* exceedingly favourable to that side, "a simoniacal election which had made him archbishop, and no man carried sordid avarice further than he. He lived most parsimoniously in his new dignity, not in order to let the poor enjoy what he refused to himself, but disgracefully to swell his savings. The most unsupportable noise to his ear was, he used to say, that made at table by teeth gnawing bones, and the harsh sound of a saw was less disagreeable to him than the continued noise of horses when eating at their manger." It was before such a man and the pope's legates that John Huss was summoned to appear, a little after his return to Prague.

"Will you obey the pope's bull and preach up the crusade?" demanded the legates. Huss replied, "There is nothing that I am more desirous of doing than to obey the apostolic commands." The legates, to whom the pope's commands and those of the apostles were one and the same thing, immediately turned round toward Albicus, and said:—"You hear, my lord archbishop, he is quite willing to obey the pope." But Huss did not leave the matter undecided; for he declared positively, that, "even were he to be burned for doing so, he would never obey the pope's orders but in as much as they were in conformity with those of the apostles." This announcement broke up the meeting.

Such was the origin of the furious troubles which burst forth in Prague; and whilst John Huss was preparing a logical and learned refutation of the bulls of John XXIII., Jerome excited men's minds by the violence of his invectives against Rome. Perhaps it is to this period that must be assigned a deplorable fact, which some historians have looked on as of anterior date. It is asserted, that, having placed in a cart two women of dissolute life with the pope's bulls hanging round their neck, and having men disguised as monks for their escort, he promenaded this burlesque cortege through the town, amidst the jeers and shouts of the multitude—then with his own hand he burned the bulls

on the square where public executions took place.*

Huss, more calm and dignified in his proceedings, published his refutation of the bulls and of the crusade.† It is distinguished by a great knowledge of Scripture and of the Fathers; by the outpouring of a firm and pure heart; and by the logic of a strong reason. It contains none of those violent invectives that disfigure some other of his writings: in it, in fact, Huss proved himself, by the force and elevation of his thoughts, the boldness of his language, and his constant appeals from the words of the pope to the language of Jesus Christ and his apostles, the veritable precursor of Luther.

We shall develope in detail this celebrated composition, in which, in the midst of much brilliant illumination, there is disclosed the struggle between these two contrary and irreconcileable principles:—the authority of the Scriptures, as the absolute rule, and that of the pope, as vicar of Jesus Christ and successor of St. Peter.

"I shall affirm nothing," said John Huss,‡ "but what is in conformity with the Holy Scriptures; and I have no intention of resisting the power which God has given to the Roman pontiff:—I shall resist nothing but the abuse of this authority. Now, war is permitted neither to the popes, nor to the bishops, nor to priests, particularly for temporal reasons. If, in fact, the disciples of Jesus Christ were not allowed to have recourse to the sword to defend him who was the chief of the Church, against those who wanted to seize on him; and if St. Peter himself was severely reproved for doing so, much more will it not be permissible to a bishop to engage in war for a temporal domination and earthly riches."

John Huss quoted the testimony of several of the Fathers in support of his words. St. Gregory, he observed, refused to join those who were exterminating the Lombards. "I fear God," said he, "and therefore I dread having a share in the death of any man."—(Greg. ep.)

St. Ambrose said, on the approach of the Goths:—"Behold, my arms are my tears; they constitute the defensive weapons of a priest: and I cannot resist by other forces."§ John Huss brought forward other texts from

---

* John Cochlœus, Hist. des Hus. liv. i. p. 129.

* Jerome, when accused of this act before the Council, denied that he was the author of it.
† The doctrine of John Huss on this point merits the more attention, inasmuch as it is equally applicable to all the bulls of crusade published against Christian populations. See the bull of pope Innocent VIII. for the extermination of the Waldenses, note C.
‡ Hist. et Monum. Hus. t. i. p. 215—234.
§ Ambros. ad Valer. imper. Epist. ii.

St. Jerome, St. Augustine, and St. Bernard; and, on the assertion made by many that Jesus Christ has granted to his Church the use of two swords, he quotes those words of St. Bernard to Eugene III.:—"You shall subdue the wolves, but you shall not domineer over the sheep;. for they have been given to you to be fed, not to be oppressed. If your heart be piously affected, make use of your tongue, and gird on the sword of the Spirit, which is the word of God." Huss maintained that the use of the double sword belonged to the universal Church alone, because it is composed of all believers without distinction. "Now," said he, "as the secular body, to whom the temporal sword alone is suitable, cannot undertake to handle the spiritual one, in like manner the ecclesiastics ought to be content with the spiritual sword, and not make use of the temporal; for if a man who has contributed, even by insinuation, to the death of any one whatever, were it even a malefactor, cannot be admitted into holy orders without a dispensation, it is a far greater infraction, on the part of a person already ordained—a priest, to kill men, whether by himself or by others."

"If the pope and his cardinals had said to Christ, 'Lord, if you wish, we will exhort the whole universe to compass the destruction of Ladislaus, Gregory, and their accomplices,' the Saviour would undoubtedly have answered to them as he did to his apostles, when they consulted him if they should take vengeance on the Samaritans: 'I am not come to destroy men's lives, but to save them.' (Luke ix.) Jesus did not smite his enemy, the high-priest's servant, when marching against him, but healed his wound.

"Let him, therefore, who pleases, declare that he is bound to obey the bull, even unto the extermination of Ladislaus and his family; for my part I would not, without a revelation—a positive order from God—raise my hand against Ladislaus and his partisans; but I would address an humble prayer to God to bring into the way of truth those who are going astray: for he who is the chief of the whole Church prayed for his persecutors, saying: 'Father, pardon them; they know not what they do!' (Luke xxiii.); and I am of opinion that Christ, his mother, and his disciples, were greater than the pope and his cardinals."

After having demonstrated how inhuman and antichristian were crusades like those prescribed, Huss attacked indulgences, as a profanation of evangelical grace. "God alone," said he, "possesses the power to forgive sins in an absolute manner; for there is only he who knows the heart, and can say whether the sinner is really changed: pardon, therefore, can be accorded for only so long as the repentance will last; and that length of time God alone can declare.

"St. Gregory replied to a lady who conjured him most eagerly to assure her that her sins were remitted: 'You ask me a thing both exceedingly difficult and useless to know:—difficult, for I am unworthy to receive such a revelation; and useless, for you cannot be set at rest with respect to your sins until the last day of your life, when you will be no longer in a state to commit any.'[*]

"St. Augustine says, in his work on Penance: 'If a man waits for the last term of a mortal malady to desire and receive the sacrament of penance, I acknowledge that, without daring to refuse him what he desires, I have no certainty of his salvation. Therefore, do penance in the time that it is possible for you to sin; for otherwise it is sin that will have quitted you, and not you it.'[†]

"When, then, those two great saints have not dared to promise remission of sins even to those who have done penance, with what countenance can Pope John, in his bull, promise the most entire remission of sins, and the recompense of eternal salvation, to his accomplices!

"If, notwithstanding the example of Christ, the pope strives for temporal domination, it is evident that he aims in that, as do those who aid him in that object. How, then, could the indulgence granted for a criminal act be of any value?"

As to what relates to the power of binding and loosening, Huss does not deny that it belongs to the true successors of the apostles; that is to say, those who, laying aside all human affection, bind and unbind only in conformity with the Divine law.

"The absolution of Jesus Christ," he remarks, "ought to precede that of the priest; or, in other words, the priest who absolves or condemns ought to be certain that the case in question is one which Jesus Christ himself has already absolved or condemned. 'A priest,' says St. Augustine, 'ought not to imagine that all those whom he has bound or unbound are so in reality, but only those whom he has bound or unbound according to the order of Jesus Christ.' The power of the keys is, therefore, limited and conditional: it supposes the proper use of the keys—a condition to which St. Peter himself did not cease to be liable. How, then, will priests who are ignorant, covetous, and whoremongers, grant, at the will of avarice, distributors of indulgences the remission of the trespass and the

---

* *Beat. Greg. in regist.* lib. iv.
† *August. in lib. Pœnit.*

penalty? 'It is not,' said St. Augustine, 'to ravishers and usurers that Jesus Christ has given this power;' and St. Gregory teaches that he who accords pardon for sins according to his passions, and not according to the state of the penitent, deprives himself of the power of binding and loosening.*

"The pope cannot know, without an especial revelation, if he is predestined to salvation; he cannot, therefore, give such indulgence to himself; it is not, besides, contrary to the faith, that many popes who have granted ample indulgences are damned. Of what value, therefore, are their indulgences in the sight of God?

"No saint in Scripture has granted indulgences for the absolution of the penalty of the trespass during a certain number of years and days: our doctors have never dared to name any of the Fathers as having instituted and published indulgences; because, in fact, they are ignorant of their origin: and if these indulgences, which are represented as so salutary to mankind, have slumbered, as it were for the space of a thousand years and more, the reason most probably is, that covetousness had not at that period, as at present, reached its highest point. A distinction must be drawn between a legitimate power, regulated by the law of God, and one usurped and exercised for a time by Divine permission: of this latter kind is the power of the devil." John Huss applied this distinction to the pope. "If," observed he, "the pope uses his power according to God's commands, he cannot be resisted without resisting God himself: but if he abuses his power, by enjoining what is contrary to the Divine law, then it is a duty to resist him, as should be done to the power of the *pale horse* of the Apocalypse, of the *dragon*, of the *beast*, and of *Leviathan*. It is better to suffer an unjust excommunication than to receive a pretended absolution. That man will be rather absolved who supports indignity and malediction even unto death, for the sake of Jesus Christ, than he who persecutes Christians in a cause like that of John XXIII. against Ladislaus." John Huss exclaimed against the strange clause in the bull, by which Ladislaus is damned to the third generation, notwithstanding this express declaration of God, (Ezekiel xviii.): *The son shall not bear the iniquity of the father.* He regarded as scandalously simoniacal the formula of the absolution which the bull accords after the act of confession and contrition. "The sin," he remarks, "cannot be pardoned to a robber unless he makes restitution; whence it follows that contrition which does not produce restitution is pretended, and that in order to grant

the remission of sins fully, the confessors ought to be able to read in the souls of the penitents —which they cannot do without a revelation."

Huss points out, by a double example, the impiety of an absolution so lightly given to those who should contribute towards the crusade. "Of two men," says he, "one has been an offender all his life; but provided he pays a sum of money, he can obtain, by means of a very slight contrition, remission of his sins, and their consequent penalty: the other is a man of worth who has never committed but venial sins; yet, if he gives nothing, he shall have no pardon. Now, according to the bull, if those two men should happen to die, the former—the criminal—will go straight to heaven, escaping the pains of purgatory; and the second—the just man—will have to undergo them. Were such indulgences really available in heaven, we ought to pray to God that war might be waged against the pope, in order that he might throw open all the treasures of the Church!"

Such was, in substance, the celebrated reply of John Huss to the bulls of John XXIII.; and it produced in Prague a prodigious sensation. It restored to Huss the favour of the people, which the withdrawal of the German students had alienated from him; but, at the same time, it drew on him the hostility of the court. The king was then at war with Ladislaus; his favour, like that of the greater part of princes, was subordinate to his political interests: he, therefore, accepted the bulls, and withdrew for a time his support from John Huss.

Prague was then divided between two powerful parties. All who had favours to expect from the king or the people declared themselves in support of the bulls; and to this period must be assigned the rupture between Huss and Stephen Paletz, an influential member of the clergy. Paletz had been his friend and disciple; but, being as anxious for the advancement of his fortune as Huss was for the progress of the truth, he preached in favour of the bulls and the indulgences. Ambition led him to an outbreak against his ancient master; and he displayed towards him as much hatred as he had previously testified affection and respect. Those marked disgraces, those base defections, irritated the multitude, and rendered their preacher still dearer to them. Huss had, besides, against his enemies, the powerful support of the nobility, several members of whom were sincerely touched by the elevation and purity of his doctrines, whilst a great number adopted them either through a spirit of opposition to the court, or through jealousy towards the high clergy, or through the hope of sharing in their spoils. But if the barons of the kingdom were favourable to him, he

---

* Greg. Hom. 26.

reckoned numerous adversaries in the university—now much weakened by the withdrawal of the Germans—and in the town-council.

Magistrates are inclined, both by their position and by necessity, to consider events in their immediate and visible effect, much more than in the hidden motive which produces them. Being bound by the duties of their office to preserve order, they almost everywhere show themselves opposed to all innovations, however called for, which might trouble public tranquillity: they support, by external means, the religions already established, though abandoned by the intimate faith of the population; and when they already behold nothing more in the edifice of the beliefs now grown old but dust and ashes, they persist in plastering up the exterior; and too frequently they command others to believe what they have ceased to believe themselves. The magistrates of Prague, therefore, blamed John Huss, and joined with the heads of the university, the court, and the clergy against him.

So many elements of discord portended fresh troubles of a more serious character than those which had already caused the voluntary exile of Huss; but no apprehension shook his resolution. He caused a placard to be put up on the doors of the churches and monasteries of Prague, inviting the public, and particularly all doctors, priests, monks, and scholars, to come forward and discuss the following theses: Whether, according to the law of Jesus Christ, Christians could, with a safe conscience, approve of the crusade ordered by the pope against Ladislaus and his followers,—and whether such a crusade could turn to the glory of God, to the safety of the Christian populations, and to the welfare of the kingdom of Bohemia ?

On the appointed day, the concourse was prodigious; and the rector, in alarm, endeavoured, though in vain, to dissolve the assembly. A doctor of canon law stood up and delivered a defence of the pope and the bulls; then, falling upon John Huss, he said—"You are a priest; you are subordinate to the pope, who is your spiritual father. It is only filthy birds that defile their own nest; and Ham was cursed for having uncovered his father's shame."

At these words, the people murmured, and were in great commotion. Already were stones beginning to fly, when John Huss interfered and calmed the storm. After him, the impetuous Jerome of Prague addressed the multitude, and terminated a vehement harangue with these words:—"Let those who are our friends unite with us; Huss and I are going to the palace, and we will let the vanity of those indulgences be seen."

All the people cried out—"What he says is true ! he speaks well."

The rector of the academy, Marcus, interfered in his turn, and conjured the crowd not to go to the palace, for fear of greater mischief being done, but to return each to his own residence. The multitude at last dispersed, the students accompanying Jerome as the more learned ; but the people following John Huss to the chapel of Bethlehem, and exhorting him to be firm and immovable.

The next day, a formidable sedition arose. The crowd assembled in a public square at Prague, and thence spread themselves through the city, insulting and threatening with death every priest that they heard crying up the indulgences. The rector sent for John Huss and Jerome to the college of St. Charles, and there, in the presence of a great number of masters of the faculties, prayed and conjured them to check, by their words, the rage of the rioters. The assessors, the doctors, and the masters, implored them at the same time,—pressing and supplicating them with tears, and invoking God and the saints. "Behold our white hairs," said they, "and thinking of your youth abandon your enterprise, before there results from it a frightful massacre, in which its authors must themselves be involved and perish." "You say well," replied Jerome, "and we will comply with your wishes; but judge, yourselves, if it be not difficult to put down the truth." "I also," said John Huss, "dread sedition. I have devoted myself to the truth, but would not dare to attempt any thing opposed to justice. It is my duty to show that those indulgences are devoid of virtue, yet I will not reject your prayer." "Dear Master John," replied the rector, "do not forget in what manner we defended you against the Germans, when no one, so much as you, was an object of hatred to the people, who complained that you had deprived them of a great profit by expelling the others. The Germans are more anxious for your destruction than for ours. They swear, in whatever place they meet you, they will kill you; and you have excited the hatred of the Emperor Sigismund, for the same reason. Postpone, therefore, your project to another time, in order to avoid a greater evil; and you will thus preserve your own life." Huss gave his assent to those words, and promised to act in conformity with them.

However, on the following Sunday a sinister report was in circulation—that three men had been thrown into prison by the magistrates, for having harangued against the pope and his indulgences. The students rose ; arms were taken up, and Huss, followed by the people and the scholars, proceeded to the town-house, and demanded that the prisoners' lives should be spared.

The magistrates deliberated in trouble and consternation, and the council replied, in the name of all: "Dear master, we are astonished at your lighting up a fire, in which you run the risk of being burned yourself. It is very hard for us to pardon persons who do not even spare the sanctuary, who fill the city with tumult, and who, if not prevented, would stain our streets with slaughter. Nevertheless, keep the people within bounds, and withdraw: your wishes shall be attended to."

Two thousand men were in arms in the square. "Return peaceably to your homes," cried John Huss to them; "the prisoners are pardoned." The crowd shouted their applause and withdrew; but, a short time after, blood was seen to flow in abundance from the prison. The senators had determined on the most dangerous course,—that of endeavouring to inspire terror, after having exhibited it themselves. An executioner had been introduced, and had beheaded the prisoners, and it was their blood which had escaped.

At this sight a furious tumult arose. The doors of the prison were burst open, the bodies taken off, and transported in linen shrouds under the vault of the chapel of Bethlehem. There they were interred with great honours, the scholars singing in chorus over their tomb,—"*They are saints who have given up their body for the gospel of God.*"

Huss at first remained silent:[*] but on the first solemn feast-day, he ascended the pulpit, and cried out, perhaps imprudently, that "they were saints and martyrs!" . . . . Indignation gradually pervaded the whole of Bohemia, and John Huss, in his violent invectives against the pope, went beyond all bounds. He attacked, in the most unmeasured language, the despotism and simony of the pontiff, as well as the debauchery and display of the priests: he rejected altogether the traditions of the Church respecting fasts and abstinence, and he opposed to every other authority that of the Scriptures.[†]

CHAPTER IV.

PROGRESS OF THE HUSSITES.—CONTROVERSIES.—SECOND RETIREMENT OF HUSS.—CONVOCATION OF A GENERAL COUNCIL AT CONSTANCE.

ALTHOUGH king Wenceslaus had withdrawn for a time his protection from the Hussites, it does not appear that he persecuted them very sharply. This grasping and rapacious prince found his advantage in secretly favouring their doctrines; and when, at the commencement of the disturbances in Bohemia, he was urged to ruin John Huss, he replied, "Let him alone; he is my fowl with the golden eggs." Some of Huss's opinions, particularly that which he borrowed from Wycliffe, respecting tithes and church property, were exceedingly to the taste of Wenceslaus. "Secular lords," he used to remark, "have the power of taking away, whenever they please, their temporal possessions from such ecclesiastics as live in habitual sin." Huss supported this maxim by the authority of the Scriptures and of the fathers, without failing to bring forward those words, pronounced in the presence of St. Bernard by the celebrated St. Hildegarde, the prophetess of Germany: "The all-powerful Father has wisely distributed all things: he assigned the heaven to celestial men and the earth to earthly ones; so that, according to this division, the spiritual men and the seculars, each possessing what suits them, do not encroach one on the other: for God is not willing to have one of his sons possessing, at the same time, the surplice and the cloak. He gave the cloak to the seculars, and the robe to the spiritual party: and when the robe and the cloak happen to get together on the same person, the cloak must be taken away and given to the poor."[‡]

As to tithes, Huss maintained, with Wycliffe, that they were nothing but alms; and he drew this conclusion, that churchmen were neither the masters nor the owners of this property, but simply the guardians and distributors of it,—that they could keep out of it, for themselves, only what was necessary for their wants,—and that, if they did not give the surplus to the poor, they would be condemned on the last day, as thieves and sacrilegious persons. Wenceslaus adopted those doctrines,—which were those of the greater portion of the Reformers, and which rendered many princes favourable to them. He, therefore,

* Several authors declare that, at the moment of this execution, John Huss was absent from Prague; and this would appear the case from some of his answers in the Council of Constance.
† *Theob. Bel. Huss.*
‡ *Hus. Hist. et Monum.* t. i. p. 155.

set himself up as the arbiter of the employment of church property; but as he cared nothing whatever for the poor, it was into his strong-box that the ill-employed riches of the clergy found their way; and when he openly came forward and supported the new opinions, his severity and his exactions swelled John Huss's party. Several wealthy ecclesiastics declared themselves to be Hussites, for, with a view to save their property, they adopted the doctrines which enjoined a good employment of it.*

Another cause of the progress of the Hussites was the profound contempt into which the dignitaries of the Church had fallen in Bohemia, in consequence of the avarice of the king, who sold all places to the highest bidder. The shameful elevation of Albicus to the episcopal see of Prague has been already seen: this unworthy archbishop, apprehending that the king might confiscate all the revenues of this charge, hastened to resell it to Conrad, bishop of Olmütz, and according to the avowal of Catholic authors themselves, the purchaser was scarcely more worthy than the seller.†

Conrad, in the beginning, displayed much zeal in opposing the new doctrines, though he embraced them at a later period, after having succeeded in alienating the revenues of his church. He forbade John Huss to preach, but the latter was aware of his strength, and, besides, did not think that obedience was due to any earthly power that prohibited the preaching of the Gospel.

He was summoned a second time to appear at Rome, but he did not even assign reasons for refusing to proceed thither.

A considerable number of Wycliffe's volumes had escaped the flames at Prague, which Archbishop Sbinko had lit up. Huss invited the people to read them, and he attacked with great vigour the condemnation of the forty-five articles extracted from the works of the celebrated English doctor; and he brought out, in the name of the faculty of theology of Prague, a powerful treatise, in which he defended Wycliffe's opinion relative to tithes and church-property, as well as to some other capital points. "They who cease to preach," said he, "or to hear God's word, will be reputed traitors on the day of judgment. Every deacon, every priest, is permitted to preach the word of God without any authorization from the apostolic see or from his bishop. In fine, every temporal lord, prelate, or bishop, living in mortal sin, ceases to be either temporal lord, prelate, or bishop."‡

Huss qualified those doctrines by the ex-

planations which he gave respecting them. His opinion on the last point, taken literally, would scarcely admit of a serious refutation; but he adds that the power of the wicked is not approved of by God, and that they are neither kings nor bishops according to his heart.

John Huss likewise preached, with the great approbation of the people, against the worship of images: he also taught that priests ought to be poor; that auricular confession was useless; that it was not necessary to inter the dead in consecrated ground, for the salvation of their souls; and that the observance of the canonical hours and abstinence from meat were mere human traditions, without any foundation in the word of God. The Catholic priests, on their part, declaimed with equal violence, so that all men's minds seemed in a blaze:—the city was daily the theatre of sanguinary scenes,—there was no longer any security at Prague for personal safety,—even the king himself thought it best to take his departure, and hurried from place to place.

However, several doctors of the faculty of theology formed at Prague a powerful league against John Huss. Amongst them the most celebrated were Stephen Paletz, already mentioned, Andrew Broda, and Stanislaus Znoïma, professor of theology, formerly John Huss's master, and once, like him, an ardent admirer of Wycliffe, whom, however, he now abused. The doctors wrote against John Huss, accusing him of belonging to the sect of the Arminians, who relied on the authority of Scripture only, and not on that of the church and the holy fathers. To this Huss replied, that on the point in question he was of the same opinion as St. Augustine, St. Jerome, and St. Gregory, who acknowledged the Scriptures alone as the foundation of their faith. They likewise declared that John Huss professed a great error relative to the authority of spiritual and temporal powers. "According to his assertion," remarked they, "the orders of popes, emperors, kings, princes, and other superior personages, are not to be obeyed, unless they are founded on evidence and reason:—a doctrine tending to nothing less than the total overthrow of established order." A formidable argument, in fact, to which John Huss opposed the example of the Maccabees, who replied that the orders of princes were not to be complied with when contrary to those of God.

"To believe our doctors," said he, "if the pope or the king commanded them to kill all the Jews in Prague, and furnished them with troops for the purpose, they would make no difficulty in obeying. Nor would they have any hesitation in cutting all our throats at the first command,—particularly mine, teaching,

---

* Cochlœus. *Hist. Hus.* lib. p. 62.
† Dunbar, *Hist. Boh.* lib. xxiii. p. 623.
‡ *Hus. Hist. et Monum.* t. i. p. 139—154.

as they declare I do, so grave an error. I cannot, however, think, that it is less allowable to hesitate about such orders, than to examine the letters of Artaxerxes, ordering the massacre of all the Jews; and I do not believe that St. Paul was bound to obey, when ordered by the sanhedrim to deliver up the disciples of Christ to the common executioner."[*]

A discussion like this serves, better than any thing else, to prove that human reason, in such conflicts, never loses its rights, and that one is almost always sure to go astray in carrying, however logically, the best principles to their farthest consequences. To admit that it is necessary always to examine and approve before obeying, is to render all government impossible; whilst, on the other hand, to forbid one's self all examination whatever, is to renounce all claim to the quality of man—is to transform one's self, according to circumstances, into a stupid automaton or a ferocious brute.

Irritated by the disobedience of Huss, and alarmed at the progress of his doctrines, John XXIII. stirred up against him the secular powers:—he wrote to Wenceslaus, to the king of France, and to the various universities. Gerson replied to this appeal in the name of the University of Paris, and wrote to Bohemia to the archbishop Conrad on the subject of John Huss. The catholic historian, John Cochlœus, has preserved to us this letter, in which will be found the impetuous passions of the period.

"Up to the present day," wrote Gerson, "various methods have been tried to extirpate heresies from the field of the Church, as with so many different scythes. First, they were torn out with the scythe of the miracles, by which God testified to the Catholic truth, in the time of the apostles. Next, they were extirpated by learned doctors, with force of argument and discussion, by the scythe of holy councils. . . . . Last of all, when the malady became desperate, it was found necessary to have recourse to the axe of the secular arm to cut down heresies, together with their authors, and cast them into the flames. It was by this merciful cruelty that the discourses of such people were prevented from being spread abroad, to their own ruin, as well as that of others. . . . . If the false doctors, who sow their heresies amongst you, demand miracles, they ought to be aware that the time for miracles has gone by. It is not permitted to tempt God, by asking him for miracles in confirmation of our faith, as if it were a new one. They have not only Moses and the prophets before them, but the apostles and the ancient doctors, with the sacred councils. They have also modern doctors assembled in the universities, particularly in the University of Paris, the *mother of studies* (*mater studiorum*), which has hitherto been exempt from the monsters of heresy, and, with the assistance of God, will be always so. They have all those things before them, and let them believe in them: if they do not, then would they not believe, even though persons rose from the dead. Besides, there would be no end of disputing with so presumptuous a set; but, as Seneca says, *by carrying the dispute too far, the people are scandalized and charity wounded*. In fine, to their shameless obstinacy must be applied the words of the poet: *the malady grows worse by the means intended to cure it* (*ægrescit medendo*). If, therefore, present remedies are useless, it only remains to put the axe of the secular arm to the root of this unfruitful and accursed tree. It is your duty to implore this arm by every possible means,—you are, in fact, under an obligation to do this for the salvation of the souls intrusted to your care."[*]

Peter d'Ailly, Cardinal of Cambray, in a work on the Reformation, touches on the precise point which rendered all those efforts useless, and gained over so many hearts to novelties, or rather to things which appeared novel. "It is," said he, "on account of the simoniacal heresy and the other iniquities which are practised at the Court of Rome, that there have arisen, in Bohemia and Moravia, sects which have spread from the head to the other members in this kingdom, where a thousand things highly insulting to the pope are publicly uttered. . . . Thus it is that the notorious vices of the Court of Rome trouble the Catholic faith, and corrupt it by errors. It is to be desired, certainly, that those heresies, and their authors, were rooted out of those provinces; but I do not see that this result can be accomplished, unless the court of Rome can be brought back to its ancient morals and its praiseworthy customs."

Peter d'Ailly here pointed out the cause of the evil and the remedy, but without suggesting the means of applying it. The schism every day furnished the partisans of John Huss with new arguments for combating the jurisdiction of the pope. "If we must obey," said they, "to whom is our obedience to be paid? Balthazar Cossa, called John XXIII., is at Rome,—Angelo Corario, named Gregory XII., is at Rimini,—Peter de Lune, who calls himself Benedict XIII., is in Aragon. If one of them, in his quality of the Most Holy Father, ought to be obeyed, how does it come to pass that he cannot be distinguished from the others, and why does he not begin by subduing them?"

---

[*] *Hus. Hist. et Monum.* t. i., Resp. ad Script. Oct. doctor.

[*] Gers. ap. Cochlœus *Hist. Hus.* p. 22.

The disturbances still continued in Bohemia, and the archbishop, perceiving that his exhortations were useless, had recourse to other means. He again enforced a decree, drawn up against the opponents, by the doctors of the faculty of theology. This publication obliged every man, invested with any public office at Prague, to sign a catholic formulary, and, at the same time, it severely repressed the Hussites. The Bishop of Litomissel, a violent enemy of John Huss, went still farther than those rigorous enactments: he recommended to have a chancellor of the University elected, to exercise a severe inquisition over the masters and the students, and whose office, besides, it should be to punish the favourers of heresy: he demanded that John Huss and his followers should be prohibited from preaching, and expelled from the chapel of Bethlehem;—that John Huss should be excluded from the society of believers;—that the books in the vulgar tongue, in which his opinions happened to be published, should be forbidden;—and, finally, that the sellers and the readers of those works should be excommunicated.

A decree, based on those points, was drawn up and published: it confounded the old and new law—applied to the court of Rome what is said in Deuteronomy of the place which the Lord had chosen—and called to mind that, whoever refused to obey the sovereign priest, was punished with death. "Every one knows," said the sentence, "that the Roman Church is the place chosen by the Lord under the New Testament,—that he has there established the principality of the entire Church,—that the pope presides there as the true and manifest successor of St. Peter,—that the cardinals, as priests of the Levitical order, are associated with him in the sacerdotal office,—and that it is to them that recourse must be had in every ecclesiastical matter. In fine, it is not the part of the clergy of Prague to judge if the excommunication of Huss be just or unjust,—they are bound to look on it as just, since it had been issued by the apostolical authority."

This decree, although approved of by the king, was without effect. The Hussites impugned it, and the clergy of the gospel refuted those of the Church of Rome. They appealed to the edict of pacification given by the princes and the king's council, and signed by Archbishop Sbinko, in which it was declared that this dignitary had found in Huss neither error nor heresy. The king was called on to have it proclaimed in all towns, that John Huss was ready publicly to assign satisfactory reasons for his faith. Should no one come forward to convict him of heresy, the kingdom ought to be purged of his accusers; and they ought to be sent to Rome to receive the reward due to their calumnies. Jesus Christ alone, and not the pope, was the head of the Church, the Hussites said; and all believers are the members of it. They added, that the clergy of Prague had condemned, without sufficient authority, the forty-five articles of Wycliffe; and that even the Roman Church itself could not be accepted as able to pronounce in the matter, because no one could, at the time, say where that Church was to be found; three popes contending amongst themselves for the chief authority. Those three popes, they further observed, were in contradiction with themselves, when they blamed us for adhering to the Holy Scriptures, and immediately after adduced the Scriptures against us. They were, in fact, punishable as forgers; because they falsified the gospel and the canons, declaring that the pope ought to be obeyed in all things, when it was most certain that several heretical popes had existed. Finally, it was absurd to pretend that the proceedings of the Court of Rome ought to be obeyed against Huss, and to assign, as a reason for so doing, that the clergy of Prague had always been obedient to them. "If that argument were to hold good, we ought to be pagans, because our forefathers were so; and the devil ought to be obeyed, because our first parents had obeyed him."

With men's minds excited to the point then observable at Prague, it was not likely that the language of reason should be still listened to. The archbishop proceeded from threats to acts, and placed the city, and all other places where John Huss should happen to sojourn, under an interdict.

This rigorous measure was feebly executed, and the customary preaching still went on at the celebrated chapel of Bethlehem. Nevertheless, Huss judged it prudent once more to withdraw, for a season, from the fury of his enemies. He retired to the place of his birth, the village of Hussinetz, the territorial lord of which was devoted to him. But there, as at Prague, he showed the same intrepidity and indefatigable zeal for the cause which he regarded as the truth.

He then wrote several remarkable treatises. The most important was that on *The Church*, which will be referred to hereafter, and from which were drawn the greatest part of the articles which caused his condemnation. He published, about the same time, a very short, but very energetic, treatise, under the title of *The Six Errors*. The *first* was the error of the priests, who boasted of making the body of Jesus Christ in the mass, and of being the creator of their Creator. The *second* consisted in declaring—*I believe in the popes and the saints;* John Huss maintaining that it was correct to believe in nothing but God. The *third* was the pretension of the priests to be able to remit the trespass and the penalty of sin to whom they pleased. The *fourth* error was implicit obedience to superiors, no matter what they ordered. The *fifth* consisted in not making a distinction, in their effect, between a just excommunication and one that was not so. And, lastly, the *sixth* error was simony, which John Huss designated a heresy, and of which he accused the greater part of the clergy.

This little work, which attacked the clergy in particular, was placarded on the door of the chapel of Bethlehem; it ran with wonderful rapidity through the whole of Bohemia, and its success was immense.

John Huss wrote also at this period his treatise on the *Abomination of the Monks*, the purport of which is sufficiently explained by its title; and, lastly, the *Members of Antichrist*, a violent and fiery diatribe against the pope and his court. His heavy trials, the obstacles which he constantly met with, and the persecutions to which he was subjected, appear to have soured his temper, all those last writings of his being distinguished by great asperity. His style, formed by a constant study of the Scriptures, being inspired by an ardent enthusiasm, which but too often degenerated into passion, frequently displayed flourishes and turns which the delicacy of modern taste would repudiate. He also abounds in figures and images, which remind one of the great prophets with whose writings he was so familiar, particularly Ezekiel. He often bursts forth and inveighs against all the inventions that swelled the coffers of the Church,—images, relics, legends, canonizations, were, by turns, the object of his vehement attack. He compared those who persecuted the living saints and compassed their death, at one time to hunters who fed on what they had killed, and afterwards eulogized it; again, to the Jews, who, after having caused the death of the prophets, ornamented and whitened their sepulchres;—or to the Romans, who first killed their emperors, and then raised up statues to them, and placed them amongst the gods. He stigmatised the worship of the saints already dead, as an invention of the devil to turn men away from the love and charity prescribed in the gospel towards the saints who are living. He concluded by those remarkable words: "This immoderate worship of the saints—a true invention of hypocrisy—is an inexhaustible source of superstitions, to the prejudice of true holiness. The virtues of the dead, whose example is far distant, are cried up, whilst contempt is inculcated for the holiness of the living, whose example would be much more efficacious. Pride, cruelty, avarice, and luxury, have given existence to this worship. Vanity is flattered by extolling the virtue of the dead, for self-love is not humiliated by the act; but envy, offended by the virtue of the living, makes every effort to tarnish its brightness. Men are generous towards the saints who are in heaven, because they are far removed above the attacks of their cruelty, and are to be feared, sitting near God; but they are cruel towards the saints living on the earth, because they are interested in crushing virtue: they are avaricious towards the latter and despoil them; yet they are profuse towards the saints in glory, who want nothing: they array bones of the latter with silk, and gold, and silver, and lodge them magnificently; but they refuse clothing and hospitality to the poor members of Jesus Christ who are amongst us, and at whose expense they feed to repletion, and drink until they are intoxicated."[*]

In the same treatise, after having alluded to the glorious transfiguration of the Saviour on Mount Tabor, he exclaims, when upbraiding the bishops with their luxury: "They love better to follow Jesus Christ on Mount Tabor than on the cross. It is to satisfy their vanity that so many ceremonies, so many feasts and bodily exercises, are administered, which are multiplied every day to dazzle the people, and amuse them with the vain hope of meriting eternal life by observing those traditions. Much better would it be to multiply acts of charity, works of mercy, and the other Christian virtues; to administer the sacraments according to the gospel, and exercise a severe discipline. But those matters cause little trouble to the scribes and Pharisees of the present day, and for this reason, that they bring them in neither worldly glory nor temporal profit." Cannot one fancy that the grand and sonorous voice of Luther is already vibrating in his ears? Have we not here those first heavy gusts of wind—that hoarse murmur of the waves, which are the certain foretellers of the storm that will shortly sweep away every thing before it?

Nothing, however, indicates that John Huss had any consciousness of the great revolution which he was preparing. To comprehend fully the vast scope of his work, and the importance of the part which he filled to the end with so much constancy and courage, as well as his influence in Europe, it is sufficient to enumerate his enemies, and estimate their power.

The most formidable of all,—he who had hoped to smite down John Huss under the thunderbolts which he launched against Ladislaus,—John XXIII., was then himself agitated

---

[*] *Hist. et Monum. J. Hus. de Myst. Iniq. Antichristi.*

by lively apprehensions in the midst of his court at Bologna, and his omnipotence, by which he opened heaven and hell, did not defend him against secret terrors; for a new emperor, strongly opposed to the abuses of the clergy, had just ascended the throne,—this was Sigismund of Hungary, brother of Wenceslaus. This prince—a zealous Catholic—had for a length of time devoted himself to the defence of the Church; and the deplorable state in which he saw it caused him constant affliction. Three popes still divided it, and whilst John XXIII., at Bologna, fulminated against his rivals, Gregory XII., at Rimini, and Benedict XIII., in Aragon, hurled back on him, with usury, all his maledictions. The simony, of which the pontiffs were giving the example, had gained on the entire mass of the clergy. Bohemia, Moravia, a part of Germany, and England, were agitated by the new opinions. No more piety could be found amongst the laity and secular clergy, but merely a rivalry in superstitions, which substituted dead practices for the regeneration of the heart. Nor was this anarchy in which Europe was plunged, the worst feature of the times; for on the frontiers might be heard the hoarse murmurs of the Mussulman hordes, which were advancing, like furious waves, to wash out so many iniquities, and efface all the pollutions of the Church, in overwhelming it.

Although affected to tears by such a spectacle, Sigismund did not, however, comprehend its real cause. In his double quality of emperor and devotee, he detested all opposition —all independence of mind; and attributed the evils which afflicted Christendom to the partisans of the new doctrines and of the schism. It was therefore against them that he brought together his forces, and he believed that a general council, convoked for the double object of putting down the schism and suppressing heresy, would again revive the palmy days of the Church. The council of Pisa was not, in the opinion of Sigismund and of the kings of Europe, a sufficient proof; for at that anterior period the imperial power and the authority of the Church were struggling with each other. The Emperor Robert had, in fact, declared against the council, and it had been too soon dissolved. The new plan was to have the temporal and the spiritual powers act simultaneously, and with a common accord,—to sustain the authority of the Church with the imperial glaive,—to convoke the whole of Christendom in a general assembly, to extinguish heresy, and reform the Church in its chief and its members.

Such was the idea of Sigismund, and such the cause of the terrors of John XXIII., who trembled the more, because he knew that

scandals of his own producing had called forth this plan, and that he was himself his own greatest enemy. He would willingly have treated the pretension of the Emperor as impious and rash, and replied to it by a new excommunication; but he saw that he must, in that case, be overwhelmed by the disastrous effects of his own fury, and, therefore, the perils to which he would be liable restrained his thunderbolts. The victorious Ladislaus, who continued to persecute him with a deadly, implacable hatred, was master of Rome, and John XXIII. had no hope against him but in the sword of Sigismund. Thus borne down, as it were, by an inexorable necessity, the pontiff appeared, in the resolutions which he took, as if struck with dizziness. It was of the utmost importance to him, for his personal independence, that the city selected for the congress should not be subordinate to the empire; but all his proceedings on the point seemed as if marked with the seal of fatality. The imperial city of Constance was proposed without his knowledge, and at once accepted by his legates; and when at last this choice became known to him, it was too late to dictate another. Penned in between Ladislaus, his enemy, and Sigismund, his defender, both of whom inspired him with an almost equal fear,—terrified at the remembrance of his past life, passed in crime, and which was on the point of being more clearly exhibited to the world—in fine, cursing himself, John XXIII. was already vanquished, when a memorable conference took place at Lodi between him and Sigismund. They both appeared there, to a certain degree, under disguise,—the one concealing his weakness under the splendid trappings of the pontifical dignity; and the other veiling his strength under the simple habit of a deacon. The discussion was long but not sincere; and the name of Constance having been pronounced, "Holy Father," said the emperor, in a determined tone, "does this city suit you?" "Yes, my dear son," replied the pope, "it does suit me." And he bowed down the head with a shudder, confirming thus, by his impotency, an expression which fell from an historian who was present at the scene, "None can escape from what God has determined."*

The convocation of a General Council was at length decided on, and the place of meeting was fixed. Sigismund proceeded further, and, on October 30, 1413, published an edict, in 1413 which he announced, that, with the perfect approval of the pope, John XXIII. (whom he designated "his most mighty lord,") a council was to assemble at Constance, on November 1,

---

* Leon. Aret. *De rebus Ital.*

of the following year, that city having been chosen as a sure place, where perfect liberty could be procured for every one. Sigismund, in his quality of defender and counsel of the Church,—titles which the canons accorded to the emperor,—invited to the council Gregory XII., Benedict XIII., the King of France, and the other sovereigns. "The malignity of mankind," said he in his letter to Charles VI., "has risen to such a point, that if a prompt remedy be not applied, it is to be feared that, at a later period, all cure will become impossible." John XXIII., in concert with the emperor, also sent invitations to all those who had any authority in Christendom to attend the council. Their project was not only to reform the Church and extinguish the schism, but also to put down the growing heresy. But there was one man in Bohemia, who, by the renown of his name, by his writings, by the boldness of his language, and, above all, by the vexatious celebrity of his virtues, repre-

sented in his own person all the innovators in Europe,—that man was John Huss. It was necessary to confound them all in his person, and accordingly he was summoned to appear before the council.

Never, since the early ages of Christianity, had so many efforts been made for so important a meeting, and never had graver questions been discussed. It was, in fact, to be decided if that man was to be accursed who should refuse to believe that an impious and simoniacal priest could, at his own pleasure, open heaven or close it;—if, in the interpretation of the Scriptures, the rights of conscience were to be respected or disowned ;—if the clergy should fix limits to the powers they had so much abused, and guaranty a prudent employment of them for the future;—and, lastly, to ascertain if Roman Catholicism could be reformed ; if the Church, which declared that no salvation was possible out of its bosom, could assure its own safety. (D.)

BOOK II.

CHAPTER I.

THE greater number of the members of the council had already arrived at Constance, when two men, hostile to each other, and as much separated by rank as by character—a pope and a poor excommunicated priest—John XXIII. and John Huss—were pursuing their way to the council, both agitated by inauspicious presentiments.

The pontiff's carriage having been overturned on a mountain of the Tyrol, from whence the eye could range extensively over Constance and its lake, John XXIII. looked on the accident as a most unlucky omen. "By the power of Satan," cried he, "behold me fallen! Why did I not rather remain quietly at Bologna!" And then, looking down at the city in the valley below, he continued—"I see how it is, that is the pit where the foxes are snared." He felt, in fact, that the extinction of the schism being the principal object of the council, it was necessary, in order to attain that object, that the three men amongst whom Christendom was divided, should make way for a new pontiff, whom it appeared to be the general wish to raise to the papal throne. Therefore was it that he feigned to convoke the council in all sincerity, in order to insure to himself the right of dissolving it.

The melancholy presentiments of John Huss were neither less cogent nor worse grounded. He neglected no legitimate means of defence; but his heart did not quail. He, first of all, loudly declared his determination to render, at Constance, testimony for his faith. A few days before his departure, in a paper affixed to the gates of the palace, he announced that he was about to depart, in order to justify himself before the council. "So that," said he, "if any one suspects me of heresy, let him proceed thither and prove, in presence of the pope and the doctors, if I ever entertained or taught any false or mistaken doctrine. If any man can convict me of having inculcated any doctrine contrary to the Christian faith, I will

consent to undergo all the penalty to which heretics are liable. But I trust that God will not grant the victory to unbelievers—to men who outrage the truth."

Huss next publicly announced that he was ready to render an account of his faith, in presence of the archbishop and his clergy; and then boldly applied for a certificate of his orthodoxy from the very person who, by his office, ought to be the most ardent to condemn him—from the Bishop of Nazareth, the grand inquisitor of the diocese of Prague. It is just as difficult to believe, as it is impossible to deny, that he obtained what he demanded. Yet so it was—and the certificate of the inquisitor, an authentic copy of which was regularly drawn up before a notary, contained, in substance, what follows:—"By these presents, we make known to all men, that we have often held converse with the honourable master, John Huss, Bachelor in Theology of the celebrated University of Prague;—that we have had several serious conferences with him relative to the Holy Scriptures and other matters;—and that we have always considered him to be a faithful and good Catholic, not finding in him, up to this present day, either evil or error. We certify, besides, that the said John Huss has declared that he was ready to render reason for his faith, in presence of the archbishop and his clergy, against any one whatever that might come forward to accuse him of error or heresy:—but that no one presented himself to support the charge. In faith of which, we have delivered to him this letter, sealed with our great seal.—Given at Prague, this 30th of August, 1412."

Armed with this paper, Huss proceeded to the abbey of St. James, where the barons and the Archbishop of Prague were assembled for the public business of the kingdom. There he besought the archbishop to declare openly if he either accused or suspected him of heresy: and, in case he did not, he conjured him to give a public testimony of the fact, which he might find use for in his journey to Constance.

The archbishop replied, that it did not fall within his knowledge that John Huss was capable of any crime or fault; but he thought he ought to purge himself from the excommunication which he had incurred.[*]

A few days after, Huss asked for permission to appear before a general assembly of the clergy of Prague, presided over by the archbishop. He offered to establish his innocence by Scripture, by the holy canons of the Church, and by the Fathers; but his application was refused, and he was not admitted.

It must be concluded, from what precedes, that the prelates dreaded another commotion at Prague, and that they reckoned on the council to give them satisfaction over John Huss. If, too, they showed themselves indulgent in the certificate which they delivered respecting his doctrines and his conduct, perhaps they yielded to the influence of the court, or to a secret wish to render the road to Constance as easy as possible,—to remove, in fact, all the obstacles that might by possibility have delayed his departure, or slackened his journey. In the month of October, 1414, Huss bade adieu to his chapel of Bethlehem, which he was no more to behold, and to his friends and disciples. He left behind his faithful Jerome, and their parting was not without emotion. "Dear master," said Jerome to him, "be firm: maintain intrepidly what thou hast written and preached against the pride, avarice, and other vices of the churchmen, with arguments drawn from the Holy Scriptures. Should this task become too severe for thee—should I learn that thou hast fallen into any peril, I shall fly forthwith to thy assistance."[†]

Huss quitted Prague, provided with a safe-conduct from King Wenceslaus, and on his way he received that which he had demanded from the Emperor Sigismund. It was couched in the following terms:[‡] "Sigismund, by the grace of God, King of the Romans, &c., to all ecclesiastical and secular princes, &c., and to all our other subjects, greeting. *We recommend to you with a full affection,—to all in general, and to each in particular, the honourable master, JOHN HUSS, bachelor in divinity, and master of arts, the bearer of these presents, journeying from Bohemia to the council of Constance, whom we have taken under our protection and safe-guard, and under that of the empire, enjoining you to receive him and treat him kindly, furnishing*

him with all that shall be necessary to speed and assure his journey, as well by water as by land, without taking any thing from him or his, for arrivals or departures, under any pretext whatever; and calling on you to allow him TO PASS, SOJOURN, STOP, AND RETURN FREELY AND SURELY, *providing him even, if necessary, with good passports, for the honour and respect of the Imperial Majesty.—Given at Spires, this 18th day of October of the year 1414, the third of our reign in Hungary, and the fifth of that of the Romans.*" (E)

John Huss was accompanied by several noble barons, Henry de Latzemboch, Wenceslaus Duba, and John de Chlum. The life of this last offers a pure model of the most touching and most devoted friendship; and his name, in the eyes of posterity, is inseparable from that of John Huss.

Enmity, however, was not slumbering, and its explosion, because deferred, was only the more to be apprehended. The bitter enemies of Huss, Stephen Paletz and Michael Causis, formerly a curé of a church in Old Prague, had preceded him to Constance, and before he had even once appeared before his judges, his destruction was already decided on.

He did not deceive himself as to his perilous position, and the very precautions that he took before his departure, prove that he had calculated the whole extent of the danger. Several farewell letters which he wrote to his friends in Prague confirm this fact.

"My brethren," said he to them, "do not suppose that I am affronting unworthy treatment for any false doctrine. . . . I am departing with a safe-conduct from the king[*] to meet my numerous and mortal enemies. . . . I confide altogether in the all-powerful God, in my Saviour; I trust that he will listen to your ardent prayers, that he will infuse his prudence and his wisdom into my mouth, in order that I may resist them; and that he will accord me his Holy Spirit to fortify me in his truth, so that I may face, with courage, temptations, prison, and, if necessary, a cruel death. Jesus Christ suffered for his well-beloved; and, therefore, ought we to be astonished that he has left us his example, in order that we may ourselves endure with patience all things for our own salvation? He is God, and we are his creatures; He is the Lord, and we are his servants; He is master of the world, and we are contemptible mortals:—yet he suffered! Why, then, should we not suffer also, particularly when suffering is for us a purification? Therefore, beloved, if my death ought to contribute to his glory, pray that it may come

---

[*] The certificate of the Bishop of Nazareth, and the language of the archbishop, are proved by the letter which the barons of Bohemia addressed to Sigismund, after Huss's death.

[†] Theob. p. 25, *Bel. Hus.*

[‡] Msc. Bruns. Leips. et Goth. ap. von der Hardt, t. iv. p. 12.

[*] The Emperor Sigismund, not being as yet crowned, was called, according to custom, King of the Romans.

quickly, and that he may enable me to support all my calamities with constancy. But if it be better that I return amongst you, let us pray to God that I may return without stain,—that is, that I may not suppress one tittle of the truth of the gospel, in order to leave my brethren an excellent example to fellow. Probably, therefore, you will never more behold my face at Prague; but should the will of the all-powerful God deign to restore me to you, let us then advance with a firmer heart in the knowledge and the love of his law."[*]

In another letter, which Huss addressed, when setting out, to the priest Martin, his disciple, he speaks of himself with the greatest humility. He accuses himself, as if they were so many grave offences, of having felt pleasure in wearing rich apparel, and of having wasted hours in frivolous occupations. He adds these affecting instructions :—

"May the glory of God, and the salvation of souls, occupy thy mind, and not the possession of benefices and estates. Beware of adorning thy house more than thy soul; and, above all, give thy care to the spiritual edifice. Be pious and humble with the poor; and consume not thy substance in feasting. Shouldst thou not amend thy life and refrain from superfluities, I fear that thou wilt be severely chastened, as I am myself—I, who also made use of such things, led away by custom, and troubled by a spirit of pride. Thou knowest my doctrine, for thou hast received my instructions from thy childhood; it is therefore useless for me to write to thee any further. But I conjure thee, by the mercy of our Lord, not to imitate me in any of the vanities into which thou hast seen me fall."[†] He concludes by making some bequests, and disposing, as if by will, of several articles which belonged to him; and then, on the cover of the letter, he adds this prophetic phrase, "I conjure thee, my friend, not to break this seal until thou shalt have acquired the certitude that I am dead."

An internal progress is manifested in those letters, which are worthy of being put on a parallel with the holy writings of the most celebrated Fathers of the ancient Church. His soul, always so upright and so pure, appears to have gained in mildness and patience. Neither in what he writes, nor what he says, is there any longer any thing of the passion of the infectious sectarian, whom the exciting and intoxicating noise of popular acclamations carries beyond all bounds. Henceforward, he is almost alone in the midst of strangers or enemies: his soul listens no longer but to the secret voice, which speaks to him in his conscience; and, turning in on itself, it gains both strength and purity. Whether it is that, in the face of extreme peril, man naturally rises above himself, or that at the approach of the last hour, Divine grace operates in the heart of the just man with greater power, Huss, from the period of his departure from Prague till his death, showed himself as grand by his patience, resignation, and evangelical sweetness, as he had previously been by the purity of his morals, his profound piety, his uprightness, and his determination. A more favourable light illuminated his noble character, and exhibited it in points of view hitherto completely unknown, or concealed in the shade.

Nothing occurred to disturb his journey, during which he enjoyed, for the last time, the satisfaction of beholding applause bestowed on his exhortations. As he attacked the abuse of certain practices of worship more than the practices themselves—the extreme consequences of certain doctrines more than those doctrines—and the vices of the ecclesiastics more than the institution itself of the clergy, his words easily found favour with the people and priests of the country parts, who had themselves suffered greatly from the despotism and avarice of the dignitaries of the Church. The prelates and doctors comprehended fully the immense bearing of the two capital points on which John Huss separated from the received doctrine; viz.—the spiritual incapacity of simoniacal or impious priests, and the appeal to the Scriptures more than to the Church: but the consequences of these two principles were above the comprehension of the vulgar; and the multitude beheld in John Huss only a man of a holy life and apostolic language, who was persecuted by the fury of the priests, because he had stigmatised their hypocrisy and avarice. Throughout this whole journey he met with the same kind reception, the same favour; and in one of his letters he himself gives an account of some of the incidents that befell him on the road.

He writes, October 20, from Nuremberg to his friends at Prague in the following terms: "Learn, that from the day on which I quitted Bohemia, I have travelled on horseback, and with my features exposed to public view. On my drawing near Pernau, I found the curé and his vicars waiting for me: when I came close to them, he drank to my health in a cup of wine. Both he and his friends listened to me with a charitable spirit; and he informed me that he had always been my friend. All the Germans beheld me with pleasure in the new town. From thence we proceeded to Weyden, where we excited great admiration amongst a very considerable crowd;[*] and when we arrived

---

[*] *Hist. et Monum. J. Hus.* t. i. p. 72, Epist. i.
[†] Ibid. Epist. ii.

[*] Habentes magnum populum in admiratione.

at Saltzbach, I thus addressed the consuls and notables of the town: 'I am that John Huss, of whom, beyond a doubt, you have heard much evil. Here I am: ascertain of the real state of the case by interrogating me yourselves.' After a great number of questions, they received most favourably all that I addressed to them. We next passed through Inspruck, and spent the night in the town of Lauff, where the curé, a great jurist, and his vicars, had come to see me. I had a conference with him; and he also received my words perfectly well. We next reached Nuremberg, where certain dealers, who preceded us, had announced my arrival; so that the people had taken up their station in the streets and public places, looking out for my coming, and inquiring which was John Huss. After dinner, the curé wrote to me to say, that he should be glad to have a long conversation with me. I invited him to come, which he did; and, afterwards, the citizens and magistrates assembled with the desire of visiting and holding converse with me. On hearing this, I immediately rose from table, and went to meet them; and as they wished to confer in private, I said to them: 'I speak only in public: they who wish to hear me have only to listen.' And from that moment until night we discussed matters in presence of the consuls and townspeople....... At last they said to me, ' Master, all that we have just heard is catholic: we have taught those things for many, many years, looking on them as true; and such we consider them still. Undoubtedly, you will return from this council with honour.'..... Learn, that I have not hitherto met with a single enemy; but that in every place where I have stopped I have been excellently received. In fact, the bitterest enemies I have are certain obscure persons from Bohemia. What more shall I say to you? The Lords Wenceslaus and John de Chlum act piously and nobly towards me. They are the heralds and advocates of the truth; and, with them, God giving his aid, all passes most suitably. We shall arrive, by night, at Constance, which Pope John is approaching. We think he follows the king at a distance of about sixty miles."*

From this letter, and some others, it appears that the populations went out to meet John Huss. The magistrates themselves escorted him in the towns; and this general eagerness was at once a homage paid to his character,

and an eloquent protest against the corruption of the clergy.

Huss arrived at Constance on November 3. He put up at the house of a poor widow, whom he compares to her of Sarepta, who received Elijah: but if she offered him a refuge, she could not insure him an asylum. However, he was not molested for several days. The Barons John de Chlum and Henry de Latzemboch notified his arrival to the pope, and informed him that John Huss was provided with a safe-conduct from the emperor. John XXIII. received them graciously, and replied: " Even had John Huss killed my own brother, I would most heartily prevent any injustice being done him, during the period of his stay at Constance." It is even asserted that he took off the excommunication from John Huss, and merely required him not to appear at the solemn masses, in order not to give occasion for scandal or popular commotion.

John Huss therefore spoke and acted with a tolerable share of liberty in the first days of his stay. Full of confidence in the safe-conduct which he possessed, he maintained his doctrines with word and pen, and said mass in a room of his lodging, where the people flocked in crowds to see and hear him. He was in hopes of being allowed to preach in public, and had prepared for this purpose two sermons, which are still preserved in his works, and which are both remarkable for prudence. In them, Huss professed to believe what the Catholic Church believed: he declared his trust in tradition, and quoted from the principal Fathers: he maintained, however, that the Holy Scriptures, well studied and understood, were the real rule of faith, and that this rule was quite sufficient for salvation: he added, that, in what regarded doctrines as to the efficacy of regeneration, the Christian faith necessarily including all acts of obedience and love, a man in mortal sin was only a Christian by name, and could not recite the creed without lying. He exhorted the Church to peace and union. As to the corruption, luxury, and simony of the clergy, his language was far more moderate than that of the principal preachers of the period; and, on certain points, his propositions were much less daring than theirs. It is beyond all doubt, that John Huss had intended to win over to himself men's minds by those two discourses; and, therefore, to prohibit him from preaching them, was to announce to him beforehand, that a determination had been taken to ruin him.

* *Hist. et Monum. J. Hus.* t. i. p. 73, Epist. iii.

CHAPTER II.

COMPOSITION OF THE COUNCIL.—SUBJECTS AND ORDER OF THE DELIBERATIONS.—CANONIZATION OF ST. BRIDGET.

THE composition of the Council was worthy of the great interests that were to be discussed. There was not a kingdom, or state, or republic, or scarcely a city or community, that was not represented at Constance.* Two popes, John XXIII. and Martin V., acted as presidents; the one at the beginning, the other at the end. There came thither thirty cardinals, twenty archbishops, one hundred and fifty bishops, and as many prelates, a multitude of abbots and doctors, and eighteen hundred priests. Amongst the sovereigns who attended in person, could be distinguished the Elector Palatine, the Electors of Mentz and of Saxony, and the Dukes of Austria, of Bavaria, and of Silesia. There were, besides, a vast number of margraves, counts, and barons, and a complete crowd of noblemen. But, amongst all, the first in rank, as in power, was the emperor. An intrepid though often unsuccessful warrior, yet deriving from his reverses a fresh vigour,—a clever and determined politician, Sigismund would perhaps be reckoned amongst those who have done most honour to their crown, had not the prejudices of a narrow and superstitious doctrine too frequently repressed in him the aspirations of his soul, and the movements of his mind.

He was forty-seven years old at the period of the council; and the maturity of his age added to the natural majesty of his person.† His manners were noble and insinuating, his mind rather elevated than enlarged, and his acquirements rare in a man of his time, and, above all, of his rank. He spoke, with facility, several languages; and conferred honour on himself by honouring literature. "I can, in a single day, make a thousand noblemen," he used to say, "but in a thousand years I cannot make a single scholar." His ardent passions, and the sanguinary instincts which he manifested in his youth, had been purified, or placed under restraint, by the rude trials which fortune had somewhat prodigally heaped on him. How-

ever, even on the throne, he preserved rather unceremonious habits; and his impetuous temper more than once had mastered his prudence. Liberal even to prodigality, it frequently happened to him, when wishing to obtain an influence over others by his gifts, to place himself in a very embarrassing dependence, by being obliged to contract loans. He was generous towards his enemies; for a prince, he used to observe, had a double interest in pardoning—he lost an enemy, and gained a friend. His mind was by nature grand and chivalrous, and yet he had adopted, like many other princes, dissimulation, as one of his rules of conduct. France, in particular, had afterwards to complain of his duplicity, and at the Council of Constance, a shameful breach of faith, with respect to John Huss, marked his name with an indelible stain. Although, in that circumstance, he was forced to submit to the yoke of the clergy, yet he exercised over the assembly a vast influence; and his will was the cohesive power which, for several years, kept united, in a single body, so many elements, and of a nature so various and so opposite.

Literature and science also had their representatives at the Council, and several of those who were the living lights of their age, appeared with honour by the side of the dignitaries of the church and of the empire. There, might be seen the illustrious scholar, Poggio of Florence, who restored to the world Quintilian and Lucretius; Thierry de Niem, secretary to several popes, and whom Providence appears to have placed near the source of so many iniquities, for the purpose of unveiling and stigmatizing them. With them must be named Æneas Sylvius Piccolomini, afterwards pope, under the title of Pius II., less celebrated in the eyes of posterity for his triple crown, than for his merit as an historian; also Manuel Chrysoloras, the learned Greek ambassador, of an illustrious origin, and an irreproachable life, and whose labours restored to light some of the writings of Demosthenes and of Cicero. He had followed Cardinal Zabarella to Constance, where both of them died.* But amongst the most learned and the most worthy, none exercised so much influence at the Council,

---

* The several kingdoms of Spain, that of Scotland, and some provinces dependent on Benedict XIII., were not represented at the Council until much later.

† Majestate regia quam in procero ostentabat corporo et liberalitate ac munificentia, quam multarum linguarum peritia, insigniorem reddidit, omnes facile suæ ætatis reges antecellebat.—Joan. Cuspin. in Sigism.

---

* See Note F, at the end of the volume.

by their personal merit, as John-Charlier Gerson and Peter d'Ailly, Cardinal of Cambray, surnamed the *Eagle of France.* The former, ambassador to King Charles VI., chancellor of the Church and of the University of Paris, was the soul of the Council, by his genius, his grand character, and his indefatigable zeal; and it was evident that he was the honour of the University of Paris, at a period when that celebrated body had become in France the last asylum of the national glory.

A crowd of men of every profession followed the members of the Council to Constance. There was also an immense concourse of strangers, so that the number of persons who repaired thither from all parts, was estimated at not less than 100,000 souls.* The eyes of Europe were fixed on a little city, where one of the most imposing assemblies ever known, a veritable Congress of Christendom, was about to decide on interests of the highest importance.

The extinction of the schism and of heresy, the union and reformation of the Church, were certainly the most serious questions that the Council had to resolve; but others were also to be submitted to it, less important perhaps in themselves, yet which, notwithstanding, excited very general attention.

One of those was the revision of the judgment passed by the Bishop of Paris in 1413, against the celebrated defence of Jean-Sans-Peur, Duke of Burgundy, pronounced by Dr. John Petit, in presence of the Dauphin, on the occasion of the murder of the Duke of Orleans.† Jean-Sans-Peur appealed to the pope, and John XXIII. committed the affair to three cardinals, who quashed the sentence pronounced in Paris. Charles VI. brought the affair before the Council, and demanded a confirmation of the sentence.

Another cause, of a great national interest, was that of the Poles against the Teutonic Knights. The knights, having been applied to by the Poles to afford them assistance against the Prussians, who were still pagans and savages, had first pursued the latter with fire and sword, and then turned their arms against the nation which had demanded their aid. A war of extermination between the Poles and

the Teutonic Order was the consequence, and the Council was chosen as arbiter between the two parties.

Besides those grand objects of deliberation, the Council had a number of other interests to regulate. But the most grave and the most pressing was, decidedly, the extinction of the schism; and to it, therefore, did the assembly, with a praiseworthy ardour, first direct all its thoughts and all its energy.

The emperor had invited Benedict XIII. and Gregory XII. to send representatives to the Council. Benedict, who still reckoned under his sway the kingdoms of Spain, Scotland, and the counties of Foix and Armagnac, proposed to the emperor to hold a conference in some city, where he could repair in company with the King of Aragon.

Gregory, on his part, declared that he was ready to resign, if his two competitors did the same.

This was to propose the problem in the same terms as previously to the Council of Pisa, when every effort made to resolve it had completely failed. The Council of Pisa, instead of extinguishing the schism, had helped to perpetuate it, by proceeding to the choice of a new pope, before it had obtained the resignation of the two others. Nearly the whole Church, and the greatest part of Europe, having concurred in the election of Alexander V., this pontiff and his successor, John XXIII., were entitled to be recognised as lawful popes. The latter, in consequence, could not be treated as Gregory XII. and Benedict XIII., whose election was considered at Pisa as vicious and invalid. The question, therefore, was less to strip him of his dignity, than to obtain from him a voluntary abdication. His temporal ambition, which had rendered the support of Sigismund so necessary to him,—his detestable reputation, which gave every one an advantage over him,—and, last of all, his troubled conscience, which deprived him of all confidence in himself, contributed more to reduce him than force possibly could have done.

It has been already seen how the emperor, by concealing from the pope his resolution already secretly decided on, had succeeded in forcing from him his consent to allow the convocation of the Council in an imperial city; but it had been necessary to entice him thither afterwards, in order to oblige him to consent to its decrees.

The pope had come in the probable expectation of predominating over the assembly by his presence,* and of giving more efficiency

---

* The concourse of persons, who flocked from all parts of Christendom, to this council, ecclesiastics and laymen, was so great that the city was insufficient to accommodate them. Booths and wooden buildings were erected outside the town, and thousands of pilgrims were encamped in the adjacent country. All kinds of shows and amusements, dramatic representations, entertainments of every description, and religious processions, were constantly going on, and thousands of persons were employed solely in transporting thither the choicest delicacies of Europe.—*Note of Translator.*

† See the Introduction, p. 18.

* Placuit Pummo pontifici ut iret Constantiam, non *judicaturus, sed judicandus.* Theod. Vrie, *Hist. Concilii Const.* lib. vi. dist. iv.—Ap. Von der Hardt, lib. i. p. 153.

to his intrigues by intriguing on the spot. A struggle, unacknowledged at first, though most deadly, was about to take place between the partisans of John XXIII. and those who agreed with the emperor, as to the policy of sacrificing this pontiff to the peace and unity of the Church. The Council was the lists where the combat was to be fought.

The most important points to be decided, and which, when once determined, would resolve all the others, were, first of all, to ascertain who was to have a deliberative voice? and, next, to declare how the suffrages were to be collected. The pope, having much less influence over the seculars than over the clergy, would have been well pleased that the former were excluded from the Council; and therefore demanded that the privilege of voting should be confined to the dignitaries of the Church. This proposition was, however, negatived. The Cardinal of Cambray (Peter d'Ailly) observed, that the Church had not been uniform, either in its mode of assembling councils, or of deliberating in them. On some occasions they had been composed of the whole community of Christians, whilst at others the members were bishops, abbots, and deacons. "If," remarked he, "the bishops had at one period a deliberative voice, it was because they had the cure of souls, and that they were learned and holy persons, elected by the Church, and not mere titular prelates, destitute of all the qualities necessary for deciding in a council."* The cardinal affirmed, that not only had doctors been allowed to vote in the Councils of Pisa and of Rome, but even secular priests, their ambassadors and proxies; and argued, that if it was intended really to reform the clergy, it would be absurd to exclude the men the most interested in the change taking place.

Cardinal de St. Marc next pleaded, with great warmth, the cause of the priests, deacons, and other inferior ecclesiastics. "According to St. Paul," said he, "the bishop and the priest have the same character, the same dignity; and the pope himself is only the first amongst priests." As to what related to kings, their ambassadors, and other seculars, they ought to confine themselves to simply forming opinions on such matters as concerned the general welfare of the Church, but to leave the clergy the decision of things purely spiritual.

Those two cardinals, in citing the Council of Pisa, employed an irresistible argument for John XXIII., who was really pope; but in his quality of successor of Alexander V., on whom

the election of a council had fallen, had the strongest interest in getting all its decisions confirmed, and in acknowledging that all which it had determined on had been executed canonically. It was, therefore, decided, that the secular princes, their deputies, the doctors, and a great number of inferior ecclesiastics, designated or accepted by the Council, should be allowed a deliberative voice.

This first point being regulated, the second, which was still more important, was to fix the manner in which the votes were to be taken. It was the interest of the pope that they should be received individually, one for each person, the Italians being all gained over to him. "The greatest number of them," said an old author, "had come poor, famished, and devoted to John XXIII., whose favours strengthened the doubtful spirits, or brought into subjection such as were rebellious." He created amongst them, it is said, as many as fifty chamberlains in one day; and as they were superior in number to all the prelates of the other nations united, it was evident, that if the pope obtained the votes per head, he would become the master of the Council. A different opinion, therefore, prevailed; and it was resolved that the votes should not be taken per head, as in the preceding council, but by nation. The assembly consisted of four nations—the Italian, the French, the German, and the English. The Spaniards had not at this period joined the Council. Each nation appointed deputies to examine the affairs nationally (*nationaliter*); and those matters were afterwards brought before the Council, and discussed in public and general sittings (*conciliariter*).

The first public sitting took place, in the absence of the emperor, on Nov. 16, 1414. The pope on that day formally opened the Council, and Cardinal Zabarella read the bull of convocation, in which it was stated, that John XXIII. assembled the Council in execution of that of Pisa. The pope next appointed the officers who were to be intrusted with the guard and defence of the Council, as well as the notaries and secretaries who were to draw up its decrees. Their names were then read aloud, and the Council having approved of what was done, the sitting was concluded.

John XXIII., a few days after, marked the end of his pontificate by an act which he was but little worthy to accomplish—the canonization of a woman named Bridget, the foundress of a monastic order, of which Jesus Christ himself had, she asserted, dictated the rules. She had already been once before canonized by Boniface IX., but the validity of that pontiff's election having been contested, it was conceived that a true pope alone had a right to

* Ex Labb. ap Von der Hardt, t. ii. part viii. pp. 224, 225.

place her amongst the saints. The Council, therefore, acknowledged her titles, and John XXIII. proclaimed them publicly, in the midst of all the pomps of the Church, on a day solemnly appointed for that purpose. This woman was, however, the very person that was accused by Gregory XI. on his death-bed, of having urged him towards Rome by pretended visions;* and it is worthy of remark, that the very Council which was assembled to put an end to the schism, commenced its labours by beatifying the woman who had originally contributed to its being brought into existence.

Whilst the guilty pontiff was thus disposing of the places reserved in heaven for the elect, he perceived, with the deepest regret, that he was totally unable to preserve his own position on earth. Excluded from the meetings where his fate was discussed, racked by suspicion at what was plotted against him outside, and torn by the action of his own disquieting thoughts, he held, with the clutch of despe-ration, to the power which was now escaping from him in every direction. Every night, when all around was silent, he called secretly around him his emissaries, and learned from them all the manœuvres of his opponents. Armed with this information, he endeavoured to win over such persons as he thought it necessary to strengthen or persuade; and those spiritual treasures which he still pretended to have at his disposal, and his temporal goods,. collected together by so many acts of rapine,. were employed in disengaging men from sworn oaths, and persuading them to take new ones. But he, by this conduct, caused more men commit perjury than he secured loyal followers for himself. Every day, too,—and this was his greatest punishment,—he perceived that the perils which encompassed him were increasing more and more, without his being able to discover any means of averting them; and he felt that, whilst he multiplied around himself spies and traitors, he multiplied also his own mortal terrors.

CHAPTER III.

ARREST OF JOHN HUSS.—ARRIVAL OF THE EMPEROR.

John XXIII. had given his solemn promise to protect John Huss; but he was rather in want of protection himself than in a condition to afford it to another. He was, besides, neither of a character nor temper to refuse any demand to the cardinals and prelates of his party; still less would he venture to endanger himself for a man accused of heresy. It is not surprising, therefore, that the moment should come when he forgot his promise.

John Huss was not mistaken when he declared, that his most bitter enemies came from Bohemia.† We have already mentioned that Stephen Paletz and Michael Causis had preceded him at the Council. Their first care, on their arrival, was to placard everywhere the documents in which Huss was signalized as a heretic and an excommunicated person. Huss complained of this to the pope, but received no satisfaction. "I cannot," said John XXIII., "do any thing in the matter: it is your own countrymen who act against you."

Paletz and Causis drew up together certain articles, which they pretended to be extracts from Huss's works, and principally his *Treatise on the Church*. Then taking an infinity of trouble, as an old author of his life expresses it, running here and there, wherever they could fall in with the cardinals, bishops, monks, and persons of the same profession,. they exhibited to them those articles; and solemnly protesting that they could, when necessary, produce others of still greater gravity, published, they affirmed, by Huss, in opposition to the pope and the Church, they produce such an effect by agitating this firebrand, that they inflamed those men, already prejudiced and irritated, and persuaded them to determine on arresting John Huss.*

On the twenty-sixth day after his arrival at Constance, whilst he was passing his time between study and the familiar conversation of his friends, two bishops, accompanied by the consul of Constance and a knight, suddenly presented themselves at his lodgings, and informed him that they were sent by the pope and the cardinals to request him to come before them, as he had often expressed a desire, and render an account of his doctrines.

"I did not come here," said John Huss, "with the intention of pleading my cause in private before the pope and the cardinals, and I never desired any such thing; but I wished

* See the Historical Introduction, p. 10
† Epist. iii. see page 52.

* *Hist. et Monum. J. Hus. t. i. p. 6.*

to appear before the general Council, in the presence of all, and there openly and plainly to reply on every point proposed to me, according as God should inspire me for my defence. Yet I do not refuse to appear previously before the cardinals; and if they act unfairly towards me, I shall put my trust in our Saviour Jesus Christ, and shall be more happy to die for his glory, than to live in denying the truth, such as it is taught in the Holy Scriptures."

Armed men had been secretly posted in the neighbouring houses, but the persons who had been sent manifested no hostile disposition towards Huss. When, therefore, they urged him to accompany them, he got on horseback with John de Chlum, and followed them to the palace of the pope and cardinals.

He accordingly appeared before them, and when he had saluted them, they thus addressed him : "Master John Huss, we have learned concerning you many things which, if true, cannot be tolerated. It is asserted that you teach the gravest errors,—the most opposed to the doctrines of the true Church,—and you have already disseminated them through the whole of Bohemia. We have summoned you to appear before us, that we may know the truth."

"Reverend fathers," replied John Huss, "learn that I would rather die than be knowingly guilty of a single error,—still more of a great number, and those of a grave character, as you express it. Well convinced of my innocence, I have come of my own free will to this council, in order to receive the correction to which I may be liable for every error that can be proved against me."

"It is well spoken," said the cardinals, as they rose to withdraw. Armed men then entered, and Huss and John de Chlum were left under their guard.

However, a certain theologian, of the order of Franciscans, an insinuating and cunning fellow, slipped through the soldiers, and, coming up to Huss, thus accosted him :— "Master," said he, "I am a simple-minded and ignorant man, anxious to gain instruction. I have heard that many opinions, foreign to the Catholic faith, have been attributed to you. Now, those things agitate my mind, and draw it in different directions, loving, as I do, the truth : therefore, I supplicate you, by the love which you profess for Christian charity and pious men, to teach me, a wretched sinner, something positive. It is confidently asserted, in the first place, that, in your opinion, after the consecration by the priest, there only remains a common piece of bread in the sacrament at the altar." "That is false," said John Huss. "How," persisted the monk, "do you not think that such is the case?" "Certainly not," was

the reply; "I believe no such thing." And when the monk repeated, for the third time, the same question, the open-hearted John de Chlum was seized with indignation, and exclaimed, in anger, "Why are you so importunate? If any one were to affirm or deny a thing to me only a single time, I should believe him; and yet you, after having heard the master express his opinion several times, still interrogate him!" "Noble lord," said the monk, "I pray you pardon me. I am only a simple and ignorant man; and what I have done, was merely with a view to gain instruction." Then, changing the subject, he proposed another doubt; and asking in what manner the divinity and humanity were united together in the person of Christ. "In my opinion," said Huss, in his own language, to John de Chlum, "this monk is not so simple as he pretends to be: he proposes to me a point of extreme difficulty." Then, turning to the monk, he said—"Brother, you represent yourself to be simple-minded; but, from what I can perceive, you smack somewhat of the double-dealer." And when the monk cried out against this—"I will prove what I advance;" observed John Huss: "Simplicity requires a certain agreement between the mind and the mouth—between the thought and the words,—which I perceive not in you. Your mouth, indeed, represents you as a simple and ignorant man; but your difficult questions plainly denote a subtle and exercised mind. Notwithstanding what I suspect, I will explain the point to you." The monk listened to the explanation, and disappeared.

John Huss then learned from the soldiers that this monk was Didacus, the most able theologian of Lombardy. "What a pity I was not aware of it!" remarked he; "I should have acted differently towards him. Would to God that all my adversaries resembled him; and, fortified by the succour of the Scriptures, I should not fear one of them!"

Huss and his friend remained thus under the guard of the soldiers, until four in the afternoon.

The cardinals were, during this time, in council with the pope. Paletz, Causis, and several others, urged and insisted, in every possible manner, that John Huss should not be set at liberty. They passed and repassed the spot where he was, insulting him and crying—"Behold, we have possession of thee; and thou shalt not escape until thou hast paid the uttermost farthing."

At the approach of night, the provost of the pontifical court announced to John de Chlum that he was at liberty, but that Huss must remain a prisoner. Furious with indignation and passion, Chlum complained, in the bitter-

8

est terms, that a most worthy and holy man had been lured, by lying representations, into a most infamous snare. He hastened to the pope to inform him of what had passed; he reminded him of the promise which his holiness had made to him and Henry de Latzembooh together, and called on him not to break his plighted faith so unworthily. The pope declared that he had not done any thing against John Huss; and pointing to the cardinals and bishops, exclaimed—"Why do you impute any thing to me, when you know well that I am myself here in their power!"

John XXIII. thus revealed the true and shameful motive of his conduct. He feared his own downfall, and flattered himself with the hope of gaining favour with a great number of cardinals and bishops, by sacrificing to them the just man whom, in the bottom of their hearts, they had already condemned.

Chlum withdrew in the utmost mortification; and, for several days, he did not cease complaining of the pope, accusing him of having most unworthily entrapped John Huss, in utter contempt of his own promise and that of the emperor.

Huss remained for a week confined, under a strong guard, in the house of the clerk of the cathedral of Constance, and was from thence conducted to the prison of the monastery of the Dominicans, on the banks of the Rhine. This prison was close to the receptacle of filth of the monastery; and from the damp and unwholesomeness of the place, he was taken so ill, that a raging fever placed his life in the utmost danger. The pope, with an intention rather cruel, perhaps, than charitable, sent his own physician to him; for "he feared," says an old historian, "that John Huss might die a natural death."[*]

John de Chlum, after having uselessly applied to the pope, appealed to the emperor, who was still absent. Sigismund shook with rage when he learned that the pontiff and cardinals had violated his safe-conduct. He immediately transmitted to his ambassador at Constance his written and formal orders:—"On the instant, set John Huss at liberty; and if resistance be made, break open the doors." This order, however, was not put into execution; and John Huss remained a prisoner. The intrepid and indefatigable John de Chlum then appealed to the public conscience, and affixed to the doors of all the churches of Constance an energetic protest, in Latin and German, against the violation of the imperial safe-conduct given to John Huss.

The pope had at first ▬▬▬ as we have seen, that he had any partici▬▬▬ in this iniquitous act; but he avowed afterwards, that John Huss, whom he offered as a victim to the fury of his enemies, had been arrested by his orders. He complained, too, that the emperor, who called himself the protector of the council and the advocate of the Church, should threaten to have recourse to force to restore a heretic to liberty.[*]

However, this baseness did not save himself; and if the hour of deliverance came not for John Huss, at least the hour of retribution was at hand. On December 24th, the Emperor Sigismund made his solemn entry into the city of Constance, and, by his presence, imparted to the council a new grandeur and majesty. The same day, the pope celebrated mass pontifically in the cathedral; and the emperor, who was present, according to custom, in his deacon's dress, read the gospel. When John XXIII. heard this formidable deacon read close to him the words—*There went out a decree from the Emperor Augustus,*[†] he grew pale and trembled. A throne had been erected in the Church, which Sigismund ascended, his empress taking her place on his right; whilst, by their side, stood the Elector of Brandenburg and the Elector of Saxony, one holding the sceptre, and the other the sword of state. After the mass, John XXIII. presented a sword to the emperor, exhorting him to use it for the defence of the council; and yet it was on himself that first fell the weight of the imperial arm.

CHAPTER IV.

STRUGGLE BETWEEN THE POPE AND THE EMPEROR.—HUSS IN PRISON.—FLIGHT OF JOHN XXIII.

ALREADY the most considerable men of the two parties had openly published their opinions. The Italian party, in the memorial which they had drawn up, demanded that measures should be taken for the reformation of certain abuses, for the maintenance of the rights of bishops,

---

* Hist. et Monum. J. Hus. t. xi. p. 6.

* Von der Hardt, t. iv. part 1st, p. 26. † Luke ii. 1.

and for the repression of simony in the pontifical court. They insisted particularly on the necessity of, first of all, obtaining the confirmation of the Council of Pisa; and, in fact, to confirm the acts of this council was, in their eyes, to recognise the rights of John XXIII. as the only lawful pope.

Their adversaries took good care not to admit a demand which tended to fortify the pontifical authority. The Cardinal of St. Marc, the Cardinal of Cambray, and the prelates of the Gallican Church, maintained, with force, that the Council of Pisa and that of Constance were completely independent of each other, and that it was not at all necessary that the first should be confirmed by the second;—that what ought then to be their great object was the union and the reformation of the Church. The Cardinal of Cambray, besides, insisted on the voluntary abdication of Benedict XIII. and Gregory XII.; and when to this was objected, that a decree had been passed at the Council of Pisa, dispossessing those two popes, on the ground of their being schismatics and heretics, he replied, that all considerations ought to yield before that of the peace and union of the Church;—that several councils having erred not only in fact, but in right, and even faith, that of Pisa, although it were legitimate, could not be reputed infallible.*

Several cardinals presented a memorial, in which a sharp censure of the habits of John XXIII. was cloaked under the appearance of great zeal for a reformation, and for a recurrence to ancient manners.

"The pope," it was there remarked, "being the rule of the council, ought to be himself better regulated than all the rest. He ought to be the first up and the last to bed; to observe the utmost courtesy in his demeanour and words, and to do nothing unless after mature deliberation. He should set apart appointed hours for reciting vespers and hearing mass, imitating in that his pious predecessors, some of whom even said their prayers in secret each night and morning. Whatever persons were admitted familiarly into the pontifical palace should be persons of irreproachable conduct. The pope, too, should rather give than receive. The ancient pontiffs, indeed, were in the habit of succouring indigent prelates; and some of them had been known to order the dishes taken from their table to be given to the poor."†

These first steps of the adversaries of John XXIII. were followed by more decisive attacks; for they resolved to establish in a formal manner the superiority of general councils over sovereign pontiffs, and thus to constrain the pope and dispose his tiara. Amongst those who most signalised themselves in this course, was remarked that same William Filastre, who, nine years before, had proved himself, in the assembly of the clergy of France, so energetic a champion of the papal power.* Named, by John XXIII., Cardinal of St. Marc, he made every imaginable effort to induce this pontiff to resign voluntarily. "He is the true shepherd," said he, "and, on that account, ought to consent to this mode of giving peace to the Church, being even obliged to sacrifice his life to procure so great an advantage." And, as John XXIII. refused to comply, Peter d'Ailly went farther than William Filastre, and declared, that the universal Church, represented by a general council, had a right to take away the pontificate from any pope, the most lawful and the most estimable, if it were not possible to restore peace to the Church by any other means.

The pope, however, refused to accede; and it is doubtful whether even so many efforts would have vanquished his resistance, had not a terrible blow suddenly disarmed him.

In a secret meeting a long list of accusations was brought forward against him, "including," says his secretary, Thierry de Niem,† "all the mortal sins, and a multitude of abominable acts not fit to be named." Almost immediately informed of this circumstance by his spies, John XXIII., in the utmost dismay, secretly assembled his most devoted cardinals, and asked their counsel, at the same time loading them with favours and promises, as if he wanted to keep off the truth after having summoned them to declare it! He confessed that some of the allegations were well-founded, but denied others, and proposed to escape from the ignominy of public inquiry into the case, by making a sincere confession before the council. The opinion of the cardinals was that he should not do any thing precipitately. However, the members of the council proceeded to deliberate on the communication that had been made to them. Several thought that the honour of the pontificate required the whole matter to be kept secret; they were even apprehensive that, by making it public, they might afford a cause for triumph to those who defended the opinions of Wycliffe and John Huss, and that the open announcement of the crimes of John XXIII. might invalidate, in the eyes of many, the acts of his spiritual power.‡

---

* Secundum magnos quosdam doctores, generale concilium potest errare non solum in facto, sed etiam in jure, et, quod magis est, in fide.—*Concl. Camer. Cerd.* ex Msc. Vindob. ap. Von der Hardt, t. ii. p. 201.
† Von der Hardt, t. iv. p. 25.

* See Hist. Introd. p. 17.
† Theod. Niem, *de Vita Joh. XXIII.* ap. Von der Hardt, t. ii., p. 391.
‡ *Ibid.*

X They said Constance was in continuation of Pisa & so could not ratify it till reformation was effected. (Creighton I 270)

This opinion prevailed, but it was determined to make every effort to obtain the wished-for abdication.

All the nations, into which the council was divided, perfectly agreed on this point, and a deputation from them waited on the pope, and laid before him the wish of the council. The pontiff, still under the influence of dreadful fear, promised all that was demanded. Two forms of abdication, drawn up by him, were rejected by the council, on account of their ambiguous language; and, at last, after long hesitation, he agreed to accept a third one, drawn up by them in the following terms :—

" I, John XXIII., pope, in order to procure rest for all the Christian world, do declare, undertake, and promise, and do swear before God, the Church, and this sacred council, that I will freely, and of my own good will, give peace to the Church, by a complete resignation of the pontificate, and carry this my promise into effect, according to the opinion of the council, whenever Peter de Lune and Angelo Corario, respectively called Benedict XIII. and Gregory XII., shall, in their obedience, equally resign all claim to the said pontificate ; or, in other circumstances, when a resignation on my part can give peace to the Church, and root out the schism."

A few days after, on the occasion of the second general session of the council, the pope officiated himself. He read aloud the solemn engagement which he had just entered into, and swore to observe it faithfully. The emperor, mastered by the emotion of the moment, and imprudently yielding to a premature exultation, rose from his throne, laid down his crown, and throwing himself at the pontiff's knees, kissed his feet, and offered him thanksgiving. The patriarch of Constantinople next arose, and, in the name of the entire council, imitated the emperor's example.

By this act of adoration, which was, in reality, nothing else than an imprudent and ill-timed show of humility, Sigismund was near losing the fruits of his former firmness; for in thus lowering himself before John XXIII., he restored courage to this man, when he already looked on himself as lost, and whose only thought was to escape from the new shackles which he had just forged for himself. There then arose between him and the emperor an unacknowledged and continued struggle, in which one employed all his means of corruption in opposition to the power that lay at his adversary's disposal, and in which both equally had recourse to address and cunning. John XXIII. being formally called upon to name his commissioners to proceed to the execution of the promised resignation, refused to comply, and endeavoured, by disguising his bitter hatred under the appearance of deep respect, to gain over Sigismund to his side. He revived for him an ancient custom of the popes, and consecrated a Golden Rose,* which he presented to the emperor, by whom it was received with every mark of respect and thankfulness. Rejoicings and fêtes took place on this occasion, and in the midst of all the pageantry, the two actors, with eyes fixed watchfully on each other, only thought how they could each deceive his adversary.

Whilst the pope was inventing new subterfuges, the terrible accusations, which had been before kept secret, were brought forward anew, and John XXIII. was again seized with apprehension. He now no longer thought of coming off victorious, but of flying. Sigismund, however, had penetrated his designs ; and he declared that no man should quit the council without having received a formal permission. Guards were stationed throughout the country round, who watched every step that the pope took outside the city, whilst, at the same time, spies rendered an account of his most secret movements.

John XXIII. then endeavoured to sow jealousy and disunion amongst the nations ; and, at last, made an attempt to corrupt the emperor himself, and purchase his liberty for a sum of money. But the nations, which had been for a moment on bad terms, united together again, when it was necessary to proceed in unison towards the same object ; and Sigismund remained immovable.

Thus hemmed in on all sides, the pontiff could only turn for support to two powerful personages,—the Archbishop of Mentz, and Frederick Duke of Austria. The latter had only arrived a few days before at the council, and the report was current that he was sold to the pope, and that the whole purpose of his coming was to deliver him and protect his flight. He denied this most energetically, but he could not lull the suspicions that had been excited, and which became still stronger when it was known that the pope declared himself to be ill. The emperor redoubled his surveillance ; and being determined not to trust any thing but his own eyes, he went and paid him a visit, assigning the great interest he took in the pontiff's health as the pretext of his coming. He found him reclining on his bed. " Holy father," said he, " how is your health at present ?" " I am quite nervous and agitated," replied the pope. " The air of Constance disagrees with me so much that I cannot exist here." " That is strange," observed the emperor ; " for the air of Constance is considered agreeable and pure." He then represented to him, that there were in the

* See Note G, at the end of the volume.

environs a number of country seats, amongst which he could choose a residence after the conclusion of the council; but that, if he had any intention of withdrawing before that period, it would not be proper to do it secretly,—he ought to impart his design to him. "Besides," pursued the emperor, "it is my duty to watch over the safety of your person, and I will go with you myself." So powerful a keeper appeared to the pope more formidable than the greatest peril; he therefore returned thanks to the emperor, and promised him not to withdraw until the council was dissolved. But in making this promise, the pope was acting with the utmost dissimulation; for, in his opinion, the council was dissolved by the very act of his own withdrawal.

Scarcely had the emperor left the presence of John XXIII., when the latter, pushed to extremities, and exasperated beyond measure by the restraint which he had placed himself under, burst forth into a violent fit of passion. "The fool!" said he, "the drunken wretch, that would have willingly sold himself, if I had purchased him!"[*] These words were conveyed to Sigismund, who, however, "feigned to be ignorant of them," said an old author, "through a magnanimity worthy of Cæsar."[†]

The firmness which Sigismund thus displayed against a grand delinquent, whom the majesty of the very highest rank protected, he was far from exhibiting with respect to a man who could only oppose his virtues to the fury of his enemies.

When the imprisonment of John Huss was known at Prague, the entire city was thrown into commotion. A number of protests were at once signed. Several barons and puissant noblemen wrote pressing letters to the emperor, reminding him, on the one hand, of the certificates of orthodoxy given to John Huss by the prelates of Prague; and, on the other, of the safe-conduct which he had received from Sigismund himself. "John Huss," observed they, "departed with full confidence in the guarantee given him in your Imperial Majesty's letter. Nevertheless, we now understand that he has been seized on, though having them in his possession; and not only seized on, but cast into prison, without being either convicted or heard. Every one here, princes or barons, rich or poor, has been astonished to hear of this event. . . . . Each man asks his neighbour how the holy Father could so shamefully have violated the sanctity of the law, the plain rules of justice, and, finally, your Majesty's safe-conduct,—how, in fact, he could thus have thrown into prison, without

cause, a just and innocent man. May your Majesty, then, deign to have John Huss restored to liberty. We conjure your Majesty to obtain for him permission to leave his prison, and to appear in a public audience of the council, where he may speak freely, and defend the truth, as he received it from God. . . . . It would be a great misfortune, not only for your Majesty, but for the whole of Bohemia, were any evil to happen to him, whom the letters you have given bind you to protect. The all-powerful God, who reads in men's hearts, knows how great would be our grief if ever we should learn any thing—which may God forefend—that could attaint your authority or your dignity."[*]

The enemies of Huss were not less active in their efforts to destroy, than his defenders to save him. They circumvented Sigismund, and dexterously took advantage of his prejudices, his blind devotion, and his zeal—more remarkable for energy than sound judgment—for the extinction of the schism. They adduced arguments of great length to prove that he was perfectly at liberty not to keep faith with a man accused of heresy: they persuaded him that he possessed no right to accord a safe-conduct to John Huss without the consent of the council; and that, the council being above the emperor, could free him from his word.[†] Yet, notwithstanding the obsession of so many men, invested, in the eyes of Sigismund, with a sacred character, he did not abandon Huss to them without a strong resistance. Two years after, he wrote to the barons in the following terms: "Why did he not enter Constance in my company? God only knows—for I am unable to express it—how much I was afflicted by his ill fortune. The active measures that I took in his favour are matters of public notoriety,—for I went so far as several times to leave the assembly in anger, and had even once quitted the city; upon which the Fathers of the council sent to inform me, that if I stopped the course of their justice, they had nothing to do at Constance. I therefore determined to abstain from any further interference; for if I interested myself further in John Huss's favour, the council would have been dissolved."[‡]

Two decrees of this assembly were issued for the purpose of proving Sigismund's conduct to be legitimate, but no rule of right can prevail in opposition to the conscience; and Sigismund, at the bottom of his heart, often felt this voice of the council, which justi-

---

[*] Theod. Niem, *De Vita Joh. XXIII.*, in Von der Hardt, t. ii. p. 395.

[†] Misc. Vindob. ap. Von der Hardt, t. iv. p. 58.

[*] *J. Hus. Hist. et Monum.* t. i. p. 96. This letter bears the signatures of nine barons, and it is said that it was signed by a great number of other persons of high rank.

[†] Von der Hardt, t. iv. p. 397.

[‡] Cochlœus, lib. iv.

F

fied him, and which he declared infallible, to be of but little real weight.

From the moment that the emperor had abandoned John Huss, nothing further stopped his enemies. Michael Causis drew up against him a criminatory memorial, in eight articles, founded on as many points of his doctrine. But his attacks did not cease there. "John Huss," said he, "has quite ruined the University of Prague, by depending on the secular authority to oppress the Germans; he has defended Wycliffe's errors; he has compromised amongst themselves the ecclesiastics and the seculars, by leading each party to suppose that it would obtain possession of the spoils of the other. For all these reasons," continued he, "if John Huss were to escape safe and sound from the council, he would do more injury to the Church than any heretic from the time of Constantine."

This memorial was favourably received, and a few days had scarcely elapsed from the commencement of his imprisonment, when the pope appointed, from amongst the prelates, three commissioners, to direct the case and interrogate him. In addition to this, doctors were named to examine his books, and report thereon.

The commissioners received the testimony of several ecclesiastics of Prague against John Huss; and they then proceeded to the monastery of the Dominicans, where he was then confined. They found him a prey to raging fever, and yet there, in the midst of his acute sufferings, he was obliged to hear the reading of the testimony produced against him by his accusers. The commissioners next presented him with a series of articles, which Paletz pretended to have extracted from his *Treatise on the Church*, but which had been designedly falsified. They told him, that he should shortly be called on to answer on all those points.

Deprived of all free communication with his friends outside, overwhelmed at the same time by the evils that affected both his body and his mind, Huss thought it advisable to apply for a legal defender. But this assistance, which is granted, as a matter of right, to the vilest criminals, and which he asked for as a favour, was refused him, under the pretext that the canons declared it to be a crime to defend any man suspected with heresy. "However," remarks an old writer of his life, "the evidence brought against him was so weak, that a serious refutation would not have been necessary, if the same men had not been, at the same time, party and judge."[*]

"I besought the commissioners," said John Huss, "to grant me an advocate. They at first granted my request, but afterwards refused it. I, therefore, place my confidence in our Saviour Jesus Christ. May he be at once my advocate and my judge!"[*]

Whilst priests were preparing to avenge in his blood the wounds which their pride had suffered, the very men that guarded him were touched with his fervent piety and Christian resignation; and several of them evinced a great eagerness to receive his instructions. He composed for them, at their request, several treatises. "Thou askest me," said he to one of them, "to give thee a few words on the state of marriage, into which thou art about to enter: it is no easy matter for me to satisfy thee as I should desire, for the subject is one on which much is to be said. My own limited faculties, the confinement in which I am placed, and my absolute want of books, are so many obstacles to my writing for thee as I should like; yet I will not leave thy demand unanswered." John Huss added to those words certain exhortations, inspired by a lively faith, and a severe sense of morality.[†]

The principal treatises which he wrote in this way, are those on the *Ten Commandments*; on *The Lord's Prayer*; on *Marriage*; on the *Three Enemies of Man*; and, finally, that on the *Body and Blood of Jesus Christ*, in which he showed, that his belief relative to the sacrament of the Eucharist was the same as that of the Roman Church. It is not without emotion that we read, at the end of those various writings, the simple names of Robert, James, and Gregory, his keepers, for whom he had written them. Several times, too, when his enemies and judges entered his prison, they found those rude and uneducated men listening attentively to his instructions, and perceived himself to be more occupied with the perils that threatened their souls, than with his own personal dangers.

John Huss, in a letter addressed to his friends, states all that he had to endure from the rage of his adversaries. "Learn," said he, "beloved, that in translating my letters, they have added to them a quantity of falsehoods; and they write against me so many untruths, that I have enough to do to reply to them from my prison. Their malice is equal to their fury." In the same letter, he exhibits a resignation truly admirable, and altogether Christian-like. "Pray to God for me," said he, "that he may come to my aid. All my hope rests in Him and in your prayers. Implore Him, therefore, to vouchsafe to me the assistance of His Spirit, that I may confess His Name even unto death. If He deigns to

* *Hist. et Monum. J. Hus.* t. i. p. 9.
* Epist. xlix.
† J. *Hus. Hist. et Monum. De Matrimonio,* t. i. p. 41.

receive me at the present time, His holy will be done! but if it be pleasing to Him that I should live, and be restored to you, may His will still be blessed! I should require His divine assistance, even were I certain of not being tempted beyond my strength; and still more, did I not feel that the peril in which I am placed is necessary for your sanctification and my own; for with such as remain firm in the truth, temptation operates salvation."[*]

Huss was about three months in prison, when a great event spread trouble and terror in the council. On March 20, 1415, in the midst of a fête given for the purpose by the Archduke of Austria, John XXIII. made his escape in a mean disguise, and fled to Schaffhausen; and there placed himself under the protection of the archduke, who soon joined him in the town, which was under his authority. Several cardinals, and all the pope's officers, at once quitted Constance to follow him.

The flight of John XXIII. disconcerted all the measures taken for the extinction of the schism; but when the fathers of the council perceived that their puissant adversary had escaped them, they redoubled their severity against their defenceless prisoner. The pope's officers, previous to their proceeding to join their master, had given up John Huss to the guards of the emperor and the cardinals; and they, in their turn, handed him over to the Bishop of Constance. Armed men transferred him, by order of this prelate, to the Castle of Gotleben, on the banks of the Rhine. He was shut up in one of the towers of the building, with irons on his feet; and at night, a chain firmly fixed to the wall prevented the captive from moving from his bed.[*]

CHAPTER V.

PROCEEDINGS OF THE EMPEROR AND THE COUNCIL AGAINST THE POPE.—SPEECH DELIVERED BY GERSON, AND CONCLUSIONS OF THE UNIVERSITY OF PARIS.—INTRIGUES OF JOHN XXIII.—MEASURES OF THE EMPEROR.—SECOND FLIGHT OF JOHN XXIII.—DECREES OF THE FIFTH SESSION.—FRESH FLIGHT OF JOHN XXIII.

ACCORDING to the opinion of John XXIII., the council was dissolved by his withdrawal; and if it were not so in principal, it was very near coming to a close in reality. Already had several cardinals followed the pope to Schaffhausen. The Italian nation, which reckoned three hundred votes, all of whom were almost to a man devoted to him, was on the point of quitting Constance; and in the three other nations, both they who feared that John XXIII., after having recovered his liberty, would resume his authority, and those others—by far the greater number—who gave way either to discouragement or disgust,—also began to think of withdrawing.

Sigismund turned aside the peril. Animated by his ardent zeal for the peace of the Church and the union of Christendom, he showed himself, immediately after the flight of the pope, worthy of the title of protector of the Council, and acted truly like an emperor.

The day after, he mounted his horse, and went through the city, accompanied by the Elector Palatine and all the lords of his court. He proceeded in great state, and, with sound of trumpet, promised to every one the same surety as before:—he declared, besides, that the council was not interrupted by the pope's flight: and that he would shed the last drop of his blood to protect its proceedings. At the same time, he gave secret orders to have a paper placarded which depicted, in strong terms, the conduct of the pope and his cardinals,—their bad faith, and their efforts to dissolve the council, or to shackle its proceedings. In this paper, John XXIII. was accused of tyranny, simony, and other crimes; and the members of the council were called on to judge him according to his merits, and in conformity with what had been practised, with the concurrence of the emperors, in the deposition of several popes.

Sigismund next assembled the nations in the cathedral, and there, in the presence of all, declared anew that he would maintain the council at the peril of his life. A deliberation was at once entered on, as to the best means of getting John XXIII. back to Constance, and forcing him to abdicate. Finally, four deputies—of whom three were cardinals, and the other, Regnaud de Chartres, Archbishop of Rheims—were sent to Schaffhausen, to lay before him the resolutions of the council. But, in order to render the measures taken to reduce the pope efficacious, it was necessary to adopt others to subdue Frederick of Austria,

* Epist. x.   * See note H.

the accomplice of his flight and his protector. The emperor, to effect this, assembled all the princes, and, in their presence, denounced the archduke as a traitor to the empire and the council, and called on them to unite with him in mastering him. The determination of his language produced a great effect on all; and not a single voice was raised in defence of Frederick. He was summoned to appear before the council and the emperor, to render an account of his conduct; and Sigismund prepared to reduce him to submission by force of arms.

The pope, however, terrified at the storm which was bursting over his head, wrote to the emperor, in submissive terms, declaring that he had come to Schaffhausen without the knowledge of the Archduke of Austria, not for the purpose of avoiding the accomplishment of his promise to abdicate, but in order to execute it freely, and without danger to his health.

But it was evident that John XXIII. would only yield to force; and, in consequence, after the emperor had employed against him, without success, his temporal authority, the council had recourse to other arms not less formidable.

The pope's flight raised anew the capital question already discussed, and once resolved at the Council of Pisa, relative to the reciprocal duties of popes and general councils, and the superiority of the latter over the former. The point was also to be decided, whether the obstinate opposition of a pontiff could annul the acts of a universal council; and whether the latter, in the interest of the Church, could not constrain a rebellious and schismatic pope. From the moment that the council, in the absence of the pope, persisted in asserting that it was legally assembled, the solution of the problem was no longer doubtful. Those persons who, through fear, had at first hesitated to declare against the pope, proceeded prudently to deprive him of those arms which he might, at a later period, turn against themselves; and they hastened to join with the men who, whilst they struggled against the papal omnipotence, only listened to the voice of their conscience. Amongst the latter, the representatives of the University of Paris were particularly noted, and in the first rank was their illustrious chancellor.

Gerson delivered, on March 23, 1415, in presence of the four nations, a celebrated sermon on this text:—"*Walk while ye have the light, lest darkness come upon you.*"[*] His discourse was the torch which gave light to the council.

Gerson exclaimed with the apostle—"Keep

the unity of the Spirit in the bond of peace. Have all of you but one body and one soul, one God, one faith, and one baptism. Let us be united in Christ, our head, from whom all the members depend, and to whom all are bound and subject."[*]

Gerson deduced, from this primary truth, twelve propositions, of which the principal are:—That ecclesiastical union depends on one only head, Jesus Christ; and that it exists through a secondary chief, called the sovereign pontiff, who is the vicar of Jesus Christ;—that the Church possesses in Jesus Christ a spouse so completely inseparable, that he can never give it letters of divorce; but that, on the contrary, the Church is not so absolutely bound to the vicar of her spouse, that they may not be separated.

"The Church, or the general council which represents her," observed Gerson, "is a rule directed by the Holy Spirit, and given by Jesus Christ, in order that every man, be he even the pope himself, should listen to her and act obediently, under penalty of being regarded as a pagan and a publican. The Church, or the council, has possessed, and still possesses, the power, in various cases, of assembling, without any express consent or authorisation of the pope, even when he may have been canonically elected, and should lead a regular life. Those cases are the following:—Should the pope, being accused and placed on trial, refuse stubbornly to assemble the Church;—should the pope, when a general council had decided that another was to be held at an appointed time, refuse to convoke it;—and, lastly, should there exist a schism or contest between several popes."

Gerson terminated in these words:—"The Church, or the general council, ought to pursue the extirpation of error, and the correction of those who go astray, without paying any respect to persons; it ought to reform the ecclesiastical order and hierarchy on the model of the heavenly hierarchy, by acting in conformity with the ancient rules; and, for this purpose, the Church has no more effectual means than to enjoin the continuance of general councils, without omitting the provincial ones."[†]

The University of Paris, in two memorials which it addressed to the council, explained itself in still bolder and more energetic language. One of those papers declared, in substance, that the Church was *more necessary* than the pope; for this reason, that no one could obtain salvation out of the Church, but that it is very possible to gain salvation with-

---

* John xii. 35.

* Ephes. iv. 3.
† Gers. Oper. t. ii. part ii. p. 201. Sermo in Vigil. Domin. Palmarum.

out the pope;—that the Church, also, was *more excellent and more useful*, because the pope was for the Church, and not it for the pope;—that the Church was *superior in dignity*, because it was the spouse of Jesus Christ, and the partner of the Lamb;—that it was *more powerful*, because the gates of hell cannot prevail against it, although they had frequently been able to hold out against popes, from their vices and heresies;—that it had *more intelligence*, because it possessed several endowments not found in a pope:—as that it was from *the Church* that the pope received the sovereign power which habitually resided in it, although it gave to the pope the power of exercising it;—that it was to *the Church* that Jesus Christ had given the keys of the kingdom of heaven, and that the pope only held them from it;—that when the Church was lawfully assembled, it could make use of those keys to judge, correct, or depose the pope, on the same principle as it was allowable to snatch a sword from the hands of a madman;—and that the Church had not conferred the keys on the pope to destroy, but to build up. The conclusion come to by the memorial was, that, in several cases, the council was superior to the pope.*

The cardinals had refused to listen to Gerson's discourse; and, from that period, they almost all kept themselves apart. They felt that, in the present state of things, the acts of the council might give a grievous blow to the authority of the Roman Church, represented in their person; and they therefore endeavoured, to the best of their power, to prepare restrictions or impediments for the decrees of the assembly.

John XXIII., on his side, had recourse to every means he could devise to defend himself. He wrote an apologetic letter to the King of France, to the Duke of Orleans, and to the University, in which he protested against the validity of the proceedings of the council. Some of the reasons which he alleged in support of his declaration were not without some plausibility. The practice of former councils had, he observed, been neglected at Constance;—the votes had been taken by nation and not by head;—every one had been admitted indifferently, ecclesiastics and seculars, married men and unmarried, persons with recognised rank or without it, men of character or the contrary:—all those things had been done, although, according to the canons, the cardinals, the patriarchs, and the prelates alone, had deliberative voices in councils. The pope accused the King of the Romans of having arrogated to himself, at

Constance, an authority which did not justly belong to him, whereas he himself was not permitted any liberty whatever. He terminated by acknowledging the complicity of the Duke of Austria, which he had denied in a former letter—that which he addressed to the emperor. Whilst he was thus negotiating with foreign powers not immediately connected with the council, he redoubled his efforts to detach from it the Italian nation, the cardinals, and all those whom their interest or chance had connected with the Holy See.

Sigismund, supported by the three other nations, forced through all opposition, and, on March 26, had the third general session opened,—the first after the flight of John XXIII. Of all the cardinals, only two were present at it—Zaberella, Cardinal of Florence, and Peter d'Ailly, Cardinal of Cambray, both of whom, and particularly the latter, manifested a real zeal for the extinction of the schism,—always reserving, however, the privileges of the Roman Church.

The Cardinal of Florence read, at the opening of the session, an act, by which the council declared, that it was not dissolved by the withdrawal of the pope, and of the greater part of the cardinals; but that it remained in all its force and authority, whatever might be ordered to the contrary, either for the present or the future. The act prohibited any prelate, or other member of the council, to withdraw from it without legitimate cause; as for such persons as might obtain permission to do so, they were enjoined to leave their powers with the members that remained behind. The act, last of all, declared that these enactments were to be observed under such penalties as were fixed by the canons, or under pain of such punishments as the council might deem it advisable to impose. The articles of this document were adopted by the deputies of all the nations united.

However, the pope continued his intrigues; and the commissioners sent to Schaffhausen returned with an answer, in which the council perceived nothing but a desire to escape from the dangers of the moment, by holding out vain hopes. John XXIII. declared that he was ready to name commissioners for the abdication which he had promised; and he offered to give a bull for the reformation of the Church. He demanded to have a court left him, and requested particularly that nothing should be undertaken against Frederick of Austria, who alone protected his independence.

Irritated by this evasive reply, Sigismund pressed on, with redoubled vigour, to reduce the pope by the decrees of the council, and by the arms of his troops. He ordered two articles

---

* Von der Hardt, t. ii. part xi. cap. iii. p. 275.

to be drawn up, for the purpose of being read in a new general session,—far more energetic and precise than those which had been adopted in the preceding session. It was therein announced, that recourse would be had to all means allowed by the canon law, to constrain and punish those who should obstinately refuse to obey the decrees of the present council, or any other general council, lawfully assembled. It was also declared, that the pope, and all the members of the council, had enjoyed complete liberty. Gerson had a strong declaration presented by the Bishop of Tolentino, attached to those articles. It declared that the flight of the pope smacked strongly of heresy and schism; and that the pontiff could not allege any fears on his part as an excuse, inasmuch as he was bound to lay down his life for his flock.

The fourth general session was announced for March 30, and these formidable preliminaries filled John XXIII. with terror. This feeling was increased when he found that the imperial troops had been put in motion. He no longer felt himself in safety at Schaffhausen—at so short a distance from the council and the emperor. He, therefore, again fled, when already several princes and cities, alarmed at the storm which threatened the archduke, his protector, had broken the feudal bond which bound them to him. From all parts arrived messengers bearing those disastrous pieces of intelligence; "and the reports of all those defections," said a contemporary author, "were so many incitements, so many strokes of the spur, to John XXIII. in his flight."[*] He proceeded towards Lauffenburg, situated on the banks of the Rhine, which he reached the same evening. But scarcely had he quitted Schaffhausen, when, ordering a notary and witnesses to appear before him, he dictated a retraction of every thing that he had done at Constance, protesting that he had neither promised nor sworn any thing in the council, but from yielding to violence or fear; and declaring, that, consequently, he was not bound to the observance of any such promises.[†] He repeated, said his secretary, this protestation in various places; and yet, regulating his language not by the truth, but by the dispositions of those to whom he addressed his letters, he wrote to them in styles altogether different, thus perpetually contradicting himself in the most shameless manner.

This second flight of the pope gave new strength to the council and the emperor. The cardinals,[‡] no longer finding any support in a leader without courage, and incapable of any resistance, perceived, that, in isolating themselves, they could only complete their own destruction; and felt, that they should be decidedly more influential when resisting, in the bosom of the council, than they could possibly be when intriguing at a distance. They, therefore, acknowledged themselves to be worsted, and only thought of rendering their defeat less disastrous.

It was then seen what address could effect against force, persevering inactivity against active perseverance. If, on the one side, it was important for the Roman party that the cardinals should be present to defend them in the council; on the other, it was of equal consequence to the emperor and the party anxious for reform, to associate the cardinals in their undertakings, and to bind them by their acts. Sigismund, therefore, employed all the means that he thought could tend towards that object, —solicitations, caresses, threats,—and his determination prevailed.

Most stormy discussions took place in the preparatory meetings, held between the emperor, the cardinals, and the deputies of the nations, which preceded the fourth general session. At those meetings, the articles which were afterwards to be submitted to the council were debated, and the cardinals obtained that the pope should not be then accused of *heresy and schism* for having fled. They demanded several other points, but all without success. The greater part of them, however, solemnly promised the emperor to attend the approaching session.

Men's minds were, at this time, in expectation of one of those events which produce an effect on remote ages. The emperor, on the one side, and the immense majority of the prelates of the three nations, who were fully convinced that the pope ought to be reduced, in order to save the Church, were preparing to inflict on the popedom one of those terrible blows which, though they do not absolutely destroy, are almost impossible to recover from. On the other side, the Italians, from being without a head, appeared divided in opinion. They did not venture openly to declare for him who had abandoned them; and yet it was repugnant to their feelings to throw up a cause which they had so long considered as their own. The greater number of them inclined towards the cardinals. These, with the exception of the French members of their college, D'Ailly and Filastre,[*] formed but one united body, and were actuated by the same views. Their

---

[*] Darherius ap. Von der Hardt. v. iv. p. 84.
[†] Th. Niem. ap. Von der Hardt. p. 84.
[‡] The Cardinal of Cambray and the Cardinal of St. Marc must always be excepted from those

who were exclusively devoted to the interests of the Roman Church.
[*] The former, Cardinal of Cambray; the latter, Cardinal of St. Marc.

interests were closely connected with the grandeur of that papal see which it was intended to humiliate. In this point also was involved a great religious question, and many of them undoubtedly were actuated by conscientious motives in their resistance to the emperor and the three nations. They shuddered at the dangers with which their Church was sure to be menaced, should the throne of St. Peter, which, in their opinion, was its firmest support, be shaken. A small number, and amongst them John de Brogni, Cardinal of Viviers, the habitual president of the council,* gave out that they were ill, and held themselves apart; thus avoiding the act of giving, by their presence, a greater authority to measures which they condemned, and which they felt they could not prevent. The others looked for more: they attended the sitting with the intention of protesting against such acts as should be too violent, and of weakening or getting them postponed. Their calculation was not altogether without foundation.

At last, the fourth general session opened, on March 30, 1415, with Cardinal Jordan des Ursius as president. The emperor was present, and with him were all the princes and the ambassadors of the various powers. The Patriarch of Antioch said mass; and immediately after the religious ceremonies, Zabarella, Cardinal of Florence, rose and read the articles which the nations, in their preparatory meeting, had determined to adopt.

They commenced thus :—" *The sacred Synod of Constance, legally assembled in the name of the Holy Ghost, forming a general council which represents the Catholic Church militant, has received, direct from Jesus Christ, a power, which every person, no matter what his station or dignity may be, even were it papal, is bound to obey in all matters relating to the faith, to the extirpation of the schism, and to the* REFORMATION OF THE CHURCH, IN ITS HEAD AND IN ITS MEMBERS."

Zabarella read with a loud voice, but when he came to this last phrase, in which mention was made of reforming the head of the Church, he suddenly stopped short, and he either had not strength, or wanted the inclination to proceed. He also omitted two other articles, declaring that they had been added contrary to the general opinion. The first was relative to the liberty which the pope had enjoyed at Constance; and the second, to the punishment which he was liable to for his obstinate resistance to the will of the council.†

Historians do not agree in their accounts of all that took place on this occasion, nor has it ever been very accurately ascertained whether Zabarella acted with design and of his own will, or in execution of what had been previously determined on by the cardinals in a secret meeting ;* yet it may be observed that the manner in which they afterwards endeavoured to take advantage of his conduct, renders the latter opinion probable. But in this way, the results of the fourth session, which the cardinals had looked to with such apprehension, were rendered null and void ; and the sitting was brought to a close amidst general agitation. Yet the Roman party gained but little ; for they only retarded their defeat a few days.

The cardinals were so imprudent as to demand that the articles omitted by Zabarella should be again brought forward for deliberation in a private meeting of the nations, before they were presented in a general session. Their object was simply to temporize ; and, in their efforts to effect that object, they forgot that delay irritates more than it wearies an uncontrolled power, and that demands increase with the sentiment of strength. They soon discovered this ; for their demand was not only negatived, but it was resolved, that the very same articles should be again brought forward the following session with greater precision and vigour.

Such were the preliminary proceedings of the fifth, and most memorable, session of the council. Cardinal des Ursius again filled the president's chair, as he had done on the preceding occasion. Eight cardinals were present, and the emperor and the princes took their seats as before. After the mass, which was celebrated by the Archbishop of Rheims, the Bishop of Posnania read the following articles:—

FIRST ARTICLE.—"The Council of Constance, lawfully assembled in the name of the Holy Ghost, and forming a general council which represents the Catholic Church militant, has received, DIRECT from Jesus Christ, a power which every person, no matter what his station or dignity may be, even were it PAPAL, is bound to obey in all matters relating to the faith, to the extirpation of the present schism, and to the general reformation of the Church of God, in its HEAD and in its members."

SECOND ARTICLE.—"Every man, whatever his station or dignity may be, even were i PAPAL, who shall stubbornly refuse to obey

---

* See Note I.

† Cum Cardinalis Florentinus veni, set ad verba de reformatione in capite et in membris, quæ na-

tiones in schedula delere omiserant, substitit, esque falsa esse et præter communem deliberationem addita asseruit.—*Schlestrat. Comp. Chron.* p. 41.

* Von der Hardt, t. iv. p. 86, 87.

the decrees which this council, and EVERY OTHER GENERAL COUNCIL, LAWFULLY ASSEMBLED, have already issued, or may hereafter issue, on the matters mentioned above, shall, if he return not to his duty, be subject to a proportionate penance, and shall be punished as he deserves; other proceedings of greater severity being employed if necessary."

THIRD ARTICLE.—"The Council forbids John XXIII. to transfer elsewhere the Court of Rome, its offices, and public officers, or to constrain them, either directly or indirectly, to follow him, without the consent of the Council: ordering, that if he has already undertaken, or shall henceforward undertake, so to do, his censures, threats, and fulminatory bulls, shall be absolutely null; and that the said officers shall exercise their functions at Constance with the most entire liberty, as long as the Council lasts."

FOURTH ARTICLE.—"All translations of prelates, deprivation of rights, revocation of benefices, or ecclesiastical censures, suits, sentences, or acts passed, or to be passed, by the said pope, to the prejudice of the Council or its members, since the commencement of its proceedings, shall be null, and are hereby broken."

FIFTH ARTICLE.—"John XXIII., as well as the prelates and all other members of the Council, have enjoyed, and do still enjoy, an entire liberty; nothing to the contrary having come to the knowledge of the Council, as it can testify in the presence of God and men."

All these articles having been at once adopted, the emperor announced that his troops were then on their march against Frederick of Austria. He offered, also, should the council desire it, to proceed in person to Lauffenburg, and bring back the pope, in spite of the archduke. The assembly burst out into loud applause at this declaration, and passed a vote of thanks to Sigismund.

The acts of the fifth session of the Council of Constance have divided the Catholic world into two parties. The Gallican Church has constantly defended them, considering them, with great justice, as the basis of its liberties; whilst the Roman Church, properly so called, has decried them, with an equal obstinacy, as illegal, injurious to the authority of St. Peter's successor; and, in fact, vicious and null. The most ardent men of this Church attempted, at a later period, to invalidate the authority from whence these acts emanated. They denied to the Council of Constance the right to assume the title of œcumenical; although it had a better claim to the epithet than the Council of Pisa, which they were obliged to acknowledge

was strictly so.[*] To all the œcumenical characters of the latter, the Council of Constance joined a canonical convocation; for a pope, legally elected, had assembled it, and another pope, also legitimate, confirmed all its decisions. It may, therefore, be declared, in conclusion, that although this controversy has given birth to innumerable volumes, and is by no means yet decided, yet it must be admitted that all Christendom recognised the celebrated decrees of the fifth session at the period at which they were issued; and that, amongst all the decisions of the general councils, there were few which might not be contested, if these could be called in question.[†]

The council, convinced of its strength, pushed on its advantages in the following session, held on April 15, and which was the sixth. It had decided that the pope owed it obedience; and, in the next step—the bringing him under subjection—the council showed with what firmness it could execute what its threats had implied.

It, first of all, adopted a form for the pontifical resignation, and next decided that this document should be presented to John XXIII. in person. Deputies were chosen from each nation, to proceed with the cardinals of St. Marc and of Florence, to carry to the pope the decrees of the council. Finally, in the seventh session, the pope was cited to come forward within the space of nine days, to fulfil his oath relative to the extinction of the schism, and the reformation of the Church in its head and its members; and to clear himself from the charge of heresy, schism, simony, improper administration of the goods of the Church, and other enormous crimes. It was declared that a safe-conduct was granted to him and his adherents, by virtue of which they should remain in safety at the council, except in what related to the course of law.

But the pontiff was no longer at Lauffenburg; for, in his terror, he had precipitately quitted that place of refuge, to protect himself behind the ramparts of Friburg. So completely had the decrees of the council struck his partisans with consternation, that the imperial troops found scarcely any obstacles to their advance, and the archduke became terrified at his own audacity, and manifested a desire to offer submission. The deputies appointed to bear the orders of the council were at last drawing near Friburg, when John XXIII., who feared them more than the emperor's soldiers, withdrew before them, dragging with him everywhere, in his uncertain and vagabond

* To attack the authority of the Council of Pisa, was to invalidate the election of John XXIII., elected in it as the successor of Alexander V.

† See Note K.

course, the mortal disgrace of the papedom. He is represented as being hurried from place to place by a kind of light-headed restlessness, seeking safety and repose even in the solitudes of forests, but nowhere finding either peace of mind or a sure asylum.*

CHAPTER VI

JUDGMENT AND CONDEMNATION OF WYCLIFFE AND HIS WORKS.

THE council which thus attacked the supreme pontiff—the vicar of Jesus Christ—burned with indignation at the thought that John Huss, a simple priest, should presume to assign limits to its power. It felt, besides, that its authority was compromised in the eyes of a great number, by the very acts which proved its strength most clearly. It was aware that all the enemies of the ecclesiastical power were about to turn to advantage against itself the sentence which it was on the point of pronouncing against the pope. It therefore hastened to confirm, by a striking example, the faith of the people in this authority, which John Huss had slighted; and the council, on this occasion, showed itself the more unrelenting; because, in defending the infallibility of the Church, it was its own that it was about to avenge.

Before, however, smiting, in the person of John Huss, such doctrines as were subversive of the double power of the priests, it was thought advisable to brand with reprobation the source from which they had been taken. The council remembered that, towards the close of the preceding century, the world had seen a celebrated heresiarch go unpunished; it recollected that Wycliffe had peaceably expired in the very country where his doctrines had been condemned; that his mortal remains reposed in consecrated ground; and that his writings were in circulation throughout Europe. In citing him before it, the council proceeded against his genius and his dead body.

Forty-five propositions, attributed to Wycliffe, and already condemned in England, had been similarly dealt with at Rome, in 1412, in a council convoked by John XXIII. These same articles were again brought forward at Constance, and formed the principal ground of the accusation laid against him. This great cause was brought before the council and judged, but without any discussion, in the eighth session.

The assembly was as solemn as any of the preceding ones. The emperor was present; Cardinal de Viviers occupied the president's chair, and the Patriarch of Antioch celebrated mass. The passage of the Gospel chosen to be read for the occasion was that beginning with the words, "Beware of false prophets."

Bishop Vital preached the sermon. He selected for his text, "The Spirit shall guide me into all truth;" and allowed himself to be so far carried away by passion as to curse the pope from the pulpit. When he had descended, the Archbishop of Genoa called to mind the terms of the Council of Lateran relative to transubstantiation, and read the forty-five articles attributed to Wycliffe, and already condemned at Rome.

The incriminated articles may be classed under a small number of principal heads. The greater part are relative to all the doctrines pointed out by Wycliffe as having been added to the simple instructions of the apostles, for the purpose of adding to the power of the pope and the clergy. Under this head must be quoted those admitting the validity of absolution or excommunication, independently of the moral state of the sinner or of the priest: those which relate to indulgences, beatification, and the obligation of university degrees for ordination; those reserving to the bishops alone the power of confirmation, of consecrating holy places, or ordaining priests; and, finally, those which establish or maintain the privileges of the Roman Church, the elevation of the pope above all bishops, and his election of the cardinals.

Five articles were so many violent attacks directed against the convents and monks of all the orders, who, under the appearance of poverty, drew together as much wealth as possible, and who were the most indefatigable champions of the privileges and the abuses of the Church of Rome. Wycliffe designated them by the appellation of Satan's synagogue. One of the articles condemned under this head, was the following:—*Monks ought to earn their livelihood by the labour of their hands, and not by begging.* This proposition was declared to be false, rash, and founded on error, because

---

* "Sic vagabundus mobilis, quærens requiem et non inveniens, ductus a spiritu, nescitur quo, in desertum." (The Black Forest.)—*Letter to the King of Poland.* Botting. See Voy. Jean de Muller, *Hist. de la Confé. Suisse,* book iii. chap. 1.

it was written that *the birds of the air reaped not, neither did they spin.* By the birds thus mentioned, said the council, were to be understood the saints who flew towards heaven.

Three other articles combated the Roman doctrine relative to the mass, and denied the bodily presence of Jesus Christ in the sacrament of the Eucharist.

Several others related to the temporal possessions of the clergy, for which Wycliffe found no justification in the gospel. His boldest proposition on this subject is the fifteenth article of the forty-five. It declares that *it is allowable for secular lords to deprive of their possessions and property such ecclesiastics as lived in habitual sin.* This article was pronounced to be heretical and sacrilegious; but the council justified the condemnation by strange reasoning, for it declared that the "property of the Church was the property of God himself, who, having been desirous of establishing on earth a kingdom, of which he was the sovereign ruler, had consecrated and set apart certain temporal goods, in order to administer them himself."

One of the incriminated articles attacked the pretensions of the Roman clergy on the point of the absolute independence of their spiritual jurisdiction. "He," observed Wycliffe, "who excommunicated an ecclesiastic because he had appealed to the king or his council, rendered himself guilty of treason towards the king." This proposition was pronounced to be false, perverse, and scandalous.

All those articles were directed against doctrines too favourable to the clergy, not to raise up the whole of that body against their author. But it was important to interest, in the condemnation of Wycliffe, the temporal lords, of whom many had voices in the council. To effect this, Wycliffe was represented as opposed to the authority of princes and magistrates; and the two following propositions were brought forward, as taken from his works:—

1st. "During the whole time that a secular lord, a prelate, or a bishop, is living in mortal sin, he is neither lord, nor bishop, nor prelate."

2d. "The people may, at their pleasure, correct their masters, when they fall into any fault."

These two articles had been imputed to Wycliffe by the clergy during his lifetime; but he had always protested against the sense attributed to them. "They did not," he said, "complete his thought. His words had been garbled; and the interpretation thus assigned to them was wanting both in exactitude and fidelity." In fact, how is it possible to admit that he who had, through the whole course of his life, defended the temporal authority against the usurpations of the clergy, could, at the same time, have maintained doctrines subversive of its privileges.*

Nevertheless, the council persisted in attributing them to him, as had been previously done by the Council of Rome, and declared them heretical and rash.

They desired, also, to show God himself interested in the condemnation of Wycliffe: and, accordingly, two articles were produced as contrary to the Divine Majesty. In one of them is found the germ of the famous doctrine of predestination, afterwards adopted by a considerable portion of the Protestant Church. It is thus conceived:—*All things happened by an absolute necessity.*

Wycliffe, in promulgating this principle, argued from the infinite wisdom of God, by which every thing must necessarily have been determined for the greatest general good, and according to his divine and infallible foreknowledge. He thus debated in his mind—the greatest problem of the Christian religion, and of all religions—a formidable mystery, from which the veil cannot be partially raised, unless there be clearly established the infinite difference which exists between *determining beforehand* and *foreseeing.*

Wycliffe's opinion on this point may lead into grave errors; yet he holds it in common with a crowd of great men before and after him; and in his idea it neither attacked the glory of God, nor the liberty of man.

The second proposition was this: *God ought to be obedient to the devil.* Wycliffe never acknowledged it as his, but himself pronounced it to be heretical. He protested against it, as having been inserted into his works by some unknown hand, and declared that it had been calumniously imputed to him by false witnesses. His disavowal on the point ought to suffice, since it is in accordance with the proceedings of his whole life; and if there was any foundation for the accusation, the article would have been pointed out by Thomas Walden, who published the best refutation of Wycliffe's opinions. But, on the contrary, this other proposition, completely different, is found there: *The devil cannot tempt men beyond what it pleases God to permit.*

The incriminated article, nevertheless, continued to be imputed to Wycliffe, and was condemned as such.

Lastly, amongst the propositions attributed to Wycliffe, and condemned, as false, at Oxford, at Rome, and in the universal Council of Constance, there is one which Christians of all denominations, whether Catholic or Protestant, admit in the present day as undoubted,

---

* Vaughan's *Life of Wycliffe.*

—it is that which declares *the decretals to be apocryphal.* The article was condemned as contrary to the decisions of the Church and the decrees of several popes. The sentence of the council on this point, approved of afterwards, with all its decrees, of a legitimate pope,—a sentence universally blamed at present,—would, of itself, be sufficient to destroy all confidence in human infallibility, if any evidence could avail against error inveterately rooted in the mind by the double force of habit and prejudice.

The condemnation antecedently pronounced at Oxford and at Rome on the forty-five articles, was confirmed by the Council of Constance. It was forbidden, under pain of excommunication, to teach these articles—to read or keep the books which contained them—or even to speak of them, unless for the purpose of mentioning their condemnation. It was ordered that the book should be burned, and particularly the works entitled the *Dialogue* and the *Trialogue.*

There was next read two hundred and sixty other articles, which were also represented to be taken from his works. They, for the most part, repeat and develope the preceding articles, particularly those relating to the pope, to monks, and to the sacrament at the altar. Some of those are generally received in the present day amongst Christians as true, and, amongst others, that *which does not exclude from the promise of salvation children dying without baptism.* Others are stained with a violent and reprehensible exaggeration: several present a dangerous meaning, as, for instance, the following: *God cannot destroy any thing, —he cannot enlarge or diminish the world,— God can create souls to a certain point, but not beyond it,—God is every creature.*

Wycliffe, it must be allowed, did not keep sufficiently free from the deplorable mania, which has afflicted so many superior and reverend men in the Church, of assigning limits and modes of action to the incomprehensible and infinite Wisdom,—a rashness which caused St. Bernard to say with good reason, "They seek into the secrets of God, even to the most secret parts." However, let us hasten to declare, that the propositions extracted from Wycliffe's writings were far from really bearing the sense which his detractors attributed to them.

In maintaining that God could not render this world greater or smaller, or create more souls than he has made, Wycliffe meant, that God has made all things as well as it was possible to make them; and when he asserts that *every creature is God, or divine,* he merely indicated by the phrase, that every created thing participates in something, and for a portion of itself, however weak it may be, in the eternal attributes of the Divinity.

It is to be regretted that these propositions could have been attributed to Wycliffe; but it is well known how easy it is to extract, from the best books, passages which, though they offer nothing reprehensible in the place where the author has placed them, yet, when considered separately, have a culpable meaning. Wycliffe, besides, was but a man, and, as such, liable to error; and in order to attribute this to him as a crime, it would have been necessary to prove him guilty of the far more serious culpability of those who condemned him,—that of declaring himself INFALLIBLE.

It is on the *ensemble* of his life and doctrine that a Christian or a reformer ought to be judged; it is the general bearing of his works which must correct and modify, in the reader's mind, the isolated thought—the particular expression; and there is not one man's life— not a single book—to which this rule is not applicable. This truth cannot be too frequently repeated, for it is constantly neglected, and, indeed, most probably will be always so. The correctness of the principle is acknowledged by all, when the passions are silent; but when the suitable moment comes, no one puts it in practice. Is the point under consideration a doctrine, which, in its totality, leads men's minds to repentance, to regeneration, to faith, to the love of God? what matters it to those who believe that in it they behold their own condemnation! Is it a question of a man's life, which is pure and holy? what do they care who thirst after his blood!

Wycliffe, if judged on higher principles, is entitled, notwithstanding his aberrations, by his genius, by his courage, and by his entire life, to the gratitude and admiration of every man that protests against the subjugation of the human conscience, against the theocratical and sacerdotal yoke—of every man that recognises in Jesus Christ the only Mediator between God and man—of every man, in fact, who looks on the diffusion of the Word of Life as the greatest of blessings, and sees, in the internal sanctification of mankind, the aim and end of Christianity.

The council committed the great mistake of condemning, *en masse,* all his works—of confounding, in its sentence, the evil with the good—what was erroneous with what was true. But it went still farther, and ordered that the remains of Wycliffe should be disinterred and delivered to the flames:—it raked up a tomb and wreaked its vengeance on a dead body. Yet, whilst we blame this barbarous decision, we must not overlook the barbarous character of the epoch; nor, whilst we are filled with indignation at the vengeance thus taken by the priesthood, must we forget the provocation that Wycliffe gave them. The seeds of the vast revolution of the sixteenth century were in his writings; and it is by the violence of the attack, and the severity of the wound, that must be explained the atrocity of the sentence.

It was executed in England more than thirty years after the reformer's death. Tra-

dition states that his bones, when disinterred and reduced to ashes, were thrown into the river Swift at Lutterworth.[*] From thence, to adopt the striking expression of Fuller, his remains were successively borne into the Severn, St. George's Channel, and the Atlantic —a veritable emblem of his doctrines, which were diffused from his province throughout the whole nation, and from his nation throughout all the kingdoms of the earth.[†]

CHAPTER VII.

ARREST OF JEROME OF PRAGUE.—HIS FIRST EXAMINATION.

The fathers of the council had, in the bottom of their souls, condemned John Huss before they condemned Wycliffe; and if they first disturbed the ashes of the latter, it was in order to succeed the more surely in destroying the other.

The ways of Providence are inscrutable— it is the blood of the martyrs which opened the way to the great truths which at first threw open the world to the word of God, and which again, in the fifteenth and sixteenth centuries, prepared Europe to receive the gospel the second time. If it was necessary that John Huss should die at Constance to render testimony to the truth, perhaps, also, it was requisite that another illustrious martyr should, in the face of death, render testimony to John Huss. The council had, at first, only demanded one victim—it got two; and the disciple followed the master.

In the public grief and agitation caused at Prague by the noise of John Huss's captivity, Jerome, his friend and disciple, had hesitated irresolutely between the desire to follow him and the dread of sharing his fate. Huss himself, in his letters, endeavoured to keep him at a distance: he recommended him to be prudent, and instanced his own position as a proof of its necessity. Jerome, at the commencement, had not despaired of his friend's deliverance; for he reckoned much on the efforts of the noblemen of the kingdom, and put faith in the honour of Sigismund. When, however, he perceived that months were gliding by, and that Huss still remained in prison —that the remonstrances of the great lords of Bohemia were disdained, and that Sigismund was forgetful of his word, Jerome thought it time that he should perform his.

Already he heard some of Huss's disciples recalling to his mind the words which, in the

effusion of his tenderness, he had addressed to his friend when receiving his farewell :— "Dear master, should any evil happen to thee, I will fly to thine aid." He no longer listened to any thing but the dictates of his courage, and the enthusiasm of friendship and faith. He set out for Constance without a safe-conduct, accompanied by a single disciple.[‡] He determined to appear before the council and plead his friend's cause.

He arrived in that city on April 4, and mingling, without being known, with the crowd of people, he overheard disastrous intelligence. It was said that John Huss would not be admitted into the presence of the council—that he would be judged and condemned in secret—that he would leave his prison only to die. Jerome was struck with alarm, and thought that all was lost. A violent terror seized on him, and he took to flight as suddenly as he had come. It is even stated, so precipitate was his flight, that he left his sword behind him at the inn where he had alighted. The news of his arrival had already begun to be spread abroad, and search was made for him in every direction; when it was ascertained, almost at the same time as his arrival, that he had departed.

Jerome did not stop until he arrived at Uberlingen. There, deeming himself more in security, he bethought him of a tardy precaution, which he should have taken before he quitted Prague, had he listened to reflection rather than to his first sudden impulse, although from it he could not expect any great result. He wrote to the emperor and to the

---

* Wycliffe was rector of Lutterworth from 1374 to 1384, the year of his death. He died there on the last day of the year.
† Vaughan's *Life of Wycliffe*, v. ii. p. 347.
‡ Reichental, *Concil. Constant.* p. 204.

council, asking each for a safe-conduct. He grounded his claim to it on the fact of his having come to Constance of his own proper movement, and without being summoned there like John Huss. "I, *Jerome of Prague*," said he, "master of arts in the celebrated academies of Paris, Cologne, and Heidelberg, notify to all persons, by this writing, that I came to Constance of my own free will, and without being forced to it, to reply to my adversaries and calumniators, who defame the most illustrious and very celebrated kingdom of Bohemia, and to defend our doctrine, which is pure and orthodox, as well as to prove my innocence in presence of the whole council. . . . . To enable me to execute so just a design, I supplicate, in the name of God, your Imperial Majesty, and the holy œcumenical council, to grant me a safe-conduct to proceed to Constance, and to withdraw from it in safety."

The emperor made the only reply that could be reasonably expected from him—he refused. The council granted the safe-conduct, in the following strange terms, in which it naïvely betrays its intention of rendering the document useless:—

"The Sacred Synod, forming a general Council at Constance, assembled by the Holy Spirit, and representing the Universal Church Militant, recommends Jerome of Prague, calling himself master of arts in several universities, to be well-conducted, even unto sobriety, and to do nothing beyond what is necessary for being well-conducted. . . . . . *As we have nothing more at heart than to catch the foxes which ravage the vineyard of the Lord of Hosts*, we summon you, by these presents, to appear before us as a suspected person, and violently abused of having rashly advanced several errors; and we order you to appear here within a fortnight from the date of this summons, to answer, as you have offered to do, in the first session that shall be held after your arrival. It is for this purpose, that, in order to prevent any violence being offered you, we, by these presents, give you a full safe-conduct as much as in us lies, *excepting always the claims of the law, and that the orthodox faith does not, in any respect, prevent it;* certifying to you, besides, that whether you appear within the specified period or not, the Council, by itself or its commissioners, will proceed against you as soon as the term shall have elapsed.—Given at Constance, in public session, the 17th of April, 1415, under the seals of the President of the Four Nations."[*]

A safe-conduct of such a character was not a guarantee, and, in addition, it did not reach Jerome in time; for, "not receiving at Uberlingen for several days any answer either from the emperor or the council, Jerome," says Theobald, "continued mournfully his way towards Bohemia, in despair at not having been of any use to his friend, and uneasy at the manner in which his return would be interpreted." He was, however, bearer of a document, in which seventy Bohemian nobles, present at Constance, gave testimony to his having come there;—that he had done all in his power to render reasons for his faith;—and that he had departed from Constance, only because he could not remain there in safety.

So many crosses and dangers had not increased his prudence. He proceeded on his way, declaiming everywhere openly, and without precaution or moderation, against the council. He was still the same man, impetuous and violent, acting and speaking according to the impulse of his heart, and never calculating the scope or effect of what he said or did.

One day, as he was passing through a town of the Black Forest, the curé persuaded him to stay and dine in his house, where he had invited several others of the clergy. There, whilst at table, the remembrance of his friend in prison occurred to him forcibly: his secret indignation burst forth in very unmeasured language, and he forgot himself so far as to call the council "a school of the devil, a synagogue of iniquity."[*] Some of the priests were deeply offended at those terms, and laid them before the officer in command of the town, by whose orders Jerome was arrested.

Other accounts[†] state simply that some officers of John of Bavaria, Count Palatine, and Prince of Saltsbach, seized on Jerome, on the 24th of April, in the city of Hersaw, whence he was taken to Saltsbach and placed in confinement. He remained there under the guard of the prince, until the council made known its wishes. An order was sent to have the prisoner transferred to Constance, which was immediately effected.

Jerome entered the city on a cart, loaded with chains, and surrounded by a guard of soldiers.[‡] He was taken in that miserable

---

[*] *Theob.* cap. xv. p. 27.—It is worthy of remark, how much less favourable was this safe-conduct, granted by the council to Jerome, than that given by the emperor to John Huss. The grand difference consists particularly in the words, *excepting*

the claims of the law, and without prejudice to the orthodox faith. With the intention of defending the council for its conduct towards John Huss, the Jesuit Rosweiden has pretended, that those same words were understood, though not expressed, in the safe-conduct granted to Huss.
* Reschental, *Concil. Constant.*
† Theob. *Bel. Hus.* p. 27; Von der Hardt, t. iv. p. 216.
‡ Venit igitur currui impositus, catenis longis ac sonantibus constrictus. *Msc. Lips.* Von der Hardt, t. iv. p. 216.

condition to the house of the Elector Palatine, brother of John of Bavaria, where he was kept until he appeared in public, before a general meeting of the members of the council.

The cardinals, prelates, and doctors, met on May 23, in the refectory of the Dominicans, and gave orders that Jerome should be brought before them. He was, accordingly, led through the city by a strong guard of soldiers, the elector himself, as if in triumph, heading the melancholy procession. So accompanied, Jerome appeared before the assembly, loaded, or rather decorated, with fetters.*

The summons sent to Jerome to come forward and answer certain charges before the council, as well as a letter, in which John of Bavaria gave an account of his arrest, having been read, one of the bishops addressed the prisoner, and inquired why he had not obeyed the order to appear, but had taken to flight. "I withdrew," replied Jerome, "because I had not obtained a safe-conduct either from you or from the emperor,—being aware, besides, that I had here a great number of mortal enemies. I never received the summons from the council. Had I known of it, I swear to you that I should at once have returned, ay, if I had already reached my own country."

At this reply the assembly rose, and a scene of great noise and confusion ensued, a considerable number of persons accusing Jerome, and volunteering to give evidence against him. He then paid dear for the triumphs of his eloquence—for the ephemeral success, which he had formerly obtained, in his journeys through Europe, by his energetic style of speaking, exercised in the contests of the schools. The rancour of the doctors was the most dangerous, because the wounds inflicted on self-love are incurable, and petty passions find an entrance into the heart of the greatest men, when they can disguise them from themselves under the pretence of the general good. The illustrious Gerson gave a melancholy example of this.

"Jerome," said he, "when you came to Paris, you fancied yourself, with your eloquence, to be an angel from heaven! You troubled the University by broaching several false propositions in our schools, particularly relative to ideas and general attributes."

"Master Gerson," replied Jerome, "the propositions which I propounded in the University of Paris, and the answers which I gave to the arguments of the masters there, were scientifically proved by me, as a philosophical thinker, and in my capacity of master in that university. If I taught errors, prove them to be such, and I will retract them."

A doctor from Cologne interrupted Jerome. "When you were at Cologne," said he, "you brought forward several erroneous arguments."

"Can you adduce a single one of them?" asked Jerome.

At this unexpected question the doctor was disconcerted. "They do not occur to my memory at the moment," said he; "but at a later period they shall be laid before you."

A third, rising in his turn, said to Jerome: —"You maintained, at Heidelberg, grave errors relative to the Trinity; you represented it under the figure of a three-cornered shield; and afterwards you compared it to water, snow, and ice."

"What I said and what I represented at Heidelberg," said Jerome, "I am ready to say and represent again. Prove that what I advanced were errors, and I will abjure them in all humility, and most sincerely."

A murmur here arose in the assembly; and several voices cried out—"To the flames with him!—to the flames!"

"If it be your pleasure that I am to die," resumed Jerome, "let the will of God be done!" "No, Jerome," said the Archbishop of Saltsburg; "for it is written, 'I desire not the death of a sinner, but rather that he may turn from his wickedness and live.'"

The noise and the vociferations were here redoubled; and, at last, when the tumult was somewhat appeased, Jerome was conducted back to prison, and the assembly broke up.*

Towards the evening Peter Maldoniewitz, better known by the name of Peter the notary, a faithful friend of Huss and Jerome, roamed about the house in which the latter was confined; and, drawing close to one of the windows, called to Jerome, who heard his voice and answered—"Welcome, brother." Peter continued—"Strengthen thy soul; be mindful of that truth of which thou hadst so often in thy mouth when thou wert at liberty, and thy limbs were free from shackles. My friend, my master, do not fear even to face death for it." "Yes," replied Jerome, "many things have I said concerning the truth, and I will maintain them."

The soldiers interrupted this moving conversation between the friends, by repulsing Peter with violence and threats. He mournfully bade farewell to Jerome, and withdrew; his heart filled with grief.

Scarcely had he gone, when another person came up—a servant belonging to John de Chlum, named Vitus. Just as he commenced speaking to Jerome, he was seized on by the

---

* Grandibus adhuc catenis ac perstrepentibus ornatus aut oneratus. Mac. Lips. ap Von der Hardt, t. iv. p. 216.

* The account of Jerome's examination is taken from old manuscripts, in part collected by Von der Hardt, t. iv. p. 216.

soldiers, and found great difficulty in recovering his liberty.*

The safe keeping of the prisoner had been confided to John of Wallendrod, Archbishop of Riga, who, the very same night, had him removed to the dungeon of a tower, in the cemetery of St. Paul, where he ordered him to be heavily ironed. His chains were riveted to a lofty beam, in such a way as to prevent his sitting down; whilst his arms were forced by fetters to cross on his neck behind, so as to force him to hold down his head. It is in this cruel position that the old authors, and those persons who actually beheld him, have depicted him in prison. He was kept for two days in that posture, living on bread and water, and without his friends from Bohemia being able to ascertain where he was. At last, Peter the notary learned from one of the keepers where he was imprisoned, and succeeded in procuring for him permission to have better food.

Jerome soon fell grievously ill; and as his state was exceedingly dangerous, he demanded a confessor. His bonds were then somewhat relaxed, and he eventually recovered from his malady, though only, like Huss, to exchange it for a public and cruel death. His confinement in this dreadful prison lasted an entire year.*

CHAPTER VIII.

SUBMISSION OF FREDERICK OF AUSTRIA.—CONDEMNATION AND DEPOSITION OF JOHN XXIII.—HIS REMOVAL TO GOTLEBEN.

WHILST the council was treating with so much severity those who questioned its infallibility, it perpetuated, within its own bosom, discussions which rendered it exceedingly disputable.

The great and constantly recurring question of the superiority of councils over popes, or of popes over councils, generated a violent dispute between the Patriarch of Antioch, who took the pope's side, and the Cardinal of Cambray (Peter d'Ailly), the indefatigable champion of the councils.

"The power which Jesus Christ has given to the mystic body of the Church," said the patriarch, "resides so completely in St. Peter, that through him it is diffused through the whole body: Leo I. affirms this; and Nicholas II., Gregory I., and others, quite agree in his opinion. It is, besides, a maxim in canon law, that the pope judges every one, but cannot himself be judged, unless he err in the faith."

"To continue obstinately in schism is a heresy," replied d'Ailly intrepidly, "and even an idolatry. Besides, is not the pope judged by a human being, in the tribunal of his own conscience?"

Amongst innumerable testimonies, which he adduced from the writers on canon law, from the Scriptures, and from the necessity of the case, D'Ailly brought forward, against the omnipotence of the pope, the celebrated argument which the reformers unceasingly advanced in denial of his supremacy—he referred to the council of Jerusalem, in which

St. Paul, he remarked, had dared to resist St. Peter to his face, although the case was not one of heresy.

This great question was discussed in writing, at Constance, by these two illustrious adversaries; for the council had already decided it by its anterior decrees, and was preparing to confirm these by a most important and most significant act—the deposition of the pope. It was, however, first necessary to complete the reduction of the prince who had afforded to the pontiff the assistance of his arms. Frederick of Austria, despairing of success by means of his troops, had given himself up for lost before he was entirely abandoned by fortune, and was now ready to submit to any sacrifice to purchase his pardon. After having protected the pope in his flight, in order to use him as a protection in his own resistance, he determined to deliver the pontiff up as a mark of his submission, and for that purpose he returned to Constance.†

On May 5, the emperor had assembled the Italian ambassadors, and a great number of the prelates of the four nations at a banquet, in the large hall of the convent of the Franciscans. He was seated at the farther end of the hall, when the vanquished prince appeared at the threshold. Frederick walked forward, conducted by Duke Louis of Bavaria and the Elector of Brandenburg, and, coming before

---

* Theobald, Bel. Hus. p. 28.

* Von der Hardt, t. iv. p. 218.—Cochlœus, a Catholic author, remarkably prejudiced, does not deny the excessive severity of Jerome's captivity.—Cochlœus, Hist. Hus. lib. iii. pp. 151, 152.
† Frederick prevented the pope from fleeing into France.—Muller, Hist. de la Suisse, lib. iii. ch. I.

the emperor, bent the knee thrice to the ground. "What do you want?" said Sigismund. "Powerful king," replied Louis of Bavaria, "the Duke Frederick, my cousin, here present, implores your royal clemency. He is ready to bring back the pope, but he requires for his honour, that no violence be offered the Holy Father." Frederick confirmed what was thus advanced, and at last moved the emperor, who tendered him his hand. The prince gave up all his domains in Alsace and the Tyrol to Sigismund, and swore fidelity to him for them, as his lord surzerain. The emperor, then addressing the persons who were present at the scene, said: "Gentlemen of the Italian nation, you are acquainted with the name and power of the Dukes of Austria; yet, observe how I tame them, and learn from this what a king of the Germans can do."[*]

Frederick being reduced, John XXIII. was sure to fall. This wretched pope was fleeing, from town to town, before the deputies appointed to notify to him the form of resignation drawn up by the council. He at last received them at Friburg, where he had returned, and endeavoured still to procrastinate, by attempting negotiations.

The council then perceived that force alone could reduce him; and it held its ninth session on the day fixed for his appearance. Prelates, appointed for the purpose, called, at the doors of the church, on John XXIII. to appear; and when no person came forward to answer the summons, three and twenty commissioners, amongst whom were Cardinals des Ursins and St. Marc, were designated to hear the witnesses against the pope.

In the tenth session, John XXIII. was declared contumacious, and suspended from all papal administration. The council decreed that thenceforward there could not be elected as pope, either Balthazar Cossa, called John XXIII., or Peter de Luna, formerly known by the name of Benedict XIII., or Angelo Corario, surnamed Gregory XII.; and it was forbidden to every person, whether imperial, royal, pontifical, or cardinal, to disobey the decree, under pain of eternal damnation.

The commissioners then heard thirty-seven witnesses, of whom twelve were bishops, the rest being men of great weight and distinction. The list of accusations on which these witnesses were examined, contained seventy points, of which only fifty were read aloud in full council. The others were held back for the honour of the Holy See and the cardinals; and the articles kept secret[†] may be judged

of by those which it was ventured to bring forward. The latter were read and examined in the eleventh session, which was considered one of the most solemn.

The emperor, the princes, the cardinals, and the ambassadors were present, Cardinal de Viviers occupying the president's chair. When mass had been celebrated, the Bishop of Posnania read the articles proved before the commissioners, with the exception of those which it had been determined should be suppressed. John XXIII. was thus publicly convicted of simony, and other criminal practices, in the acquisition and exercise of his offices—of a frightful tyranny, accompanied with depredation and murder, in his legation of Bologna—and of wilful squandering of the property of the Roman Church, as well as of the other churches in Christendom. It was shown that, in 1412, he had sent a laic dealer into Brabant, with authority to levy the tithes of the ecclesiastical revenues in several dioceses, and with power to have excommunicated or interdicted, by sub-delegates, such persons and provinces as might refuse to obey:—that he had permitted this dealer to choose out, for persons of both sexes, according to his own will, confessors, to give them a general absolution on payment of certain dues; and that he had by such means obtained immense sums of money. It was, in fine, declared in the same articles, that John XXIII. was looked on by every one as the oppressor of the poor, the persecutor of the law, and the prop of all those guilty of simony—that he was fondly devoted to sensual pursuits, the enemy of all virtue, the mirror of infamy, a person spoken of by all who knew him as a devil incarnate. From this, the council came to the conclusion that John XXIII. was stiff-necked and stubborn; a hardened and incorrigible sinner, and a favourer of schism; and that, in consequence, he had rendered himself absolutely unworthy of the pontificate.

The Bishop of Posnania read all those articles, one after the other, adducing, as he went on, the evidence of the witnesses, and the proofs which had been given in support of each. They were in succession adopted by the council, and the cardinals themselves affixed to them their signatures. Five out of that body were appointed to notify to the pope this result, as well as the suspension pronounced against him in the preceding session.

Frederick of Austria—who, from being his defender, had become his jailor—had brought

* Müller, Hist. de la Suisse, lib. iii. chap. i.

† A list of the secret crimes of Pope John XXIII. may be found in various manuscripts, extracted by Van der Hardt, t. iv. pp. 196, 198, and

248. We shall not lay them before our readers; merely confining ourselves to this one fact, that amongst the crimes to which the witnesses bore testimony, and which the council threw a cloak over, was that of his having got rid of Pope Alexander V. by poison.

him from Friburg to the strong fortress of Ratolfeel, within two leagues of Constance. There, three bishops, delegated by the council, took possession of his person; and John XXIII., abandoned to himself, no longer offered any resistance, but displayed the most despicable cowardice.

Struck with consternation and grief at the sight of the delegates of the council, he affected contrition and remorse of conscience, refusing to read the act of accusation. "He repented with all his soul," he said, "of having so shamefully quitted Constance: he would rather have been struck dead than have caused the scandal of that act: he had no intention to oppose the resolutions of the council, which he recognised as just and INFALLIBLE: his sentence might be sent him, and he would receive it with all submission, and bareheaded: he was quite ready to resign his dignity; but he implored the compassion of the council and the emperor for his person and his honour."

The commissioners demanded the pontifical seal—the annulus piscatorius—and the book of petitions from the datary's office; all of which John XXIII. delivered up. He then wrote a letter to Sigismund, in which cringing meanness contended with falsehood.

He reminded the emperor that he had contributed to his elevation. "I acted so, my beloved son," said he, "from the very particular and completely disinterested predilection which I felt for you, and for which the most precious return that I could meet with would be a feeling of affection on your part . . . . . . All my vows tend towards you, as being, after God, the only refuge of my hopes; and, therefore, I address to you my most fervent prayers, demanding love for love. We conjure you, by the bowels of Divine mercy, not to forget your promise; for in it we have placed all our expectations. We shall thus be consoled in our abasement."

It was too late—this humble and submissive language did not deceive the emperor, whose feelings were soured by the multiplied abuse and defamation of which John XXIII. had shown himself culpable towards him.[*] "Men then beheld," says a contemporary writer, "the confirmation of this expression of the Roman historian—that 'there is but little security in majesty without power;'[†] and the emperor acted towards the pope as suited the dignity of Cæsar."[‡]

Sigismund vigorously urged on the proceedings; and the twelfth session, in which the pontiff's fate was irrevocably decided, opened in his presence.

All the princes, cardinals, and ambassadors,

were present at this memorable session, which was held on May 29, 1415. During mass, the portion of the gospel which was read commenced with this formidable passage:—"Now is the judgment of this world: now shall the prince of this world be cast out."[*] When the religious ceremony had terminated, the Bishop of Lavaur rose and read aloud the reply of John XXIII. to the delegates of the council; after which, the Bishop of Arras, Martin Poreous, read the act of the pope's deposition. The principal charges were first enumerated in it, and the sentence was drawn up in the following terms:—"The council hereby declares John XXIII. to be deposed and stripped of his pontificate, and releases all Christians from their oath of fidelity to him. . . . . . It condemns him to remain in some suitable place, under the guard of his most Serene Highness Sigismund King of the Romans, and advocate of the Church; reserving to itself, in addition, the task of punishing him for his crimes according to the canons of the Church, and as the law may demand."[†]

The president repeated this sentence in the name of the college of cardinals; four bishops repeated it after him in the name of the four nations; and the whole council signified their approval of it by pronouncing the placet. The armorial bearings of John XXIII. were then effaced, and his seal broken; and, finally, five cardinals were appointed to notify to him his deposition, and to exhort him to submit quietly, under pain of a more rigorous punishment.

The next day they repaired to Ratolfeel; and appearing before him who had been John XXIII., but who was now only Balthasar Cossa, they presented him with a copy of his sentence, and demanded if he acquiesced in it. Balthasar took it, read it over in silence, and then requested some time to give his answer. After a lapse of two hours, he ordered the cardinals to be called before him, and informed them, that after having attentively perused and examined the sentence of the council, he approved of it, and, of his certain knowledge, ratified it; adding, that he acquiesced in his deposition. He then placed his hand on his heart, and, of his own proper motion, and at full liberty, swore never to offer the slightest obstacle to the decisions of the council, and that he absolutely, and of his own free will, renounced all claim to the pontificate. "Would to God!" exclaimed he, "that I had never mounted to such a height! Since then, I have never known a happy day!"[‡]

* Theod. Niemens.   † Titus Livius.
‡ Apud Von der Hardt, t. iv. p. 252.

* St. John xii. 31.
† MSS. Brunsv. Lips. Goth. ac Vindob.; ap. Von der Hardt, t. iv. pp. 280, 281.
‡ MSS. Lips. et Goth. Von der Hardt, t. iv. p. 295.

The council, dreading his intrigues, had him brought nearer to Constance; and three days after his deposition, the fallen pontiff was transferred to that same castle of Gotleben, in which the unfortunate John Huss, arrested by his orders, had languished for the last six months, in the expectation of his trial and of a certain death. There, separated from his friends, and deprived of all his domestics, except one, Balthazar endeavoured to re-establish a secret intercourse with some friends remaining at Constance. The latter, however, returned no answer, through prudence, and also because the man who implored their aid, in his disgrace, had, in the time of his prosperity, disdained their exhortations.[*]

What a contrast was then offered by the two men confined within those walls! That haughty pontiff, who, not long since, had denied that any human authority had a right to judge the vicar of God, was now in the power of his enemies, shrinking under their threats, and basely abandoning the prerogatives of his throne, for which honour and religion commanded him to die! There he was, without any support within himself against external ignominy, endeavouring to ransom himself from a severe captivity by concessions still more despicable than his late avowals, acknowledging with his lips, in a rival power, that privilege of infallibility which the successors of St. Peter then only attributed to themselves!—There he was crushed to the earth—despairing of all—exhibiting marks of bitter regret, rather than of remorse—through terror degrading himself before men, rather than before God—filled with far greater solicitude for the miserable remains of his temporal life, than for the state of his soul in eternity—a hundred times more crushed by his infamy than by his chains!

A few paces from him, and under the same bolts, another man—a poor priest—displayed against his enemies, in the interests of truth alone, an immovable firmness. He refused to acknowledge himself culpable of certain errors laid to his charge; because such an avowal, he said, in the first place, would have been a falsehood, and, next, because his disciples might find in it an occasion of scandal and backsliding. This man's life is pure, and yet his sins disquiet him far more than his perils. His thoughts turn on his soul, on his disciples, on his friends, and above all, on his God. It is to God alone that he turns in his distress. He knows that, should he persist in refusing the base avowal that is required, the fate reserved for him will be a slow and frightful death; and yet he persists in so

* Theod. Niem. ap. Von der Hardt, t. iv. p. 297.

doing, and still has hope. His soul is firm; for God is his hope and strength. And now, that destiny brings him on terms of comparison with his persecutor, and appears to place them on a level, he soars above him, and predominates by the majesty of his virtues; and by it they are now more separated from one another than they ever were by worldly dignity and power.

History does not say whether they then met. It is to be presumed that the oppressor, in his degradation, shunned the regard of him whom he had contributed to crush; but he could not conceal his disgrace from his fellow-captive. John Huss, in his letters to his friends, pours forth freely all that was suggested to him by the unveiled crimes of John XXIII. and their punishment, and draws an argument from them in favour of his own doctrines. "Courage," said he; "you can now give an answer to those preachers, who declare that the pope is God on earth—that he can sell the sacraments, as the canonists assert—that he is the head and heart of the Church, by vivifying it spiritually—that he is the fountain from which all virtue and excellence issue—that he is the sun of the Holy Ghost, and the sure asylum where all Christians ought to find refuge. Behold! already is this head, as if severed with the sword—already is this terrestrial God bound in chains—already are his sins unveiled—the gushing fountain is dried up—the heavenly sun is dimmed—the heart is torn out, that no one may again seek an asylum there."[*]

John Huss next refers to the cruel persecution of which he was the object, as well as to the corruption of his judges; and in doing so, expressed, in strong terms, the indignation with which his soul was filled. "The council," remarked he, "has condemned its chief —its proper head—for having sold indulgences, bishoprics, in fact, every thing; and yet, amongst those who have condemned him are many bishops who are themselves guilty of this shameful traffic! . . . O profligate men! why did you not first pull out the beam from your own eye? . . . They have declared the seller to be accursed, and have condemned him, and yet themselves are the purchasers! They are the other party in the compact, and they remain unpunished![†] . . . Why did the cardinals elect such a man pope, and permit him to traffic in holy things? And why did none of them dare to resist him before his flight? Because then they feared him, and dared not act. But when, with the permission of God, the secular power had seized on him, then they conspired together, and de-

* Epist. xiii.   † Ibid.

termined that he should not escape. .... Such are those spiritual princes, who declare themselves, forsooth, to be the true vicars and apostles of Christ,—who give themselves the appellation of the Holy Church and the most sacred and infallible council; which, however, proved itself fallible enough when they adored John XXIII., and bent the knee before him, kissing his feet, and calling him the 'Most Holy!' when all the time they knew him to be a homicide, a man of most flagitious life, stained with simony, and a heretic, as their judgment declares. .... May God forgive them! for with such knowledge of the man they named him pope! ... And now Christendom is without a head on earth,—possesses Jesus Christ alone, as chief to direct it; as the heart to give it life; as the fountain to water it with the seven gifts of the Holy Spirit; as the always sufficient refuge to which I have recourse in my misfortunes, firmly believing that there I shall always find direction, assistance, and plenteous vivification; and that God will fill me with an ineffable joy in delivering me from my sins and from a wretched existence. .... Happy, then, are they who, in observing His law, perceive and detest the vain pomp, avarice, and hypocrisy, of the Saviour's enemies, and patiently wait for the coming of the sovereign Judge and his angels!"[*]

---

[*] *Hist. et Monum. Joan. Hus.* t. i. p. 81, Epist. xix.

BOOK III.

CHAPTER I.

THE CUP.

IMMEDIATELY after the deposition of John XXIII., the council condemned the cup in the communion, as a practice opposed to the rule established by the Roman Church.

The communion, in the primitive Church, as is well known, was administered after the repast, and in the two kinds—bread and wine. Afterwards a different custom prevailed, the communion being received fasting; and next, the priests alone took the communion with the two kinds, administering the sacrament to the laity under the form of bread alone.

The Eastern Church preserved the ancient practice, which was appealed to by the greater part of the reformers, and re-established in many countries. But no nation clung to it with so much ardour as Bohemia, where the communion in the two kinds had never been altogether abolished. Bohemia, in fact,—converted to Christianity in the ninth century, by Greek monks, sent there by the Empress Theodora and the Emperor Michael, her son,—preserved, for a length of time, in its worship, certain practices peculiar to itself; and when it attracted the serious attention of the Roman pontiffs, the work of conversion was already almost accomplished. They, nevertheless, interfered, because, pretending, as they did, to universal empire, they interfered everywhere and in every thing; yet at first they manifested toleration for the practices of Bohemia, and their indulgence originated in a grave motive. The Eastern Church had recently separated from that of Rome; and it was to be apprehended that Bohemia, already united to the former by strong ties, might withdraw her obedience altogether from the latter. The Church of Rome, therefore, tolerated the practices already established in the country:—the Bohemians preserved their Sclavonian Bible, and continued to celebrate their religious service in their national language. They thus guarded certain habits of independence in their worship, and were easily enabled to compare its doctrines with the sacred text.

When time had rendered Bohemia more docile to the yoke of the papal see, the latter became more exacting: tolerance gave way to severity, and Gregory VII. enjoined an exact conformity to the Roman practice. In a celebrated letter which this pontiff wrote, in 1079, to Wratislaus, Duke of Bohemia, he thus expresses himself:—"Learn, that from frequent meditation on the Holy Scriptures, we have discovered that it is the pleasure of the all-powerful God that the language of the sacred worship shall be hidden, in order that it may not be understood by every one, and particularly by the simple."[*] Gregory adds, that the contrary practice engenders contempt and heresy.[†]

A schism then arose amongst the people of Bohemia, the higher classes adopting the Latin ritual, whilst the heart of the multitude, in preference, adhered to that of the Greek Church; and when the cup was formally prohibited to the laity, many churches in Bohemia still continued to use it, as more in conformity with the commands of Scripture and with ancient tradition.

However, in the fourteenth century, under King Charles IV., the Latin practice prevailed everywhere; and the communion by the two kinds was no longer given, except in the secrecy of private dwellings or in the depths of forests.

But when the Eastern schism had shaken the pontifical authority, and brought back the minds of many to the sacred sources, the question of giving the cup to the laity was again discussed. The difference between the ancient and the modern practice—between the institution of Christ and the custom of the Church—was evident; and it seized on the mind of the multitude with the greater force, from falling more immediately under the

* It would be difficult to reconcile this assertion of the pope with the text of St. Paul's 1st Epistle to the Corinthians, chap. xiv.

† This letter may be found amongst those written by Gregory VII., in vol. xxvi. of the Councils, in the Louvre.

80

senses; so that, wherever the reformation triumphed, the communion of the cup was restored.

This practice became, in the fifteenth century, the distinctive mark of the Hussites in Europe. It was not, however, John Huss who brought about the return to the ancient custom on this point. He was absent from Prague, and already prisoner at Constance, when two doctors, both of them his friends and disciples, Peter of Dresden and the celebrated James of Misa (or Jacobel, as he was surnamed), called on the people to partake of the communion in the two kinds.

If Dubravius, the Catholic historian, be believed, John Huss at first looked on this conduct of his disciples as a serious act of hostility against the Church, and exceedingly calculated to augment the animosity of the council against himself; his exclamation being, when speaking of them,—"They have at length found a cup to hasten my death."[*] However, he afterwards wrote to Prague to approve of Jacobel's conduct.[†] His judges were not aware of his having written; and it does not appear that he was ever called on to answer for it before them.

It was one of his bitter adversaries, the Bishop of Litomissel, who lodged a complaint against Jacobel before the Council.

The assembly named a commission of doctors, who presented a report under six heads.[‡]

The doctors allowed the fact of the communion in the two kinds in the primitive Church; they next declared that the contrary custom, although originally established without any formal decision of the Church, ought to be considered equivalent to law. According to St. Augustine, they alleged, Christ had left the communion quite undecided as to time; whilst, as to manner, a great miracle, they said, could be adduced in favour of their opinion. It occurred, they stated, in this way:—Some monks wished to take the communion in the two kinds. The priest having broken the bread, it came to pass that the communion plate became filled with blood; and when the priest afterwards put together the two pieces of the sacramental wafer, the blood immediately returned to it, so that not a drop remained in the plate. A celebrated doctor of the thirteenth century, Alexander Hale, had guarantied the truth of this miracle : and the question of the holding back the cup was thus decided. This practice, the doctors declared, had been in-

troduced for reasonable causes :—it had been approved of amongst various celebrated persons —by Richard Middleton, Peter of Tarentaise, Thomas Aquinas, and other great doctors; it had, besides, prevailed for several centuries— so that no person could speak against it without the authority of the Church; and its opponents ought to be looked on as heretics, and punished accordingly.[*]

These conclusions of the commissioners were vigorously refuted. Jacobel, in his reply, brought forward doctors against doctors, St. Augustine against St. Augustine, and Jesus Christ against the Church. "The miracle mentioned by Dr. Hale might," he observed, "be doubted; and it is impossible to deduce any argument from it in contradiction to the certain practice and the precise commands of the sovereign Teacher. The most illustrious fathers—St. Augustine and St. Cyprian—have declared that practice ought to yield to truth. Perhaps you will oppose to me the custom enjoined by Pope Gregory; but our Lord has declared, *I am the way, the truth, and the life,* and not, *I am the custom.* Three other popes— Urban II., Marcelline, and Symmachus—as well as St. Augustine, have affirmed that it was not permitted either to pope or emperor to change any thing of what was commanded in the law and the evangelists. The blame rests, therefore, with those who have withdrawn the cup from the people, contrary to the institutes of Jesus Christ and the practice of the ancient Church—with those who had suppressed the communion in the two kinds, and not with those who are anxious to re-establish it."

Next, assuming the defence of the University of Prague, which appeared anxious to return to the primitive institution of the Lord's supper, Jacobel was not sparing of sharp censures on his adversaries:—"The members of our university," said he, "do not strut about in a remarkable and sumptuous costume, in order to set off their dignity the more. They are not of that class of whom our Lord speaks, as loving the first places at feasts and synagogues, in order to be saluted in public places, and hear themselves called Master. Is it not a disgrace to the Church, as St. Jerome says, to preach Jesus Christ, poor, crucified, in want of every thing—with bodies loaded with fat, with well-fed faces and vermilion lips. If we are in the apostles' places, it is not merely in order to preach their doctrines, but also to imitate their mode of life. And men like these dare affirm that such persons as think differently from themselves are liable to punishment as heretics! But, in the primitive Church, were not all who followed Jesus Christ—his

* Illos tandem reperisse poculum, quod sibi mortem accelerarct.—(Dubrav. Hist. Boh. p. 622.)
† Epist. xvi.
‡ Theolog. Const. Concil. contra Jacobum de Misa. Ex Antiq. Cod. Msc. Acad. Helmstad. ap. Von der Hardt, t. iii. p. 586.

* Von der Hardt, t. iii. p. 608.

11

disciples, his apostles, nay, Jesus Christ him-self—declared heretics by the priests, and punished as such!"

Jacobel quotes Isaiah, Ezekiel, St. Cyprian, and St. Chrysostom, to prove that the priest-hood of the Romish Church conducted them-selves exactly like the priests of the Jewish Church, in persecuting the true disciples—the faithful servants of God.

"If, by a miracle," said he, "Jesus Christ should suddenly appear in the midst of the Council of Constance, with the members of the primitive Church, and should address the assembly in the words pronounced by him at Capernaum, *If you eat not of the body of the Son of man, and drink of his blood*, &c.; and if he desired to administer the sacrament in that place, such as he had instituted it, do you suppose that the persons present would allow him to speak, would permit him to proceed? They would withdraw, like those whom his words offended at Capernaum,—they would accuse him of heresy,—they would condemn him, declaring, *What you are doing there is not the practice!* Just see what manner of acting they have adopted. First of all, they calumniate; next, they summon before them; after that, they excommunicate; and, last of all, they remove from office. They devote the soul, as far as in them lies, to the demons, and deliver up the body to the secular power; and, as the Jewish priests formerly declared, *If thou let this man go, thou art not Cæsar's friend,* so they, in the present time, say to the tem-poral magistrate, This man comes under the jurisdiction of your tribunal; he ought to be punished by the secular arm! Damnable and dangerous hypocrisy! They err at their own peril, says St. Augustine,[*] who fancy that those alone are murderers who kill with their hands—the Jews did not themselves put our Lord to death. 'We are forbidden,' said they, 'to cause the death of any one;' and yet the death of the Lord is justly to be imputed to them; for they killed him with their tongue, in say-ing, *Crucify him!*

"Our Lord has said, 'Beware of men, for they will deliver you up to the councils, and they will scourge you in their synagogues; and ye shall be brought before governors and kings for my sake: ye shall be hated of all for my sake.'——O King of kings, Lord of lords, Eternal Father, on every side do I behold dangers! If I listen to thy well-beloved Son,—if I believe in his holy word,—if I act in conformity with the practice of the early Christians,—I shall be excommunicated, and declared a heretic: I shall be condemned and burned, or put to death in some other way, by

this Roman Church, which no longer is even aware of what were the manners and customs of the primitive Church. If I disobey the Scriptures, I have to dread eternal perdition, and those flames which never cease to burn. What, then, must I do? What decision must I take? Ah! I know that it is better to fall into the hands of men than to sin against God."[*]

Jacobel, and the doctrine of the commu-nion in the two kinds, found in the council a more formidable adversary than the Bishop of Litomissel and the doctors appointed to in-quire into the matter. This was Gerson, whose name and acts recur perpetually in all the grand questions which were discussed at Constance. To the arguments of the doctors, Gerson added others—first, by word of mouth, and afterwards in writing, in a remarkable treatise, which he published two years after-wards at the request of the council, and which is inserted in his works.[†]

After having discussed the question in the double point of view, of the Scriptures and of tradition, Gerson enumerated the incon-veniences that would arise from allowing all believers to participate in the cup. "There are various dangers, of different kinds," said he, "likely to arise from this practice, which ought to be guarded against;—the danger of the wine being spilt in taking it from place to place:—the danger of its being frozen, or be-ing insufficient in quantity:—the danger of its 'turning sour, in which case, the pure blood of Jesus Christ would no longer be there;[‡]—the danger of its being spoiled, or of flies being engendered in it, by heat:—and the danger of some of it adhering to the long beards of the laity." Gerson asks where vessels could be found in sufficient abundance for the commu-nion of 20,000 persons; he declares, too, that he sees a grave peril in a practice which would lead believers into various errors; as, for in-stance, in their supposing that the laity are of equal dignity, in the communion, with the priesthood;—that the learned men, doctors and prelates, who have inculcated a contrary practice, have falsified the Scriptures, and are damned;—that the virtue of this sacrament does not reside more in the consecration than in the participation;—that, finally, the Roman Church, and the general and private councils, have been mistaken with respect to the sacra-ments.

---

[*] Treatise on Penance.

[*] Jacob. de Misa, *Apol. pro Commun. pleb. sub utr. spec.* Ex Cod. Msc. Acad. Lips. ap. Von der Hardt, t. iii. p. 561.
[†] J. Gerson, *Oper.* t. i. p. 457, 467.
[‡] Quoniam posset in vase acetum generari, et ita desineret ibi esse sanguis Christi; nec suscipien-dum esse, nec noviter consecrandum sine missa; et fieri posset quod daretur acetum purum pro san-guine Christi.—*Ibid.* p. 466.

Such, in substance, were the principal arguments brought forward on both sides before the council, in the famous question of withholding the cup,—a question which gave birth to innumerable volumes, and caused oceans of blood to be shed.

The council, on June 15, 1415, in its thirteenth session, pronounced its decree, the tenor of which is not particularly respectful to Jesus Christ:

"The Sacred Council, wishing to provide for the eternal safety of the faithful, after a mature deliberation by several doctors, declares and decides, that, although Jesus Christ instituted and administered to his apostles the venerable sacrament, after the Lord's supper, in the two kinds, of bread and of wine, nevertheless, the laudable authority of the sacred canons, and the practice countenanced by the Church, have held, and still hold, that this sacrament ought to be received only when fasting, unless in case of malady, or some other necessity, admitted by the law of the Church,—a custom which has been reasonably introduced in order to avoid certain perils and scandal. In the same way, although in the primitive Church this sacrament was received by the faithful in the two kinds, yet it can be clearly proved, that afterwards it was received in that manner only by the officiating priests, and was offered to the laity under the form of bread alone, because it must be believed firmly, and without any hesitation or doubt, that the whole body and the whole blood of Jesus Christ are truly contained in the bread as well as in the wine. Wherefore, this practice, introduced by the Church and by the holy Fathers, and observed for a very great length of time,* ought to be regarded as a law, which it is not permitted to reject or change without the authority of the Church."

The council terminated by decreeing that the punishment to which heretics were liable should be put in force against all infringers of the rule thus laid down.

By this celebrated decree, the practice of the communion when fasting, and in one kind, was legally established; and since then it has had the force of law in the Church. The council hoped to put down the discussion, by deciding the question; but the opponents appealed from the power which had drawn up the decree, to the sword. Thence resulted a frightful war; and the question, kept down in the fifteenth century under streams of blood, revived in the century following more formidable than ever. The obstinacy of the Roman Church, on this very secondary point of doctrine, contributed, in no small degree, to the success of the Reformation; and if the council, which declared itself infallible, had been endowed with second sight, it may be doubted that it would have acted so as to separate from Romanism one-half of Christian Europe, not in order to maintain the integrity of tradition, or of the tenets of the Church, but merely to preserve a uniformity of practice.

CHAPTER II.

ABDICATION OF GREGORY XII.

Of the three popes whose pretensions held Christendom in suspense, and whom the council had determined to constrain to a resignation, or to depose, only one had submitted,—induced in such a course, principally, by a dread of the punishment which his crimes deserved. The fall of John XXIII. removed an obstacle to the abdication of Gregory XII., who now, at the advanced age of eighty-eight, probably felt himself too feeble to struggle against the formidable assembly, which held at its disposal the forces of the emperor and of the kings. Perhaps, too, when thus standing on the brink of the grave, he was not unwilling, by offering a tardy, but striking, sacrifice to the peace of the world, to expiate the misery and scandal which his obstinacy had occasioned; and after having for eight years contended, in the face of Europe, with his rival, Benedict XIII., in pride and ambition, there is every reason to suppose that he endeavoured, for once, to bear off the palm from him, in self-denial before God.

On June 16, 1415, Charles Malatesta, Lord of Rimini, captain-general and procurator of Gregory XII., made his public entrance into

* It is not easy to see how the council could take on itself to declare, that a very great length of time had elapsed since the practice of taking the communion under one kind only had been introduced into the Church. Can 200 years at most—which was the period that the practice had prevailed, and that not even generally, nor without contradiction— be called a very great length of time, particularly if that period be compared with twelve entire centuries, during which the Church gave the communion in the two kinds.—(Lenfant, *Concili de Constance*, t. ii. p. 371.)

Constance with a brilliant escort, and was received with great magnificence. Gregory had not, however, deputed him to treat with the council: for he did not recognise that assembly, as it had not been convoked by him —he had directed his envoy to address himself to the emperor only. He laid down two conditions on which he would resign his pontificate—one, that the council should agree to be convoked by him; the other, that a cardinal of his jurisdiction should occupy the president's chair; and he forbade his procurator to appear before it, unless the latter clause was accepted.

The council agreed to the first condition, and rejected the second; it thought it better, for this time only, to ask the emperor to preside. But, in avoiding one difficulty, it fell into another; for, on the one hand, as it had not the slightest intention that its acts, anterior to this last convocation, should be invalidated, so, on the other, it was unwilling to have it said that the emperor had presided at the session of an œcumenical council. It was, therefore, determined, with the consent of all parties, to deprive the present session of the sacred character of the preceding ones, by suppressing, at its opening, nearly all the religious services that had been celebrated at the commencement of those which had already taken place.

Matters having been thus regulated with extreme circumspection to preserve the rights of all, the sitting opened with Sigismund in the president's chair. The emperor, seated right in front of the altar, had on his right Charles Malatesta, Gregory's procurator, and on his left the Cardinal of Ragusa, one of his legates. A few hymns having been sung, the two bulls of Gregory XII. were read. One authorized the prelates and great officers to recognise the assembly at Constance as a general council, as soon as it should have been anew convoked by him:—the other conferred full power on Malatesta to effect and conclude whatever he might deem most advisable for his master's interests and those of the Church.

The bulls having been read, Gregory's legate rose and said:—"I, John Cardinal of Ragusa, with the authority of my lord the pope, *as much as it regards him*, do hereby CONVOKE the sacred general council—I authorize and confirm whatever it shall do for the union and reformation of the Church, and for the extirpation of heresy."

The Archbishop of Milan next spoke; and, in the name of the council, approved of this new convocation in the following words:— "The principle and motive being the capital point in all things, the sacred Council of Constance, lawfully assembled in the name of the

Holy Spirit, and representing the Catholic Church, having, for its governing principle, the desire to do every thing it possibly can for the union of the Church; and in order that the two obediences—they who maintain that John XXIII. has been pope, and they who declare that Gregory XII. is so at the present moment—may be united together under Jesus Christ, their chief—hereby does fully admit the convocation just made, in the name of him called Gregory XII., *inasmuch as the matter may regard him*, and orders that the two bodies of persons already alluded to, under the jurisdiction of the said popes, be, and remain, united."

As soon as the council had been thus convoked, the Cardinal of Pisa celebrated mass, and all the ceremonies that were usual at the opening of each session were regularly gone through. The emperor resumed his usual place: Cardinal de Viviers took his place as president; and the fourteenth session commenced.

Several decrees were then read, by which the council forbade any one whatever to proceed to the election of a new pope without its permission, and suspended, for this one occasion, all the usages, rights, and privileges, authorized by preceding councils, in the said elections. The council reserved to itself the faculty of regulating the time, form, and place, of this election. It decided, besides, that it should not be dissolved until a pope was elected, and requested the emperor to employ himself efficaciously to maintain and defend it.

The emperor declared that he should comply with the wishes of the council; and he, accordingly, after the sitting, published an edict, threatening, with the severest penalties, whoever should attempt any thing against the security of the council or the liberty of the pope's election.

The council next ratified all that Gregory had done canonically in the places within his real jurisdiction; and declared that it was not through incapacity, but for the promotion of general peace, that Gregory had been excluded, in the twelfth session, from the right of being elected anew. The council recognised him as cardinal; and confirmed in their dignities the six cardinals who had adhered to his jurisdiction.

Then Charles Malatesta rose and addressed the assembly. In allusion to the name of Angelo, which was that of Gregory XII., he took for the text of his observations those words of St. Luke—"*And suddenly there arose with the angel a great multitude of the heavenly host.*" When he had concluded, he ascended an elevated seat, arranged as if for Gregory himself, and solemnly declared that his master abdicated the sovereign pontificate, without being induced by any other motive than an ardent desire to procure peace and union for the Church.

The council terminated its fourteenth session by the reading of a decree, summoning Peter de Luna, called Benedict XIII., to keep his promise, and abdicate the pontificate within ten days, under pain of being proceeded against as schismatic, incorrigible, devoid of faith, and perjured. Should he prove contumacious, the emperor was required to act against him in pursuance of this judgment.

Gregory, after having resigned the tiara, appeared relieved of a great burden—the crown, in fact, weighed more heavily on his conscience than on his brow. As soon as he learned what had taken place at Constance, he assembled his cardinals, priests, and household, and putting off in their presence his mitre and pontifical ornaments, took a solemn oath that he would never resume them. He was made Cardinal of Oporto; and, two years after, he died, at the age of ninety, at Recanati, in the march of Ancona, of which he was legate.

The theologians of Italy have availed themselves of the concession made by the council to Gregory, to declare all its anterior acts null and void, and, in particular, the decrees of the fifth session, which established the superiority of a general council to the pope. Such a pretension on their part is easily comprehended; but it cannot be in any way justified.

To have the acts of the preceding sessions invalidated, the council ought to have declared them to be so in the fourteenth or following sittings; and, above all, it ought to have reckoned them only from the new convocation. It, however, did the very opposite—it continued to count the sessions in the same order as previously; and, in the end, had all its acts confirmed by the mouth of a new pope. It even required, in order that there should exist no pretext for equivocation or doubt, to have this clause :—" In as much as that regards Gregory XII.," maintained in that pontiff's decree of convocation.

Besides, we do not find that Gregory himself, after his abdication, regarded what had taken place antecedently to that act as invalid,[*] or that he believed, for instance, that, in order to invalidate the deposition of John XXIII., it was requisite to depose him anew. Gregory, undoubtedly, desired to treat with tenderness and respect what he owed to himself, in order to justify his long resistance. He was anxious, too, as far as it depended on him, to preserve intact the prerogatives of his supreme rank, which have been abandoned by his former competitor. Though vanquished, he knew how to reap honour from his defeat; and when his downfall was forced, he covered himself with a certain degree of glory in making it appear as voluntary—in gracing a real constraint with an appearance of liberty. Balthazar Cossa had been ignominiously precipitated from his high position, and resigned his crown like a groveling coward: • Angelo Corrario yielded up his in a manner worthy of a pope:—and it may be declared of him, that he descended with dignity from the throne, rather than that he was constrained to abandon it.

CHAPTER III.

JOHN HUSS BEFORE HIS TRIAL.

AFTER having done much for the extinction of the schism, the council now turned all its efforts to put down heresy.

Already, in condemning Wycliffe and his works, it had attempted to stigmatize his new doctrines at their very source; and it now remained to exercise severity against those persons who dared to propagate them. Notwithstanding the vast difference between Wycliffe and John Huss as to dogmas, the public considered the latter as the disciple—the successor—of the great arch-heretic of England; and, looking closely at the matter, it must be allowed that Huss was, in effect, the continuer of Wycliffe. He defended, as Wycliffe had done, the authority of the Scriptures, and of the conscience, against that of the priesthood; he departed, it is true, but very slightly on any other point, from the doctrines of the Roman Church. He merely laid down a principle, of which the consequence was, that any one might dissent from them if his conscience made it a duty to do so. This was amply sufficient—in such tenets there were the seeds of a revolution, which it was thought necessary to crush. His ruin was, therefore, determined on; and never had a great cause a nobler victim.

---

* See a curious letter of Gregory XII., quoted in Martine's Anecdotes, vol. ii. p. 1646.

No affliction was spared Huss whilst waiting for his trial. The arrest of Jerome of Prague, his pupil and friend, had been to him a severe shock. The consolation of an imprisonment in common was refused them; and whilst Jerome languished in chains in the tower of the cemetery of St. Paul, Huss remained at Gotleben, under the guard of the Bishop of Constance.

All his letters, and all the testimony of contemporary writers, serve to prove, that at this last period of his life, his angelic meekness and resignation were as constant as his misfortunes. If indignation had formerly characterized some of his acts and writings with an impress of extra violence or bitterness, these defects had given place to their opposite virtues; and, through the sanctifying power of the Spirit, he had never been more meet for the crown of immortality in heaven than at the moment when his enemies were preparing to inflict martyrdom on him on earth. Never did any one manifest a faith more full of hope and gratitude, in the midst of trials in which carnal men would have beheld only motives for lamentation and despair. "This declaration of our Saviour," said he, "is to me a great source of consolation: ' Blessed are ye when men shall hate you, and shall reproach you, and cast out your name as evil, for the Son of man's sake. Rejoice ye in that day; for, behold, your reward is great in heaven.' "[*]

John Huss, like most men of a sincere piety, united to a great courage that elevation of mind and enthusiasm, in which we frequently perceive a direct influence of the Divine Spirit, and by which man is enabled to surmount the greatest obstacles, and to sustain the most poignant anguish. But this ecstatic development of the higher faculties—this unusual exaltation of soul, which human knowledge has so much sneered at and run down, because it feels itself powerless to explain its operations, did not in any way alter Huss's humility.

Already, when he had been driven from Prague, and was wandering about in the villages of Bohemia, followed by crowds of the population, attentive to his words, he used to speak thus: "The wicked, with their ecclesiastical censures and citations, have caught the *poor bird*[†] in their nets. But if this domestic and peaceful animal, whose flight is not lofty, has broken through its snares, how much more will they be torn asunder by others who soar aloft. In place of a feeble bird, the truth has sent forth keen-sighted and high-flying eagles, that will gain over many to Jesus Christ, who will furnish them with strength."[‡]

* Luke vi. 22, 23.
† Huss, in the Bohemian tongue, signifies *goose.*
‡ Epist. vi. J. *Huss,* Script. tempore anat. et interd. pontif.

Huss also was visited by visions and prophetic dreams. One night, in his dungeon, it seemed to him that the priests wanted to efface the figures of Jesus Christ which he had got painted on the walls of his chapel at Bethlehem.[*] "The next day," said he, "methought I perceived several painters busied in retracing those pictures of the Saviour, so as to make them more numerous and more brilliant than before; and, as they did so, they were crying out, ' Now, let the bishops and the priests come forth! Let them efface these if they can !' and the crowd was filled with joy, and I also."[†]

"Occupy your thoughts with your defence rather than with visions," said John de Chlum, when he heard this one narrated. John Huss, in replying to his friend, quoted the text of Scripture, "*Place no faith in dreams.* And yet," said he, "I firmly hope that this life of Christ, which I engraved in men's hearts at Bethlehem, when I preached his word, will not be effaced; and that, after I have ceased to live, it will be still better shown forth, by mightier preachers, to the great satisfaction of the people and to my own most sincere joy, when I shall be again permitted to announce His gospel, that is, when I shall rise from the dead. . . . . . As to my defence, I intrust it to the Saviour, to whom I have appealed before the commissioners, saying, ' Let the Lord, who soon shall judge you all, be my advocate and my judge : to him do I confide my cause, as he confided his own to his Father.' It is he who has said, ' Take no thought how or what ye shall speak. Think not of what ye shall answer, for I will place in your mouths a wisdom and a virtue which your adversaries shall not be able to resist. Be ye not afraid or disquieted. Ye shall indeed walk to the combat, but it is I who will fight for you.' "[‡]

The day of his trial did not, however, arrive. His most determined enemies, and amongst them Paletz and Michael Causis, dreaded the influence of his eloquence on the assembly: probably they were also afraid that a public retractation might rob them of their victim. They had discovered in the canon law that an advocate could be conscientiously refused to a heretic: and they would equally have found that they might justly condemn him without hearing him, if they deemed it necessary. Sigismund, on the other side, clearly perceived how injurious to his character and glory would be the issue of a public trial: the safe-conduct

* Balbinus ascribes this vision to Huss before his captivity, and he perceives in it only the presage of the calamities which were about to burst over the Church and over Bohemia. (*Epit. ser Bohem.* p. 412.)
† Epist. xliv.
‡ Epist. xlvi.

which he had granted, weighed on his conscience, and in gaining time for John Huss, he gained it also for himself. The barons, however, and other noblemen of Bohemia, and amongst them all, the brave John de Chlum, always displayed the same zeal for their unfortunate countryman, and they renewed their energetic instances with the council and the emperor.

" "John Huss," pleaded they, "is wrongfully accused of having openly preached at Constance, where he lived in the same lodging as the Lord John de Chlum, who never quitted him; which that nobleman is ready to swear to, and prove at his own risk and peril, in any manner that may be required. John Huss came freely to the council to make a public confession of his faith,—he came with the intention of joining the holy Church on the points in which he should be found to differ from her." The barons also appealed to the certificates of orthodoxy delivered to him at Prague, and then produced the following protest from John Huss :—

"Anxious, above all things, for the honour of God and of the holy Church, and being most desirous of remaining a faithful member of our Lord Jesus Christ, who is the Head and Spouse of the Church which he has redeemed, I do hereby protest, as I have already done, that I have never obstinately sustained, or shall sustain, what is contrary to the truth. I have always believed, I still believe, and I desire always firmly to believe, all the truths that ought to be admitted; and before I take on me to defend any error contrary to this, may I, with a hope in the Lord and in his divine assistance, undergo death. I am therefore ready, with the help of God, to expose my miserable life for the law of Christ, which I believe to have been literally given to us by the inspiration of the Holy Trinity, and promulgated by the saints of God for the salvation of mankind. I believe in the articles of the divine law, as the Trinity teaches them to us, and orders us to believe them. In my theses, my answers, and my public actions, I have always been, am, and shall be, subject to the prescriptions of that holy law—fully prepared to revoke all that I can have said contrary to the truth."*

"Now," said the barons to the council, "the intention is to condemn John Huss on mutilated passages, perfidiously extracted from his works, and erroneously interpreted, by his most deadly enemies, and in direct violation of the emperor's safe-conduct. We conjure you, Reverend Fathers, to allow John Huss to be brought from his cruel prison, and placed in the hands of some bishops or commissioners designated by you, in order that he may regain strength and health, to enable him to be interrogated by you. In faith of which, we, nobles and barons of the kingdom of Bohemia, offer to give whatever guarantees you may demand, and good security that the aforesaid John Huss will not withdraw, but will, fully and satisfactorily, reply to all questions put to him by your commissioners."

They sent a letter, couched in similar language, to the emperor. His answer has not come down to us; but the Patriarch of Antioch replied, in the name of the council, that the result would show whether John Huss's protest was imposture or truth—that, with respect to the guarantees or security which the barons were ready to offer for him, were a thousand presented, the deputies of the council could not, in conscience, receive them for a heretic; —they could, however, promise, that Huss should be taken from Gotleben on the 5th of June, and brought to Constance, to be publicly interrogated.

This last determination ought to be attributed particularly to the emperor, who gave the same assurance with his own lips to the barons of Bohemia. John de Chlum quitted this prince, full of hope, and hastened to write thus to Huss :—

"Beloved brother in Christ, learn that it has been resolved between the emperor and the deputies of the nations, that you shall have a public hearing. Your friends insist on your being removed to an airy and wholesome residence, in order that you may, to a certain degree, recover your tranquillity, and have some relaxation. Therefore, in God's name, and for the sake of the truth, take good care not to desert the holy cause, through any fear of losing this wretched life; for it is for your great benefit that God visits you by this trial."*

Notwithstanding the engagement which the council and the emperor had just taken, Huss's enemies persisted in opposing the promised hearing, and spread abroad a report that a sedition was to burst forth on his arrival. They persuaded the council to send deputies to Gotleben, to interrogate him, hoping that some avowal might be drawn from him, which would render the public audience unnecessary. In the secret interrogatories that took place, every means were tried—even to insult and violence —to shake his firmness; and his friends were not without disquietude as to the result. Huss thus set their minds at rest, in one of his letters, which depicts, at the same time, the severity and annoying nature of this secret in-

---

* J. Hus. Hist. et Monum. vol. i. p. 15.

* Oper. Huss. Epist. xlvii. vol. i. p. 91.

quisition:—"Let my friends," said he, "be under no alarm on the score of my answers. *I firmly hope, that the matters which I have uttered in the shade, will be hereafter preached on the house-top.*[*] Every one of the articles has been presented to me separately, and the question has been asked, whether I persisted in desiring to defend it. My answer was, that I would not do so, but would await the decision of the council. God is my witness, that no reply has appeared to me more suitable, since I gave it under my own hand, that I did not wish to maintain any thing obstinately, but was disposed to let myself be instructed by any one. Michael Causis stood by with a paper in his hand, urging the patriarch to use force to make me reply to his questions. The bishops then came in, and interrogated in their turn. . . . God has permitted Paletz and Causis to rise against me, for my sins.[†] The first examined and remarked upon all my letters, and the second brought forward conversations which had taken place between us many years back.. . . . The patriarch would insist on it that I was exceedingly rich ;[‡] and an archbishop even named the very sum that I possess—namely, 70,000 florins. . . . . Oh! certainly my sufferings to-day were great! One of the bishops said to me, ' You have established a new law ;' and another, ' You have preached up all those articles.' My answer simply was, Why do you overwhelm me with outrage ?"[§]

Amongst those who manifested the greatest bitterness against John Huss, were the doctors of France. Being consulted by the council on nineteen articles attributed to him, their conclusions, signed by Gerson, were severe, and called on the author a rigorous condemnation. The greater number of the deputies of the Church and of the University of Paris at the council belonged to the school of *Nominalists*,[||] who, after a struggle of two centuries, were gaining the advantage in France over the rival school. Several of them reproved in Huss the *realist*, at least as much as the heterodox preacher. Perhaps they forgot, that formerly their own school had been condemned by the Church, in the persons of Roscelin and Abelard :[*] or rather they remembered it but too well ; and when they instigated the council against John Huss, they probably fancied that they could thereby efface their ancient disgrace, and avenge their humiliating defeats. These paltry calculations undoubtedly never entered into the mind of Gerson ; but the strongest minds are not closed against prejudices, and Gerson imputed to the great doctor of Bohemia exaggerated offences. These conclusions of the University of Paris, on that account, weighed heavily on the mind of Huss ; and in one of his letters, after declaring them calumnious, he exclaimed : "Oh! that God may grant me time to reply to the false imputations of the Chancellor of Paris!"[†]

At last, the council appeared disposed to give him the desired hearing; and on June 5, he was removed from Gotleben to the monastery of the Franciscans, where he remained in irons until his death. However, the day before that appointed for the public audience, the cardinals, the prelates, and almost all the members of the council, assembled in this place, and resolved to pronounce, first of all, on the incriminated articles, without Huss being present.

The good notary, Peter Maldoniewitz, the friend and disciple of Huss, happened to be there, and he, at once, hurried out and ran to inform John de Chlum and Wenceslaus Duba. "John Huss," said he to them, "is going to be condemned before having been heard."

The two barons gave information of the matter to the emperor, who, on the instant, sent the Elector Palatine and the Burgrave of Nuremberg to the assembled members. Sigismund ordered them to suspend the inquiry in the absence of John Huss, and called on them to transmit to him, by his messengers, the incriminated articles, in order that he might get them examined by doctors of acknowledged learning and probity. The assembly acceded to the first point, giving orders.

---

[*] *Spero quod qua dixi sub tecto prædicabuntur super tecta.* The disciples of Huss looked on those words as prophetic.

[†] Michael stabat et tenebat chartam et instigabat patriarcham ut responderem super interrogatis. . . . Deus permisit ipsum et Paletz propter peccata mea consurgere.

[‡] Several letters, in which Huss prays his friends to pay for him some trifling debts, prove, on the contrary, that he was very poor.

[§] Epist. xlviii.

[||] Scholastic philosophers, who sustained, in contradiction to the realists, that the object of dialectics was words or names, and not things. This school commenced in the ninth century, and had Ocana for its head.—*(Note of Translator.)*

[*] Peter Abelard was born near Nantes in 1079. He opened at Paris, in 1103, a celebrated school, where he taught theology, rhetoric, and philosophy, and formed some distinguished scholars, amongst whom were Berenger, Arnaud de Brescia, and Pope Celestin II. He was condemned in 1140 by the Council of Soissons for heterodox opinions, and retired to the Paralilete in the diocese of Troyes, where he died in 1142. His amour with Heloise, the niece of the Canon Fulbert of Paris, and his subsequent misfortunes, have made him even more celebrated than his great acquirements as a theologian, grammarian, historian, mathematician, poet, and musician.—Roscelin was also a distinguished leader of the Nominalist theory.—*(Note of Translator.)*

[†] Epist. i.

to have Huss brought before them, but refused the second.* John de Chlum and Wenceslaus then handed to the Elector Palatine the volumes of Huss's writings whence the articles of his doctrines were pretended to be taken, and prayed him to produce them in the assembly, that it might be verified if the extracts were faithfully copied. The Elector and the Burgrave, after having handed in the volumes, withdrew, and all things having been regulated as has been just related, John Huss was introduced.

CHAPTER IV.

TRIAL OF JOHN HUSS.—FIRST AND SECOND AUDIENCES.

WHEN John Huss appeared before the assembly, his books were presented to him, and he was asked if he acknowledged them to be his production. He examined them and answered—"I acknowledge them to be mine; and if any man amongst you can point out any mistaken proposition in them, I will rectify it with the most hearty good will."

The reading of the articles then commenced. An article was read, and the names mentioned of some witnesses who supported the charge against it. Huss proceeded to reply; but he had scarcely uttered a word when there burst forth, throughout the whole assembly, so furious a clamour, that it was impossible to understand a word he said. One would have said, if Maldoniewitz, who was present at the scene, may be believed, that those men were ferocious wild beasts, rather than sage doctors, assembled to discuss grave and important questions. When the tumult had somewhat subsided, Huss made an appeal to the Holy Scriptures, which occasioned a general outcry from all parts of the council, every one crying out—"That is not the question!" Some of them uttered accusations against him, whilst others laughed him to scorn. Huss made no attempt to speak, and already his enemies were enjoying their triumph. "He is dumb," cried they; "it is evident that he has taught the heretical proposition contained in the article." "All," said Luther, in his energetic language, "all worked themselves into rage like wild boars—the bristles of their back stood on an end; they bent their brows and gnashed their teeth against John Huss."†

He, however, in the utmost astonishment, but perfectly motionless, sadly turned his eyes round the assembly, where he expected to behold his judges, but found only enemies. "I anticipated," said he, "a different reception, and had imagined that I should obtain a hearing. I am unable to make myself audible over so great a noise; and I am silent, because I am forced to it. I would willingly speak were I listened to."

The fathers, seeing that they could not agree on what was to be done, because they were too much agitated to proceed calmly, broke up the sitting. The Bohemian noblemen gave the emperor an account of what had taken place, and conjured him to be present at the succeeding sitting, in order to maintain order there by his presence. Sigismund promised that he would attend.

The next audience took place on June 7. On that day an eclipse, which was long afterwards spoken of in Europe, completely darkened the sun's disc; and it was not until after the darkness had altogether disappeared, about an hour after noon, that the council assembled in the hall of the Franciscans, where it had before met. John Huss was led there by a numerous body of soldiers.

The emperor was present—and no one had a more painful part to play on the occasion than himself. He beheld, right in front of him, loaded with chains, that same John Huss for whose liberty he had pledged his imperial word. He came with the hope of saving from condemnation the man whose trial he reproached himself for not having prevented; and, without doubt, he firmly believed in the influence which he should exercise over the prisoner. His desire to be of service was rendered abortive by two circumstances—one, that Huss was inexorable; and, next, that the whole council appeared animated against him with the same hostile feeling as distinguished his most cruel adversaries, Michael Causis and Paletz. The latter two had neglected nothing to procure a capital sentence; and the coming of the emperor excited them to redouble their efforts, through apprehension of the shameful defeat they should experience, if their victim escaped. John Huss, however,

---

* Theobald, *Bel. Huss*, chap. xvii.—The refusal of the council ought to be imputed, either to the fear which it felt as to the emperor's sentiments in favour of Huss, or to the apprehension that Sigismund might take on himself to act as judge in an ecclesiastical court.

† Script. in. fin. liter. J. Huss, Mart. Luth.

perceived some friendly visages in this formidable assembly. He recognised in the emperor's suite, his faithful disciple, Peter the notary, whose zeal no peril intimidated; and, standing immediately behind the emperor, he saw his brave protectors, Wenceslaus Duba and John de Chlum, both more experienced in combats in the field than in wordy war, but who, nevertheless, in this contest, so novel to them, and where the means of defence were so exceedingly circumscribed, gave proofs of address and courage.

Michael Causis read the act of accusation, which commenced thus :—

"John Huss, in the chapel of Bethlehem, and in various other places in the city of Prague, has taught the people various errors, partly drawn from Wycliffe's works and partly from his own invention, and has defended them with the greatest obstinacy. The first is, that after the consecration of the wafer in the sacrament, the bread remains material."

This fact was attested by several ecclesiastics, whose names Causis read aloud.

John Huss declared, on oath, that he had never taught this doctrine relative to the Eucharist. He acknowledged, however, that the Archbishop of Prague having forbidden him to make use of the term bread in consecrating the host, he had thought it his duty to refuse compliance, because Jesus Christ, in the sixth of St. John, calls himself the living bread, which had descended from heaven to give itself for the life of the world. He denied, positively, that he had called this bread material bread.

The Cardinal of Cambray, Peter d'Ailly, then stood up to speak. This celebrated man, who, in other respects, possessed an upright mind and a well exercised reason, was self-opinionated, positive, and prone to passion, and often showed more of the doctor than of the Christian.[*] An ardent Nominalist, he was tinctured with all the prejudices of his time; and, in his religious discussions, made use of the niceties and refinements of the schools, and the rigour of an inflexible and pitiless logic, which had procured him the surname (glorious in that day) of the hammer of heretics.[†] He questioned John Huss; and whoever is not aware of the passions peculiar to theologians, and to what a point the spirit of cavilling stifles in many the pure and meek spirit of the gospel, will scarcely be able to imagine that such an interrogatory could have

taken place for the purpose of ascertaining if Huss were a Christian.

"John Huss," said the cardinal, "do you admit the universals, à parte rei, as belonging to the thing itself of which they are the universals?"[*] "I admit them," replied Huss, "for this reason, that St. Anselme, and other great doctors, have admitted them." "If that be the case," retorted the cardinal, "it must be concluded that, after the consecration, the substance of the material bread remains; and I can prove it thus"——The cardinal then entered into a long scholastic dissertation in support of his assertion, and terminated by proposing an embarrassing dilemma.

John Huss replied, with great simplicity, that transubstantiation was an act contrary to the natural order of things, the substance disappearing in that case, though remaining in all others. In this Huss was in accord with the Scotist[†] theologians, all of whom admit the universal à parte rei.

Some English doctors then proceeded to declaim against the prisoner; and one of them gave a second edition of the cardinal's argument. He was not satisfied that Huss's profession of faith relative to transubstantiation was in accordance with the tenets of the Roman Church;—he could not allow that a man whose opinions relative to the universals was such as Huss had just stated, could believe that the material bread disappeared after the consecration. "Such argument is quite puerile," replied Huss, "a child could answer it."

A second doctor was not more fortunate; and a third stood up and reproached him with sharing the opinion of Wycliffe on this point. When Huss denied this with great energy, the doctor inquired if he believed the body of Christ to be totally and really in the sacramental wafer. "Yes," said John Huss, "the very body of Christ which was born of the Virgin Mary, was crucified, dead and buried, rose on the third day, and is now sitting on the right hand of God, the Father Almighty."

This reply ought certainly to have satisfied

---

[*] See a comparison between Gerson and D'Ailly by Elie Dupin.—(Gers. Oper. vol. i. p. 48.)

[†] Porro autem Alliacus dum viveret dicimerunt aquila Franciæ et malleus a veritate aberrantium indefessus.—(J. Launoii Reg. Navar. Gym. Hist. p. 476.)

[*] The Realists regarded abstract ideas as real things, and applied to them the term universals, whence the scholastic term, universalia à parte rei. The Nominals, on the contrary, saw in the universals nothing but words and names—simple abstractions of the mind.

[†] The disciples of Duns Scotus; who, from his abilities as a disputant on theological and metaphysical subjects, acquired the name of "the most subtle doctor." He was appointed Regent of the Theological Schools of the University of Paris, and had previously lectured at Oxford. He died in 1308, leaving behind him twelve volumes in folio, which are now looked on as a melancholy example of perverted learning and ingenuity. His followers formed one of the two great sections of the Nominalists, the other being called Thomists, from Thomas Aquinas, the head of the division.—(Note of Translator.)

the most fastidious, and yet it did not appear sufficiently explicit; and, on both sides, there were still many remarks made relative to the universals.

At last an Englishman, named Stokes, declaring that the doctrine now professed in words by Huss must be considered canonical, attacked him for what he had stated about it in his writings. "I saw at Prague," said he, "a certain treatise of this same John Huss, in which it was expressly asserted, that the material bread remains, after the sacrament at the altar, in the consecrated wafer." "That is absolutely false," replied John Huss.

It was found necessary to return to the written declarations. One of the witnesses, John Protiva, curé of Prague, accused Huss of having spoken of St. Gregory with irreverence. Huss replied, that it was doing him foul wrong to say so, as he had always considered Gregory as one of the most holy doctors of the Church.

After this, a moment's silence took place, and the Cardinal of Florence, Zabarella, then addressed the prisoner. "Master John Huss," said he, "you must know that it is written, that what is in the mouth of two or three witnesses must be considered as a veritable testimony. Now, here are twenty persons worthy of confidence, who declare that you have preached this doctrine which is imputed to you. The greater number of them adduce, in support of their assertions, unanswerable proofs; is it possible that you defend yourself against them all?"

John Huss replied, "I appeal to God and my conscience that I have never preached, and that it never entered my mind to teach, what is brought against me here, although these men dare aver that I said what they never heard themselves. Were they infinitely more numerous than they are, I should esteem far more the testimony of my own conscience, and of my God, to the judgment of my enemies."

"We cannot decide," rejoined the cardinal, "after your conscience, but on clear and well-established evidence. You are wrong, too, in your estimation of those who oppose you, for they are not in any way actuated by hatred. When you reproach Master Stephen Paletz with having acted perfidiously, and made false extracts of certain articles from your writings, you do him a great injustice; for, in the greater part of these articles, he has used your own expressions. Your opinions are equally erroneous relative to several others, and it is confidently asserted, that you regard with suspicion the illustrious Chancellor of Paris, whom no person in Christendom can surpass in merit."

Huss's answer is not given in the minutes

of the council;* but, in one of his letters, he says, "Should I live, I will reply to the Chancellor of Paris : if I die, God will answer for me at the day of judgment."†

The second charge against Huss was that he had taught and obstinately maintained, in Bohemia, Wycliffe's errors. This charge was unjust, in what regarded the dogmas of the Catholic Church which Wycliffe had rejected; but it was well-founded with respect to three points, which Huss had admitted, as has been seen, with all the simplicity of a candid mind, not comprehending that the Roman Catholic Church rested altogether, internally and externally, on those points which he rejected. These were,—the infallibility of its decisions, be they in comformity with the Scriptures or opposed to them—the spiritual authority of the priests, whether their way of life was evangelical or infamous,‡—and lastly, their right to hold temporal possessions, no matter what use they made of them. John Huss also declared that tithes were nothing but alms, and that they could be withdrawn from the priests if they made a bad use of them. But, in other respects, Huss did not adopt the bold opinions of Wycliffe on several dogmas of the Roman Church,—he admitted the latter; but blamed their abuse. He, therefore, denied most strongly, that he had either taught or preached the dogmatic errors of the great English reformer; and when it was objected to him as a heinous offence, that he had opposed their condemnation, he observed—"I refused to recognise as false and scandalous all the articles extracted from Wycliffe's works, because I hold several of them to be true—amongst others, that which declares that Pope Sylvester and the Emperor Constantine erred in endowing the Church as they have done—and that which establishes that *tithes* are not demandable by divine right, but are merely alms."

Huss added, that he had not given his approval to the condemnation of Wycliffe's articles, in consequence of its not having been pronounced according to reasons drawn from *the Holy Scriptures ;* and when several members of the assembly attributed to him, as a

* Mac. Lips. ap. Von der Hardt, t. iv. p. 310. The article touching the Eucharist was probably one of the two which the council struck out. "Deleti sunt *articuli* duo ; jam spero de gratia Dei, quod plures delebuntur." (*J. Huss*, Epist. xxxvi.)

† Epist. xli.

‡ Huss, as will presently be seen, defended himself with success on this point : but, the indecision and obscurity of his way of thinking are very apparent in his writings; and it has been allowed that this was really the weak side of his doctrine. (Vol. i. p. 75.)

grievous fault, his having expressed a doubt of Wycliffe's damnation, at the time his books were publicly burned, he replied: "These were my words on that occasion: 'I cannot affirm if Wycliffe will be saved or lost—I would willingly, however, have my soul where his is.'"*

A noble answer, which ought to have touched the assembly; but which was greeted with an insulting roar of laughter!

Accused of having asserted, like Wycliffe, that a priest in mortal sin neither baptizes nor consecrates, he replied that "he had modified this article in one of his books, by saying that such a priest baptized unworthily." He appealed to the book itself, a copy of which was produced, and it was ascertained that his statement was correct.†

Accused of having appealed from the sentence of the popes Alexander V. and John XXIII. to Jesus Christ, he said: "I swear, that no appeal can be more just and more holy. Is not an appeal, according to law, to have recourse from an inferior judge to a higher and more enlightened one? But, what judge can be superior to Christ? Is there in any one more justice than in Him, in whom neither error nor falsity can be found? Is there any where a more assured refuge for the wretched and the oppressed?"

Whilst John Huss answered thus, in a grave yet earnest tone, he was overwhelmed with mockery and insult.

Accused of having called on the people, in his sermons, to take up arms in defence of his doctrines: "Yes," said he, "I certainly did invite the people to arm themselves to support the truth of the gospel, but only with the arms spoken of by the apostle,—the helmet and sword of salvation."

Accused of having ruined the University of Prague, in the affair of the three votes taken from the Germans, and made responsible for that event by a doctor named Nason, one of the most inveterate of his adversaries, he replied that he had acted in the matter according to justice,—for the interest of his countrymen,—and in obedience to the king's orders.

Accused, finally, by this same Nason of having caused sentences of banishment to be pronounced against a great number of learned men, removed to Moravia by Wenceslaus: "How could I have done that," said he, "as

* Tamen in spe vellem meam animam ibidem ubi Joannes Wycliffe esse. *Hist. et Monum. J. Huss*, vol. i. p. 17; Msc. Lips. ap. Von der Hardt, vol. iv. p. 311.

† Such a proof, though quite sufficient to procure an acquittal, was, however, in general, exceedingly incomplete. Huss's works had been transcribed by several different hands, and no copy could with justice be considered as authentic, if not written or approved of by the author.

when they were banished I was not at Prague."

John Huss was then given over to the keeping of the Archbishop of Riga, under whom was already his friend, Jerome of Prague. As the soldiers were leading him away, he was called back to appear before the emperor, by the Cardinal of Cambray, who thus accosted him: "John Huss, I have heard you affirm, that if you had not come to Constance of your own free will, neither the Emperor nor the King of Bohemia could have forced you to do so." "Reverend father," replied Huss, "what I said was, that there were in Bohemia many nobles who wished me well; and that they could have kept me, and concealed me in such a manner, that no person could constrain me to come to Constance, not even the King of Bohemia, or the emperor himself."

At this answer, the Cardinal of Cambray grew crimson with anger, and exclaimed, "Do you hear the audacity of this man?"

The assembly murmured, and a commotion arose amongst the members, when John de Chlum resolutely stood forward, and dared to defy the emperor himself, in order to succour his friend. "John Huss," said he, "has spoken well. I am but an insignificant person in Bohemia, compared with many others; and yet, if I had undertaken it, I should engage to defend him for a year against these great sovereigns! What, therefore, would they have done who are far more powerful than I, and who possess impregnable fortresses?"

"Enough has been said," said the cardinal. "As to you, John Huss, I exhort you to submit to the sentence of the council, as you have promised to do. Do so, I recommend you;—your person and your honour will fare well therefrom."

The emperor himself endeavoured to move John Huss, and to justify himself; but from the very first words that he uttered, it was easy to perceive the secret trouble which agitated him. "Several persons," said he, "pretend that you were in prison a fortnight, when you obtained from me a safe-conduct. Nevertheless it is certain,—I allow it, and many are aware of the fact,—that this safe-conduct was granted before your departure from Prague. It guarantied you the liberty of explaining frankly before the council, as you have just done, your doctrines and your faith; and we have to thank the cardinals and the bishops for the indulgence with which they have heard you. But as we are assured, that it is not allowable for us to defend a man suspected of heresy, we give you the same advice as the Cardinal of Cambray. Submit yourself, therefore, and we shall take care that you shall withdraw in peace, after having undergone a moderate correction. Should you think fit to refuse, you will furnish the council with arms against yourself; and as to me, be certain, that I would sooner burn you with my own hands, than any longer put up with this stubbornness, which you have given too many proofs of. Our counsel, to you, therefore, is, that you unreservedly submit to the authority of the council."

"Magnanimous emperor," replied John Huss, "I shall first of all return thanks to your Majesty for the safe-conduct which you gave me——"

Dreading what was to follow such an exor-dium, John de Chlum interrupted his friend, and said, "Confine yourself to offering a justi-fication for the stubbornness of which the emperor accuses you."

Huss then repeated with mildness his usual defence, and said, "I did not come here, ex-cellent prince, with the intention of defending any thing with stubbornness. God is witness to the truth of what I assert. Let any thing better, or more holy than what I taught, be shown me, and I am perfectly ready to retract."

At these words, the soldiers led him out, and the sitting was at an end.

CHAPTER V.

CONTINUATION OF THE TRIAL OF JOHN HUSS.—THIRD AND LAST AUDIENCE.

In the third audience, John Huss had to reply, first of all, to a series of articles taken from his treatise *On the Church*. In this work, as in all his sermons, he protests that he is catholic; and his doctrine differs but little, as to dogma, from that of the Church of Rome. Six-and-twenty articles were produced before the council, as extracted from this book, and as being all stained with heresy or error. They may be classed under these two prncipal heads,—*predestination*, and *the power of the pope and the priesthood.**

Amongst these articles are several which offer precisely the same meaning, and they all may be reduced to the following propositions:

1°. *The predestinated, whatever fault they may fall into, nevertheless do not cease to be members of the Church of Christ, it not being possible for grace to be lost or fall away.*

2°. *No human election or any external dig-nity renders a man a member of the Holy Catho-lic Church.*

Huss replied to this point, that it was pre-destination and grace, and not any sensible mark, which rendered a man a veritable mem-ber of the Church. Judas Iscariot, although he received his election from Jesus Christ him-self, was not, however, his true disciple. He was, as St. Augustine remarked, a wolf in sheep's clothing. This was, according to Huss, what would be found in his book.

3°. *St. Peter neither was, nor is, the head of the Holy Catholic Church.*

Huss affirmed that he had simply declared, that the stone on which the Church is built is Jesus Christ himself, and that St. Peter had obtained the strengthening of it by faith.

4°. *The papal dignity owes its origin to the Roman Emperors.*

This article was denied altogether by John Huss, who declared that he had never con-sidered the institution of the pope as proceed-ing from the emperor, except with respect to external lustre and temporal possessions.

5°. *The power of the pope, as vicar of Jesus Christ, is null, if the pope does not act in con-formity with the lives of Jesus Christ and St. Peter, by his conduct and morals.*

Huss gave an explanation on this article, which was deemed satisfactory, by saying, that the power of such a pope is null, as to merit and reward, but not as to the office itself.

6°. *The pope is not most holy because he holds the place of St. Peter, but because he possesses great riches.*

Huss denied this article, affirming that what he said in his book, on the contrary, was this, that "the pope was not most holy because he held the place of St. Peter, and possessed great riches; but that if he imitated Jesus Christ in his meekness, his patience, his good works, and his charity, then was he holy."

7°. *No heretic, after being censured by the Church, ought to be abandoned to the secular arm, to be punished corporeally.*

8°. *The great personages of the world ought to oblige the priesthood to observe the law of Jesus Christ.*

9°. *If any man, who is excommunicated by the pope, should appeal to Jesus Christ, this ap-peal prevents the excommunication from being detrimental to him.*

---

* See in Note L, at the end of this volume, the complete list of the articles produced against John Huss, as extracted from his works.

John Huss denied that this article could be found in his book;—but he allowed that he had himself appealed from the pope to Jesus Christ.

10°. *A priest who lives according to the law of Jesus Christ ought to continue to preach, notwithstanding a pretended excommunication.*

This article Huss acknowledged, but he affirmed that he meant to allude to an unjust excommunication only.

11°. *The ecclesiastical censures, called fulminatory, which the clergy have invented to exalt themselves, and bring the people under subjection to them, are antichristian.*

This article was denied as to form, but acknowledged in substance.*

12°. *The people ought not to be laid under an interdict; because Jesus Christ, who is the sovereign Pontiff, did not lay the Jews under one, on account of the persecutions which he underwent himself.*

Such are the propositions which are contained in the six-and-twenty articles presented by the adversaries of Huss, as extracted from his treatise *On the Church.* Out of the whole number, Huss refused to acknowledge five, all relating to the power of the priests. He manifested indecision with respect to the cruel doctrine relating to heretics, and of which he saw himself on the point of experiencing the severity.† "The heretic," said he at last, "cannot be corporeally punished, until after he has been charitably instructed, by means of arguments drawn from Scripture."

While he was still speaking, one of his judges reproached him with having, in one of his works, compared the high priest and Pharisees, who delivered up Jesus to Pilate, to such persons as abandoned to the secular arm an unconvinced heretic. On this, a great tumult arose amongst the cardinals and bishops, who cried out: "Whom do you compare to the Pharisees?"

"Those," replied Huss, "who hand over an innocent man to the secular sword, as the scribes and Pharisees gave up Jesus Christ to Pilate."

"Truly," observed the Cardinal of Cambray, "they who extracted those articles showed great moderation: for there are in the writings of this man other matters far more horrible and detestable."

The assembly next proceeded to consider the articles of the book written by Huss, in reply to the attacks of Paletz. These articles, seven in number, were a recapitulation of the preceding ones, and in them was found the seeds of the doctrine of predestination. In one, he said, "The assembly of those predestinated, whether they be in a state of grace or not, alone constitutes the true Church of Christ." He said in another, "The grace of predestination is an indissoluble bond, by which the body of the Church, and each of its members, are united to the head."*

In his reply to Paletz, John Huss inveighed, in very forcible language, against the impious custom of giving the title of "most holy" to an unworthy pope; and he repeated with Wycliffe, what he had so often asserted: "If a pope, a bishop, or a prelate, be in mortal sin, he is neither pope, nor bishop, nor prelate." Huss invoked, in support of this assertion, the authority of the most illustrious fathers, St. Augustine, St. Jerome, St. Gregory, St. Cyprian, and St. Bernard, all of whom have declared that a man in mortal sin is not a Christian; and, much more, is neither pope nor bishop. "It was to guilty men like these," said John Huss, "that the prophet referred, when he said, 'They have reigned, but not by me; they have been princes, but I never knew them.' I have allowed, nevertheless, with the support of those great authorities, that although a wicked priest be an unworthy minister of the sacraments, God, however, baptizes, consecrates, and operates by his ministry. I will, however, go still farther, and declare, that a king in mortal sin is not worthily a king before God, as may be perceived by the divine judgment pronounced by Samuel on Saul: 'Since thou hast rejected the word of the Lord, the Lord hath rejected thee from being king over Israel.'"†

During this energetic reply, the emperor was conversing, in a low voice, in the embrasure of a window, with the Elector Palatine and the Burgrave of Nuremberg; and he was overheard to say, "There never was a more dangerous heretic." He called on Huss to repeat his last assertion;‡ and Huss having done so, with some restrictions, the emperor, by an effort, restrained himself, merely saying, "No person is exempt from sin."

Irritated at so much boldness, the Cardinal of Cambray exclaimed, "What! are you not satisfied with endeavouring to shake the whole

---

* Duas vocant in processibus suis *fulminationes.* Lenfant, whose quotations are, in general, so very exact, does not appear to have given the sense of this article with his habitual accuracy. *Hist. du Concile de Const.* vol. ii. p. 329.

† In the articles condemned by the doctors of Paris, Huss said: "According to the doctrine of Jesus Christ, heretics ought not to be punished with death." The doctors had condemned the article as scandalous and rash; and Gerson had signed the declaration.

* The opinion of Huss on predestination was that of a great number of orthodox theologians, and, amongst others, of Gerson.—(See Introduction, p. 24.)

† 1 Samuel xv. 26.

‡ Von der Hardt, vol. iv. p. 321.

Church with your doctrine, but you must also attack kings ?"

Paletz joined the cardinal in his censures; and after explaining the words of Samuel to Saul, he said, "A pope can be truly a pope, and a king truly a king, and yet not be a Christian."

"If John XXIII. was a true pope," retorted John Huss, "why have you deposed him ?"

Six articles, extracted from a treatise addressed by John Huss to his old master, Znoïma, were next produced. Huss acknowledged five of them,—all treating, like the greater number of the preceding ones, of the authority of the pope; and it would seem, that in them this question, then so embarrassing for the greatest enemies of the popedom, and which Huss himself had so much difficulty to decide, is presented in a clearer and more precise point of view. The principal inculpated articles declare, "1°. That there is no necessity for the Church militant always to possess a single visible head, who shall direct spiritual matters.* 2°. The apostles and faithful ministers of Jesus Christ have very well governed the Church, in all matters necessary to salvation, before the office of pope was introduced; and they could do so until the day of judgment, if there was no pope in existence. 3°. In fine, Jesus Christ is alone the head of the whole Church, and he will govern it uninterruptedly, until the day of judgment, by vivifying it by his Spirit. The Church subsisted without a head, and lived in the grace of Jesus Christ from the time of *Agnes*,† for a space of two years and five months. Could it not remain so for a longer time? Jesus Christ would govern it better by his true disciples, who are scattered through the world, than by such monstrous heads as these."

Huss himself repeated these latter words; and whilst he spoke, the fathers shook their heads disdainfully, and a voice cried out, "Do you hear him? He is acting the prophet!"

"Yes," replied he, with animation, "I affirm that the Church was much better governed in the time of the apostles than it is at present. And what is there to prevent Jesus Christ from governing it still by his true disciples, without these monstrous chiefs? But why do I ask the question? The Church is, at this present moment, without a visible head; and yet Jesus Christ does not cease to govern it."

The reading of the articles, and of the depositaries in support of them, being concluded,* the Cardinal of Cambray addressed John Huss:—"You have heard how many atrocious crimes you are accused of. Reflect now, and make your choice—if you submit, with humility, to the judgment and decision of the council, we shall act towards you with humanity, particularly on account of the most gracious emperor here present, and of the King of Bohemia, his brother; but if, contrary to the feeling of so many wise and illustrious men, you determine to defend some of the articles which have just been read, you will do it at your own great peril."

Huss having replied, in a submissive tone, that he only asked to be instructed, the cardinal added—"The council requires three things;—first, that you humbly confess that you have erred in all the articles that have been here laid to your charge;—next, that you swear never to teach them more;—and, lastly, that you abjure them publicly."

Several other members sided with the cardinal, and exhorted Huss to comply with what was demanded. He thus replied:—"I repeat to you that I am ready to receive, with submission, the instructions of the council. But in the name of Him who is the God of all of us in common, I pray and conjure you not to constrain me to do what my conscience forbids me,—what I cannot do but at the peril of my eternal salvation; do not force me to abjure all those articles brought against me. I have read, in the Catholic doctrine, that to abjure, is to renounce errors which one has entertained. As I have never either admitted or taught several of those articles, how can I conscientiously abjure them? But as to those which I have acknowledged and avowed, if any one can teach me better doctrine, I will most readily do what you require from me,"

These dignified and touching words were not comprehended by the assembly. The emperor replied:—"What can you fear in abjuring all these articles? For my part, I have no hesitation in disavowing all kinds of errors; but does it follow that I have entertained them?"

"Excellent prince," replied Huss, "to *disavow* is not the same thing as to *abjure*."

"You shall have submitted to you," said the Cardinal of Florence, "a form of abjuration easy to sanction. Will you obey?"

John Huss repeated what he had previously answered.

---

* Huss, in reply to this article, pretended that, when the pope was a simonist and a reprobate, the only true spiritual head of the Church was Jesus Christ.

† Pope Joan. See note M, at the end of the volume.

* Huss was not accused of having authorized the administration of the Eucharist to the laity under the two kinds; for, as has been stated, he had left Prague when Jacobel, his disciple, maintained that this mode of communion was the only one in conformity with the example of Christ; and the letter, dated from Constance, in which John Huss approved of what Jacobel did, had not been yet made public.—(Book iii. chap. i.)

"You are old enough to see what is right," said the emperor; "and you ought to comprehend me when I tell you, that if you are wise, you will submit to all that is required from you:—if not, you will be sentenced according to the law of the council."

"That law is clear enough," said an aged bishop of Poland; "it is the law which inflicts the punishment due to heresy."

John Huss, for the third time, replied as he had done before.

A priest then rose up and said :—"John Huss ought not to be permitted to retract his opinions; for his oath cannot be trusted, he having himself declared, when writing to his friends: 'If my tongue swore, my heart would take no oath.' "

"That is false—is altogether calumnious"—rejoined Huss; "and I protest solemnly, that my conscience does not reproach me with any error."[*]

Paletz returned to the charge, and accused John Huss anew of having publicly given his approbation to several of Wycliffe's doctrines, and then he denounced him for having pronounced the funeral eulogium of certain rioters, who had been decapitated during the troubles at Prague.

Huss did not deny this double accusation. Paletz then again rose up and cried out—"I call God to witness, in presence of the emperor and the sacred council, that I have said nothing here through hatred to John Huss, nor through any malevolent feeling, and that I have not set myself up as the adversary of so many errors, but through zeal for the Catholic Church.

Michael Causis repeated the same oath.

The inflexible resistance of John Huss had irritated the emperor, who besides admitted, to its fullest extent, the doctrine of the Church with respect to heretics :—anger and superstition stifled the cry of his conscience. "You have heard," said he, addressing the assembly, "the errors which this man has taught—many of which are crimes deserving of the severest punishment. My opinion, therefore, is, that, unless he abjures every one of them, he ought to be burned to death. . . . . If any of his followers should happen to be at Constance, they also ought to be severely put down, and chiefly, amongst them all, his disciple Jerome."

"Yes, yes," cried several voices: "the master being punished, the pupil will be found more tractable !"

With these words, the assembly broke up, and John Huss was conducted back to prison.

When he arrived there, he could scarcely stand, so much was he overcome with illness and the fatigue of so lengthened an examination. The trusty John de Chlum followed him, to give him encouragement. "Oh !" said John Huss, in alluding to this circumstance, in one of his letters, " what a consolation was it to me, in the midst of my trials, to see that excellent nobleman, John de Chlum, stretch forth the hand to me, miserable heretic, languishing in chains, and already condemned by every one."[*]

CHAPTER VI.

FIRMNESS OF JOHN HUSS.—LAST INTERVIEW.

A FORM of retractation had been drawn up by order of the council, and was sent the next day to John Huss by Cardinal de Viviers, the president. It was couched in the following terms :—"I, John Huss, in addition to the protestations which I have made, and all of which I adhere to, do hereby protest anew, that although several things are imputed to me which I never thought of, I submit myself with all humility to the merciful orders and correction of the sacred council, touching all things that have been objected or imputed to me, or drawn from my books, or, in fine, proved by the depositions of witnesses—in order to abjure, revoke, and retract them, and to undergo the merciful penance imposed by the council ; and, generally to do all that its goodness shall judge necessary for my salvation, recommending myself to its pity with an entire submission."[†]

The character of John Huss then displayed itself openly in its most admirable point of view ; and the distinction to be drawn between him and others who had been condemned as great heretics is altogether to his praise. Several had died before him in defence of new doctrines and dogmas which they had themselves brought before the world, and perhaps the stimulus of self-love had contri-

---

* Theob. Bel. Hus. chap. xviii.; Von der Hardt, vol. iv. p. 326,327.

* Epist. xxxii.
† Oper. Hus. vol. i. p. 70; Von der Hardt, vol. iv. p. 329.

buted to their remaining firm. But John Huss had not proclaimed any new dogma—it was, in general, much more respecting the abuse of certain doctrines than relative to the doctrines themselves, that he adduced the authority of the Scriptures in opposition to that of the Church; and, in this respect too, he had been preceded by Wycliffe. He had explained, like the Roman Church, the doctrine of the Eucharist, and had modified, in a manner deemed satisfactory, his opinion relative to the spiritual power of bad priests. His self-love, therefore, had no interest in his firm persistance; and it was evident that he offered himself to death for the truth, such as it was understood by his reason. He strove, therefore, from the purest motives; and, in his struggle, he towered aloft and became remarkable in the eyes of his contemporaries, and of posterity, by the unalterable firmness of his soul; and what contributed most to his strength also constituted his glory. "I cannot sign this form," said he; "first, because I am called on to condemn, as impious, several propositions which I hold to be true; and, next, because I should thereby cause a scandal to the people of God, to whom I have taught those truths."

A man, supposed by some to be Cardinal de Viviers,* and by others, with better reason, to be a Polish doctor, named John Cardinal, a friend of Huss, strongly urged him to abjure, as was required.† Huss replied to him:

"If Eleazar, who was a man of the old law, would never consent to affirm, contrary to the truth, that he had eaten of the forbidden meat, through a fear of offending God and of giving a bad example to posterity, ought I, a priest of the new law, although an unworthy one, through fear of a temporary punishment, to transgress the law of God by so great a sin as perjury? Most certainly I should far prefer being put to death:—and as I have appealed to Jesus Christ, the almighty Judge, I shall abide by his sentence, well persuaded that he will not decide either on false testimony, or according to councils subject to error, but according to the truth."‡

Huss persevered to the end in the same sentiments, never affirming that his writings were exempt from error, but refusing to acknowledge with his lips any to be blameable before he had felt it to be so in his conscience.

Alarmed at the impression that would be produced in Bohemia, in Germany, and, indeed, throughout Europe, by the capital punishment of so celebrated a man, and whose holy life presented such a contrast with that of the greater number of his judges, the cardinals and bishops spared no effort to obtain a retractation from his mouth. "The council," remarked several of them, "is the supreme arbiter in cases of conscience; and if the act which it demands is a perjury, it alone will be responsible in the sight of God."

John Huss was quite willing to allow that the council was sovereign judge in points of right; but he maintained that it was not so also in points of fact. He declared that the author of a book ought to know, better than any one, if he had taught or not, and published in his work, the doctrines which were imputed to him. He defended, against the council, precisely the same cause that was supported three centuries later in France by men as remarkable for their knowledge as their virtues;* and, like them, he also failed. The council, like the pope, pretended to be infallible in fact, as well as in right; and one of the members, an inflexible doctor, seeking to persuade John Huss to comply, carried the rigour of his principles in this respect to such a point, as to make use of the following strange argument. "Even supposing," said he, "that the council were to affirm that you had only one eye, when you have in reality two, you would be obliged to agree with it in its assertion."†

"As long as God shall preserve my reason," replied John Huss, "I shall take good care not to say any such thing;—no, not if the whole universe should endeavour to force me to it."

From this period, he had no other thought than to prepare for death, and to mitigate, for his friends, the bitterness of the cruel separation that was about to take place, by fortifying their confidence and hope in God. In a letter which he wrote to his faithful disciples in

---

* Luther is of this number.
† See, on this subject, Lenfant, *Conc. de Const.* vol. i. p. 343, &c.
‡ Epist. xxxix.

* The persons here alluded to are the Jansenists, who were persecuted in the seventeenth and eighteenth centuries, by the Jesuits. Jansen had been at first professor of theology at Louvain, and was appointed Bishop of Ypres in 1635, where he died in 1638. He was an able writer, and published several works on the Scriptures; but that which made most noise was his *Augustinus*, in which he endeavoured to develop St. Augustine's opinions on grace. This work gave birth to the greatest difference of opinion among Catholic theologians; and Urban VIII. proscribed it in 1642. The chief residence of the Jansenists was Port-Royal, which, under D'Arnauld, Sacy, Nicole, Semaistre, and others, became so celebrated as a place of education. The Jesuits had sufficient credit to get it closed in 1656; and it was eventually razed to the ground by Louis XIV. in 1709. The followers of Jansen had refused to acknowledge that five propositions, condemned by the pope, had been taken from the bishop's work. This quarrel was extremely bitter, and lasted for nearly a century.—*Note of Translator.*
† *Huss. Hist. et Monum.* vol. i.

Bohemia, he thus expressed himself: "Beloved, I conjure you to obey God, to glorify his holy Word, to adhere constantly to the truth of Him of whom I have spoken to you in my writings and my oral instructions. I pray you, that if any one of you has heard a word fall from me which appears contrary to the truth, he may at once reject it. I beseech whatever person may have observed any levity in my words or acts, not to imitate me in that, but to pray God to pardon me. I conjure you to love and respect all priests who live a moral life, and to honour, in particular, those who suffer for the love of God. I pray you to offer thanks to the worthy barons of Bohemia, Moravia, and Poland, who came forward as the defenders of the truth in my case, and who struggled courageously against the whole council for my deliverance, and particularly to Wenceslaus Duba and John de Chlum. Believe whatever they shall tell you of me. I write this letter in my prison and with my fettered hand, expecting my sentence of death to-morrow, but with a full and entire confidence that God will not abandon me;—that he will not permit me to outrage his holy truth, by confessing what false witnesses have wickedly alleged against me. When, with the assistance of Jesus Christ, we shall again meet in the delicious peace of the future life, you will learn how merciful God has shown himself towards me, how effectually he has supported me in the midst of my temptations and trials. I know nothing of Jerome, my faithful and well-beloved disciple, unless that he too is held in cruel chains, awaiting death like me, on account of his faith. Alas! it is by our own countrymen, by natives of Bohemia, our implacable adversaries, that we have been both delivered into the hands of our enemies: I ask for them your prayers. Remain, I conjure you, attached to my chapel of Bethlehem, and use all your endeavours to have the gospel preached there as long as God will permit it. Love ye one another. Never turn any one aside from the divine truth; and watch that the good be not oppressed with violence."[*]

It is evident, from this letter, and many others, that this man, who astonished and baffled the great council by his firmness, united to the intrepidity of a heroic heart all the tenderness of a Christian and affectionate disposition. No remembrance struck on his heart more bitterly than that of his friendship having been betrayed; and to strengthen himself against this recollection, in another of his letters he called to mind the prediction of our Saviour: "And the brother shall deliver up the brother to death, and the father the child,. and the children shall rise up against their parents, and cause them to be put to death. .... "Alas!" said he, "the wounds which we receive from those persons in whom our soul had placed its hope, are the most cruel: for, to the sufferings of the body are joined the pangs of betrayed friendship. In my case, it is from Paletz that my most profound affliction proceeds."[*]

The poignancy of such a grief must be experienced, in order to comprehend fully to what a point John Huss carried his forgiveness of injuries, and his humility. Many others have, when dying, pardoned their enemies. Huss is perhaps the only person that. ever chose out, for the purpose of giving him absolution before God, the very man to whom he had himself to forgive so much before the world. "Paletz," said he, "is my greatest adversary: it is to him that I wish to confess myself."[†] This request was refused, and the bishops sent him a monk, whom he speaks well of, and who, after having given him absolution, recommended him to submit, but. without absolutely commanding it.[‡]

Paletz, when applied to, had refused: he had recoiled from the painful task which Huss's humility had imposed on him. He was, however, vanquished by such greatness of soul, and he determined to visit his victim.. When Huss saw him, he addressed him in a mild and melancholy tone. "Paletz," said he, "I uttered some expressions before the council, that were calculated to offend you— Pardon me!"

Paletz was much affected, and he himself supplicated Huss to abjure.

"I conjure you," said he, "do not look to the shame of a retractation, but only to the good that must result from it."

"Is not the opprobrium of the condemnation and of the punishment," replied John Huss, "greater in the eyes of men than that of the abjuration? How then can you suppose that it is a false shame which prevents me? But, I put the question to yourself—if errors were falsely imputed to you, what would be your course? Would you abjure them?"

"That would, certainly, be hard to do!" replied Paletz; and he shed tears.

"Is it possible," rejoined Huss, "that you, who are now in this state before me, could have said in full council, when pointing to me, ‘That man does not believe in God?'"

Paletz denied it. "You said so, however," repeated Huss; and, in addition, you declared that, ‘since the birth of Jesus Christ, there

<hr>

* J. Huss. Hist. et Monum. vol. i. Epist. x. p. 77.

* Epist. xlvi. Paletz had been the friend and disciple of Huss. See p. 40.
† Epist. xxxi.   ‡ Ibid.

never was seen a more dangerous heretic.' Ah! Paletz, Paletz, why have you wrought me so much ill?"

Paletz replied, by again exhorting him to submit; and he then withdrew, weeping bitterly.[*]

Amongst all those who exerted themselves to obtain a retractation from John Huss, none showed more anxiety than the emperor. When his first burst of passion had passed away, and particularly when he had got beyond the precincts of the council, which exhorted him to act severely, and of which he shared, in a certain degree, the superstitious intolerance, he turned his thoughts inwards, and bethought him that John Huss had come to the council on his word and safeguard. He feared, in delivering him up to the flames, not only the secret reproaches of his conscience, but also the cry of the indignant population. If, on the contrary, he should shield him with his protection, after having abandoned him to his judges, and should save him from punishment, after having permitted him to be condemned, he saw that he should raise up against himself the whole council, whose will, both his narrow prejudices and his title of defender of the Church ordered him to execute. The abjuration of John Huss could alone free the emperor from the difficulty; and therefore, to obtain it, he spared neither prayers, nor persuasion, nor threats. All were in vain;—his efforts only inspired John Huss with a melancholy pity. "Place not your confidence in the princes of the earth!"[†] wrote he to his Bohemian friends; and, on another occasion, he said—"Truly did they say that Sigismund would himself deliver me up to my adversaries;—he has done more, he has condemned me before them. . . ."

John Huss, by his firmness, forced the emperor to undergo the disgraceful consequences of the violation of his faith, and had vengeance on him, so to speak, in taking from him the power to rescue him from the funeral pile.

It is worthy of remark—and it is not one of the least striking proofs of the justice of Huss's cause—that, at the very time that his enemies, as if alarmed at their triumph, were calling on him to live, by escaping from the sentence which they had pronounced against him, his friends were exhorting him to persevere to the end, and die. The emperor, in the hope that their wishes would coincide with his own, prayed John de Chlum and Wenceslaus Duba to accompany four bishops, whom he had charged with the task of persuading John Huss to submit. He thought it more than probable that Huss would listen to their representations. They repaired to the refectory of the Franciscans, where Huss was brought before them. John de Chlum first addressed him.

"Dear master," said he, "I am not a learned man, and I deem myself unable to aid you by my counsels; you must, therefore, decide yourself on the course which you have to adopt, and determine whether you are guilty or not of those crimes of which the council accuses you. If you are convinced of your error, have no hesitation—be not ashamed to yield. But if, in your conscience, you feel yourself to be innocent, beware, by calumniating yourself, of committing perjury in the sight of God, and of leaving the path of truth through any apprehension of death."

Huss was much affected, and replied with a flood of tears. "Generous lord!"—said he —"O my noble friend!—I call the Almighty God to witness, that, if I was aware of having taught or written any thing contrary to the law or orthodox doctrine of the Church, I would retract with the utmost readiness; and, even at this present time, I desire most vehemently to be better instructed in sacred literature. If, therefore, any one will teach me a better doctrine than I have inculcated myself, let him do it—I am ready to hear him; and, abandoning my own, I will fervently embrace the other."

"Do you, then, believe yourself," said one of the bishops, "to be wiser than the whole council?"

"I conjure you, in the name of the all-powerful God," replied John Huss, "to give me as my instructor in the Divine Word the least person in the council, and I will subscribe to what he says, and in such a manner as that the council will be satisfied."

"See," said the bishops, "how stubborn he is in his heresy!"

They withdrew; and John Huss was, by their orders, again consigned to his dungeon.[*]

John de Chlum, from this time forth, never ceased exhorting and consoling his friend; and Huss expressed a desire that he would extend his devotedness to the point of witnessing his death.

"O thou, the kindest and most faithful friend," said he, "may God grant thee a fitting recompense! I conjure thee to grant me still this—not to depart until thou has seen every thing consummated. Would to God that I could be at once led to the stake before thy face, rather than be worn away in prison, as I am, by perfidious manœuvres! I still have hope—I still have confidence—that Almighty God will previously snatch me from their hands to himself, through the merits of his saints. Salute all our friends for me; and let them pray to the Lord that I may await my death with humility and without murmuring."[†]

[*] J. Hus. Epist. xxx. xxxi. xxxii.   [†] Epist. xxxiii.   [*] Theobald, Bel. Hus. c. xvi.   [†] Epist. xxxv.

CHAPTER VII.

JOHN HUSS TAKES LEAVE OF HIS FRIENDS.—HIS CONDEMNATION.—HIS DEATH.

THE day on which judgment was to be passed was approaching, and John Huss remained inflexible in his resolution to die, rather than lie to his conscience. It was in such sentiments that he wrote these lines to one of his friends:—"My last resolution is to refuse to acknowledge as erroneous the articles which have been truly extracted from my work, and to abjure those which have been falsely attributed to me. I detest and condemn all false interpretation, which may happen to be given to the former, contrary to my intention. I submit to the correction of our Divine Master, and I put my trust in his infinite mercy."[*]

"To justify myself," said he, in another of his writings, "I recall to my memory the great number of holy men, of the old and new covenant, who have undergone martyrdom rather than transgress the law; and I, who for so many years have preached up patience and constancy under trials—I, to fall into perjury! —I, so shamefully to scandalize the people of God! Far, far from me be the thought! The Lord Jesus will be my succour and my recompense."[†]

In some of his letters to his friends, he pours out, in most affectionate terms, his feelings of gratitude for their kindness—he bids them farewell in the most affecting manner— and addresses them with exhortations to live piously, and watch over their own safety. "May God be with you!" is his letter of adieu to his noble protectors; "may he grant you all imaginable felicity for the kindnesses with which you have loaded me. Do not permit the Lord John de Chlum—that loyal knight—my dearest and best friend—my other self—to expose himself to danger through love for me. I conjure you to live according to the word of God, and to obey His precepts, as I have instructed you. Return thanks from me to his Majesty the King,[‡] for all the benefits I have received from him.[§]

He wrote to the priest Martin, his disciple, saying:—"Fear not to die, if thou desirest to live with Christ; for he has himself said, 'Fear not them that kill the body, but who cannot kill the soul.'" And yet Huss gave to his friend this rare counsel, as remarkable for prudence as for modesty:—"Should they seek

after thee, on account of thy adhesion to my doctrines, make them this reply: 'I believe that my master was a good Christian; but as to what regards his writings and his instructions, I have neither read all nor comprehend all.'"[*]

Huss in his adieus showed no respect of persons, but remembered his most obscure disciples, and evinced as much gratitude and feeling for their friendship as for that of the most illustrious personages. In his last letter to Martin the priest, he says, "I recommend to thee my very dear brethren. Thou wilt salute Peter, with his wife and family, and all who belong to the church of Bethlehem; Catherine, that holy maiden; Maurice Volzer; and all the friends of the truth. . . . . . . Let all those who have, or shall have, any of my books in their possession, be prudent. . . . . . . Salute all my beloved brethren in Christ, the doctors, the public scribes, the cordwainers, and others: recommend them to be zealous for the love of Christ, to advance with humility in wisdom, and not to indulge in comments of their own making, but to recur to those of the saints. . . . . "

Huss bequeathed some legacies to his most intimate friends: he prayed them to pay some debts of his; and the details into which he entered on this point sufficiently contradict the reproaches of those who accused him of being rich.[†] The esteem with which he looked, to the last, on the books of Wycliffe, may be proved by the bequests which he made of some of them to one of his most devoted friends, Peter the notary, to whom also he left a sum of money. "It is not," said he, "that I pretend to recompense in this way thy lovely and unalterable love for the truth—the various services which thou hast rendered to me—and the consolations which thou hast lavished on me in my difficulties. May God be thy great recompense for all these things, for I have nothing to offer thee that is worthy of them."[‡]

Huss pardoned all his enemies, of whom the most inveterate was Michael Causis. He wrote to his friends thus, on June 23:— "Michael has been several times in my prison, and said to my keepers, 'With the grace of God, we shall soon burn this heretic.' Learn that I have no wish for vengeance—I leave

---

[*] Epist. xx.
[†] Hist. et Monum. J. Hus. Epist. xli. p. 50.
[‡] The King of Bohemia.   [§] Epist. xxiv.

[*] Epist. iii.   [†] Epist. xxix.   [‡] Ibid.

him to God, and pray for this man most affectionately."

But, notwithstanding his courage, John Huss was human, and did not always feel himself weaned from life, and intrepid in looking at death. "Certainly," wrote he, in this same letter, "it is a difficult matter to rejoice, as says the apostle St. James,[*] in the midst of trials, and look on them as so many subjects of rejoicing. He, who was the most patient and the most intrepid, although knowing that he should rise again on the third day—should vanquish his enemies by his death—and should redeem the elect—even He was troubled in spirit after the last supper, and his words were, *My soul is exceeding sorrowful, even unto death.* And an angel strengthened him in his agony, and a sweat, as it were great drops of blood, flowed down from his body.

"O divine Jesus! draw us, then, to thyself! Feeble as we are, if thou drawest us not, we cannot follow in thy steps. Strengthen my spirit, that it may be ready and determined. The flesh is weak: let thy Spirit prevent, assist, and accompany me! For without thee we can do nothing, and are incapable of braving for thy name a cruel death. . . . . Written in chains, the eve of the day of St. John the Baptist, who died in prison for having condemned the iniquity of the wicked.[†]

"JOHN HUSS,

"In hope, the servant of JESUS CHRIST."

In another letter, written nearly at the same period, he resumes all his confidence and courage. After having anew enumerated the holy men of the Old Testament, who were miraculously delivered by the Lord, he says, "And I, also, wretched that I am, if that could contribute to his glory, to the advantage of believers and my own good, could be also delivered by the Lord from chains and death. The power of Him who freed from prison, by an angel, St. Peter, when ready to die at Jerusalem, and who caused the chains to fall from his hands, is not diminished. But the will of the Lord be done! May it be accomplished in me for His glory and for my sins!" And farther on he cried, like the Psalmist,[‡]—"The LORD is my light and my salvation; whom shall I fear? The LORD is the strength of my life; of whom shall I be afraid."[§]

John Huss remained for thirty days in prison, after having publicly replied to his judges; and it was on July 6 that he appeared for the last time before the council, in the fifteenth general session, in order to hear his sentence pronounced.

The Cardinal de Viviers presided; the emperor and all the princes of the empire were present; and an immense crowd had assembled from all quarters to view this sad spectacle. Mass was being celebrated when Huss arrived; and he was kept outside until it was over, lest the holy mysteries should be profaned by the presence of so great a heretic. A high table had been erected in the midst of the church, and on it were placed sacerdotal habits with which John Huss was to be invested, in order to be stripped of them afterwards. He was directed to seat himself in front of this table on a footstool, elevated enough to allow him to be seen by every one. On taking his seat, he made a long prayer in a low voice; and, whilst he was employed in this self-communion, the Bishop of Lodi ascended the pulpit. This prelate, who acted as official preacher of the council, and whose language was virulent and declamatory, seized, with equal eagerness, on all occasions of rejoicing or mourning to display his eloquence. On the day in question, he took for text this passage of St. Paul—*That the body of sin might be destroyed.[*]*

His sermon was so violent against the schism and its authors, that, at first, one could imagine that he aimed at having the antipopes burned, and not John Huss. He concluded, however, with these words, addressed to Sigismund:—"Destroy heresies and errors, and, above all," pointing to John Huss, "this obstinate heretic. It is a holy work, glorious prince, that which is reserved to you to accomplish—you, to whom the authority of justice is given. Smite, then, such great enemies of the faith, in order that your praises may proceed from the mouth of children, and that your glory may be eternal. May Jesus Christ, for ever blessed, deign to accord you this favour!"[†]

Immediately after the sermon, a bishop read the decree, by which the counsel demanded silence:—and nothing testifies more strongly than this the omnipotence which the council arrogated to itself, and the humiliation in which the kings and the emperor were held in its presence. This decree is thus worded:—"The holy Council of Constance, lawfully assembled by the influence of the Holy Spirit, decrees and orders every one, with whatever dignity he may be invested, whether imperial, royal, or episcopal, to abstain, during the present session, from all language, murmur, and noise, which may trouble the assembly, convoked with the inspiration of God; and this, under pain of incurring excommunication, and imprisonment of two months, and to be declared an abettor of heresy."[‡]

---

[*] Rom. vi. 6.
[†] *Hist. et Monum, J. Hus.* vol. i. p. 34.
[‡] Macs. Brunsw. Lips. et Goth. Von der Hardt, vol. iv. p. 400.

---

[*] St. James i. 2.   [†] Epist. xxx.
[‡] Psalm xxvii. 1.   [§] Epist. xxxii

This decree having been read, Henry Piron, the proctor of the council, rose up and demanded, in its name, the condemnation of John Huss and of his writings.

The council had first sixty articles of Wycliffe, extracted from the books already condemned, read aloud; and it condemned them afresh. It then proceeded to the works of John Huss, and thirty articles were gone through which had not been previously read in public, but several of which were a mere repetition of those on which he had been already interrogated.

Huss wished to reply to each separately; but the Cardinal of Cambray ordered him to be silent, declaring that he could reply, at the end, to all of them together. Huss represented to him that so great an effort of memory was absolutely impossible, and was proceeding to enforce his request to be allowed to speak on each article as it arose, when the Cardinal of Florence stood up, and exclaiming, "You are stunning us!" gave orders to the ushers of the council to seize him, and force him to keep silence. Then John Huss, with a loud voice, and his hands raised to heaven, cried out, "In the name of the Almighty God, I conjure you to afford me an equitable hearing, that I may clear myself before all whom I see around me from the reproach of these errors. Grant me this favour, and then do with me what you will!"

He was a second time prevented from speaking; and, finding that he was not to be permitted to repel so many accusations, he kneeled down, and, raising his hands and eyes to heaven, recommended his cause to the Sovereign Judge of the universe.

After the reading of the articles had been gone through, the depositions of witnesses were proceeded to, and these were designated by their titles and qualities, and not by their names. The accusation previously brought against him, relative to his doctrine on the administration of the sacrament, was again adduced, although he had victoriously refuted it, and had been pronounced orthodox on the point. He was also accused, amongst other absurd charges, of having given himself out as the fourth person of the Trinity. This accusation was supported by the testimony of a doctor, whose name was not given. John Huss replied by repeating aloud the Athanasian creed.

His appeal to Jesus Christ was also again laid to his charge as a heavy crime. He, however, repeated it, and maintained that it was a just and proper proceeding, and founded upon the example of Jesus Christ himself. "Behold!" cried he, with his hands joined together and raised to heaven, "behold, O most kind Jesus, how thy council condemns what thou hast both ordered and practised; when, being borne down by thy enemies, thou deliveredst up thy cause into the hands of God, thy Father, leaving us this example, that we might ourselves have recourse to the judgment of God, the most righteous Judge, against oppression. Yes," continued he, turning towards the assembly, "I have maintained, and I still uphold, that it is impossible to appeal more safely than to Jesus Christ, because He cannot be either corrupted by presents, or deceived by false witnesses, or overreached by any artifice." When they accused him of having treated with contempt the excommunication of the pope, he observed: "I did not despise it; but as I did not consider him legitimate, I continued the duties of my priesthood. I sent my procurators to Rome, where they were thrown into prison, ill treated, and driven out. It is on that account that I determined, of my own free will, to appear before this council, under the public protection and faith of the emperor here present."

John Huss, in pronouncing these last words, looked steadfastly at Sigismund, and a deep blush at once mounted to the imperial brow.[*]

Huss's refusal to abjure having been publicly repeated before the council, two sentences were pronounced, one of which condemned all his writings to be publicly burned; and the other devoted him to degradation from his sacred office, as a true and manifest heretic, proved guilty of having publicly taught errors which had been long condemned by the Church of God—of having advanced several things that were scandalous, rash, and offensive to pious ears, to the great opprobrium of the Divine majesty, and to the detriment of the Catholic faith;—in fine, of having stubbornly persisted in scandalizing Christians by his appeal to Jesus Christ as to a sovereign Judge, in contempt of the Apostolic See, and of the censures and the keys of the Church.

During the reading of the sentence, Huss, who was listening very attentively, exclaimed against it several times, and, in particular, repelled the accusation of stubbornness. "I have always desired," said he, "and am still most anxious to be better instructed by the Scriptures. I declare that my zeal for the truth is such, that if, by a single word, I could overturn all the errors of heretics, there is no peril

---

[*] The remembrance of this circumstance was long preserved in Germany, and was not without influence in the ensuing century, in the success of the Reformation commenced by Luther; for when, at the celebrated Diet of Worms, the enemies of that great man pressed Charles V. to have him seized, in contempt of the safe-conduct which he had given him—"No," replied the emperor, "I should not like to blush like Sigismund."

that I would not encounter for such a result."
He then fell on his knees, and said, "Lord
Jesus, pardon my enemies! Thou knowest
that they have falsely accused me, and that
they have had recourse to false testimony and
vile calumnies against me;—pardon them from
thy infinite mercy!"

This prayer produced feelings of indignation in some of the members of the council,
and called forth mockery in others, particularly amongst the heads of the assembly.

Then commenced the afflicting ceremony of
degradation. The bishops clothed John Huss
in sacerdotal habits, and placed the chalice in
his hand, as if he was about to celebrate mass.
He said, in taking the alb: "Our Lord Jesus
Christ was covered with a white robe, by way
of insult, when Herod had him conducted before Pilate." Being thus clad, the prelates
again exhorted him to retract, for his salvation
and his honour; but he declared aloud, turning towards the people, that he should take
good care not to scandalize and lead astray believers by a hypocritical abjuration. "How
could I," said he, "after having done so,
raise my face to heaven! With what eye
could I support the looks of that crowd of men
whom I have instructed, should it come to pass,
through my fault, that those same things which
are now regarded by them as certainties, should
become matters of doubt—if, by my example,
I caused confusion and trouble in so many
souls, so many consciences, which I have
filled with the pure doctrine of Christ's gospel,
and which I have strengthened against the
snares of the devil? No! no! It shall never
be said that I preferred the safety of this miserable body, now destined to death, to their
eternal salvation!"*

The bishops then made him descend from
his seat, and took the chalice out of his hand,
saying: "O accursed Judas! who, having
abandoned the counsels of peace, have taken
part in that of the Jews, we take from you this
cup filled with the blood of Jesus Christ!"

"I hope, by the mercy of God," replied
John Huss, "that this very day I shall drink
of his cup in his own kingdom; and in one
hundred years, you shall answer before God
and before me!"†

His habits were then taken off, one after the
other, and on each of them the bishops pronounced some maledictions. When, last of
all, it was necessary to efface the marks of the

tonsure, a dispute arose amongst them whether
a razor or scissors ought to be employed.
"See," said John Huss, turning towards the
emperor, "though they are all equally cruel,
yet can they not agree on the manner of exercising their cruelty."

They placed on his head a sort of crown or
pyramidal mitre, on which were painted frightful figures of demons, with this inscription,
"THE ARCH-HERETIC," and when he was thus
arrayed, the prelates devoted his soul to the
devils.* John Huss, however, recommended
his spirit to God, and said aloud: "I wear
with joy this crown of opprobrium, for the love
of Him who bore a crown of thorns."

The Church then gave up all claim to him,
—declared him a layman—and, as such, delivered him over to the secular power, to conduct him to the place of punishment. John
Huss, by the order of Sigismund, was given
up by the Elector Palatine, vicar of the empire,
to the chief magistrate of Constance, who, in
his turn, abandoned him to the officers of
justice. He walked between four town-ser-
jeants to the place of execution. The princes
followed, with an escort of eight hundred men,
strongly armed, and the concourse of the people was so prodigious, that a bridge was very
near breaking down under the multitude. In
passing by the episcopal palace, Huss beheld
a great fire consuming his books, and he
smiled at the sight.

The place of punishment was a meadow
adjoining the gardens of the city, outside the
gate of Gotleben. On arriving there, Huss
kneeled down and recited some of the peni-
tential psalms. Several of the people, hearing
him pray with fervour, said aloud: "We are
ignorant of this man's crime; but he offers up
to God most excellent prayers."

When he was in front of the pile of wood,
which was to consume his body, he was recommended to confess his sins. Huss consented, and a priest was brought to him, a man
of great learning and high reputation.† The
priest refused to hear him, unless he avowed
his errors, and retracted. "A heretic," he
observed, "could neither give nor receive the
sacraments." Huss replied: "I do not feel
myself to be guilty of any mortal sin, and now
that I am on the point of appearing before God,
I will not purchase absolution by a perjury."

When he wished to address the crowd in
German, the Elector Palatine opposed it, and
ordered him to be forthwith burned. "Lord
Jesus!" cried John Huss, "I shall endeavour

---

* J. Hus. Hist. et Monum. vol. i. p. 36.
† This prophecy was noted down on a celebrated
medal, struck in Bohemia in 1415, immediately
after John Huss's death, and the period of which is
guarantied by many authors, and amongst others,
by M. Bizot, author of Histoire Metallique de
Hollande. Luther came a century after John
Huss.

* Animam tuam diabolis commendamus. (Theob.
Bell. Huss. p. 42.)
† This priest's name was Ulrich Schorand.
(Reichental, Concil. Constant. p. 206.)

to endure, with humility, this frightful death, which I am awarded for thy holy gospel,—pardon all my enemies." Whilst he was praying thus, with his eyes raised up to heaven, the paper crown fell off: he smiled, but the soldiers replaced it on his head, in order, as they declared, that he might be burned with the devils whom he had obeyed.

Having obtained permission to speak to his keepers, he thanked them for the good treatment he had received at their hands. "My brethren," said he, "learn that I firmly believe in my Saviour: it is in his name that I suffer, and this very day shall I go and reign with him !" His body was then bound with thongs, with which he was firmly tied to a stake, driven deep into the ground. When he was so affixed, some persons objected to his face being turned to the east, saying that this ought not to be, since he was a heretic. He was then untied and bound again to the stake with his face to the west. His head was held close to the wood by a chain smeared with soot, and the view of which inspired him with pious reflections on the ignominy of our Saviour's sufferings.

Fagots were then arranged about and under his feet, and around him was piled up a quantity of wood and straw. When all these preparations were completed, the Elector Palatine, accompanied by Count d'Oppenheim, marshal of the empire, came up to him, and for the last time recommended him to retract. But he, looking up to heaven, said with a loud voice: "I call God to witness, that I have never either taught or written what those false witnesses have laid to my charge,—my sermons, my books, my writings, have all been done with the sole view of rescuing souls from the tyranny of sin; and therefore, most joyfully will I confirm with my blood that truth which I have taught, written, and preached;—and which is confirmed by the divine law and the holy Fathers."

The elector and the marshal then withdrew, and fire was set to the pile ! "Jesus, Son of the living God," cried John Huss, "have pity on me !" He prayed and sung a hymn in the midst of his torments, but soon after, the wind having risen, his voice was drowned by the roaring of the flames. He was perceived for some time longer moving his head and lips, and as if still praying,—and then he gave up the spirit. His habits were burned with him, and the executioners tore in pieces the remains of his body and threw them back into the funeral pile, until the fire had absolutely consumed every thing; the ashes were then collected together and thrown into the Rhine.*

Thus perished, at the age of five-and-forty, one of the men whose character throws most honour on the Christian church; and it is not easy to discern, at the first glance, the real causes of his death. The following words were found in an old manuscript copy of his works : "*As long as John Huss merely declaimed against the vices of the seculars, every one said that he was inspired with the Spirit of God; but as soon as he proceeded against ecclesiastics, he became an object of odium, for he then really laid his finger on the sore.*" Yet many others had, before his time, come forward with impunity against the abuses of the Church,—against the vices of the pope and the clergy : and to be convinced of this fact, all that is necessary, is to peruse the writings of his contemporaries, of Peter D'Ailly, Clemangis, Gerson, and a crowd of other priests and doctors revered by the Church. In their treatises, and even in the sermons which several of them delivered in presence of the council, there will be found a crowd of expressions fully as violent and as offensive as any of those which fell from John Huss. In the language of the most catholic among them, the Roman Church is openly designated as a hole of iniquity; and the pope is said to be as wicked as antichrist. John Huss, besides, fully admitted the dogmas of the Roman Church; and as he was already in prison when Jacobel gave the communion under the two kinds to the laity at Prague, the approbation which he gave to this practice, as being established on the authority of the Scriptures and of tradition, was not known to the council until after his death. When interrogated on transubstantiation and the Trinity, he replied according to the Catholic formula: and on the other points of belief, such as the sacraments, the confession, the intercession of saints, the adoration of images, works, purgatory, and tradition, the replies of Huss to the council, as well as his letters and writings, prove that he did not secede from the opinions received in the Church. As to his doctrine touching the absence of the spiritual character in bad priests,—a doctrine so long obscure in his own mind,—he finished by giving it a catholic explanation, declaring that, in the ministry of an impious priest, God operates worthily and efficaciously by unworthy hands : and, finally, with respect to indulgences, he did not refuse to the pope the

* All the details that are here given, relative to the trial and death of John Huss, are faithfully extracted from the Brunswick, Leipsic, and Gotha

manuscripts, collected by Von der Hardt; from the *History of Huss's Life*, published by an eye-witness, and inserted at the beginning of his works ; and from the *Histoire des Hussites* of Theobald. They were never contradicted by any of his contemporaries, and the pious intrepidity of the martyr is attested by the Catholic writers, Eneas Sylvius Piccolomini, Reichental, and John Cochlaeus. —See note N.

power to grant them;[*] he merely denied that they were of any value, when given for improper purposes. He refused to acknowledge, as his, some propositions attributed to him by the council: and as to those which he avowed, he modified the strongest of them in such a manner, that they possessed, with respect to faith, but a very secondary importance. John Huss, in a word, as we have already declared, did not attack the Catholic doctrines in themselves, but in their extreme consequences,—not in the principle, but in the abuse,—and in that he did not want imitators amongst the most celebrated Romanists.

In presence of these facts, the question is asked, with an astonishment mingled with terror, what could have induced the council to employ so much severity towards a man of the purest life, alike estimable for his knowledge and his piety? Two causes may be assigned—each of which excited against him in the highest degree the hatred and implacable resentment of the priests. In the first place, John Huss, like Wycliffe, beheld the source of the excesses of the clergy in their riches: he assigned to the secular power the right of enforcing a good employment of the property of the Church, or of taking it away altogether from such ecclesiastics as made an unworthy use of it;—this gave a mortal blow to the priesthood in their external influence, in their temporal authority. In the second place, though he professed himself obedient to the council, he affixed a condition to his submission;—he insisted that the voice of his conscience should approve of what the council ordained. Huss desired ardently to be convinced of his errors, in order to abjure them: but, in order that he should acknowledge them, it was not sufficient that the council pointed them out: for he refused, in point of fact, to avow himself guilty of any erroneous article imputed to him, if, in the tribunal of his conscience, he did not feel that it was justly attributed to his doctrine.[†] As to the right

of the matter, before he admitted that any proposition was heretical or false, he required to have its falsehood demonstrated by Scripture. This was to recognise in the divine word, interpreted by private judgment, an authority superior to the decisions of the Church,—it was to attack the clergy in their spiritual authority. It is in this respect, above all—or rather, indeed, altogether—that John Huss is connected with the communions separated from the Roman Church. His doctrine on this last named point is the common root of the dissenting sects—the bond which connects them together, though without many of them being aware of it. Strange destiny of Huss! Most curious problem! In his way of thinking, all separation from the old trunk of the Church is a heresy worthy of hell; and yet the separated churches reckon him, with pride, amongst their martyrs! He protests his devotedness for the Roman Church, even unto death; and that Church condemns him to death! It is here that the situation proves stronger than the individual, and the consequences of a first act carry inevitably to the end, which his eyes do not yet distinguish, and far beyond the limits within which his will retains him. So true is it, that between the two grand families of Christendom, the real and only question is this: "Who is to interpret the law of God? Who is at last to deduce from it the rules of faith—of life? Is it the priesthood or the conscience?" John Huss considered himself a Catholic, and yet he appealed from the Church to his conscience and to God! He was a Protestant without knowing it. The Church condemned in his person, not the heretical consequences of the right of examination, but the right itself: and the flames of his funeral pile instructed Europe in the information, that the appeal to the conscience was henceforward placed in the rank of heresies.[*]

---

[*] Nec etiam est intentionis meæ potestati datæ a Deo Romano Pontifici resistere.—(*J. Huss. Hist. et Monum. Disput. adv. indulg. papal.*)

[†] The witnesses who attributed to him the propositions which he denied he was the author of, were neither confronted with him, nor even named.—See on this subject Lenfant, *Hist. du Concile de Constance,* vol. i. p. 413, and the following.

[*] Note O.

CHAPTER VIII

THE AFFAIR OF JOHN PETIT.—GERSON ACCUSED OF HERESY.

WE read, in a manuscript history of the Council of Constance, that the day after the execution of John Huss, the following writing was affixed to the doors of all the churches in the city: *The Holy Ghost to the believers of Constance, greeting: Pay attention to your affairs; As to us, being occupied elsewhere, we cannot remain any longer in the midst of you.—Adieu.**

The severe opinion expressed in these lines, found but few to echo it at Constance, and the sacerdotal spirit had so completely taken the place of the evangelical one in the religious world, that the most violent and cruel means of constraint excited no horror in the minds of those who did not entertain the condemned doctrines.[†]

The very different opinion entertained in the present day by the most part of Christians, as to the employment of fire and sword to bring souls under subjection, is not the least convincing proof of the progress of Divine truth; and if the good faith of the judges in the frightful drama of Constance be an excuse for their conduct, it is also a strong condemnation of the spirit of their time. The counsel seriously believed, that the human sacrifice which it had accomplished would draw down on their labours the divine blessing; and, in consequence, it ordered, on the occasion, solemn processions. Yet, in the very same session in which John Huss was condemned, the assembly, which pretended to receive its inspirations from the Holy Ghost only, gave a remarkable proof of the facility with which it yielded to other influences.

It has been seen,[‡] that amongst the great affairs submitted to the council, was the too celebrated apology of the murder of the Duke of Orleans by the Duke of Burgundy. This justification of the murder of his own brother, was admitted or rejected by the feeble Charles VI., according as the faction of Burgundy was triumphant or vanquished at Paris. The Orleans party having had the advantage in 1412,

the University of Paris condemned seven propositions, faithfully extracted by its chancellor, Gerson, from the pleadings of John Petit. The king, in consequence, ordered Gerard de Montaigne, Bishop of Paris, and John Polet, inquisitor of the faith in France, to join with themselves such a number of doctors of the university as they might think advisable, to examine these propositions, and give judgment on them. In this way was established the celebrated assembly, called the *Council of the Faith,* and which opened its sittings at the episcopal palace, on November 30, 1413.

Its proceedings were pursued with vigour and justice; all the manuscripts of John Petit's pleadings that it could procure were compared with the seven propositions already extracted and condemned. The author was dead, but the assembly received the testimony of two of his secretaries, who declared that they had written the work under his dictation. The grand majority of the doctors decided that thirty-seven propositions, just as dangerous as the first seven, could be extracted from the apology. They, however, reduced them to nine, comprised under the three following heads:

1°.—It is lawful for any subject, according to moral, natural, and divine laws, to kill, without any order, every tyrant that, by witchcraft or malice, hatches evil against the corporeal safety and power of the king, his sovereign lord.

2°.—The king ought to recompense him who kills the aforesaid tyrant, by riches, honour, and love, after the example of the remunerations accorded to St. Michael, the archangel, for expelling Lucifer from Paradise, and to the noble Phinehas for the cutting off of Zimri.

3°.—In case of covenant, promise, or oath, no matter of what description, made from one knight to another, should the enagement turn to the prejudice of one of the parties so pledged, he is not obliged to guard it. The letter kills, but the spirit vivifies.*

These propositions, and the apology from which they were extracted, were condemned to be publicly burned; which was duly executed, and the king ordered the parliaments of the kingdom to inscribe the sentence in their registers.

---

* MS. See Lenfant, *Histoire du Concile de Constance,* book iii.

† There is, however, shown in the choir of the church at Constance, a monument, with which an affecting tradition is connected:—it is the tomb of an English bishop, who, it is said, died of grief at witnessing the death of John Huss.—*Rev. Suisse,* 1839.

‡ Page 54.

* See the nine propositions in note P.

The Duke of Burgundy appealed to the Apostolic See, and three cardinals—of Florence, of Aquileia, and Des Ursius—were appointed by John XXIII. to examine into the affair. They quashed the sentence of the Bishop of Paris. Charles VI., on his side, desired to have it confirmed at Constance, where he named, for his own ambassadors, two bishops and several doctors, amongst whom the most illustrious was John Gerson, the Chancellor of the University of Paris. Jean-sans-Peur also had himself represented at Constance; and two persons were particularly noted in the defence of his cause—Martin Poreus, Bishop of Arras, whose zeal for the doctrines of John Petit had procured him his bishopric; and Peter Cauchon; who became afterwards too celebrated, for his own misfortune and that of France, as Bishop of Beauvais and judge of Joan of Arc, and whose defence at Constance, of an execrable murder, served as a fitting prelude to the most frightful of judicial assassinations. The reaction of the factions, which still agitated France, thus made itself felt in the council, where the dispute between Burgundy and Orleans was brought forward under a new and vivid aspect. But there the influence of the powerful personages, who carried on this great struggle elsewhere by the sword, was also perceptible; and the votes of the council on this question exhibited less the injustice or the equity of John Petit's cause, than the influence of the house of Burgundy in Europe. The grand culprit himself, under pretext of hunting, had come into the neighbourhood of Constance, whilst the English were already invading the kingdom. Jean-sans-Peur had taken up his residence under a tent in the great forest of Argilly, in order, he remarked, that he might hear the stags belling by night,* but really to watch the proceedings of the council, and hold a check over his adversaries by coming near them.

Amongst the latter, Gerson set the example to all. This great affair had become, in a measure, a personal matter to him, and he therefore pursued, with extraordinary energy, the condemnation of John Petit's doctrines. And it was not merely because he was the king's servant and ambassador at the council that he acted so; for he was, on the contrary, invested with that dignity because, from the very beginning, these guilty doctrines had raised in his soul indignation and horror, and because he had, at the earliest moment, denounced to the king, to France, and to Europe, the apology of the murder as more dangerous than the murder itself. Every consideration faded away in his mind before the sense of

duty; and he was not turned away from what he conceived was his path of action, even by the strongest obligation to noble minds—the feeling of gratitude.* This sense of uprightness, and this masculine firmness, actuated him in all his acts; and his greatest anxiety at Constance was to be consistent with himself.

Gerson, besides, since the execution of John Huss, had to render a severe account to God and his conscience. The ardent desire to found the authority of the Church on the infallibility of councils, the horror which he entertained of heresy, the universal prejudices of the age, which caused the punishment of a heretic to be regarded as an act of piety,—all had contributed to arm Gerson against John Huss. Nature had, however, formed their souls worthy of each other, and sometimes when the passions of the theologian were at rest—where an inflexible logic was less listened to, the sad image of Huss at the stake— of the victim pardoning his executioners, and offering up prayers to Heaven in the midst of the flame,—presented itself to his judge.

It is impossible that this dismal vision could have found Gerson always equally firm— equally insensible; and no doubt he was occasionally agitated by poignant reminiscences. At those moments he must have examined his conscience most searchingly; and if he found himself actuated by other interests than those of religion and duty,—if he perceived that he was guilty of some weakness,—if, in fine, he could have employed less zeal, in other circumstances, against the crime of puissant personages, than he had exhibited against the heresy of John Huss, the judgment of the latter must have fallen on his heart with all the weight of remorse.

This melancholy state of mind—this internal conflict between an inflexible sense of duty and praiseworthy regrets, was often displayed in the course of the stormy discussions which followed. The placid style of him who wrote the tender pages of *De parvulis ad Christum trahendis*, became bitter and virulent: the passionate expressions which he employed, betrayed his internal agitation; and several

* Lefebvre de Saint-Remy.

* "After God, I owe every thing to the Duke of Burgundy," said Gerson, when speaking of Philip II., the father of Jean-sans-Peur. Therefore, nothing could equal the affliction which Gerson experienced at the crimes committed by his benefactor's son. What, then, was to be his conduct relative to the apology of this crime? Religion, morality, and society, were on one side, and on the other, a powerful prince, who seemed protected by gratitude and fear. The chancellor remained faithful to public morality, and determined to prosecute, at his risks and perils, and with all his power, the homicidal doctrines promulgated in the name of the Duke of Burgundy.—(Prosper Faugères, *Eloge de J. Gerson*.)

times, in beholding the failure of his efforts against certain mistaken or dangerous men, he cried out, in the bitterness of his soul,—"John Huss was less guilty."[*]

The council at first appeared favourable to the wishes of the king and the University of Paris. Martin Poreus, the Bishop of Arras, Peter Cauchon, and the other deputies of the Duke of Burgundy, exerted themselves, in every possible way, to get the cause considered altogether unconnected with the faith. "It was nothing more," they said, "than a simple question of morality; and religion had no connection with it." The council, at the commencement, did not agree in that opinion.

In consequence of the heresies and new doctrines that were springing up on every side, a commission of twelve members had been named, under the titles of *Commission of the Faith* and *Reformatory College*, to examine into all causes relating to faith, morals, and the reformation of the Church, and to judge them, subject to the definitive sentence of the council. Some time after, when Gerson had applied to have John Petit's doctrine condemned, and the sentence of the Bishop of Paris confirmed, two of the three cardinals to whom the affair had been previously submitted—the Cardinal des Ursius and the Cardinal of Aquileia —were added to the Commission of the Faith,[†] which act was to confound this cause with those having faith for their object. The French influence then predominated; and although Gerson, at the most violent part of the discussion, had never pronounced a direct accusation against the Duke of Burgundy, his early benefactor, yet the party which he acted for aimed at nothing less than bringing that prince before the council as a heretic.

But this state of things was of short duration: the advance through France of Henry V. King of England, the ally of Jean-sans-Peur— the bribery of the latter—the constantly increasing anarchy of the kingdom—and, finally, the sanguinary and disastrous battle of Agincourt, modified, not the spirit of the doctrines that were incriminated, but the dispositions of the judges. The council refused to implicate in the matter the powerful Duke of Burgundy, or any of his partisans; it did not even venture to pronounce the name of his apologist, John Petit; it merely condemned, in general terms, the principal proposition of the apology, conceived in these terms:—*It is allowable, and even meritorious, in any casual or subject, to kill a tyrant, by ambuscade or otherwise, notwithstanding all promises or treaties sworn to with him, and without waiting for the sentence and order of any judge.*

The council declared this doctrine to be heretical, scandalous, and seditious, and that it could only tend to authorize lies, treachery, imposture, and perjury.

This sentence eluded the question, instead of deciding it; and although the general proposition was, in the eyes of the council, the summary of the doctrine professed by John Petit, still his partisans—the favourers of the Duke of Burgundy—could deny that it was so; and deny it they did. The Apology itself escaped all condemnation; and the sentence of the Bishop of Paris was broken and of no avail. According to this sentence, if it were forbidden to kill a man without a judgment being passed on him—without a legal mission —in the circumstances stated by the sentence of the council, it did not follow that it was prohibited to commit murder in the cases defined by John Petit. This consequence, which was clearly deducible from the conduct of the council, was monstrous, unheard-of, and yet just. A conclusion so dangerous and disastrous, revolted all honourable minds, and filled that of Gerson, in particular, with indignation and grief. "The council," he unceasingly remarked, "had two weights and measures. It had condemned Wycliffe and John Huss for errors far less grave, and less subversive of social order. What will the world think and say ? what supposition will the princes form ? Every one will say, that the errors of Huss were condemned because they were contrary to the interests of the priesthood, and that those of John Petit were respected, because they were only prejudicial to the secular body and kings."[*]

No human power, not even that which he represented, could move Gerson. "The University of Paris, maltreated by the bishops, or gained over by the Duke of Burgundy, turned its coat," said Stephen Paquier;[†] but in vain did it disavow its chancellor, and demand his recall; in vain did the king, reconciled with the murderers, give orders to suspend the proceedings. With Gerson, the voice of insulted justice, morality, and religion, was far stronger than all—or, rather, he heard nothing else. He pursued his ungrateful task, and devoted himself to it with all the immovable determination, which a profound sentiment of a duty, fulfilled towards God and men, always produces.

* For every thing relating to the affair of John Petit in the Council of Constance, see the third part of the fifth volume of Gerson's Works, collected by Dupin.

† The third, the Cardinal of Florence, was already a member.

* Additur hic quod principes dicere possent Joannem Hussum et errores suos fuisse damnatos quia erunt contra prælatos et clerum ; sed demittunt istos Joannis Parvi quia sunt contra principes et seculares.

† *Recherches de la France*, edition of 1633, p. 353.

His adversaries were devoid neither of talent nor shrewdness; and the most dangerous of them were Martin Poreus, Bishop of Arras, and a Franciscan friar, named John de Rocha, doctor in theology of the University of Toulouse, an old comrade and a grand partisan of John Petit.

Martin Poreus said, "The nine propositions, attributed by Gerson to John Petit, are probable, and are not false. Besides these nine propositions have been improperly deduced from the eight propositions of the Apology, which are all true, as may be proved by comparing them: Gerson, therefore, has garbled and falsified the Apology, to make the author say what he never had any idea of saying.* If John Petit's propositions were false, it would follow, that, in a case of imminent danger, it would be necessary to refrain from killing a murderer; and yet if it be an evil to kill a man, it is much worse to allow one's sovereign to be murdered.† Finally, if these propositions are condemned, war will be resumed between the King of France and the Duke of Burgundy."

Martin Poreus and John de Rocha next brought forward, against the sentence of the Bishop of Paris, a series of objections, each of which involved a grave theological question. "The propositions of John Petit," they declared, "were quite distinct from matters of faith; and if they belonged to it, the Bishop of Paris was not the person to condemn them—he had encroached, in doing so, on the rights of the Apostolic See and of the council. If bishops imagined that they possessed the right of deciding in matters of faith, what one might have approved of, another would condemn, and thence would arise schisms and heresies,—the articles of faith would be multiplied without end, and the Christian religion would be charged with a new and insupportable yoke. It was a heresy to command persons to believe, as an article of faith, what was not really one, and what had not been decided to be so by the Church. Every article, which had not been condemned by the Church, was held as doubtful, and ought to be referred to the Apostolic See." This deplorable discussion thus exposed fully to view one of the most feeble—most vulnerable points of the Church. The bishops, the doctors, all allowed it the right—which it made use of without measure—of judging and condemning in every matter relating to faith; but they could neither come to an understanding on what was within the jurisdiction of the faith, nor on the authority, which in the Church was proper to judge them.

To the objection of his adversaries, Gerson opposed excellent, if not victorious reasons; and in that he was strongly seconded by Peter d'Ailly, the Cardinal of Cambray, his friend and former master. D'Ailly, a member of the Commission of the Faith, had been refused by the Bishop of Arras, and, from being judge, had become one of the parties in the suit. He published a strong memorial, in which he maintained that each of the propositions of the Apology ought to be condemned, as well as the general one; and he brought forward in favour of that opinion the two commandments, "*Thou shalt not kill: and thou shalt not swear falsely;*"* and the verse from the Bible, in which it is said, "*But if a man come presumptuously on his neighbour and slay him with guile, thou shalt take him from mine altar, that he may die.*"† D'Ailly also brought forward against Martin Poreus two passages of St. Augustine (in which that doctor declares to be a homicide, whoever kills any one by his private authority, were it even a poisoner, or a robber, or a heretic), and a formal decree of the Council of Lyons against assassins. He declared, finally, that the doctrine of John Petit merited condemnation infinitely more than the proposition of Wycliffe, which asserts, that if princes fall into error, their subjects may reprehend and correct them.‡

Gerson, in a close piece of argumentation, took up in detail, one after the other, all the arguments of Martin Poreus and of Rocha. "Even they," he said, "who regard the propositions of the Apology as probable, could not help declaring them to be rash; and a probability could not authorize a murder. Let it not be said that their condemnation would trouble the recent peace between the King of France and the Duke of Burgundy. What tranquillity, what peace, could be hoped for, if such maxims were spread abroad with impunity? It was false and heretical to maintain that morals did not belong to the faith; for the Church had condemned, as so many heresies, several propositions purely relating to morals, extracted from the works of Wycliffe and John Huss. Besides," continued Gerson, "every proposition contained in Scripture belonged to the faith; and to maintain the contrary was an error." As to the objection that the universities and the bishops had not right to condemn, with respect to faith, doctrines which had not been condemned by the Church, Gerson re-

---

* John Huss maintained the same thing with respect to the extracts taken from Wycliffe's works and his own.

† Gers. Oper. *Acta in Concil. Constant. circ. damnat. propos. Joan. Parvi,* vol. v. p. 403.

* Exodus xx. 13; Levit. xix. 12.

† Exodus xxi. 14.

‡ Gers. Oper. *Acta in Concil. Constant. circ. damnat. propos. Joan. Parvi,* vol. v. p. 481.

K

plied, that the council had decided the contrary, by approving of the condemnations passed in England and Bohemia. If it were not permitted to diocesans to pronounce in matters of faith, it would follow, amongst other inconveniences, that the mendicant monks would be masters of every thing, because at the court of Rome they were both judge and party. Should the objection be made that bishops could err, might it not be replied, that the pope himself might err; and had not the present council sufficiently proved the fact![*]

More ample details cannot be given here; it is sufficient to add, that Gerson, in the meetings of the nations, and in several general sessions, engaged in four-and-twenty public discussions on the same subject. He appeared each day in the breach with new energy; and he would, beyond a doubt, have triumphed, had he had only his antagonists to conquer, had he not had to combat in the council against the most formidable auxiliaries of their eloquence—the cupidity which the secret bribes of the Duke of Burgundy kept on the alert, and the apprehension inspired by his power.

The deputies of the prince, having only Gerson and D'Ailly to dread, did not hesitate to employ every possible means to ruin them: and at last they had recourse to that which was most abused in those days—they accused them both of *heresy*. Gerson, the most Christian doctor, the light and soul of the council,—D'Ailly, surnamed the Eagle of France, and the harrower of heretics, accused of heresy!—seriously denounced and prosecuted at Constance in that same council which had hitherto been by their eyes and spoken by their mouth! This ought to appear incredible; yet so it was: and no stronger argument than this fact can be adduced against this execrable rage, which is often found to exist amongst Christians, to persecute and condemn each other for mere words,—to heap curses each on his neighbour for vain speculative opinions, totally unconnected with all laws of morality, and deduced not from the *ensemble* of a doctrine, but from certain scattered or mutilated fragments of speeches or writings.

It does not appear, from the historical documents of the council, that the accusation against D'Ailly was carried any further: the Roman purple, with which he was invested, placed him out of the reach of his enemies. The proceedings against Gerson were more serious, since he was obliged to defend himself before the Commissioners of the Faith. The Bishop of Arras and John de Rocha presented against

him five-and-twenty charges, all drawn from some extracts of his numerous treatises.

The principal ones are the following:—

1°. *Neither the pope, nor any other person, ought to pretend that the canons of positive right, or the other canonical traditions, are observed everywhere, and by the whole Church.*

This proposition was held to be erroneous, as tending to prevent Christians from obeying the pope, and to discredit the statutes and traditions of the Church.

2°. *Should any one, in passion, or through fear of death, deny with his mouth any truth of the faith, and should not be inclined or able sufficiently to purge himself from this offence, he does not cease to remain a believer.*[*]

"A man is catholic," said Gerson, "when he guards the faith in his understanding." "A most dangerous maxim," retorted John de Rocha, "inasmuch as it tended to encourage hypocrisy and apostasy."

3°. *Jesus Christ, who is the Spouse of the Church, cannot be taken away from it and from his children, in such a way as that the Church should rest in a single woman.*[†]

This proposition was judged rash, erroneous, scandalous, and contrary to faith and piety; because it was piously believed, that during the days of our Saviour's passion, the Church subsisted in the Virgin Mary alone.

4°. *The retrenchment of a single member of the Church affects it with a grievous imperfection.*

A false and scandalous proposition, they said, because the Church every day lost several members by their own obstinacy and impenitence, without its losing any of its beauty.

5°. *Were an angel of God to descend from heaven and announce to the author of these assertions any thing contrary to his opinion, he would not believe him; and, what is more, he would not believe God himself in such a case.*

Gerson maintained that he had spoken, not of what was opposed to an opinion, but to the catholic faith in general; and he referred in his defence to the Epistle of St. Paul to the Galatians.[‡] John de Rocha asserted that there were both temerity and blasphemy in this proposition: St. Paul, besides, only spoke of an angel from heaven, and not of God.[§]

6°. *If John Huss had had certain advocates, he would not have been condemned.*

This proposition, Gerson remarked, ought not to be taken in a literal sense, but John de Rocha replied that it was most insulting to the council; for, were its wisdom admitted, it was

---

[*] Gers. Oper. *Acta in Concile Constant. circ. damnat. propos. Joan. Parvi,* vol. v. p. 403.

[*] Gers. Oper. vol. v. p. 453.
[†] Gerson, *De Auferibilitate,* vol. ii. p. 212, 213.
—Gerson says the contrary in his treatise, *De Mod. de uniendi ac reform. Eccles.* vol. ii. p. 189.
[‡] Gal. i. 9.   [§] J. Gerson, vol. v. pp. 443—449.

impossible that John Huss could escape in any way.

What an example for the age, for the council, for Gerson himself! What a lesson for all, to behold this great man, reputed one of the shining lights of the Church, prosecuted like him whom he himself not long since attacked and condemned, and having recourse to the same means to escape from his adversaries!

His position, however, in other respects, was in every way different, as he incurred no serious danger in a council composed of so many of his friends and admirers. The proceedings instituted against him were directed, less with a view to ruin him, than to shake his credit, and he felt, with respect to his enemies, besides the certitude of his innocence, the conviction of his strength.

The high and dignified position in which he stood, dictated to Gerson his line of defence, and in some noble words which he uttered, there appeared more of disdain for such accusations, than of eagerness to repel them. "Notwithstanding that I possess ample means," said he, " to reply to calumny, I should consider it a shame for me, who am but dust and ashes, if, like Jesus Christ, the Master of us all, I did not pass over the personal insults directed against me, to occupy myself with those relating to God and the faith. I have determined, besides, not to stop and discuss the facts. I shall let this holy council judge of itself on what side is the truth, and the falsehood. To take the pains of refuting all that is false—to give bite for bite—is a brutal, frivolous, and insane struggle, unworthy of Christian gravity."[*]

Gerson came out of the discussion victoriously: but, if before the world he had gained his cause on this point, in his secret soul he felt himself already vanquished on another, of almost equal importance in his eyes. The authority of general councils was, in his opinion, the anchor of salvation, of Catholicity: he had devoted his talents, his strength, his life, to get it recognised as the first of the powers of the Church,—as the only one that was infallible—and in the affair which he had most at heart, in which he appeared as the representative of the King of France, he had seen the influence of virtue and truth—the inspiration from above—at first balanced, and then smothered by mundane and degrading influences, and in the bitterness of grief he was forced to exclaim, " *I would rather have Jews and Pagans for judges in matters of faith, than the deputies of the council!*"

This cry of indignation from a mind inflexible in its love of justice, was, however, rash and ill-advised in his case, as it was immediately seized on by his enemies, and brought forward against him as the last charge.

He was, as we have said, the victor in this personal conflict; but could he have deceived himself as to the nature of the victory? Must not his strong common sense have told him that this result was owing more to the place at which the council was convoked, than to its infallibility: and that, though he was absolved at Constance, he should have been condemned at Rome?

CHAPTER IX.

JOURNEY OF THE EMPEROR.—BENEDICT XIII.—CAPITULATION OF NARBONNE.

THE principal object of the council—the extinction of the schism—was not yet attained. John XXIII. had subscribed to his deposition, and Gregory XII. had abdicated; but the inflexible Benedict XIII. was not yet under submission. His jurisdiction still comprehended several kingdoms—Aragon, Castile, Navarre, Scotland, and the counties of Foix and Armagnac. As he had resisted all the persuasions made to him by Christendom to resign the tiara, when worn by several, it was not probable that he would give it up of his own accord when he found that it was only on his own brow. It was evident that all the efforts of the council for the union of the Church would end in nothing, if it elected another pope before it had dispossessed Benedict.

As all hope of a voluntary abdication seemed desperate, it was deemed necessary to employ coercive measures, and to persuade the kings under his jurisdiction to consent to them. One man alone, from the ascendency which his high rank and character gave him, was qualified to undertake this task with success: that person was the emperor; and he devoted himself to the wishes of the council with heart and soul. He immediately announced, with great form, that he was about to set out, to confer on matters relative to the peace of the Church, with the most powerful prince of those who supported Benedict XIII.—with Ferdinand IV., King of Aragon.

The decree which the council issued in its seventeenth general session, for the safety of

---

* *Éloge de Gerson,* Faugères, p. 37.

the emperor during his journey, was, with good reason, looked on as strongly invasive of the rights of the sovereigns.* "*The Sacred Council threatens with excommunication, and with the deprivation, IPSO FACTO, of their dignities, whether secular or ecclesiastic, whoever—whether king or prince, bishop or cardinal—shall, in any manner, impede the journey of the emperor or his suite.*" It was difficult to put forward, in fewer words, more lofty pretensions; and it was impossible, whilst the deepest interest was manifested for the first of the temporal sovereigns, more effectually to brave the rest.

The council next decreed a solemn mass and procession every Sabbath, during the emperor's absence, for the fortunate issue of his journey. It accorded one hundred days' indulgence to all who should attend those devotional exercises, and forty to every one who should, each day, say a *pater* and an *ave* for the same purpose. The emperor, before setting out, appointed the Elector Palatine to be the protector of the council during his absence; and finally, on July 14, 1415, he left the city with great pomp, in the midst of public prayers and wishes.†

He found, at the appointed place of meeting, neither the King of Aragon nor Benedict—the first was dangerously ill; the second could not make up his mind to come; and let himself be long waited for. He at last arrived, escorted with soldiers carrying halberds and swords, and with a troop of cavalry; less formidable, however, from this external force with which he had surrounded himself, than from that which was within himself. Nature appeared to have conspired against the union of the Church, in giving this little old man, so mean and delicate in appearance, a vigour such as was rarely found in all the fire of youth. He collected an unextinguishable ardour from the possession of power, and wearied out, by his indefatigable power of speaking, all who attempted to persuade him. It is said that he spoke, on one occasion, seven hours consecutively, without the slightest alteration being perceptible in his voice or appearance. He would consent, he said, to yield; but on conditions which could not possibly be complied with. He stipulated that "the Council of Pisa should be declared null; the Council of Constance be dissolved, and a third convoked in a city chosen by himself." He required, besides, that, "before proceeding to a new election, his own should be recognised." Then, suddenly changing his tone, he declared, that "he was the true

pope; and that, in order to terminate the schism, all that was necessary was to recognise him. A new election would renew the schism; and he could not, in conscience, abandon the boat that God had confided to his care. The older he was, the more he was bound to do his duty, and resist the tempest. If, nevertheless, another pope were necessary, he alone could elect him, because, having remained the only one of all the cardinals promoted before the schism, he was also the only one whose promotion was incontestable."*

It was in vain that the kings, the ambassadors, and deputies of the council employed every means to induce him to yield on the same terms as Gregory had done. Threats had no better effects on him than entreaties; but seeing that, after both had been ineffectually used, recourse was about to be had to other and stronger measures, Benedict secretly quitted Perpignan, and shut himself up in the fort of Collioura, a few miles distant, on the sea-shore. He was immediately pursued thither; and almost all his galleys having been destroyed, to prevent his fleeing farther, he received in this place a fresh summons to yield, from the council and the kings.

Up to this period, the King of Aragon, if Thierry de Niem's account is to be believed, had secretly encouraged Benedict XIII. in his resistance;† but, without doubt, supposing that he could not any longer support him in this conjuncture, he joined the other princes and nobles under Benedict's jurisdiction, in their endeavours to constrain him.

Already the most of the cardinals of this pontiff had abandoned him, the princes were now falling off, yet he still remained true to himself. Finding that he was near being forced in Collioura, he ordered the ambassadors of the King of Aragon to be introduced; and after having heard their summons, he said, "Gentlemen, you are welcome. I have listened attentively to what you have said. I am going to Saint-Mathein, where I shall deliberate, and I will send an answer to the king who has sent you."

He embarked in a galley, with only four cardinals, who had remained faithful to him, passed the night in the harbour, and the next morning, at sunrise, set all the sail he could for Peniscola.‡ There, thinking himself in security, as being far distant from the emperor, and on the territory of Spain, he ceased to feign; and on his receiving a last summons

* Maimbourg, *Histoire du Grand Schisme*, second part, p. 247.
† Magnâ cum pompâ. inter preces et vota. Von der Hardt, vol. iv. p. 582.

* Ex Msc. Vindob. et Al. ap. Von der Hardt, vol. ii. part xviii.
† Theod. Niem, *Vita Joh. XXIII.* ap. Von der Hardt, vol. ii. p. 429.
‡ Letter of François de Conzié, Archbishop of Narbonne, to the Cardinals of Ostea, Cambray, St. Marc, Chalons, and Saluces.

from the Kings of Aragon, Castile, and Navarre, he sent a clear and bold reply. " He could not, in conscience," he said, " recognise the Council of Constance, because it had been convoked in a city dependent on the emperor. It was equally impossible for him to accept another council composed of the cardinals of Gregory XII. and John XXIII., because that would be to join schismatics with Catholics, to the grand scandal of the Church; and, for these reasons, to yield up the pontificate would be to offend God. He protested strongly against any measures adopted against him, under pretext of extirpating the schism; and he addressed himself to the King of Aragon in particular, reminding him that he held his status from him, as pope—that he was his feudatory, and would not, he was convinced, become a rebel." Benedict declared, besides, that "he was exceedingly anxious to have the union of the Church effected : This," he said, "he proved by convoking a council for the month of February following; and he conjured Ferdinand, in the bowels of compassion of God, not to prevent the prelates from being present at it." He terminated by inveighing, in strong terms, against Gerson, who had accused him of having maintained some propositions which were not very orthodox. He protested his inviolable attachment to the faith of the Church, and submitted himself to its judgment.*

To reply in this strain, was to presume on the patience and docility of the kings; and they forthwith drew up the articles of a treaty of union, and despatched them to the emperor at Narbonne.

These articles were the basis of the celebrated Capitulation of Narbonne, by which the kings, nobles, cardinals, and prelates, under the jurisdiction of Benedict XIII., made their submission. The emperor and the council, in convoking them to Constance, refrained, through regard for them, from giving the name of General Council to the assembly held in that city, before the adhesion of the Spaniards. The principal clauses of the capitulation declared, 1°. That the emperor and the prelates of Constance would respect the interest of the kings, prelates, and others, under the jurisdiction of Benedict, except with respect to the deposition of this pope, to the election of a new pontiff, the reformation of the Church, and the extirpation of heresy. 2°. That the council should confirm all the grants, dispensations, and favours, accorded by Benedict XIII., to all persons, whether ecclesiastic or secular. 3°. That the cardinals of Benedict should be treated at the council as true cardi-

nals, and should enjoy all the privileges attached to their dignity.

The capitulation of Narbonne was received at Constance with great joy, and solemnly sworn to on February 4, 1416. The proceedings against Benedict XIII. were continued at the same time as the negotiations, which were about to complete the union with the council of all those under his jurisdiction.

Peter de Luna was summoned to appear at Constance within a space of two months and ten days; and two Benedictine monks, Lambert Stipilz and Bernard Plancha,* were charged to carry the summons to Peniscola. The recital which they gave of their mission, showed clearly enough that they were amongst his most inveterate enemies. Benedict seeing them draw near, clothed in black, according to the statutes of their order, said to those who were around him, " Let us hear the ravens of the council !" " There is nothing surprising," replied one of the monks, boldly, " that ravens should come near a dead body !"

In a letter to the Archbishop of Riga, one of them thus gives an account of the interview :—

" We repaired to Peniscola without a safe-conduct from the pope and without escort, with three apostolic notaries, a notary of the King of Aragon, two nobles, and other honourable persons, as witnesses. A certain doctor came to us, requesting us to defer our entry until the next day, assigning as a pretext for the application, that his master wished to receive us more honourably. We refused to comply..... These devils imagine they have gained every thing, if they can postpone the union a single hour !† As we were entering the town, a nephew of Peter de Luna, escorted by two hundred well-armed soldiers, came to meet us. What an honour for us to find this Peter de Luna, so long frightened at the approach of two defenceless monks, as to think it necessary to prepare such an armed force ! We had an audience the next day. He had with him his three cardinals, some bishops, some priests, and about three hundred laymen. Then, making a profound reverence, but without bending the knee, I read aloud, and word by word, the citations of the council. When, in reading, I named him heretic and schismatic, he testified an inexpressible impatience, saying at one time, That is not true ; at another, They lie. . . . . Peter de Luna replied, in Latin and in French, that the matter was of importance; and that he should deliberate on it with his cardinals. He had, he said, four things to allege in his

* Ex Msc. Vindob. ap. Von der Hardt, vol. ii. p. 521.

15

* Von der Hardt, vol. iv. p. 116.
† Isti diaboli videntur salvari, quando possent materiam unionis differre etiam per horam. Marten. Anecd. vol. ii. p. 1699.

justification; but he only mentioned three, and moved about in such a way whilst speaking, that the fourth was lost under his cap. In truth, this man is made up of wickedness..... He, first of all, related the history of a certain abbot, whom his disciples could not put in a passion, except in calling him *heretic*. He said the same thing might be said of himself. 'The Council of Constance is null,' he added; 'its members not having any lawful authority; for they are either under my jurisdiction, in which case they are excommunicated, according to the principles of the council; or they are under that of Rome, and then they were excommunicated by Gregory..... I am no heretic, since I am guided by the judgment of the Church: and if I do not give myself up at Constance, as they require, it does not follow that I am a heretic; for the Church is not at Constance, but at Peniscola. It is here,' said he, striking his seat with his hand, 'it is here that is the ark of Noah and the true Church. The folks at Constance pretend that I am schismatic and heretical, because I will not deliver the Church over into their hands: —I shall take right good care not to do so. Six months ago, peace would have been restored without them; it is therefore they who are guilty of schism and heresy, and not I.'* ... This man is more obstinate than ever, and is bent only on evil; but, whatever may be said to the contrary, he is in the power of the King of Aragon, although being in a strong fortress, and having men-at-arms about him. They are in despair at having been ruined by him; and soon not a single man will remain with him. Therefore, let him be deposed forthwith. ... It is thus that two black monks summoned for judgment to the infernal regions the great devil Beelzebub."[†]

The council, in fact, deposed Benedict, but not for a year afterwards—in its thirty-seventh session.

The emperor was absent from Constance during the continuance of the proceedings against Peter de Luna; for immediately after having signed the capitulation of Narbonne, he had proceeded to Paris.

France was then in a most deplorable state, and suffered all the evils that a country could suffer under a king weak in intellect and absolute. She was, like the court, divided amongst the factions of the princes, and had become the prey of whatever party could succeed in seizing on the person of the imbecile monarch: she groaned under the effects of both intestine and foreign war, and endured, with the greatest grief, the consequence of the disaster at Agincourt.

Sigismund, seeing that the Turks were advancing into Europe, and had invaded his hereditary kingdom of Hungary, comprehended clearly how much the disorders of Christendom favoured their progress. His chivalrous spirit had conceived the idea of a new crusade, which he hoped might be effected: but for that, it was, first of all, necessary to have the the Church united; and, next, that peace should reign amongst all Christian princes. He had almost attained the first point,—the extinction of the schism,—and he was now going to prosecute the second, which was, in fact, the cause of the journey to France and England.

He was received in the first of these kingdoms with the greatest honours; and after having there exerted himself to bring about the union of the two nations, and concluded a treaty of alliance with Charles VI., he crossed over to England. There he evinced but little scruple, relative to the engagement which he had just entered into; for though he undoubtedly continued to negotiate the peace, he concluded it on conditions onerous to France. Finding that his designs were strongly resisted, he at last joined England against France by the treaty of Canterbury, and alleged, as the motive of his conduct, that the kings of France unjustly retained certain lands belonging to the empire.*

Whatever may have been the conduct of Sigismund in this circumstance, and however merited may have been the reproach of duplicity which he has incurred from the French writers; it is impossible, without injustice, to refuse him the honour of having nobly devoted himself for the peace of the Church. He gave, by the capitulation of Narbonne, a new pledge to the cause of the union, and it was he who induced the Spanish nation to join the council. He never allowed himself to be turned aside from his purposes by the disasters which took place in his hereditary kingdom from the ravages of the Turks; and, in thus abandoning for some time his own subjects to themselves, in order to re-establish and cement the union amongst the Christian princes, he gave proofs of that quality which is of such rare occurrence, and peculiar to great characters—a readiness to sacrifice a present and personal benefit, for more distant advantages of a general interest.

---

* Potius sunt heretici et schismatici quam ego.
† Marten. *An.* v. ii. p. 1669, and the following.

* Lenfant (*Hist. du Concile de Constance*, vol. ii. p. 10, 20) has endeavoured to exonerate Sigismund from the reproach of want of faith, which is brought against him by the French historians. He has succeeded in proving that the emperor had never lost sight of the peace between the nations; but not that he took the best means of attaining that object, in holding the balance even between France and England.

CHAPTER X.

BOHEMIA AFTER JOHN HUSS'S DEATH.

THE great task undertaken by Sigismund exceeded his strength; and, whilst he was bringing Spain under subjection to the council, a violent tempest had arisen at the other extremity of Europe, against both the council and himself.

The execution of John Huss offered a fresh proof of the inefficiency of violent means for putting down doctrines amongst a people disposed to embrace them; for the flames which consumed him gave new life to his word, and the fire raised at his stake set Bohemia on fire.

When the news of his punishment reached Prague, the exasperated multitude flocked in crowds to the chapel of Bethlehem, and this man, whom the council had burned as a heretic and an unbeliever, was honoured by the people as a martyr and a saint in heaven.*

Nor was it merely a blind, misjudging crowd that rendered a striking homage to his memory, but the barons and nobles of the kingdom met together, and with their hand on their sword, swore to avenge him whom they regarded as the Apostle of Bohemia. The University of Prague also assembled, and its doctors indignantly appealed to the whole of Europe against the sentence of the council, and the reproaches directed against themselves. "In the midst of our innumerable and poignant subjects of grief," said they, "we consider it to be an imperious necessity to defend the insulted reputation of our university, hitherto always esteemed so pure, against the attacks of blasphemers. To all the other motives which induce us to adopt this course, is added the remembrance of the honour and virtue of that man who is now lost to us for ever. . . . . . We desire to do this, in order that the great renown of one of our children, John of Hussinetz, surnamed Huss, should not fade away, but shine forth more and more in the eyes of the universe. . . . We desire the more ardently that our words may be heard by all believers, because the presence of so great a man amongst us has produced so much good before God and before men. . . . For his life glided on before our eyes from his very infancy, and was so holy and pure that no man could show him to be guilty of a single fault. O man, truly pious, truly humble! thou who wert conspicuous with

the lustre of such great virtues—who wert accustomed to despise riches and to succour the poor, even to experiencing want thyself—whose place was by the bedside of the unfortunate—who invitedst, by thy tears, the most hardened hearts to repentance, and soothedst rebellious spirits by the inexhaustible mildness of the word—thine it was to root out from every heart, and particularly from that of a clergy, rich, covetous, and haughty, their manifold vices, by applying to them the ancient remedy of the Scriptures, which appeared new doctrines in thy mouth—thou, in fine, following in the footsteps of the apostles, restoredst the morals of the primitive Church in the clergy and the people. . . . Ah! beyond a doubt, nature had loaded this man with all her gifts, and the Divine grace was so abundantly shed around him, that not only was he virtuous, but it is even permitted to assert that he was virtue itself!* But why employ words, when acts speak? A frightful death, inflicted by his enemies, and supported with such wonderful patience, proves that he placed his trust on a heavenly foundation. . . . It is in fact a divine thing—it is the effect of a courage inspired by God alone, to endure so many outrages, so many tortures, and so much infamy, for the Divine truth, to receive all these insults with a visage calm and serene, to shine forth by the greatest piety in the face of tyrants, and thus to terminate an irreproachable life by the most bitter death."†

The barons assumed a loftier tone, and, with unanimous consent, in an assembly held, according to some authors, at Sternberg, and, according to others, at Prague, they despatched to the council this warlike defiance:—

"As, by natural and divine right," said they, "no one ought to do to others what he would not that others should do to him; and as it is written, 'Love thy neighbour as thyself,' we wish to apply this Divine precept to our dear and very venerable master, John Huss, bachelor of theology, and preacher of the Holy Scriptures, whom lately, in the Council of Constance, you, inspired by we know not what feeling, to the shame of our most Christian kingdom of Bohemia, and of the most

---

* Theod. Vrie, *Hist. Conc. Const.* ap. Von der Hardt, vol. i. p. 181.

* Certe fecit in eo natura quod potuit, divinæque munificentiæ gratiosa effecit liberalitas, ut nedum virtuosus, sed dici possit ipsa virtus.

† J. Huss. *Monum. Testim. Univers. Pragens.* vol. i. p. 410.

illustrious Marquisate of Moravia, did condemn, as an obstinate heretic, to a cruel and most disgraceful death, without having convicted him of any error, and only on the false accusation of his enemies and of confirmed traitors."

The barons then eulogized, in the highest terms, the character and preaching of John Huss and Jerome of Prague, ... "whom," continued they, "you have also seized on, imprisoned, and perhaps, by this time, cruelly put to death." They next repelled with indignation the charge of heresy made by the council against the kingdom. "Placing," pursued they, "our firm hope and our most orthodox faith in our Lord Jesus Christ, and making one only exception in favour of our Prince and Lord, Sigismund, King of the Romans and of Hungary, brother and successor of our sovereign in the kingdom of Bohemia, we make it known by these presents, to your reverence, and all believers, that whoever, of whatever rank, dignity, or condition he may be, shall pretend that error or heresy has been spread abroad in Bohemia, and that we are polluted with it, lies in the throat like a villain—like a traitor to our kingdom—like a dangerous heretic, and a child of the devil, who is the chief liar and the father of lies.* Leaving vengeance to God, to whom it belongs, we shall ulteriorly carry our complaints to the lawful and indubitable apostolic pontiff, that God, we trust, will give to the Holy Church, and whom we shall obey with respect, like submissive sons, in every thing just, honourable, and conformable to reason and Divine truth.... We declare, besides, that, in spite of all human ordinances, we shall support the humble, devoted, and faithful preachers, who shall make known the words of our Divine Lord Jesus Christ; and we shall defend and protect them fearlessly, even unto shedding of blood.†—Given at Sternberg, on St. Wenceslaus' day."

Fifty-four signatures, which are given in the collection of John Huss's works, were appended to this haughty epistle.

In these grave circumstances, the man who evinced the greatest want of resolution was he whom it most imported to determine on some decided course of proceeding—the King of Bohemia. Wenceslaus, wholly given up to vices of every kind, was incapable of a noble or vigorous resolution. We have seen him abetting or rejecting the reformers through motives the most foreign to the welfare of the

Church and of religion;—such as he was then, such he remained to the end.

In the midst of the disturbances and agitation excited throughout his kingdom by the death of John Huss, he remained the prey of the most contrary interests. He feared the council—he feared the emperor his brother—he feared also the consequences of a popular agitation, commenced by such inauspicious violence. But if this, when unrepressed, was attended with dangers, it foreboded others if these were repressed; and Wenceslaus, already twice hurled from the throne, dreaded a third downfall. His avarice, besides, and his cupidity, suggested to him, that if the authority of Rome was restored in Bohemia, he would have to render an account of the property confiscated from the clergy. To these latter causes was added a just resentment; for Wenceslaus was incensed that the council should have delivered up to the executioner one of his most illustrious subjects, without any regard for the protection which he accorded him, and without having even condescended to lay before him the grievances complained of. Anger, therefore, carried the day in a mind incapable of listening to cool reason, and completely a stranger to restraint. He permitted matters to take their course at first, with the intention afterwards of being guided by events.

This prince, at that time, had amongst his chamberlains a gentleman of good birth, named *John de Trocznow*, who had signalized himself in war when exceedingly young. He had obtained the cognomen of *Ziska*,* because he was blind of one eye, from a wound received in battle, and under this name he subsequently became the terror of a part of Europe. This fear-inspiring man detested the licentiousness of the priests. He had a sister, a nun, who was seduced or forced by a monk, and this circumstance redoubled his horror of the Roman clergy, and inspired him with a furious and unextinguishable hatred against that order. The death of John Huss, whom he loved and looked upon as the great doctor of Bohemia, affected him profoundly; and as he was one day walking in the court of the palace, lost in thought, the king saw him, and asked what was the subject of his reflections. "I was thinking," replied Ziska, "of the dreadful affront that has been offered to the kingdom, by the treatment inflicted on John Huss and Jerome."

"Neither you nor I," rejoined Wenceslaus, "are in a position to avenge them. If, however, you are aware of any means of accomplishing it, take courage, and avenge your Bohemians."†

---

* Mentitur in caput suum.

† Alias datum Prague 1415, die 2 Septembris, in pleno concilio magnatum, baronum, procerum et nobilium Regni Bohemiæ et Marchionatus Moraviæ.—(*Huss. Monum.* vol. i. p. 99.)

* ZISKA, in Bohemian, signifies *one-eyed*.

† Balbinus, *Epit. rer. Bohem.* p. 424.

Notwithstanding these words, and the extreme irritation of men's minds, the sword did not yet quit the scabbard. The barons held another assembly, on September 5, at Prague, at which their letter to the council was read, and unanimously approved of. They then adopted the following resolution, which strongly testifies the sincere intention of the nobles of Bohemia to remain united to the Roman Catholic Church, and at the same time their entire ignorance of the foundation on which that Church was established. They agreed to allow the word of God to be freely preached, according to the Holy Scriptures, in all places under their jurisdiction—to punish all priests convicted of teaching error—to admit an appeal from the judgment of the 'shops before the University of Prague—and to repel by force, if necessity required it, all unlawful censures launched against them, in hatred of the evangelical truth. They concluded by expressing a wish that God would

speedily accord a pope to the Church, whom they pledged themselves to obey in every thing that would not remove them from the word of God.

The nobles of the kingdom thus evinced their desire not to break with the Roman Church, and their sincerity could not be doubted. But, at the same time, they placed above the prescriptions of that Church their private interpretations of the divine word. They professed, like John Huss, to be members of the Catholic Church, and they certainly considered themselves to be such; but they denied its infallibility; and in that they adhered, by anticipation, to the fundamental principle of the reformation of Wycliffe, and of that of the succeeding century. A strange period, and fruitful in storms, was that in which the greatest of crimes in the eyes of men was heresy, and in which the half of a nation were heretics without being aware of it!

CHAPTER XI.

JEROME OF PRAGUE.

THE menacing letter of the nobles of Bohemia produced a lively agitation in the council, and at first held the fathers irresolute as to the conduct they should have to observe towards Jerome of Prague, whom they still kept in irons, in the tower of St. Paul's cemetery.

Irritated at the contents of this letter, they would willingly have despatched Jerome to execution, but they were apprehensive that vengeance would follow the threat. They, therefore, first sought for a pretext to dispense with punishing him, and every thing was employed to prevail on Jerome to abjure.*

He had for six months been pining away in chains; no severity had been spared him in his noisome dungeon, and his legs were already afflicted with incurable sores.† It was hoped that sufferings of such duration and rigour would have depressed his soul, and subdued his courage. He was taken out of prison, and summoned, under pain of being burned, to

abjure his errors, and subscribe to the justice of John Huss's death.

Human weakness prevailed—Jerome was afraid, and signed a paper by which he submitted himself to the council, and approved of all its acts. This retractation of Jerome proves, by the very restrictions which it contains, how much it must have cost this unfortunate man to consent to it. He subscribed, it is true, to the condemnation of the articles of Wycliffe and John Huss; but he declared that he had no intention of bearing any prejudice to the holy truths which these two men had taught; and, as to Huss in particular, he avowed that he had loved him from his tenderest years, and that he had always been ready to defend him against every one, on account of the mildness of his language, and the good instructions he gave the people. Better informed at present, he had no wish to stand forward as the partisan of his errors. Whilst, however, he condemned them, he honoured his person, his excellent morals, and various fine expressions that had issued from his mouth.

Such restrictions as these were but little calculated to satisfy his judges. They demanded a more precise retractation, and drew up a new form, which was presented to Jerome, and read by him aloud in full council

---

* Concilii patres, viso ex novissimis Bohemorum litteris per Bohemos ex Hussi cineribus orto incendio, Hieronymum ad recantandum omnibus modis invitare, eoque fine e carcere in cæmeterio Sancti Pauli sito productum, concilio sæpius sistere, ne novo statim fuso sanguine oleum denuo igni affunderent.—(Msc. Helmst. ap. Von der Hardt, vol. ix. p. 497.)

† Theobald: Bell. Hussit. cap. xx.

in the nineteenth general session. He had
next to answer on certain propositions that
looked like heresy. Jerome, as well as his
master John Huss, belonged, as we have seen,
to the Realist school. This school, two centuries before, was sovereign in the universities,
and signalized, as heretical, the opposing
party—the Nominalists: the latter triumphed
at present, and counted, as its chief followers,
the greatest doctors of the council,—it was
now the turn of the Realists to give proofs of
their orthodoxy. Jerome, strongly attacked
as John Huss had been on the famous doctrine
of *universalia à parte rei*,[*] protested that he
did not consider it necessary for salvation;
and when the charge was made against him
of having badly defined the faith, he was forced
to allow that his definition applied less to the
faith itself than to a certain knowledge of the
beatifical vision.[†] Who could suppose that
such subtleties should become matters of life
and death, and that the rage of disputation
could have seized on the world to such a
point.

Jerome swore to live and die in the truth of
the Catholic faith, and he anathematized those
who should maintain any thing against it.
"I swear," said he, "to teach nothing against
my retractation; and should it happen to me
to do so, I submit to all the rigour of the
canons, and to eternal punishment."

After this positive declaration, Jerome was
led back to prison, and treated with less severity.

There was every reason to expect that the
council would rest satisfied with what had
been done; and it was so at first: but enmity
demanded more than this. At the instigation
of Peter Paletz and Michael Causis, monks
came from Prague, and, on their bringing forward new charges against Jerome, his enemies demanded to have the proceedings revised. The council was again divided in
opinion; and as, without doubt, it no longer
entertained any hope of preventing, by pru-
dential measures, the outbreak of popular
resentment in Bohemia, the majority gave
themselves unreservedly up to their persecuting instincts.

The most prudent members of the assembly,
and particularly the first commissioners, the
Cardinals of Cambray, Des Ursins, Aquileia,
and Florence, represented that he had obeyed
the council, and insisted on his being set at
liberty. A loud murmur greeted this demand;
and Dr. Nason, strong in his orthodoxy, was
bold enough to remark to the cardinals, "We
are much astonished, reverend fathers, to find

you interceding for this pestiferous heretic,
from whom we have received so much injury
in Bohemia, and who could very easily cause
as much to yourselves. Is it possible that
you have been gained over by bribes from the
King of Bohemia, or from the heretics? Can
they have purchased from you the liberty of
this man?"

At these words the cardinals rose up, and
demanded to be discharged from their office
as commissioners in the proceedings against
Jerome. New commissioners were elected,
and amongst them were John de Rocha, the
implacable adversary of Gerson, and the Patriarch of Constantinople, the most ardent
persecutor of John Huss.

Jerome then comprehended, that, in order to
safe his life, he should be obliged to plunge
deeper into perjury. Indignation restored him
strength—the love of the truth prevailed over
the love of life—and he at once made up
his mind to adopt an heroic resolution. He
refused positively to reply to his new judges,
and demanded a public audience, at which he
might clearly and fully expose his sentiments.
This application was consented to; and, on
23d May, he was taken to the cathedral church,
where the council was assembled. The new
commissioners, at the instigation of his enemies, brought forward against him seven heads
of accusation. The plot, remarked an old
author of his life,[*] was designedly framed in
such a manner that it was impossible for him
to escape. The act of accusation, which was
read by John de Rocha, charged Jerome with
having honoured Wycliffe as a saint and a
martyr;—with having contemned the authority
of the Church, in administering the sacrament
in Prague, at the very time that he was excommunicated in Austria;—with having shown
himself the abettor of John Huss;—with
having counterfeited the seal of the University
of Oxford, in order to give a favourable testimony to Wycliffe;—and, above all, with having committed violence and sacrilege, by publishing libels against the pope and the princes;
—by having fomented sanguinary insurrec-
tions at Prague;—and by having excited the
nobles to despoil the clergy.

In addition to these accusations, relative to
the conduct of Jerome, several persons inculpated his opinions on transubstantiation, the
real presence, indulgences, the worship of
images and relics, the authority of the priests,
and the Trinity. He had, on this last point,
it was said, certainly confessed the Athanasian
creed; but the further explanation which he
gave of it smacked of heresy. As to the power
of the priests, he had, said the act of accusa-

* See pp. 74, 90.
† Von der Hardt, vol. iv. p. 499; Theob. Bell.
Hussit. cap. xxi.

* Oper. Huss. vol. ii. p. 505.

tion, sustained, like Wycliffe and John Huss, that excommunication was only to be feared by those who incurred that of God himself; and as to relics, Jerome, it asserted, had dared to uphold that no worship was due to them; and that the veil of the Virgin was not more worthy of the homage of Christians than the skin of the ass on which Christ had ridden.

The proctor of the council, Henry Piron, enumerated these latter grievances, and added several others; above all, accusing Jerome of having been intemperate in his prison. He represented his retractation as worthy of suspicion, and insisted on his being obliged to reply by a single word, yes or no, to each article: he advised the torture to be employed in case of necessity. "Should the prisoner," concluded he, "persevere in his error, let him be treated as an obstinate heretic, and be delivered over to the secular authority."

The demand of the proctor was complied with, and Jerome was authorised to reply to each article, but in the briefest manner. He, however, was firmly resolved not to express his opinions, until he was allowed to expose them with perfect freedom.

He, therefore, demanded permission to explain himself at full. "Confine yourself to give a simple reply," was the general exclamation, "and answer forthwith." "God of goodness!" said he, "what injustice! what cruelty! You have held me shut up three hundred and forty days in a frightful prison, in the midst of filth, noisomeness, stench, and the utmost want of every thing; you then bring me out before you, and, lending an ear to my mortal enemies, you refuse to hear me. Is it astonishing that they have persuaded you that I am the most stubborn of heretics, the enemy of the faith, the persecutor of priests? I have never been able to obtain, notwithstanding my most humble entreaties, a single moment to justify myself; and before you made the slightest attempt to ascertain what I am, you have treated me as an unbeliever. And yet you are men, and not gods—you can fall into error, and be mistaken. If you be really wise men, and the lights of the world, take care not to sin against justice. As to me, I am only a feeble mortal—my life is but of little importance; and when I exhort you not to deliver an unjust sentence, I speak less for myself than for you."

A great noise followed these words, and Jerome was peremptorily ordered to remain silent; but the fathers at last agreed that he should be permitted to explain himself freely, after he had replied to each article.

Two entire sittings, the 23d and 26th of May, were occupied in this most trying examination, during which each of the hundred and seven articles was successively brought before him. All the historians, Catholic or Hussite, agree in stating that he replied with marvellous ability and presence of mind; discussing every fact, rejecting some as false, and admitting others as true. "It is incredible," said the celebrated Poggio of Florence, who was an ocular witness of the whole; "what a multiplicity of authorities and reasons he alleged in support of his opinions. Not once, during the whole time, did he express a thought which was unworthy of a man of worth; so that, if his sentiments on the faith were in conformity with his words, there was no reason to accuse, much less to condemn, him. When he heard himself branded as an enemy of the Roman pontiff, the adversary of the cardinals, and the persecutor of the prelates, he rose and cried out, with a pathetic voice, and stretching forth his hands, 'To what side shall I turn, O fathers! from whom shall I expect support and succour? whom, in fact, shall I supplicate? Is it you? Alas! my cruel enemies have already alienated your minds from me, by representing me as your persecutor. They have said to themselves, The charges against this man are too slight to warrant his condemnation to death; let us depict him as the enemy of his judges, and he is sure to be condemned. O Lord! thy will be done!'"

He recognised, he said, that the right to preach the gospel belonged to laymen, as well as to priests; but he denied that he had suspended the pope's bull round the neck of certain abandoned women. The pope, in his opinion, had a right to grant indulgences; but it was not allowable for him to dispose of them for money. Several of his answers were exceedingly Catholic; and when he was interrogated relative to the substance of the sacrament of the Eucharist, he replied, "Before consecration it is bread; but after, it is the body of Jesus Christ."

Perfectly in possession of his mental powers, notwithstanding so many sufferings, he at one time confounded his judges by the vigour of his eloquence; and, at another, provoked their smiles by some keen pleasantry.

At last, on the second day, May 26, all the articles having been read, Jerome obtained, though not without great difficulty, the permission which he had so long applied for in vain—that of speaking without constraint.

First of all, addressing his prayers to God, he conjured the Supreme Being to place in his thoughts and in his mouth only such words as should be advantageous to the well-being and safety of his soul; and then, turning towards

* Theobald. *Bello Hussit.* p. 58.—Pogg. Flor. Leonard Aret.

the assembly, he said, "Reverend fathers, many excellent men have, in all ages, suffered most unworthy treatment—have been oppressed by false witnesses, and condemned by perverse judges." He then referred, in turn, to the death of Socrates, the captivity of Plato, the flight of Anaxagoras, the tortures of Zeno, and the condemnation of very many of the Gentiles, whose unmerited deaths Boëtius has narrated. Next, passing to the Hebrews, he enumerated the misfortunes of Moses, the liberator of that people; the trials of Joseph, of Isaiah, of Daniel, and of almost all the prophets—the victims of unjust resentments, and condemned as seditious persons and the enemies of God. Arriving, lastly, at the holy men of the New Testament, he showed John the Baptist, and the Saviour himself, condemned on false testimony—after them, Stephen, put to death by a college of priests—and the apostles, persecuted and punished, as the exciters of disturbance, the enemies of the gods, and the workers of iniquity. "It is," said he, "an odious thing to have a priest condemned by a priest; but the crowning point of iniquity is, when he is so by a council of priests—and yet that has been seen, that has been done."

As the whole case rested on the declarations of witnesses, Jerome gave excellent reasons why their depositions were to be considered as unworthy of confidence—their expressions have been suggested, and coloured by hatred, and not by truth.[*] He exposed the motives of his enemies with such force, that he was on the point of persuading the assembly. In fact, men's minds were evidently affected and inclined towards pity. Jerome added, that he had come, of his own free movement, to the council, to justify himself. He recalled to the minds of his hearers his long course of study, and his whole life consecrated to his duties and the practice of well-doing. "In the ancient Church," said he, "the most learned and most holy doctors were divided in opinion touching doctrine; and these differences did not tend to the ruin of the faith, but to its advancement. In this way, St. Augustine and St. Jerome were divided, and even opposed to each other; and yet no suspicion of heresy was ever entertained with respect to them."

Every one thought that he would clear himself of the accusation, either by a retractation or by humbly asking pardon; but nothing of the kind took place—he refused to acknowledge himself to be guilty of any error; and maintained that it was not for him to retract the accusations of his enemies. He spoke in the very highest terms of John Huss. "I knew him from his childhood," said he; "and there was never any thing wrong in him. He was a most excellent man, just and holy;—he was condemned, notwithstanding his innocence;—he has ascended to heaven, like Elias, in the midst of flames; and from thence he will summon his judges to the formidable tribunal of Christ. I, also—I am ready to die: I will not recoil before the torments that are prepared for me by my enemies and false witnesses, who will one day have to render an account of their impostures before the great God, whom nothing can deceive."

The greatest agitation reigned amongst the persons present, when they heard him speak thus, many being most anxious to save the life of a man of such great merit; but he did not appear to feel any care about his life; or, rather, seemed to aspire after death, "Of all the sins," added he, "that I have committed since my youth, none weigh so heavily on my mind, and cause me such poignant remorse, as that which I committed in this fatal place, when I approved of the iniquitous sentence rendered against Wycliffe, and against the holy martyr, John Huss, my master and my friend. Yes! I confess it from my heart; and declare, with horror, that I disgracefully quailed, when, through a dread of death, I condemned their doctrines.[*] I therefore supplicate and conjure Almighty God to deign to pardon me my sins—and this one, in particular, the most heinous of all—according to the promise which he has made us, 'I will not have the death of a sinner, but rather that he may turn from his wickedness, and live!' You condemned Wycliffe and John Huss, not for having shaken the doctrine of the Church, but simply because they branded with reprobation the scandals proceeding from the clergy—their pomp, their pride, and all the vices of the prelates and priests. The things which they have affirmed, and which are irrefutable, I also think and declare, like them."

---

[*] It is worthy of remark, said Poggio, that, after having been so long shut up in a place where it was utterly impossible for him either to read, or even to see, and where the perpetual anxiety of his mind would have been quite sufficient to deprive any other of memory altogether, he could, notwithstanding, have been able to quote, in support of his opinions, so great a number of authorities, and learned testimonies of the greatest doctors, so that one would have said that he had passed all that time in perfect repose, and at full liberty to devote himself wholly to study.—*Letter of Poggio of Florence to Leonard Aretin.*

[*] Jerome, in approving of the doctrines of Wycliffe and John Huss, nevertheless, excepted that of Wycliffe touching the Eucharist. Some authors have erroneously supposed that this exception also applied to the doctrine of John Huss. We have seen that John Huss was an orthodox Catholic on this point. Theod. Vrie, a contemporary author, exceedingly Catholic, declares formally, that Jerome designated Wycliffe's doctrine alone as erroneous on this dogma.—(Theod. Vrie, ap. Von der Hardt, vol. i. p. 184.)

At these words, the assembly shook with anger. "He condemns himself!" was exclaimed from all sides. "What need is there of further proof? We behold with our own eyes the most obstinate of heretics!"

"What!" resumed Jerome. "Do you suppose that I fear to die? You have held me for a whole year in a frightful dungeon, more horrible than death itself. You have treated me more cruelly than a Turk, Jew, or pagan, and my flesh has literally rotted off my bones alive; and yet I make no complaint, for lamentation ill becomes a man of heart and spirit; but I cannot but express my astonishment at such great barbarity towards a Christian."

A fresh burst of clamour then arose against him, and he remained without speaking until silence was again restored. He then resumed, in so firm and lofty a tone, that one might have supposed that he had nothing to apprehend for himself. "His voice," remarks the illustrious Poggio, "was touching, clear, and sonorous; his gesture full of dignity and persuasiveness, whether he expressed indignation or moved his hearers to pity, which, however, he appeared neither to ask for nor to desire. He stood there, in the midst of all, the features pale, but the heart intrepid, despising death, and advancing to meet it. Interrupted frequently, attacked and tormented by many, he replied fully to all, and took vengeance on them, forcing some to blush, and others to be silent, and towering above all their clamours. Sometimes, too, he earnestly besought, and at others forcibly claimed to be permitted to speak freely—calling on the assembly to listen to him whose voice would soon be hushed for ever."[*]

When he had at last concluded his address, he was carried back to his dungeon, where he was more strictly fettered than before. His hands, his arms, and his feet, were loaded with irons;—and they who had heard him speak remarked to each other, "He has pronounced his own sentence!"[†]

CHAPTER XII.

SENTENCE AND EXECUTION OF JEROME.

A DEATH voluntarily suffered for a just and holy cause is the more worthy of admiration, as it had been previously shunned and dreaded. It is this circumstance which throws so great an interest round Jerome's last moments—an interest superior, perhaps, even to that which belongs to the death of John Huss.

The latter, endowed with an almost superhuman constancy, evinced, in the midst of his sufferings and his agony, rather a vague hope of life than an apprehension of death, and the most dreadful anguish did not draw from him the slightest mark of weakness. Jerome, on the contrary, always completely given up to the emotion of the moment, after having braved destruction from a movement more generous than prudent, had then shrunk from the idea of confronting it.

Another cause helps to show why he manifested less constancy in his intrepidity than his master. John Huss had near him, in his difficulties, his most faithful disciples; and he himself, in his letters, acknowledged, with the liveliest gratitude, how greatly he was indebted to their devotedness. What had now become of the noble barons Wenceslaus Duba, Hussinetz, and John de Chlum, his most attached friend, all of whom had accompanied John Huss to the council? They had departed, beyond a doubt, after his death—they had returned to Bohemia to avenge his death. Neither is it known what became at this period of Peter Maldoniewitz, the good notary. We have seen how he risked his life to aid Jerome; what, then, was he doing now? Was he still at Constance? Or had he already quitted this fatal place, where attachment to an unfortunate friend was deemed a crime worthy of death? History makes no mention of him, and Jerome was, therefore, alone in the midst of his mortal enemies, without any support against them, but what he found in his own mind. How, then, was it possible for him not to give way—he who already had twice appeared to shrink back in the face of death—he who was less steeled than John Huss against its terrors? But also how truly great did he stand forth when he rose from his fall—when he triumphed over his terror, and rushed forward to martyrdom! By his final display of courage, he made up for all his weakness.

Struck by his eloquence, and astonished by his great abilities, the cardinals and bishops came in crowds to visit him in his confinement, conjuring him to save his life by subscribing to the sentence passed on John Huss, and by

---

[*] Theod. Vrie, ap. Von der Hardt, vol. i. p. 183. Pogg. Flor. Leonard Aret.
[†] Huss. Act. et Mon.—Narratio de Hieron. p. 527.

16

L

abjuring his doctrine. "I will abjure," said he, "if you demonstrate to me by the Holy Scriptures that it is false." '

"Can you be to such an extent your own enemy?" inquired the bishops.

"What!" replied he; "do you suppose that life is so precious to me, that I fear to give it for the truth, or for Him who gave his for mine? Are you not cardinals? are you not bishops? and can you be ignorant what Christ has said: 'He that does not give up all for my sake, is not worthy of me. . . . . Behind me, tempters!'"

The Cardinal of Florence presented himself last. He sent for Jerome, and said to him: "Jerome, you are a learned man, whom God has loaded with his choicest gifts—do not employ them to your own ruin, but for the advantage of the Church. The council has compassion on you, and, on account of your rare talents, would regret to behold you marching to execution. You may pretend to high honours, and be a powerful succour to the Church of Jesus Christ, if you consent to be converted, like St. Peter and St. Paul. The Church is not to such a point cruel, as to refuse a pardon, if you become worthy of it; and I promise you every kind favour when it shall be found that neither obstinacy nor falsehood remains in you. Reflect whilst it is yet time: spare your own life, and open your heart to me."

Jerome replied: "The only favour that I demand—and which I have always demanded —is to be convinced by the Holy Scriptures. This body, which has suffered such frightful torments in my chains, will also know how to support death, by fire, for Jesus Christ."

"Jerome," asked the cardinal, "do you suppose yourself to be wiser than all the council?"

"I am anxious to be instructed," rejoined Jerome; "and he who desires to be instructed cannot be infatuated with ideas of his own wisdom."

"And in what manner do you desire to be instructed?"

"By the Holy Writings, which are our illuminating torch."

"What! is every thing to be judged of by the Holy Writings? Who can perfectly comprehend them? And must not the Fathers be at last appealed to, to interpret them?"

"What do I hear!" cried Jerome. "Shall the word of God be declared fallacious? And shall it not be listened to? Are the traditions of men more worthy of faith, than the holy gospel of our Saviour? Paul did not exhort the priests to listen to old men and traditions, but said,—'The Holy Scriptures will instruct you.' O Sacred Writings, inspired by the Holy Ghost, already men esteem you less

than what they themselves forge every day! I have lived long enough. Great God! receive my life; Thou who canst restore it to me!"

"Heretic!" said the cardinal, regarding him with anger. "I repent having so long pleaded with you. I see that you are urged on by the devil."[*]

Jerome was once more taken back to his dungeon, where he remained until May 30, on which day the council held its twenty-first general session.

The report spread that day that Jerome was going to be condemned, and immediately the whole city was on the alert. The emperor was still absent, but the Elector Palatine replaced him, as protector of the council; and by his orders, the troops were called out, and placed under arms. The Bishop of Riga then had Jerome conducted into the cathedral, where he formally called on him to retract what he had lately said in public.

Jerome exclaimed: "Almighty God! and you who hear me, be witnesses. I swear that I believe all the articles of the Catholic faith, as the Church believes and observes them; but I refuse to subscribe to the condemnation of those just and holy men, whom you have unjustly condemned, because they have denounced the scandals of your life; and it is for that, that I am about to perish."

Jerome then repeated aloud the Nicene creed and the Confession of Athanasius, and spoke for a considerable time with as much ability as eloquence.

All were lost in admiration at his knowledge and his admirable language. Several drew near to him, and presented him with a new form of retractation, exhorting him to allow himself to be prevailed upon; but he refused to listen to any exhortation on that point.

Then the Bishop of Lodi[†] ascended the pulpit, and chose for his text this verse: "Afterwards he appeared unto the eleven as they sat at meat, and upbraided them with their unbelief and hardness of heart."[‡]

When the frightful severity of Jerome's captivity is borne in mind, it is difficult not to perceive in the discourse of the bishop a long and cruel irony. However, the preacher certainly meant it seriously; and to understand it, it must be remembered, that, in all religions, persecuting priests have always professed to be actuated by motives of compassion towards

---

* Te a diabolo agitari video. Theob. Bell. Hussit. chap. xxiv. p. 60.

† According to Theobald, the sermon was pronounced by the Bishop of Lyons (Bell. Hussit. p. 60); but contemporary authors contradict it.

‡ Mark xvi. 14.

those whom they have overwhelmed with the greatest evils, and to pardon them torments which they did not inflict.

"Reverend fathers," said the bishop, "and you, believing Catholic and orthodox noblemen, as it often happens that a slight correction is powerless, and that a severe chastisement produces more effect, it is necessary that they, with whom mildness can do nothing, should be treated rigorously. Isidore has declared, that with minds which cannot be cured by a gentle treatment, violent and painful means must be employed. . . . When the iron does not assume the desired shape with facility, it is submitted to the action of a hotter fire, and a more weighty hammer. It is on this account, Jerome, that having beheld your prolonged obstinacy, and having heard your last most perverse reply, I can say of you what Isaiah declares, ' I know that thou art obstinate, and thy neck is an iron sinew, and thy brow brass.'[*] But wait for what is to follow: the hardened heart shall be visited with afflictions at the end, and he who loves danger shall perish in it.

"Be assured, nevertheless, that although my voice externally appears formidable and terrible for you, yet, in the bottom of my soul, there lies a fund of tenderness, made up of kindness and charity. Do not, therefore, suppose that I wish to increase affliction in the heart of the wretched, nor to stir up fire with a sword; but in order that you may the better understand with what charity you have been chastened—with what love—what long and pious mildness, you have been reprehended and exhorted, I have chosen for my text these words: ' He upbraided them with their unbelief and hardness of heart.' "

The bishop then expatiated at great length on all the evils that result from a haughty presumption, which misleads the wisest; and in which it was easy, he remarked, to see the source of Jerome's errors, and the cause of his ruin.

"Jerome," continued he, "I have resolved to strike you on both cheeks; but with that charity, however, which cures whilst it wounds. Wherefore, turn not on me a hardened visage, but rather remember the precept of the gospel, ' If any one strike thee on the one cheek, present to him the other.' I will, therefore, smite you, Jerome; and may it be the will of God that I may thus be able to effect your cure.

"I shall commence by flinging your own filth into your face, in order that you may know how culpable you are."[†] The bishop

here gave way to the most violent invectives against John Huss and against Jerome. "What temerity !" pursued he, "what insolent presumption in these men of obscure extraction, of low birth—in these vile plebeians, to dare stir up the noble kingdom of Bohemia, to raise the barons and princes, to sap the ancient foundations of the state, to divide the population, to provoke dissensions amongst the citizens, to commit, or at least occasion, homicides, and profane the altars! Happy kingdom of Bohemia, had these men not been born there! . . . How many evils has not the pride of these two peasants been the cause of!" The bishop had not the slightest difficulty in attributing to them all the disorders and excesses of which Bohemia had been the theatre from the period of their imprisonment, and in making Jerome responsible for them. He then added, "Jerome, I have struck you on one cheek; now, stretch forth the other, and learn to appreciate the mildness of your judges. It is well known with what severity men suspected of heresy ought to be treated. They are kept in a rigorous imprisonment, and witnesses of all kinds—even robbers, abandoned women, and infamous characters—are received against them. Should that not prove sufficient to convince them, they are subjected to the torture, and interrogated in the midst of their sufferings,—they are held altogether apart, and all public audience is refused them. If they repent, they must be mercifully pardoned; but if they persist in their error, they are condemned, and delivered over to the secular arm. But with you—who are more guilty than Arius, Sabellius, and Nestorius;—with you, who have infected all Europe with the poison of heresy, grand indulgence has been practised. You have been detained in prison only from necessity; honourable witnesses alone have been listened to against you, and the torture has not been employed, which was a great fault. Would to God that you had been tortured !—You would have denied your errors in your torments; and suffering would have opened your eyes, which your crime held closed. No hinderance has been made to any one that desired to console and exhort you, to visit you at all seasons;—several public audiences have been granted you, and they have turned to your ruin, from redoubling your audacity. You have shut the mouths of those who desired to save you, and who, in order to defend you, represented you as mad. One must be mad one's self to declare a man who could speak so well out of his senses; but it was necessary that your de-

---

[*] Isaiah xlviii. 4.

[†] Primo quidem projicio stercus non alienum super faciem tuam, sed tuum proprium, ut tua

possis ad tui emendationem crimina intueri.—(Ex Antiq. Cod. Msc. Cæsareo Vendob. et Brunswic. ap. Von der Hardt, vol. iii. p. 35.)

fenders should thus be reduced to silence, and convinced by your own words .... We have all here felt the utmost compassion for your fate; but you have fought against yourself—you have been your own greatest enemy. You have not blushed to praise John Huss, after having condemned and anathematized him! With what countenance have you dared exalt a malcontent, a heretic, an abetter of homicides? You have often said that John Huss was neither a man given to intemperance, nor a fornicator; but of what use is it not to get intoxicated with wine, when one is intoxicated with pride, anger, and hatred;—of what advantage is it not to commit fornication or adultery? What is the most important is not to fall into heresy; and the greatest adultery is to sin against the Catholic faith! Why did you not observe silence? What stronger testimony can there be against you than what you have given in declaring yourself, by your lying revocation, perjured, heretical, and relapsed into error? Wherefore, the Sacred Council, to which belongs judgment over the whole world, will judge you *according to your deserts.*"[*]

After this harangue, Jerome, in order to be better heard by all, mounted on a bench, from which he addressed the assembly. He energetically repelled all the accusations of the prelate, relative to the disturbances in Bohemia. He repeated that he should die Catholic, as he had lived; but he expressed his abhorrence of the assent given by him to the sentence of John Huss, and again cursed it. " I only gave it," said he, " from a dread of being burned—from the fear of that dreadful punishment. I :evoke that culpable avowal; and I declare it anew, that I lied like a wretch, in abjuring the doctrines of Wycliffe and of John Huss, and in approving of the death of so holy and just a man. As to you, you cannot cite a single point on which my doctrine has been either erroneous or heretical. You wish to see me die, because I honour upright men who have stigmatized the pride and avarice of the priests. Yet is that a sufficient cause to warrant my death? Why, before you found in me any evil whatever, you had resolved that I should die! Courage, therefore, and proceed! But believe me, that, in dying, I will leave you a sting in your hearts, and a gnawing worm in your consciences. I appeal to the sacred tribunal of Jesus Christ, and within a hundred years you shall answer there for your conduct to me."[†]

The Patriarch of Constantinople then read Jerome's sentence, founded wholly on his re-

tractation, and on the approbation which he had publicly given to the doctrine of Wycliffe and John Huss, with the exception of the opinion of the former on the sacrament at the altar. "He has returned like a dog to his vomit," said the sentence, "and, therefore, the sacred council orders that he shall be torn from the vine, like a barren and rotten branch." It declared him heretical, backsliding, and excommunicated; it condemned him as such, and cursed him; and, finally, it abandoned him to the secular judge, in order to receive the just punishment due to so great a crime. However, although this punishment was capital, the council expressed its trust that it was not too great.

Then, if some historians are to be believed, the emperor's chancellor, Gaspard Schlick, advanced into the middle of the assembly, and protested, in his master's name, against the condemnation of Jerome, threatening the persons engaged in it with all the anger of Sigismund. This tardy interposition was not attended to, and the chancellor retired without having obtained any thing.[*]

Jerome was at once handed over to the secular power. A high crown of paper, on which were painted demons in flames, was brought in. Jerome, on seeing it, threw his hat on the ground in the midst of the prelates, and taking it in his hand, placed it on his head himself, repeating the words which John Huss had pronounced—"Jesus Christ, who died for me a sinner, wore a crown of thorns. I will willingly wear this for him." The soldiers then seized on his person, and led him away to death.

During the passage from the cathedral to the place of execution, he repeated with a firm voice the Apostle's Creed, his eyes upraised to heaven, and his face radiant. He next chanted the Litanies, after that a hymn in honour of the Virgin; and when he arrived at the place where John Huss had suffered, he fell on his knees near the image of his master, carved on the stake to which he was himself about to be bound, and there he prayed to God.

The executioners raised him up, whilst still praying, and having bound him to the stake with cords and chains, they heaped up around him pieces of wood and a quantity of straw. Jerome sang the hymn, *Salve, festa dies tota venerabilis ævo,* &c.—He then repeated the creed, and, addressing the people, he exclaimed, "This creed which I have just sung is my real profession of faith; I die, therefore, only for not having consented to acknowledge that John Huss was justly condemned. I declare

---

[*] Ezek. vii. 3.
[†] Theobald. *Bell. Hussit.* p. 61. *Act. et Monum.* J. Huss. et Hier. Prag. vol. ii. f. 527; p. 353.

[*] This fact has been collected by Von der Hardt, vol. iv. p. 765.

that I have always beheld in him a true preacher of the gospel."

Seeing a poor husbandman bringing a fagot, he smiled, and said, "O holy simplicity! a thousand times more guilty is he who abuses thee!"

When the wood was raised on a level with his head, his vestments were thrown on the pile, and, as the executioner was setting fire to the mass behind, in order not to be seen, "Come forward boldly," said Jerome; "apply the fire before my face. Had I been afraid, I should not be here." When the pile had taken fire, he said with a loud voice, "Lord, into thy hands do I commit my spirit!" Feeling already the burning heat of the flames, he was heard to cry out in the Bohemian language, "Lord, Almighty Father, have pity on me, and pardon me my sins; for Thou knowest that I have always loved thy Truth!"[*]

His voice was speedily lost; but by the rapid movement of his lips, it was easy to see that he continued to pray.

At last, when he had ceased to exist, all that had belonged to him, his bed, cap, shoes, &c., were brought from the prison and thrown into the flames, where they were reduced to ashes with himself. These ashes were then collected and thrown into the Rhine, as had been done

* Theob. *Bello Hussit.* p. 61 ; Pogg. Flor. Leon. Aret.

in the case of John Huss. It was hoped, by this means, to remove from the followers of these two great martyrs every article that might, by possibility, become in their hands an object of veneration; even to the last particle of their bodies and clothes, every thing was made away with; but the very ground where their stake was placed was hollowed out, and the earth on which they had suffered was carried to Bohemia, and guarded with religious care, as of another Holy Land.[*]

The sanguinary annals of the human race do not, perhaps, present any spectacle more odious than the funeral pile of Jerome. We have studiously abstained from all reflections in the course of this lamentable recital. The most eloquent commentary would say less than the simple facts, which are summed up in the following brief account of the matter:—An assembly of priests cast a man into the flames for having refused to subscribe to the condemnation of his master and friend.

* The recital of Jerome's sentence and death has been indiscriminately taken from Protestant and Catholic authors. The latter, and amongst others, Æneas Sylvius Piccolomini, Theod. de Niem. Theod. Vrie, and Poggio of Florence, have all equally paid homage to the heroic courage and pious sentiments manifested by him in his last moments—"An object of commiseration to all," said Theod. Vrie, "except to himself!"—(Theod. Vrie, ap. Von der Hardt vol. i. p. 202.)

BOOK IV.

CHAPTER I.

DISPUTES CONCERNING THE REFORMATION OF THE CHURCH AND THE ELECTION OF THE POPE.

THE council, assembled for the union and reformation of the Church, had now been sitting for eighteen months, and, during that long space of time, had been particularly occupied with extending and strengthening its own authority: it had proclaimed itself superior to kings, emperors, and popes. It had acted in consequence, and was recognised as such. Two dethroned popes—one of whom had resigned when forced to it by defeat; and the other had voluntarily abdicated—were a living proof of its omnipotence. It was now about to let fall the weight of its arm on a third pontiff, and, for that purpose, had at its disposal all the spiritual and temporal forces of Christendom.

This absolute power which the council exercised externally over mankind, it equally attributed to itself over their consciences; it wanted to direct the minds as well as bodies, —thoughts as well as acts. In its design of subduing all resistance, every means appeared to it legitimate; and we have seen it employ, to that effect, by turns the censures of the Church, the arms of the empire, and the fire of the funeral stake.

The council, it is true, could not, without being invested with an immense power, have attained the double object for which it had been convoked; but it was affected with the drawback common to all human authority, that is, without counterpoise;—it recognised no limit, and the less avoided the dangers arising from that pretension, that it considered its decisions as directly emanating from the Holy Ghost. All opposition was, in its eyes, a rebellion against God himself,—it measured the offence by the attributes of the party offended, and regarded it as a duty to proportion the chastisement and vengeance to the greatness of Him whom it thought it was avenging. It has been seen into what deplorable excesses the abuse of this principle had led it; and it may be easily conceived in what

manner a multitude of men, in other respects estimable, were, by adopting it as their rule of conduct, induced to forget every sentiment of humanity. The council, at the period of the judgment of Jerome of Prague, had attained the apogee of its power;—it has been seen how it arrived at that point, and it now remains to show in what manner it acted, when there.

Two opposite opinions were beginning to manifest themselves amongst its members; but the struggle was hidden and unacknowledged, on account of a common object which it was, first of all, necessary to attain in concert, before giving free career to their contradictory pretensions;—that object was the extinction of the schism. In that, all agreed. All likewise allowed that the next thing to be effected was, to unite the Church under a new pontiff, legitimately elected, and to operate sage reforms ; but, in the opinion of some, the most pressing object was the election of the common head,—of others, the reformation. At the head of the first division were the cardinals, in whose minds the general welfare of the Church was always confounded with the private interests of the Roman Church, to which several abuses were a source of profit. They were, therefore, in haste to reconstitute this Church, and to restore to it its strength, by giving it a head. In the front rank of those who were desirous of seeing the reformation of the Church precede the election of a pope, was the emperor, who, better than any other, could appreciate the evils resulting from the excesses of the Roman court, and its unbounded pretensions. The most important reforms were to be applied to the innumerable means which that court employed to draw gold from the several kingdoms,—the question, in fact, was to dry up the thousand channels which supplied the wealth of the clergy. Little dependence was to be laid, in effecting this, on the aid of him whose treasure was augmented by it;—in a word, in order that the reformation should be serious and beneficial, it was necessary that it should be brought about without the pope, and even before he was elected.

This difference of opinion was long partially concealed; but after the death of Jerome of Prague, the two parties showed themselves somewhat more openly, guarded, however, and restrained, until after the complete adhesion to the council of the powers and the nations under the jurisdiction of Benedict XIII.

Several general sessions, after the twenty-first, in which Jerome was condemned, were, in a great measure, consecrated to the proceedings against Peter de Luna, and to important negotiations with the princes who still recognised him. They successively joined the council, and Benedict beheld Aragon, Scotland, and the county of Foix, fall off from him by turns. The adhesion of the Castilians brought about that of the Spaniards, who thenceforward formed a fifth nation in the Council; and, a few days after, in the thirty-seventh session, on January 26, 1417, Benedict was solemnly deposed. Though abandoned by all, he never bent, but continued to brave all Christendom on his rock of Peniscola, whence the stubborn old man, exasperated by his disgrace, daily launched forth his impotent fulminations on his enemies.

For a length of time the two great parties, between whom the council was divided, were silently studying each other, and preparing for an open struggle. The cardinals depended on the Italians, always interested in the grandeur of the popes and of their court; whilst the emperor was supported by the English, and still more by the Germans, for whom, for several centuries, resistance to the temporal despotism of the sovereign pontiffs was a national interest. The former party gained over to their side the Spaniards and the French, and the latter, in their turn, the English nation.

Amongst those who demanded that the election of a pope should precede the reformation, the greatest number, particularly amongst the Spanish and French nations, were sincerely anxious that the latter should take place; several cardinals even shared this desire, and they who thought differently did not venture to avow it. Every one appeared to agree as to the result that ought to be effected; they only differed in opinion on the choice of the proper moment. Many did not perceive, that on the second question depended the first; and the apparent unanimity of the wishes of all for the reformation, rendered the council less attentive to the only means of effecting it.

A commission had been named to investigate all abuses, and draw up a plan of reform: it had assumed the title of *Reformatory College,*

and met with no opposition from any quarter. Ardent preachers ascended the pulpit, and thundered forth in the midst of the council against the vices of the clergy, with a rudeness of language and a violence of invective never surpassed by the strongest expressions of Wycliffe or John Huss. A French Benedictine monk, named Bernard, drew a most frightful picture of the crimes of the priests, all of whom, with very few exceptions, he declared to be under the power of the devil. "What was the council," asked this preacher, "if not an assembly of new Pharisees, who mocked religion and the Church, under the veil of processions and of a multitude of external devotions! Alas!" continued he, "in the present age the Catholic faith is reduced to nothing: hope is a wild presumption: the love of God and of one's neighbour has disappeared: in the world, deception reigns triumphant; among the clergy, cupidity is the supreme law; with the prelates nothing can be found but malice, ignorance, pride, avarice, simony, luxury, ostentation, and hypocrisy. The Pharisees who are here mount to the temple; but they do nothing there but sleep, laugh, look haughty, and lie."

A few days after, it was the turn of another doctor, who passed so far beyond all the bounds of decency, that his extraordinary invectives cannot be given here with propriety.* Several others held forth on this inexhaustible topic; and all came to the conclusion that a prompt and complete reformation, which should cut away the evil at the root, was absolutely required. In no case was there found any one to oppose this view of the question.

The men, who at the bottom of their souls were attached to the abuses by which they lived, took care not to raise their voice against those who stigmatized them, knowing that by doing so they must allow their real opinions to be suspected. They placidly allowed every thing to be said and done; and this formal or tacit avowal on their part was only a fresh manœuvre added to so many others. They had the art to engage in their quarrel one of the most powerful men of the council—one who had shown, with the greatest authority, the extreme importance and urgency of a reform in the Church. This person was Peter d'Ailly, who, unfortunately, at this decisive moment, remembered rather his dignity of cardinal and of member of the Court of Rome, than of his principles of reformer and Gallican prelate.

D'Ailly was a man of the schools, always armed with his syllogism; and when he put forth a false principle, he followed it out intrepidly to its remotest consequences. Ascend-

---

* Von der Hardt, vol. i. p. 898.

ing the pulpit on August 25, St. Louis's day, he branded with reprobation the disorderly conduct of the clergy, in terms which did not yield to any person's language in violence;[*] he called anew for a reformation of the Church in its chief and its members, but pretended that this could not be effected, if the Church remained without a pope. "The election of a pope," said he, " is the first article of this reformation, inasmuch as the greatest deformity in a body is not to possess a head. What can there be more irregular, than to deprive the Church of its pontiff, and not give it another? Can we reform a chief that does not exist; and what reformation is greater, than to unite the Church, by providing it with a head, by a canonical election? Let us fear what Scripture says, ' That a kingdom divided against itself cannot stand.' " D'Ailly forgot the Council of Pisa in his wishes for reform,—he ought rather to have feared that a pope, once elected, would not allow himself to be reformed.

His discourse had an immense influence, and strongly contributed to keep the French nation united to those who wished to proceed without delay to the election of a pope. Emboldened by this success, the cardinals and the Italians redoubled their activity, making a great noise about the union of the Church, particularly since the deposition of Benedict XIII., and representing as an enemy of this union whoever should cause any obstacle to the election of the new pontiff. The emperor himself was not spared. His opinion was alleged against him as a crime; and it was asked, if it was not contrary to divine right, when the Apostolic See was vacant, to postpone filling it up—whether this error did not partake of the heresy of John Huss—and whether it was not tacitly to acknowledge that the Church could be governed without a pope?

Sigismund disdained those cloaked and insidious attacks, and even in the midst of the opposing nations he found some support. "Beware of those," said the Archbishop of Genoa, " as of your most dangerous enemies, who, by their promises and manœuvres, are endeavouring to turn you aside from your holy design of reforming the Church."

However, these persevering endeavours succeeded with the greatest number. Each day the emperor beheld the circle of those who shared his opinion diminishing; and he lost one of the prelates most devoted to the proposed reformation, in the person of Robert Hallam, Bishop of Salisbury, who died at

Gotleben, Sept. 4, 1417. The English nation, whom this bishop had restrained by the authority of his words and of his character, passed shortly after his death over to the party of the cardinals. Exulting in this victory, those who were in favour of an immediate election no longer thought it necessary to observe any decorum. In a meeting of the nations, held on Sept. 9, 1417, a strong protest from the cardinals was read, couched in language very disrespectful to Sigismund. "What matter is it," said they, " that his opinion differs from ours? He is not the person to decide—these questions are not within the competency of the emperor."

Sigismund, in great irritation, rose up, and before the whole document was read through, left the meeting, followed by the Patriarch of Alexandria, and some others. As he withdrew, this sinister sound struck his ears: "Let the heretics depart!"

Sigismund then beheld, with dismay, that the design to which he had consecrated so much exertion, was on the point of miscarrying. In his just indignation against the cardinals, he had some thoughts of having some of the bishops arrested and banished; but they, who were thus threatened, held firm. The emperor, they said, was irritated against them, because he wanted to have a pope devoted to himself—which he should never obtain as long as they could prevent it. They declared, therefore, that no feeling of apprehension should induce them to yield, and that nothing should turn them from pursuing their plan of effecting the union of the Church until death.[*]

It does not appear that the emperor acted with severity against any one; but he had their protest answered by a memorial, in which all the abuses and excesses that rendered a reformation necessary, were represented with extreme virulence. It was necessary, it said, to proceed to effect the change forthwith, as otherwise the new pope, however holy he might be before his election, could not fail to sully himself afterwards in the midst of such filth.

This memorial was presented in the name of the German nation, the only one that remained faithful to the cause defended by the emperor; but the cardinals, taught by experience, encouraged by success, and knowing, besides, that, in acting in a multitude, it is sufficient to gain over the leaders, in order to draw with them the flock, tampered in secret with the two men whose influence was greatest in this nation—the Archbishop of Riga and the Bishop of Coire. Both allowed them-

---

* Væ et iterum væ vobis quia hæc omnia vitia in clero experimur. Quid dicemus in hoc fœdo et infami tempore, quo fidei fervor, spei vigor, et charitatis ardor in servis et ministris ecclesiasticis fere totaliter evanuit?—(Petr. de Allia. Panes. in S. Ludovic. ap. Von der Hardt, vol. iv. p. 1400.)

* Schlestrat, p. 64.

selves to be seduced,* and their defection produced that of the Germans; so that the emperor was thus left alone. All resistance then became impossible: he yielded, therefore, but with the formal condition, that the pope should occupy himself with the reformation of the Church, before his coronation—that he should labour at it in concert with the council:—and that he should not leave Constance until it was accomplished.

Yet, though the election of the pope was decided to take place before the reformation of the Church, the Reformatory College continued to pursue its labours. It will be seen afterwards what points it signalized as principally calling for a reform; and the council itself, before proceeding to the choice of a new pontiff, passed, in its thirty-ninth session, some important decrees, destined to serve as a curb on the future pope.

The first ordered the periodical and regular convocation of œcumenical councils, in the following manner: A first council was to assemble within five years; a second, seven years later; and, at least, one should assemble every ten years afterwards. Each council, in concert with the pope, or without the pope, should indicate the place and time of the succeeding council's meeting. The pope could not change the place thus appointed, without an evident necessity, such as war or plague, or other contagious disease; and even then he could not do so but with the consent of his cardinals. This decree was termed *a perpetual edict;* and of it, it may be said, that it confirmed the famous decrees of the fifth session, in making the pope subordinate to the council.

The second decree regulated the conduct to be observed in case of schism. Should it happen that two or more persons declared themselves to be lawful popes, the term marked for the convocation of a council was to be advanced to the year immediately following that on which the schism declared itself: the emperor, the kings, and the princes, were to be bound to repair to it, as if to extinguish a general conflagration; none of the competitors should preside over the council as pope, but their powers should be declared suspended from the moment the assembly opened. In case a pope should be elected by violent means, his election was to be null. The car-

dinals, however, were not to proceed to any new election until the council had given permission: every city, were it Rome itself, that should suffer violence or coercion to be shown to the electors of the pope, was to be struck with an interdict.

The third decree gave the form of the profession of faith to be pronounced by the pope, before his public election. It was short and insignificant, and contained nothing more than an oath to adhere, until death, to all the articles of the Catholic faith, according to the tradition of the apostles, councils, and fathers. It is more remarkable for the matters which it omits, than those which it expresses; and no mention whatever is made in it of the Holy Gospel or the Bible. The Reformatory College proposed to substitute for this profession of faith that of Boniface VIII.,* and to add to it some articles restrictive of the pontifical authority.

The fourth decree referred to translation of benefices, procurations,† and revenues of vacant cures. The translations were to be permitted only for just causes, and with the consent and signature of the majority of the cardinals. The pope was forbidden to appropriate to himself either the procurations or the revenues of the benefices which happened to become vacant.

Thus terminated the thirty-ninth general session, remarkable only for being the last in which the council manifested, by serious proceedings, a real zeal for a reformation. From the very day on which it was decided that the election of the pope should be proceeded to, the cause of the desired reform was lost, and that of the Roman court gained. The cardinals triumphed; but the efforts for victory cost his life to one of the most illustrious members of their body. After a most stormy discussion, from which he came out exceedingly heated, Zabarella, Cardinal of Florence, was taken ill, and died. It was he who, with the celebrated Emmanuel Chrysolorus, had most contributed to have Constance, a city independent of the pope, chosen for holding the council. From that time, his good intentions and sincere desires for a reform in the Church were unceasingly opposed by the prejudices of his order, and by a timid respect for the privileges of the Roman Church; and after having prepared the way for a reformation, he

---

* The cardinals gained over the first by promising him the bishopric of Liege, should he consent to the election of the pope before the reformation of the Church. As to the Bishop of Coire, he could not resist the hope of being put in possession of the archbishopric of Riga as soon as the pope was elected.—(Lenfant, *Concile de Constance*, book v. sect. lxxv.)

* See note Q.

† By procurations was meant what was gratuitously furnished to the bishops, for their wants and expenses in their pastoral visitations. The popes, under pretext of being masters of all ecclesiastical goods, often appropriated to themselves these procurations, and even sent collectors round to demand them.

contributed to render it impossible. Univer-sally esteemed, he was acknowledged to be worthy of the tiara; and it is asserted, that he would have obtained it had he lived. To appear less worthy of it, all he wanted, per-haps, was to have worn it.[*]

CHAPTER II.

DECREES RELATIVE TO THE REFORMATION OF THE CHURCH AND THE ELECTION OF THE POPE.—THE CONCLAVE.—ELECTION AND CORONATION OF MARTIN V.

THE emperor was not present at the fortieth general session. In it the council decided that a reformation should be effected, according to the plan of the Reformatory College, on eighteen principal heads, of which it drew up a list.[*] Under an apparent zeal for this change, it showed that it was overcome with fatigue and lassitude at its prolonged sittings; and this frame of mind of the council contributed, pro-bably more than any other cause, to precipi-tate the election of the pope. The following decree was first passed :—

"The council orders that the future pope, in concert with it, or with deputies named for the purpose by the nations, shall reform the Church, in its head and in the court of Rome, according to equity and the good government of the Church, before the Sacred Council shall be dissolved; and this reformation shall be effected on the articles determined on by the nations in the Reformatory College. These deputies being elected, it shall be permitted to the other members of the council to withdraw to their homes, with the authorization of the pope."[†]

Thus the council built up with one hand, to pull down with the other. It declared that the reformation of the Church should precede its own dissolution; and, at the same time, it ex-pressed its determination to dissolve itself absolutely before that great object was even commenced :—it confided the care of effecting the necessary reforms to the future pontiff, the very person most interested in their not taking place :—it was itself to withdraw just as he was appointed ;—and, finally, when the am-bitious court of Rome was with difficulty restrained by the whole assembly, what was to be expected from it when only opposed by a few deputies, whom it could gain over by drawing them into its own circle ?

The council next ordered that the election of the pope should be proceeded to in ten days; and decided that, for this time only, there should be adjoined to the twenty-three cardi-nals, as electors, six prelates or distinguished ecclesiastics from each nation, and that the election should be decided by the two-thirds of the whole number of votes. The forty-first general session was almost entirely devoted to regulating, to the most trifling details, the conduct of the electors in the conclave—the number of their servants, the quality and quantity of the dishes which were to be served to them ;—in fine, in taking all the necessary measures for insuring their complete isolation. The council passed enactments for their acts during the day and their repose by night.

The sermon was preached by the Bishop of Lodi; and in his enumeration of all the quali-ties with which the future pope ought to be gifted, he displayed just as much imagination as he had given proofs of a few months before, in his famous discourse against Jerome of Prague.

He chose for his text these words from the Book of Kings—*Look even out the best and meetest,*[†] and exhorted the electors, in order to do so, to cast far from them—as if the poison of serpents—cupidity, ambition, and all un-lawful ties. "Search, therefore," said he,

* The objects designated in this list were, 1st, The number, quality, and nation of the cardinals; 2d, The reservations of the Holy See; 3d, Annats; 4th, The advowson of benefices and reversionary favours; 5th, The confirmation of elections; 6th, The suits that ought to be decided at the Court of Rome; 7th, Appeals to that Court; 8th, The of-fices of the chancellor's and penitentiary's depart-ments; 9th, The exceptions given, and the incor-porations made, during the schism; 10th, Bene-fices *in commendam;* 11th, The intermediates or revenues disposable during the vacancy of bene-fices; 12th, The alienation of ecclesiastical pro-perty; 13th, Causes for which the pope ought to be deposed; 14th, Simony; 15th, Dispensations; 16th, Provisions for the pope and the cardinals; 17th, Indulgences; 18th, Tenths. This list, de-cided on by the council, embraced fewer objects than the vast plan of the Reformatory College, as will be seen in the following chapter. (Msc. Brunsw. Lips. Vindob. Dorran. Wolf. ap. Von der Hardt, vol. iv. p. 1452.)

† Hoc adjecto, quod facta per nationes deputatione prædicta, liceat aliis de licentia papæ libere ad pro-pria remeare. (Mac. Vindob. Dorran. ap. Von der Hardt, vol. iv. p. 1410.)

* See the conduct of Zabarella, in the fourth general session, p. 67.
† 2 Kings x. 3.

" carefully into your souls, in order to banish from them evil practices, disgraceful compacts, quarrels, and cabals. . . . . Several have come here rather to a market than to a council; and, in place of thinking of the general good, are earnest only after their own interest. Such is not the manner in which you ought to be. Be pure, be sincere, be devoted: think that you hold in your hands the safety or ruin of the world; the entire universe has its eyes fixed on you! Remember that, according to your votes, you must render an account to God and men. Moses, in choosing his successor, not amongst his own people, but from another tribe, has shown that the authority of the Lord ought to be conferred on virtue alone. Therefore, look even out the best; choose a man uniting these three great perfections—holiness, wisdom, and knowledge. . . . . . What greater abuse can there be, than to be obliged to give the title of Most Holy to a man of abandoned habits, a villain, a person absolutely infamous! Beware, therefore, of choosing, as an occupant of St. Peter's seat, a Judas, a Simon, a Gehazi, unless you are determined to sell Jesus Christ a second time, and to crucify him anew at Rome. In a vessel like ours, where the poop is damaged, the sail in pieces, the anchor lost, and the mast broken, we are in extreme want of a skilful pilot;—in the contagion, which is wasting us away, it is a great physician that can alone cure us. Like sheep straying far from the pasture-grounds, when the keepers have lost their way, and we have followed them, we want the most excellent of pastors. The clergy are in affliction, religion is suffering, the whole Church is in tears—select, therefore, a man sincere, generous, upright, vigilant, inflexible, of pure morals, patient, severe, and faithful, who may be to the kings a John the Baptist, to the Egyptians a Moses, to fornicators a Phinehas, to idolaters an Elias, to misers an Elisha, to liars a Peter, to blasphemers a Paul, and to simonists another Jesus Christ." It was still too small a quantity of so many rare qualities; for the preacher enumerated forty-six other perfections; and expressed a wish that they might all fall to the lot of the future pope, so that he was, in fact, to be exempt of all human weaknesses, and to unite all the virtues in his own person. A learned and conscientious historian naïvely remarks on this subject: "The portrait is admirable—it is a great pity that it is but a dream."†

In this same session, the names of the fifty-three electors, of whom twenty-three were cardinals, and thirty deputies of the nations, were read aloud. The council also provided

by some decrees for the liberty and validity of the new election, by pronouncing dreadful penalties against any one that should attempt to trouble it by violence. It besides prohibited to pillage the house of him who was elected,* and suspended all business during the election. The very same day the electors entered the conclave.

They proceeded there in great pomp; and when they arrived in front of the cathedral they kneeled down, whilst the Patriarch of Antioch came forth from the church in his pontifical habits, and, at the head of all his clergy, advanced towards them, and gave them his benediction. They then arose, and directed their steps towards the conclave.

The exchange, or public meeting-place of the merchants, had been disposed for this object. Fifty-three chambers had been constructed there, in such a way as that no light could enter from the exterior: all the windows, except one, had been walled up, so that the electors were obliged to enter by the light of flambeaux. The emperor stood at the entrance, and gave the hand to each as he showed him in, conjuring him to elect the most worthy. He administered to all a solemn oath that they would choose a pope remarkable for piety, of good morals, capable of reforming the Church, and well inclined to do so. Having done this, he withdrew, and the conclave was securely locked.

No precaution was omitted to leave the electors to themselves.† Count de Papenheim, marshal of the empire, accompanied by the consul of Constance, going through the city at the head of four heralds, published an edict from the emperor, forbidding all persons to go near the conclave. Two princes and the Grand-Master of Rhodes guarded the doors day and night, having the keys suspended from their neck; and armed soldiers kept watch on the steps in the most profound silence. In front of the building was placed a table, round which were seated the bishops and doctors charged with the task of examining the dishes carried into the conclave, in order that no letter or notification could reach the electors by that means. The Grand-Master of Rhodes himself carried the dishes and cups to the only window by which the members of the conclave could hold communication with the exterior, and from thence the servants placed them before their masters. The object of such extraordinary precaution was to keep away from the electors all other influence than that of the

* Negociantibus.
† Lenfant, Hist. du Concile de Const. book v.

* This savage act was repeated at each new election of a sovereign pontiff, under the pretext that the elected, thenceforward possessing every thing, no longer wanted any of his former property.
† Each was allowed to have with him but a single servant.

Holy Ghost. But had the members laid aside their passions when they crossed the threshold of the conclave? Had they left behind their prejudices, pride, ambition, and the thousand weaknesses which flesh is heir to? If they thought so, they erred, and this was perceived to be the case, from the very beginning of their proceedings. For, notwithstanding the noble exhortation made to them by Cardinal de Vivier, not to pay regard to any thing but the public good, scarcely had they met, when they began to dispute, and continued to do so, for not less than ten days, during which time each elector showed himself to be more anxious about the interests of his own nation than about those of Christendom.

At last, an example of self-denial and sacrifice was given by those belonging to the German nation, who gave up their own candidate, to join with the Italians: this induced the English and the Spaniards to do the same. Finally, the French yielded, and on the morning of the eleventh day, whilst the emperor, the princes, and the priests were singing the *Veni creator* at the door of the conclave, the German electors cried out, *Behold, the Holy Ghost is operating on us!* They all agreed in favour of Otho de Colonna, cardinal and deacon of St. George with the golden veil. Otho was immediately proclaimed pope; and he ordered himself to be called Martin, in honour of the saint whose fête was to be celebrated that same day,[*]—he was the fifth pontiff of that name.

He was then about fifty years of age, and descended from the famous Colonna, who were illustrious for their struggle with the popes and emperors, and who had been excommunicated by Boniface VIII. to the fourth generation. Several historians concur in speaking well of him: they extol his knowledge, his mildness, his justice, and his ability in managing both men and affairs: one even adds—and it is no feeble eulogium—that he became still more affable and upright, after his proposition to the cardinalship. Some others, however, are less favourable to him. Leonard Aretin declares that he had only the outside appearance of goodness; and Windek, a councillor of Sigismund, informs us, that Otho of Colonna was the poorest and most modest of cardinals, but that Martin V. became the most wealthy and most grasping of popes.[†]

Scarcely was he elected, when one of the officers of the conclave had a breach made in the wall, and cried out from thence, so as to be heard at a considerable distance, *We have a pope—it is Otho de Colonna!* Long acclama-

tions replied to this announcement, which the world was expecting for forty years, and which proclaimed the end of the schism, and the union of the church. Not less than eighty thousand persons, says an ocular witness,[*] crowded to the spot, and the immense multitude shouted out, with one voice, "Long live Pope Martin V.!"

The people, being requested to retire, streamed to the vast cathedral, where they returned thanks to Heaven, all the bells pealing forth, all the time, with full volley, while the emperor, followed by the princes and nobles, entered the conclave to pay their respects to the newly elected pope.

There, Sigismund, in the first effusion of his joy, if we are to believe the account of two historians,[†] addressed his thanks to all the electors for the excellent choice they had made, and, without any regard for his proper dignity, prostrated himself before the pontiff, and even kissed his feet with all the marks of the most profound respect. The pope embraced him with brotherly affection, and returned him fervent thanks for having, by so many efforts and cares, restored peace to the Church of God.

This conduct of the emperor put an end to the last hopes of a serious reformation. Sigismund, from this day, was no longer himself: whether it was that he found in the unanimous accord of nations to elect a pope, before the Church was reformed, a motive of discouragement or a decree of Providence; or that he recognised, in the choice of the new pontiff, the certain and immediate working of the Holy Ghost, he no longer appeared that emperor, who, although often subjugated by his prejudices and by the irresistible ascendency of the puissant council, nevertheless knew how to impart to that assembly a vigorous impulse; and the King of the Romans, the fierce successor of Hohenstauffen,[‡] disappeared completely, to show nothing but the submissive son,—the first soldier of the first of priests.

---

[*] November 11—St. Martin's day.
[†] Windekius *In vit. Sigism.* chap. lxxvii. ap. Von der Hardt, vol. iv. p. 1483.

[*] Dacherius, ap. Von der Hardt, vol. iv. p. 1483.
[†] Platina, His. devit. pontif. Roman.—Vanclerus.
[‡] A German family, originally from the castle of Hohenstauffen, in Suabia, and possessing also the castle of Wibling, whence their partisans were also called Wiblings, corrupted into Ghibelines. The family was rendered illustrious by Count Frederick, who, by his services, obtained the hand of the daughter of the Emperor Henry IV., and who was created Duke of Suabia, in 1030. His son, Conrad III., was afterwards elected emperor, and it was in his reign that arose the two celebrated parties, the Guelphs and Ghibelines,—the former, the partisans of Welf or Guelph, Duke of Bavaria, who was warmly supported by the pope, and the latter of the emperor. The Guelph family is the stock from which sprang the houses of Este, Modena, Tuscany, Brunswick, and others, and from which the reigning family of England is descended.—(*Note of Translator.*)

The pope being elected, the next step was to enthrone him, and the council proceeded to this ceremony, with the most solemn pomp, and with honours, both excessive and imprudent. The conclave proceeded in a body to the cathedral, accompanied by the clergy, the princes, and the nobles. Every one was on foot, except the pontiff himself, who came after the clergy, and before the secular body, mounted on a white horse, covered with rich scarlet housings, from whence he scattered his benedictions to a distance amongst the crowd. His bridle rein was held, on the right, by the emperor, and on the left, by the Elector Palatine, who thus conducted the pontiff to the cathedral, where he was elevated on the high altar, to be adored according to custom, to the sound of musical instruments and universal acclamations.

Afterwards succeeded, in their turns, and with the same pomp, the ceremonies of the ordination, of the homage rendered by all, and of the consecration. The last took place on Nov. 21, at midnight, in the cathedral, amidst the pealing of bells, and in the presence of all the clergy, the nobles, the princes, and the emperor. Mass was celebrated by Cardinal de Viviers, and the sermon was preached by Philip Malla, an Aragonese doctor, who chose for his text the following words, to which he gave a symbolical signification: *Him that overcometh, will I make a pillar in the temple of my God.** And this other verse: *And there appeared a great wonder in heaven: a woman clothed with the sun, and the moon under her feet, and upon her head a crown of twelve stars.*† The preacher thus interpreted the words of his text,—the *Column* meant Otho de *Colonna*, chosen to be the support of the Church of God; the *moon* was Benedict XIII., Peter de *Luna*, who had just then been deposed: and lastly, the *twelve stars* were nothing else but the twelve kings present at the council, in person, or by their ambassadors.‡ The Church, on this occasion, again displayed unusual pomp.

Martin V. being consecrated, next expressed his wish to have his coronation proceeded with; and Sigismund was the first to forget the express condition which he had himself laid down, for the meeting of the conclave; namely, that the reformation of the Church was to precede the pope's coronation.

This ceremony surpassed all the rest in splendour. A lofty throne, surmounted by a golden canopy, had been prepared for the pope, in the court of the pontifical palace, lower seats being placed for the princes and prelates. Martin V. appeared in the midst of a most imposing cortege, and took his seat on the throne, amidst the flourish of trumpets and the sound of musical instruments. The crowd of princes and nobles placed themselves by his sides, whilst the Patriarch of Antioch and three cardinals knelt down before him. Three other cardinals, aided by the Grand-Master of Rhodes, took the tiara and placed it on the pope's head, the clergy, at the same time, thundering forth the *Te Deum*. When the ceremony had concluded, Martin V. mounted on horseback, and was led in procession through the city, preceded by the clergy, followed by the princes, and escorted by the whole people; the emperor and the Elector of Brandenburg holding his reins, and walking on foot through the mud.*

However, in the midst of all this worldly magnificence, a lesson, which an ancient usage authorised to be given to the pope, was not forgotten. One of the cardinals, who had remained kneeling before him, previous to the coronation, presented to him, on the end of a wand, a small quantity of burning tow, which was consumed in an instant. "Holy father," said he, "so passes the glory of the world!" But of what use was it to show to the pontiff all this glory under a fugitive emblem, when every one pressed forward in emulation to make him savour its intoxicating delights? of what advantage could such an exhortation to humility be to him, when every visage, from that of Cæsar to the lowest priests, humbled itself at his feet?

Not only did Sigismund neglect to avail himself of this unique occasion, to recover the ancient privilege which his predecessors had possessed, of confirming the election of the popes, but he suffered the pope to confirm his. A short time after the coronation, the emperor bent the knee before him, and Martin V. recognised him as lawful king of the Romans; further deigning to declare, that he would himself supply, by his pontifical authority, whatever deficiencies might have been found in that prince's election.

In the excess of his inconsiderate devotion, Sigismund, without doubt, thought that he could not do too much to render Martin V. the object of universal veneration. He forgot to what a degree extreme adulation tended to corrupt the mind; and, wholly occupied with the task of gaining for the new pontiff the respect of the universe, he took a certain means of rendering him less worthy of it.

---

* Rev. iii. 12.   † Rev. xii. 1.
‡ The King of the Romans, Sigismund, who was also King of Hungary, the kings of France, Aragon, Castile, Navarre, Portugal, Poland, Bohemia, England, Denmark, Sweden, and Naples.

* Sigismundus, Romanorum Rex, duxit equum papæ pedester in *magno luto*, in parte dextra. (Mac. Vindob. Dorrian. ap. Von der Hardt, vol. iv. p. 1490.

M

This was soon discovered; Martin V. swore to the profession of faith of Boniface, and pledged himself, at the same time, to observe the article added by the Reformatory College. This oath comprehended the suppression of the most crying abuses of the court of Rome, and yet he, who thus promised to abolish them, almost immediately again put in force the two celebrated regulations which sanctioned them all. He had a table drawn up of the rules of the Roman chancery, the impure source of simony and of the usurpations of the popes, and the object of the merited animadversion of the prelates, princes, and populations. By that act was confirmed all that existed relative to the reservations of the popes, reversionary favours, vacancies, dispensations, annats, tithes, indulgences, all, in fact, that had been near destroying the Church, and which, it was supposed, the Council of Constance would apply a remedy to. These rules of the chancellor's department, which Martin V. had so early drawn up, were not, however, published till the beginning of the following year; and at the very time that his secret efforts were disposing every thing to oppose the reformation of the Church, he feigned to forward it as much as possible. A few days after his election, the five nations demanded from him the reforms which he had promised to carry out, according to the plan laid down by the Reformatory College. Not daring, openly, to refuse this demand, he pretended to greet it with favour. He ordered the nations to designate deputies, to labour at this grand affair, in concert with six cardinals, whom he should appoint himself. The latter took care to procrastinate the proceedings, either by the slowness incidental to such matters, or by disputes, adroitly originated amongst the various nations. It will be shortly seen to what this grand undertaking was reduced to, and how the council responded, in this most important matter, to the expectation of all Christendom.

Worn out by so many delays, and irritated by the evident want of good will on the part of the pontiff, the French, in the beginning of the year 1418, sent a deputation to the emperor, to complain and to pray him to hasten on the work of the reformation, so anxiously desired. He replied to them with great good sense: "When I pressed you to have the Church reformed, before a pope was elected, you refused to consent—you would have a pope, before the reformation. Now, you have one. Go, therefore, to him yourselves, and obtain from him what you desire." It was to tell them, in other words, that their hopes were fallacious.

Thus, after three years that the council was assembled, the union of the Church under a single pope was the only result, though an important one, of all their labours; and this sovereign body appeared to have taken possession of all authority, only for the purpose of laying it down at the feet of a master.

CHAPTER III.

THE REFORMS.

THE council having decreed in its fortieth general session that the reformation of the Church, in its head and in its members, should be effected, according to the plan determined on by the Reformatory College,* it was difficult for the pope, however anxious he might be to elude all reforms, not, at least, to agree to some. The Reformatory College had terminated its labours—all the nations, with the exception of the Italians, were murmuring at the delays of the pontiff—the Germans had become sensible of the grave fault which they had committed, and they presented a strong memorial in favour of the most urgent reforms—in fact, all Christendom was in expectation;—what would be said if the council should be dissolved before it had fulfilled one of the principal objects for which it had been convoked? All these reasons spoke loud and ought to suffice; but there was another, of a more secret nature, which alone, perhaps, more than all the rest together, forcibly influenced the mind of the pontiff.

Benedict XIII., abandoned by all, and protesting alone, against the council, on his rock of Peniscola, was a cause of great uneasiness to Martin V. The Spaniards were discontented; the fidelity of the King of Aragon not very well assured; the schism might again revive; a spark might rekindle it, and the refusal of the pope supply the motive.

He was unwilling to give this plausible pretext to an enemy—he, therefore, himself, drew up a plan of reform, in sixteen articles, based, in a great measure, on the memorial of the Germans; and he presented it to the coun-

* See page 130.

cil, in January, 1418, with an appearance of sincere zeal, but with a mental reservation to postpone it or render it useless, by ulterior and secret manœuvres. To properly appreciate the reforms which he accomplished, it will be necessary to state those proposed by the Reformatory College.

Three cardinals, and four deputies of each nation, prelates or doctors, composed this college, which commenced its proceedings on June 15, 1415, and prolonged its labours for upwards of thirty months. The rank of its members, and the time which it bestowed on its work, are a double and sufficient guarantee, not alone of the care which it took not to omit any useful reform, but of the absolute necessity which existed for those which it proposed.*

The Reformatory College embraced in its vast plan, the councils, the pope, the court of Rome the prelates, the religious orders, the inferior clergy, and the laity, in their intercourse with the Church. It proposed what follows:

Councils and synods:

Every three years, at least, provincial councils should be assembled, and should last eight or ten days: the archbishops and bishops should attend, under pain of being deprived of their jurisdiction and their revenues. Every year synods of bishops should assemble, and should last, at least, five days. Should the archbishops and bishops neglect to convoke these councils and synods within the prescribed term, they should answer for it to the general council, which could strip them of their offices.

2°. The pope:

The Roman pontiff should decide nothing of importance, without the advice of the cardinals; and, in certain cases, he should await the decision of a general council. He should not take the title of *most holy*, unless he showed himself worthy of it, by an irreproachable conduct. He could be punished, and even deposed, by an œcumenical council, not only for heresy, but also for simony, or any other notorious crime, of which he should have been solemnly warned, in case he proved himself incorrigible one year after the said warning was given him by two-thirds of the cardinals assembled in their college, or by three nations, subject to three different kings.

3°. Cardinals:

There should be but eighteen cardinals.

They were required to be distinguished for their learning, morals, and experience; their age must, at least, have reached thirty years ... they should not be, when appointed, either relatives by blood or marriage to any other cardinal living at the time, to the second degree inclusively; they should not, with the exception of one, be chosen from amongst the religious orders; their election should be made by ballot, and by public examination, and subscribed to by the majority of the cardinals.

4°. Officers of the chancellor's court and of the apostolic chamber:

Their charges were specified, and their number fixed by the Reformatory College.

5°. Reservations:

They were to be abolished: the popes were for ever prohibited from reserving to themselves the property left by bishops, and the revenues of benefices, whilst unoccupied, as well as the procurations or provisions destined for bishops, during the period of their making their visitations. The college broke all grants, by which the advowsons of vacant benefices had been reserved to the apostolic chamber, to the prejudice of such persons as had the right to dispose of them. Should the court of Rome not execute this decree, it should be suspended from its authority, until restitution was made, and its officers were excommunicated, *ipso facto.**

6°. Dispensations:

The popes were not, for the future, to grant dispensations to bishops and abbots, when elected, to take orders within the term of three months, prescribed by the canon law, unless with the concurrence of the majority of the cardinals; and as to dispensations of age for orders, they were not to be extended beyond three years; the dispensations granted to children to hold bishoprics and other ecclesiastical dignities were to be regarded as null; bishops and abbots should hold but one bishopric or one abbey: the pope was not to grant any dispensations for residence.

7°. Ecclesiastical justice, appeals to Rome:

The popes should no longer impede the course of justice: they were neither to protract nor annul suits, after having been judged, unless for very legitimate causes. No person, whether ecclesiastic or secular, should be summoned, in virtue of a pope's order, beyond the towns of the diocese to which he belonged, unless in the cases marked down by the bull of Boniface VIII.

---

* The original documents, from which the resolutions of the Reformatory College are taken, have been extracted from manuscripts in the library of Vienna by Dr. Von der Hardt. They will be found enumerated in the *Hist. du Conc. de Constance*, by Lenfant, vol. ii. p. 309, and following.

* The college made no *mental reservations* of the popes amongst the collection of benefices, be cause they were not invented until afterwards, in the time of Julius II. and Leo X.—(Fra. Paol. *Hist. du Conc. de Trent*, book viii.)

8°. Tenths:

The popes were prohibited from imposing them, without the authorization of a general council.

9°. Exemptions, translations, reserved cases:

The popes should no longer exempt either priests or monks from the jurisdiction of the bishops, nor bishops from that of archbishops. All such exemptions, accorded without the concurrence of the cardinals, were to be broken. Translations of bishoprics and benefices were prohibited. The cases reserved for the pope's judgment were reduced to an exceedingly small number.

10°. Simony:

Every ecclesiastic, of whatever condition or dignity he might be, found guilty of simony, should be deprived for ever of his charges and benefices. Laymen falling into this crime were to be excommunicated *ipso jure*.

The object of the preceding articles was, in particular, to effect a reform in the pope and his court. The Reformatory College next treated of the reform of the prelates, the inferior clergy, the monks, and provided for it by a set of articles, which treated, in detail, of the election of prelates, which was to be effected by the chapters, at full liberty, without the intervention of the pope and the secular powers—of the conditions necessary to obtain bishoprics or abbeys—of the number of prebends, and of those entitled to hold them—of residence, which was rendered obligatory—of the exactions of the prelates and canons on the inferior clergy, which were severely prohibited, as well as the employment of abbeys, churches, and monasteries, for temporal purposes; and bishops were no longer to issue an interdict on places, or excommunication on persons, on account of insolvency.

The Reformatory College next regulated the jurisdiction of the bishops, and, first of all, separated the ecclesiastical jurisdiction from the civil; and distinguished the suits which the bishops ought to be acquainted with, and decide on. They were:

1°. Suits relating to benefices, even when laymen should have the right of patronage. 2°. Every thing concerning ecclesiastical persons, or the property of the church, whatever its nature might be. 3°. Matrimonial suits, dowries, and donations for marriage. 4°. Suits relating to widows, wards, and paupers. 5°. Heresies, schisms, and even public crimes, when they remained unpunished, or cloaked by secular courts of law. 6°. Suits in which the secular justice is one of the parties pleading, which was to be proved by the oath of the demandant, in presence of two witnesses. 7°. All civil suits, where the parties voluntarily referred the matter to an ecclesiastical judge,

crimes confessed before the ecclesiastical judge, legacies, and donations for pious purposes.

The Reformatory College regulated, in all these cases, the best mode of rendering justice. The ecclesiastical judge was to acquit without any charge, and if he should happen to impose a fine, he was to employ the sum so obtained in pious uses, under penalty of being deprived of his charges and benefices. Prelates, priors, archdeacons, and others having ecclesiastical jurisdiction, were to choose for judges and officials only such persons as were learned in the law, of acknowledged probity, unmarried, and above all suspicion of being united to the bishop by blood or marriage.

The national and provincial synods were to provide for the maintenance of ecclesiastical liberty and of union amongst the prelates. These were forbidden to undertake any war, unless obliged to do so by the authority of their sovereigns; or that the offender could not be reclaimed by means of law proceedings and ecclesiastical censures.

The Reformatory College next directed all its attention to the morals of the priesthood, and gave directions to bishops to exercise a strict surveillance over those found offending, and to punish them. Every priest living with a concubine was to lose his benefice, if within the space of a month he did not send away his paramour; the children of priests were not to be admitted into orders, nor should obtain benefices or prebends, unless by a dispensation from the see of Rome from extraordinary motives.

Residence was rendered imperative on curés; they were always to wear the ecclesiastical habit, and no man was to be curé in a parish of which he did not speak the language.

The college regulated every thing relating to the state of canons, their age,[*] their revenues, and the mode of their election; it broke all unjust oaths imposed as the condition of the choice that was to be made of them. If bishops should have been so unfortunate as to swear similar oaths, they were not bound to observe them. At the death of a bishop, the canons should not seize either on his furniture, jewels, or money.

As the clergy united its voice to that of the laity to denounce the almost general corruption of the monks, and as conflicts for authority were perpetually arising between them and the secular priests, the Reformatory College placed them under severe regulations. It, first of all, broke all the exemptions accorded, since the schism, to the monasteries, and all other religious houses, without the consent of the diocesans. It ordered the monks, under heavy

---

[*] The college decided that they should not be younger than eighteen.

penalties, to observe the rules of their order, and to adhere to the three essential points, *obedience, charity,* and *poverty*; it prescribed the regular convocation of meetings of chapters, for the purpose of visiting and inspecting the convents; and it forbade any one to be received in the convents, unless the perpetual vow was taken. The regular monks and canons should not rule in parishes belonging to commanderies, beyond the territory of their monastery, and should not establish themselves, on any pretext, as judges amongst the laity. The college annulled the privileges granted to several abbots to wear the mitre, the pastoral staff, the cross, ring, and sandals, this privilege belonging to the bishops only.

As to the ecclesiastical powers of the monks, the college referred to the bull of Clement V. It forbade all friars to hear confession and to administer the sacraments, without an express permission of the curé.

The superiors were not to exact any pecuniary retribution from the religious persons in their establishment, under pain of excommunication, which could not be taken off, but by the pope, and *in articulo mortis.*

In the mendicant orders, the provincials should be chosen in preference amongst those who were graduates, and each year they should assemble their chapter.

The college next regulated what regarded nuns, their age, their conduct, their living in common, and the mode of punishing them.

Next, passing to the laity, the college showed that they felt considerable apprehension lest they should endeavour to make some inroads on the privileges and jurisdiction of the ecclesiastics, and particularly on their property.

When a man was to present himself to receive sacred orders, the college prescribed that a strict inquiry should be instituted, as to whether he, his father, or his grandfather, might not have exercised or sanctioned some violence against ecclesiastics or their goods, in which case he was not to be admitted without a dispensation from the Apostolic See.

If the temporal should think fit to intermeddle in proceedings of matrimonial suits, or raise obstacles to the spiritual punishment of the crimes of heresy, adultery, fornication, perjury, usury, etc., they were to be warned canonically, and, in case they persisted, an interdict was to be laid on their estates.

The Reformatory College also ordered that a stop should be put to the abuses observable in the consecration of chapels, and in the variations from the canon of the mass: and it terminated its labours by some regulations relative to feast-days, of which it diminished the number—relics, which it forbade to be exposed

to view—and alms-collectors, whom it repressed altogether.

As its last act, it published a curious decree concerning the Jews. This unfortunate people were exposed to frightful treatment, on account of their religion, if they remained Jews, and, on the other hand, if they became Christians, they were stripped of their property, under the pretext that they should, in that way, give satisfaction for the usury exercised by themselves *or their fathers.* Several generous voices had been already raised against this odious practice, and Peter d'Ailly, in particular, had demanded to have it abolished. The college took a middle course,—it recognised the abuse, but only put an end to it, by half. Its decree on this point is a melancholy monument of the prejudices of the age. It is thus worded : " When a Jew is converted, and adheres to Christianity, he shall give up only half his property, whether landed or personal, in restitution of the usury practised on Christians; and he shall charitably be allowed to retain the other half, for the support of himself and his family."

The acts of the Reformatory College were important and extensive, and yet they gave no satisfaction whatever to the wishes of the populations on certain capital points. Thus, they were altogether silent on the abuse of excommunications, interdicts, and indulgences:— they regulated the employment of ecclesiastical property, but they did not diminish the sources from which it proceeded; they did not declare that the extreme corruption of the clergy owed its origin to the very excess of their wealth. The college reduced the number of the offices and privileges of the court of Rome, but did not suppress the tax which nourished its luxury, and which called forth the most animated protests and representations from the kings, parliaments, and churches;—it remained silent relative to the annats, thus tacitly preserving them—it subjected the monks to severe regulations, but it did nothing to lessen their number, or to suppress the abuses arising from the perpetually multiplied foundations of new orders and religious houses :*—

* Peter d'Ailly thus expresses himself on this point :—" Videtur quod tanta religiosorum numerositas et varietas non expediat, quæ inducit ad varietatem morum, et quandoque ad contrarietatem, et repugnantiam observationum, et sæpe ad singularitatem et ad superbiam et vanam excellentiam unius status super alium. Et maxime videtur necessarium ut diminuerentur ordines mendicantium, quia tot sunt et in numero conventuum, et in numero suppositorum, ut eorum status sit onerosus hominibus, damnosus leprosis hospitalibus ac aliis vere pauperibus, quibus convenit jus et verus titulus mendicanti, ipsis quoque curatis parochialibus et si bene consideretur etiam prejudicialis omnibus Ecclesiæ statibus.—(Petr. Alliac. *Op. Gers.* vol. ii. p. 911.)

finally, it assigned limits to the pope's puissance, but only to profit that of the prelates, to whom it preserved a jurisdiction of immense extent, at the expense of that of the secular power. It is indeed difficult to conceive, that at a period when the immorality of the episcopal body was recognised to be so profound and so general, the college could imagine that an unlimited power might be placed in such abandoned and corrupt hands, without danger.

The college had hoped to obviate the evil, by multiplying the precautions that were taken to assure freedom in elections and a good choice of electors: but, in a vast body, which renders an account only to itself, which has no foreign intervention to dread, nothing can supply the place of a check on morals; and of all corruptions, the most incurable, perhaps, is that of an electoral body, when the very persons who could alone repress and punish it are also those to whom it is profitable.

In place of one absolute master, the Church gave itself, in the bishops, a multitude of little sovereigns, almost independent—it dried up one abundant fountain of abuses to supply nourishment to several smaller ones. However, in the regulations of the Reformatory College, the simony of the high clergy met with numerous obstacles, and the licentiousness of the inferior clergy, powerful impediments. There was, therefore, reason to hope, that the surveillance of the national synods, regularly convoked, on the one hand; and the useful balancing of power between the councils and the Roman court, on the other, would gradually cause the most crying abuses, and the extreme immorality, to gradually disappear; and, taking every thing into consideration, it would have been difficult to expect much more in the way of reforms, from an assembly of men, all belonging to the very order which it was designed to amend. Let us now see what was really obtained.

The Reformatory College demanded less than Christendom: the council, in its fortieth session, applied for less than the college; the pope offered for less again; and he gave less than he offered, as far as reforms were concerned; but the shadow was scarcely given, for the plan presented by the pope to the council, in the beginning of the year 1418, only comprised the reform of the high clergy and of the Roman court, and on most points it emasculated the resolutions of the Reformatory College.

The college limited the number of cardinals to eighteen; the pope fixed them at twenty-four;—the college abolished altogether the *reservations* of benefices to the Roman court; the pope maintained a certain number;—the college allowed a free course to the judicial proceedings of the bishops, and did not intend

their judgments to be reversed or revised by the Holy See; the pope maintained appeals to his court, and specified the cases in which they were to be admitted;—the college observed silence on the article of annats, which the Gallican doctors had demanded to be formally abolished; the pope maintained them, specifying on what property they were to be imposed;—the college, on the other hand, restricted to a very small number the cases of conscience reserved for the decision of the sovereign pontiff; whilst the pope never even alluded to this important article; to make up for it, he promised to use, with moderation, the treasure of *indulgences*. In what concerned *exemptions*, *in commendams, dispensations*, and *tenths*, the plan of the pope was almost the same as that of the college: but on the capital matter—that authorizing the pope to be punished in case of his *infringing the laws of the council*—there was a complete dissidency: the Reformatory College specified the cases in which the sovereign pontiff could be deposed, whereas the pope's plan made no mention of such a matter, nor even admitted that such a clause could be at any time lawful.

However little calculated to give satisfaction was the pontifical plan, the pope found it too complete, and became afraid of his own production; whether it was, that he feared, in presenting it for the approbation of all the nations united together, to contrast, by so doing, too serious an engagement; or whether he apprehended calling forth disagreeable representations, it was long before he submitted it to a general discussion. He contrived to divide the nations, and to multiply the difficulties when he assembled them. He knew that he should be stronger when treating with each separately, than with all united; and he adroitly gave them to understand that they would find it their advantage to agree to such a course;[*] he then withdrew his plan, and made with all, except the Italians, separate concordates. In them were reproduced, in part as to the principle, the chief dispositions of the pontifical plan, but they were, designedly, exceedingly different in form and extent.

In addition to the concordates passed separately with the nations, Martin V. published some general constitutions obligatory on the whole of Christendom, and which he caused to be read in the forty-third general session. They annulled the collations made, the unions prescribed, the exemptions and dispensations accorded, in an illegal manner, during the

---

[*] Dicebat enim rem ipsam maturitate et consilio indigere; quia, ex Hieronimi sententia, unaquæque provincia suos habeat mores, suos sensus, qui tolli sine perturbatione rerum subito non possunt. (Von der Hardt, vol. iv. p. 1412.)

schism;—they interdicted the secular habit to the priesthood;—they abolished the exactions of the tenths from the clergy, except in case of an extreme necessity, and with the authorization of the prelate of the district;—and, finally, they enacted severe penalties against simony. Every priest, were it the pope himself, was to be excommunicated by the very fact, if he received money for conferring a benefice.* This concession, though great in appearance, was, in reality, illusory, for a few days before, Martin V., in a secret consistory, passed a *perpetual constitution*, by which it was not allowed any one whatever to appeal from the sovereign pontiff to a future council. Not to allow any one the right of appealing from the pope's decision, was to refuse to all the power of condemning him.†

Last of all, the pope passed the concluding decree, thus conceived: "We declare, with the approbation of the council, that we have satisfied the articles of reform contained in the decree of Oct. 30, 1417, by the decrees which have just been read in this session, as well as by the concordates which we have passed, separately, with each nation in particular."

Cardinal de Viviers declared that the council approved of this decree; whether he had really consulted it, (which the minutes of the proceedings do not specify,) or, which is more probable, he had construed this silence into approbation.

Such was the insignificant result of so many vigorous efforts. The pope, in not permitting the articles relating to the *reform* to be freely discussed in the general assembly, appeared to concede, of his own will, those which he

accorded. He was well aware that a constitution granted has not the force of one consecrated by a synallagmatic contract, and he who gives supposes also that he can take away. In passing separate concordates with all the nations, except the Italians, he remained nearly free and absolute in the country where he was most interested to be so: he divided in the rest of Europe the interests and suits of the nations, and according as each should appear obedient or hostile, formidable or weakened, the pope reserved to himself the power of confirming or withdrawing its privileges, without the others having any right to complain, or to reap advantage from it for themselves.

The general reforms consented to, for all times and all places, were, as has been shown, limited to a very small number of points—the most of them of secondary importance. Some contemporary authors, on this occasion, have quoted the expression of Scripture: *They strained at a gnat and swallowed a camel*—and have applied it to the reformers of the council.

But how could they have done more? Where could the council have found, after the election of the pope, the necessary determination and force? It had been deficient in these qualities before, and now they should have still greater occasion for them. Besides, in the midst of the general corruption of morals and doctrines, what result could be hoped for in an evangelical point of view, from plans in which every thing was treated of except the gospel: and what serious reforms could be expected from an assembly which flung into the flames the real reformers?

CHAPTER IV.

AFFAIR OF THE POLES AND THE MONK FALKENBERG.—DECREES AND BULLS OF MARTIN V.—CLOSE OF THE COUNCIL.

AMONGST the important suits submitted to the council, was, as has been seen, that of the Poles and the Teutonic Knights.‡ For about

two centuries the Poles had been sustaining a continual war, waged on them by the Prussians, a people, at that period, still savage and pagan: they had, at last, been obliged to call to their aid the Teutonic Knights, agreeing to cede to them all the territory they might be able to subdue. This donation was confirmed by the Emperor Frederick II., and by the popes, Honorius III. and Gregory IX., who at the same time granted to the knights bulls of indulgences for the conversion of the infidels. But with men who made warfare their occupation, at that period, to convert was tantamount to massacre. The knights selected, in particular, each year, for their excursions against the Prussians, two days consecrated

---

* Martinus, etc. . . statuentes usuper quod dantes et recipientes eo ipso facto sententiam excommunicationes incurrant, etiamsi pontificali aut cardinalatus præfulgeant dignitate. (Msc. Brunsw. Goth. Lips. et Wolfenb. ap. Von der Hardt, vol. iv. p. 1537.)

† See Gers. *Dialog. apolog.* vol. ii. p. 390, and *Tractat. quonod. et an liceat in caus. fid. a sum. pontif. appell.* vol. ii. p. 303. Gerson is the only author present at the council who has mentioned this constitution of Martin V. He speaks of it in his *Dialogue apologetique*, in rather an obscure manner, but afterwards, in the treatise which he composed to refute it, his testimony is formal and cannot be called in question.

‡ Page 54.

to the Virgin—the feasts of the Purification
and the Assumption. They thought that they,
thereby, performed signal acts of devotion to
the mother of the Saviour, in visiting every
thing amongst the Prussians with fire and
blood. They, in the end, fell on the Poles
themselves, who had called them to their aid,
and a frightful war ensued, in which the
knights met with several sanguinary defeats.
But their ambition had greater influence on
them than their disasters, and each reverse
filled their minds with fresh fury.

Ladislaus Jagellon, King of Poland, and
Alexander Withold, the Grand-Duke of Lithuania, denounced to all Christendom these
acts of violence on the part of the knights;
and, at last, both parties agreed to refer the
matter to the council, and abide by its arbitration. Two questions were submitted for
decision, one, of right : *Is it allowable to convert infidels by force of arms, and do the lands of
the infidels belong to the Christians?* and the other,
of fact, and relative to the *conduct itself* of the
knights.

The most remarkable advocate of the Poles,
at the council, was Paul Voladimir, doctor of
canon-law, rector of the University of Cra-
cow, and one of the ambassadors of the King
of Poland. He published a memorial, in
which are found arguments superior to the
opinions generally received at that period, and
their very superiority contributed, without
doubt, to their failure. Voladimir inveighed
against that doctrine of the canonists which
declares that, since the coming of Jesus Christ,
all jurisdiction has passed into the hands of
believers. He, on this point, opposed the
right of nations to the bulls of the popes and
the ordinances of the emperor. "Although
infidels," said he, " do not belong to the fold
of the Church, they still are in the number of
the sheep of Christ, and the successor of St.
Peter is bound to protect and succour them . . .
Right cannot spring either from injustice or
violence. . . . Natural law declares to us, 'What
one man occupies cannot be justly occupied
by another;' and divine law says, 'Encroach
not on the lands of thy neighbour !' It is not,
therefore, allowable to forcibly take from the
infidels their property and jurisdiction, for
they hold them from God. The letters of the
emperors and the bulls of the popes, which
give the lands of the infidels to the Christians,
confer on them no right, but only deceive them,
for no person can give what he does not possess. . . . It is by gentleness and not by violence that souls are converted ; . . . and under
pretext of performing a holy work, acts of impiety must not be committed—they who act
so, labour much more for themselves, than for
God." . . . Voladimir then proceeded to de-

nounce as an abominable sacrilege the choice,
which the knights made, of the feast days of
the Virgin, and of Sabbaths, to visit the infidels
with fire and sword. "It is absurd and impious," said he, " to affirm that the infidels
are incapable of jurisdiction, honour, and government—such a doctrine opens the road to
rapine and homicide." . . . . He, however,
excepted from the class of impious wars those
of the Spaniards against the Moors, because
the former did nothing but recover from the
Moors what the latter had deprived them of :
and the crusades to the Holy Land, because
Palestine had been, at first, possessed by the
Christians ; and because it was not proper to
have Mahomet obeyed in a place where Jesus
Christ had been adored.*

The memorial of Paul Voladimir, though so
highly to be praised for morality and reasoning, clashed with the prejudices of the time,
and wounded the pretensions of the Roman
court ; its conclusions being much more favourable to the rights of humanity than to
those of the ecclesiastical power. It was read
for the first time in the assembly of the nations,
on July 15, 1415, the very day that the council
had just proved, by the execution of John
Huss, that all other interests disappeared, in
its opinion, before that of the privileges and
power of the clergy. The Poles, besides,
had but little credit in that assembly, whilst
the knights had acquired a considerable share
by their intrigues, and had rendered themselves
formidable by their audacity ; so that the memorial of Voladimir remained without result.
The affair was again brought forward on the
13th February following, without any better success; pretexts, rather than reasons, having been
recurred to, to postpone it. The knights, however, excited against the Poles and their king
the licentious pen of a Dominican monk named
De Falkenberg. This shameless fellow addressed a frightful libel to all the kings,
princes, and prelates in Christendom. "Ladislaus," said he, " is an idol, and to obey him
is idolatry. The Poles and their king are
heretics and impudent dogs, and it is more
meritorious to kill them than the pagans. The
secular princes who shall get them hanged,
will be worthy of celestial glory, and they
who tolerate them will be damned."†

The deputies of the nations condemned this
infamous pamphlet; and the Poles were, on
this occasion, warmly seconded by the ambassadors of the King of France, and particularly
by D'Ailly and Gerson, who reproduced against
the author the same arguments that they had

* *Opposit. Paul Volad. demonstr. erunfer. Ord.
Teuton.* Ex antiq. cod. mec. Cæsar. Vindob. ap.
Von der Hardt. vol. iii. p. 9, and the following.
† Dugloss, *Hist. Polon.* book xi. p. 377, 461.

before advanced against the apologist of the Duke of Burgundy. John Petit and John de Falkenberg were, in fact, champions of the same cause—that of murder; one justified the crime and the other exhorted to commit it.

The sentence, signed by the deputies of the nations, and all the cardinals, ordered that Falkenberg's pamphlet should be publicly burnt, as seditious, impious, cruel, and heretical: and it was announced, that this decision, taken by the assembled nations, would be confirmed in full council.

Otho de Colonna had signed it, like the other cardinals; and when he became pope, every one thought that he would confirm the sentence which he had rendered as cardinal. This, however, was not the case—for whether the knights gained him over, or terrified him, Martin V. did not ratify the signature of Otho de Colonna; and no argument or expostulation could obtain from him the condemnation either of Falkenberg's libel or of John Petit's apology for the Duke of Burgundy.

This twofold denial of justice filled the mind of Gerson with a poignant affliction. He gave full career to his indignation, and pointed out the dangerous consequences of such conduct in these terms: " After having so often entered into engagements to extirpate heresies, not to condemn similar maxims, is to give reason to think that concession has been made to terror. —it is to call forth just reproaches from the Bohemians, against whom vigorous measures have been put into execution—it is to furnish justification for homicides, treasons, and perjuries—it is to give ample scope to believers as well as pagans to laugh and mock, particularly to Peter de Luna and his supporters, who will assert that error has been tolerated in full council on matters of the highest importance, and that, after the election of a pope, chosen chiefly to extirpate errors, they were less openly combated than before. Others will behold in such conduct the abandonment of the Catholic truth, and an assent given to heresy: for not to oppose an error is to adhere to it.*

Not only the council of the pope did not approve of Voladimir's doctrine, against the extermination of infidels or their conversion by arms, but the pope even published a crusade bull, which sanctioned the opposite doctrine.

It exhorted, by the advice of the cardinals,† all Christendom to second in Africa the conquests of King John of Portugal, against the Moors. Martin V. invited, by the shedding of the blood of Jesus Christ, all emperors, kings, dukes, princes, marquises, barons, and others, to take up arms valiantly, and assist that monarch in his design of exterminating infidels, with a promise to grant them, for their efforts in forwarding so excellent a work, *spiritual munificences*, that is to say, indulgences and remission of their sins.

This bull, thus commanding a crusade against the infidels, was followed by a terrible decree of the council, in twenty-four articles, and by a new bull of the pope against a Christian people. The execution of John Huss, far from putting down heresy in Bohemia, had doubled its strength, and the death of Jerome of Prague carried the public irritation to the highest pitch. After it had been vainly attempted to stifle the independence of men's minds, by the blood of these two men, it was now deemed necessary to crush their revolt in the blood of the people. The decree of the council, drawn up for that object, ordered, amongst other things, what follows:

"The clergy of Bohemia shall be re-established in their charges and property. The principal disciples of Huss, pointed out by name, shall be cited to appear before the court of Rome; all the condemned works of Wycliffe, John Huss, and Jacobel, shall be delivered up to the legates; all the practices relative to divine worship, images, and the veneration of relics, shall be enforced. Whoever, whether priest or layman, shall preach or defend the condemned heresies, or render to John Huss, or to Jerome, the worship paid to the saints, shall be treated as a relapsed heretic, and burnt to death.* Every secular, when duly warned, shall be bound to lend assistance in the execution of this decree, or shall be punished as an abettor of heresy."†

This order of the council was accompanied by a bull from the pope, addressed to all archbishops, bishops, and inquisitors of the faith; and the latter is a model of inquisitorial procedure. Martin V. in it ordered suspected persons to be interrogated and forced to reply, with the hand on the gospel, on the crucifix, or relics of saints, and to swear in that manner, if they held any of the errors declared reprehensible in the forty-five condemned articles of Wycliffe, and in the thirty articles attributed to Huss.‡

To these seventy-five questions, the pope

* Gers. oper. Dialog. apolog. vol. ii. p. 390.
. † De fratrum nostrorum consilio.—The bull, dated in the month of April, does not bear the approbation of the council.—(Lenfant, *Hist. du Conc. de Const.* book vi.)

* Tanquam hæretici relapsi puniantur ad ignem.
† Ex msc. Vindob. ap. Von der Hardt, vol. iii. p. 1514.
‡ Amongst the errors attributed to John Huss, is the following article, which appears orthodox, and of which we do not find that any mention was made at his trial: The two natures, divinity and humanity, are in one Christ.

added thirty-nine, of which only a few shall be mentioned here.

Every suspected person was to be asked:

If he was not acquainted with Wycliffe, John Huss, or Jerome, during their lifetime; and if he had not been on terms of friendship with them.

If he had not prayed for them after their death.

If he had not some of their books in his possession, or knew those who possessed them, in which case he was *bound to denounce* them.

If he believed, that all which the sacred Council of Constance, representing the universal Church, had approved of, in all points belonging to the faith and salvation of souls, ought to be accepted and observed by all Christians; and that the matters which the council had condemned as contrary to the faith and moral practices, ought to be held as justly and properly condemned.*

If he believed that the sentences passed on Wycliffe, John Huss, and Jerome of Prague, were according to right and justice.

If he believed that after the consecration, by the priest, in the communion, under the appearance of bread and wine, there was neither material bread nor wine, but this same Jesus Christ, who suffered on the cross, and who is now seated on the right hand of God.

If he believed that after the consecration, the true flesh of Jesus Christ, *his blood, his soul, and his divinity,* Christ altogether, and the same body, were found without distinction under one and the other kind.

If he believed and affirmed that it was lawful for believers to *venerate* the relics and images of saints.

If he believed that in case of obstinate disobedience, the prelates had the power to issue an *interdict,* to invoke the aid of the *secular power,* and to *insist* on the execution of their sentences.

If he believed that to deprive a priest of evil life of his property was a *sacrilege.*

If he believed that it was allowable for the laity, men and women, to preach freely the *word of God.*†

This bull was conceived in terms most likely to produce irritation, for it obliged each to swear that a perjury knowingly committed to save his own life, or that of others, was a mortal sin; and yet it placed every person between perjury and martyrdom, making for one

convert a hundred hypocrites, or a hundred rebels.

However, from all quarters, ambassadors of princes and republics arrived at Constance to offer their congratulations to the pope and to make requests. They, whose coming excited in the highest degree the general attention, were the envoys of the Greek emperor Manuel Paleologus, and of Joseph, Patriarch of Constantinople. The chief of this embassy, George, archbishop of Krovia, was accompanied by several Turkish and Tartar princes and by nineteen bishops of the Greek Church.

For a considerable length of time, a general council had been looked to as the only remedy for the schism which separated the two Churches, and Gerson, in particular, had insisted on its importance for this object.

The Greek deputies were received with signal honour, in the expectation of the union, which was so much desired. The emperor, princes, and clergy went out to meet them, and during their stay at Constance, full liberty was allowed them to exercise their own worship. "The general opinion was," says a contemporary author,* "that the union would have taken place, if the reformation had not miscarried." This is, however, problematical. It is difficult, on the other hand, to reconcile the honours paid these schismatics, and this toleration for their religion, with the barbarous treatment inflicted on other parties, reputed schismatics and heretics—Huss and Jerome. The reason of this double fact is that which sways so many events—the privilege of force. The Bohemians were weak, and they were struck down; the Greeks were powerful, and they were loaded with honours.

In the midst of the homage which he received from all parts, Martin V. had a serious motive for uneasiness. Benedict XIII. still continued to call himself pope, and to brave all Christendom, from the summit of his rock of Peniscola. The council again sent deputies to him, and the pope despatched a legate to summon him to resign. But Benedict, retrenched behind the walls of his fortress, again had recourse to his shuffling tricks: he acted with Martin V. as he had formerly done with Gregory XII. "He should wish," he said, "to confer, relative to the union of the Church, with the elected of the council, and since the latter was a reasonable man, he doubted not that he should induce him to hear reason."

Benedict felt himself not without support when he used such language. The King of Aragon alone could have brought him under

---

* This question, which Martin V. ordered to be put to every suspected person, has always been regarded as a new confirmation of the acts of the council.

†*De inquisitione in Huss et Bohem.* Msc. Vindob. ap. Von der Hardt, vol. iv. p. 1527—1529.

* Dacherius, ap. Von der Hardt, vol. iv. p. 1511.

subjection, but Ferdinand IV. was dead, and his son Alphonso V. could not resist the temptation of keeping in his power, as a useful instrument, the fallen but unsubmissive pontiff. Immediately after the election of the pope, Alphonso represented to him the extent of his father's services and his own. "Both," said his ambassadors, "had expended large sums for the peace of the Church," and under this pretext, Alphonso demanded the perpetual disposal of the benefices of Sicily and Sardinia, with a dispensation of all service or rent, therefore, to the Apostolic See—a great part of the ecclesiastical property belonging to the See of Rome in the kingdom of Aragon—and some fortresses of the domain of the Knights of Rhodes, and amongst the rest, Peniscola.

These demands went beyond all reasonable limits, and the pope only granted some, rejecting the rest. Alphonso avenged himself by covering Benedict XIII. with his protection, at first, in secret, and afterwards avowedly. Spain became unsettled, being discontent with the council and the pope, and divided between weariness of the schism and the attraction of independence—and Peter de Luna lived to be a menace and a check on Martin V.

The council approached its close, and the pope, who had done so little to respond to the expectations of Christendom, put a stop to most important demands and representations, by attaching to himself, by favours, the most powerful of those who could have urged them to a conclusion. Thus, through a desire to propitiate Sigismund, he granted to John of Bavaria, bishop of Liege and sub-deacon, a dispensation to marry the duchess of Luxembourg, the emperor's niece. About the same time, however, he disposed of another for twenty thousand crowns, contrary to Sigismund's wish, to John, duke of Brabant, to marry his first cousin. Anger, on this occasion, called to the emperor's mind what he had forgotten, when he interested himself in the marriage of the Bishop of Liege. "Holy Father," he asked the pope, "why are we at Constance?" "To reform the Church,"[*] coolly replied the pontiff. "One would never suppose so," rejoined the emperor. "You can pardon sins, but not sanction them."

The discontent of Sigismund soon disappeared, for Martin V. found a sure means of appeasing him—he granted him a year's tenths from all the churches of Germany, although he had formally promised not again to impose any without their concurrence.

Finally, the pope renewed, in favour of

Sigismund, the empty ceremony of the golden rose, which he consecrated with great pomp, and which Sigismund received publicly from his hands, as he had formerly accepted it from the hands of John XXIII., with respect and great devotion.

In the midst of such acts, the assembly concluded its labours. The pope, in the forty-fourth session, appointed Pavia as the place of meeting for the next council, and on April 18, 1418, he opened, in presence of the emperor, the forty-fifth and last session, which was marked by a grave incident. Mass had been said—the pope had pronounced an exhortation, and Cardinal Raymond Brancaccio, by his order, was in the act of formally announcing that the assembly was that day to be dismissed, when Gaspard of Perousa, the advocate of the sacred consistory, rose, and in the name of the ambassadors of the King of Poland and of the Grand-Duke of Lithuania, humbly exposed to the council the disastrous and most insulting proposition, and the cruel heresies contained in the pamphlet of John de Falkenberg. It had, he observed, been condemned, first of all, by the commissioners appointed for matters of the faith ; and next, by the five nations and the cardinals: he, therefore, had to beseech the pope to have it also condemned by the council, previously to its dissolution. The council, he said, had been assembled to extirpate heresies, and could not therefore refuse to stigmatize an infamous doctrine, which tended to the massacre of kings and the destruction of kingdoms. If, however, contrary to all justice, this demand should be rejected, the ambassadors of Poland and Lithuania would appeal to the next council.

At this determined language, a great tumult arose in the assembly. The patriarchs of Constantinople and Antioch, who always declared themselves to belong to the French nation, and a Spanish Dominican friar, took the part of the pamphlet, and declared that it had not been condemned in their nations:—two law-officers publicly declared that assertion to be false. Then the Polish ambassador, Paul Voladimir, rose, and requested permission to speak, to complete, he said, the statement that had been but imperfectly made by Gaspard of Perousa. He then commenced reading an energetic protest, in the midst of great noise and confusion. The pope ordered all to be silent, and said : "I shall inviolably observe all that in the present council has been determined on, and concluded relative to matters of faith, synodically (conciliariter) but not otherwise."[*]

---

[*] Lenfant, *Hist. du Conc. de Const.*; Vindek, *Hist. Msc. de la vie de Sigismond*, ch. xiv.

[*] Dixit quod omnia et singula determinata et conclusa et decreta in materiis fidei per presens

The pope meant to imply by these words, that as the pamphlet of Falkenberg had not been condemned by the council in a general session, he should not condemn it either. Voladimir did not permit himself to lose courage, but went on with the reading of the protest, declaring loudly with the apostle that it was better to obey God than men.

The pope interrupted him anew, and ordered him to be silent, under pain of excommunication. "I appeal then to the next council," cried Voladimir, "and I demand to have my motive of appeal formally registered."

But the pope had provided, by anticipation, for such a case, in the secret consistory, in which he had drawn up the perpetual constitution, which prohibited all appeal from the sovereign judge, the Roman pontiff, the vicar of Jesus Christ on earth, to any other power whatever.

"This constitution, or bull of the pope," said Gerson, with grief, "overturns, from top to bottom, all that was done in the councils of Pisa and of Constance, particularly, relative to the election of the sovereign pontiff, and the rejection of intruders."[*]

When calm was restored in the assembly, the Bishop of Ancona, general of the Dominicans, delivered the sermon on this text: *Ye now, therefore, have sorrow: but I will see you again and your hearts shall rejoice.*[†] The bishop, by these words, made allusion to the separation of the present council, and the union of the succeeding one, to finish the work of *reformation.*

It was, however, difficult to comprehend how this great undertaking, having miscarried twice, in the midst of the most favourable circumstances, could be brought to an end, by a council, at any other place or any other time.

The pope next took leave of the illustrious assembly, from which Europe had expected such great results, and had the following bull read out:[‡] "We, Martin, bishop, servant of the servants of God, with a perpetual remembrance of this great event, and at the request of the sacred council, do hereby dismiss it,

giving to each member liberty to return home. By the authority of Almighty God and the blessed apostles, St. Peter and St. Paul, and by our own, we grant to all who have been present at this council a full and entire remission of their sins, once during their lifetime, so that each of them may enjoy the benefits of this absolution for two months after it shall have become known to him. We grant them the same grace when *in articulo mortis,* both to them and their servants, on this condition, however, that they shall fast all the Fridays in a year for the absolution, at the point of death, unless they be legitimately prevented: in which case they will perform other acts of piety. After the second year, they shall fast the Friday for the rest of their life. . . . If any one shall rashly oppose this absolution and this concession, which we give, let him learn that he will thereby have incurred the indignation of Almighty God, and of the blessed apostles, Paul and Peter."

The council which had burnt Wycliffe and John Huss—the one dead and the other living —ought to have looked on itself as morally bound to present, to the respect and faith of the world, decrees and doctrines superior to the opinions and works which it had condemned. Yet, after reading this bull, which terminates its labours, if it be conscientiously examined, it will be impossible to find in it any thing of real piety. One would suppose it to be dictated by some enemy of the council, rather than by the pope of its choice.

Cardinal de Viviers pronounced the *placet,* and approved of the bull, in the name of the council. Then the emperor, through his advocate, Arduin de Navarre, recapitulated all that he had done for the union of the Church, his expenses, his journeys, his labours, his dangers, and declared that he did not regret them, since this union, so anxiously desired, had been, at last, accomplished. He thanked the cardinals, ambassadors, and deputies of the academies, for their perseverance, and promised to remain, to his last breath, inviolably in the obedience of the Roman Church and the pope.

Thus was closed, on April 22, 1418, the celebrated Council of Constance, after three years and a half's duration.

A few days after, Sigismund and Martin V. took their departure from the city, with great pomp—the first with the design of consolidating all that had been done there, and the second, of weakening and annulling in several points the work of the council, and even his own.

---

sacrum concilium Constantiense conciliariter, et non aliter, observare volebat. (Msc. Lips. ap. Von der Hardt, vol. iv. p. 1557.)

[*] Minuta quædam sub forma bullæ destruens fundamentale penitus robur, nedum Pisani, sed Constantiensis concilii, et eorum omnium, quæ in eis præsertim super electione summi pontificis, et intrusorum ejectione, attentata factave sunt.—(J. Gerson, *Oper. Dialog. apolog.* vol. ii. p. 308.)

[†] St. John xvi. 22.

[‡] Ex Msc. Vindob. Dorr. Brunsw. Lips. et Wolfenb. ap. Von der Hardt, vol. iv. p. 1560.

CHAPTER V.

GENERAL CONSIDERATIONS ON THE COUNCIL OF CONSTANCE.—RESULTS OF THE COUNCIL AND OF THE SCHISM, RELATING TO THE GALLICAN CHURCH AND THE REFORMATION.

THE council had been convoked to extinguish the schism, to extirpate heresy, to effect the union of the Church, and to reform it. For nearly four years, these great results were the objects of the efforts of the princes, prelates, and doctors of Europe, assembled at Constance. To attain this end, the council forced one pope, Gregory XIII., to abdicate—deposed two others, John XXIII. and Benedict XIII.—elected a new pontiff, Martin V., whom it got recognised by almost the whole of Christendom—employed, against its adversaries, spiritual thunders, the imperial arms, and the fires of the funeral stake—signalised, in innumerable public acts and decrees, all the sores of the Church, and the urgency of reforming them; and yet its efforts, in a great measure, miscarried—it left incomplete and unfinished nearly all it had undertaken.

The schism, it is true, was nearly extinguished, but the union of the Church was far from being cemented, and the new troubles that arose, almost immediately after, proved that the council had sown in the Church the seeds of a division more profound and lasting than that which it had put down. Heresies were not extirpated: those which struck the most serious blow at morality and the repose of empires were only imperfectly condemned, and the authors of them escaped the censure of the council. Never could France, whose representatives had directed that body in every thing that it effected for the general good, obtain, by the organ of Gerson, the condemnation of John Petit, the apologist of the murder of the Duke of Orleans;[*] never could the pope be induced to condemn John de Falkenberg, who, in his dreadful libel, had devoted the King of Poland to death, by promising celestial glory to his assassin. On the other hand, the doctrines reputed heretical, and which directly attacked the clergy in their fortune and power, drew down, on their authors, all the severity of the council: but they swelled into much greater importance, from the very violence employed to crush them, and finally they set Bohemia and Germany in flames.

As to the reforms, most of them came to naught. The vices, which were universally acknowledged to exist in discipline and morals,

were but feebly repressed; and the powers, the abuse of which had caused so much scandal, and called forth so many complaints, received, almost every one, a new recognition from the acts of the council; no restriction was imposed on the use of indulgences, or excommunications, or interdicts; the clergy preserved the right of waging war on their own account, of employing the censures of the Church in support of its terrestrial puissance, and of calling on the secular power to aid it in spiritual decisions—it was not forced to accept any bridle to its authority, or any limit to its wealth.

The council, therefore, to which so many hopes were directed, fell far below what was expected from it, and yet it is famous in history, for it passed the decrees of the fifth century, and lit up the funeral piles of John Huss and Jerome of Prague—two things which are imperishable.

The decrees of the fifth session, of which the Gallican doctors were the principal authors, have established and consecrated, in a solemn manner, this maxim, already recognised at the Council of Pisa, that the pope is subject to the judgment of every universal council, *in all matters relating to the faith, to the extinction of schism, and general reformation*—"a maxim taught in France from time immemorial,"[*] says Fleury, "but which had not, up to that period, been promulgated by the authority of the assembled church." The acts passed at Pisa, and, still more, the decrees of Constance, afterwards confirmed at Basle, raised this maxim to the dignity of a dogma, and thus gave the most imposing authority to the principle which consecrated the most important of the liberties of the Gallican church. This grand principle was admitted as a fundamental rule in France, in her intercourse with Rome, and but a few years separate the Council of Constance from the assembly of Bourges, where was decreed the celebrated pragmatic regulation, which adopted the decisions of Constance and Basle for the reformation of the Church in its head and in its members—admitted the superiority of general councils over the Roman pontiff—and maintained the liberty of electing bishops and the abolition of appeals to the pope.

---

* The council, however, condemned the general proposition of the apology.

* Tenth discourse on ecclesiastical history, tit. xv.

The decrees of these famous councils became still more important when they were contested, and afterwards in some measure annulled, by other decrees.

They did not, of themselves, shake the authority of the whole Catholic Church; they merely weakened the power of the Holy See and of the Church called Roman. This one had always combated and rejected the principle of the superiority of general councils, and it was natural to suppose that it would make the greatest efforts to revoke them, or at least to render them null.* The proof of this was evident, as soon as the pope was elected, for Martin V. placed himself, as Gerson remarks, above the council, by his bull against all appeals from the judgments of the pope; and his successor, Eugenius IV., followed his example. The Council of Florence, and the fifth general Council of the Lateran, passed decrees relating to the power of the sovereign pontiff—decrees which were, with good reason, considered as subversive of those of Constance.† The Council of Trent confirmed them, under the immediate influence of Pope Paul III., and he, in publishing shew the famous bull, *In cœna Domine*, excommunicated all who should presume to think a general council superior to the pope, or dare to appeal from him to the council.‡ This bull was regularly published

during a period of two centuries in the pontifical states: but these councils and these imprudent popes did not thus fortify the authority of the Holy See, and of the visible head of the Catholic Church, but at the expense of the very infallibility of catholicism.

An exclusive church, which pretends to be infallible, has a marked disadvantage, in one point, when compared with religious communions, which do not lay claim to the same privilege. In the doctrine of the latter, a slight contradiction was of no serious consequence, and an error on one principle by no means compromises the rest; but in the church, which gives all its dogmatical decisions as inspired by God himself, and therefore infallible, every error and every acknowledged contradiction testifies against its infallibility, and ruins its authority; it is on this account that the councils and popes, attributing to the See of Rome the superior and absolute authority, which the proceedings of Constance only accorded to the general council, inflicted, in a logical point of view, a most serious blow on the doctrine of their Church—on its infallibility; and still more, they destroyed, with the same blow, its unity.

The maxims solemnly sanctioned at Constance, and which were, from time immemorial, taught in many countries, and particularly in France, had penetrated too deeply into their doctrines and morals, to allow any possibility of rejecting them, when condemned by Rome. France, therefore, would never receive the contrary decrees; and the liberties of the Gallican church, in spite of so many efforts of the popes to destroy them, had much less to fear, after the Council of Constance, from the usurpations of the Holy See than from those of her own kings. Pius II., who published the bull *Execrabilis*,* Paul III., who had the pragmatic dragged through the kennels of Rome, were less formidable to these liberties than Louis XI. and Francis I. France, in fact, found in the decrees of Constance a new support against the popes: she made a shield, as Pasquier expresses it, of two grand principles against the assaults of the court of Rome; to the ancient one of the right of appeal to the king,† she added the other, laid down as a

---

* "To tell the truth, such persons as were in the habit of being always at the court of Rome, could not take this medicine kindly."—(Pasquier, *Recherches de la France*, p. 154.)

† The Council of Florence clearly declared that the pope possesses an absolute and sovereign power over the whole church. The terms in which this declaration is couched are not susceptible of any other sense: *Ipsi (Romano Pontifici) in beato Petro, pascendi, regendi ac gubernandi universalem Ecclesiam, a Domino nostro Jesu-Christo plenam potestatem traditam esse, quemadmodum etiam in gestis œcumenicorum conciliorum et in sacris canonibus continetur.* At the Council of Trent no person thought of giving them any other meaning, and on that account the French prelates constantly refused to express the authority of the pope in these terms.—(Fleury, disc. x. sect. xvii. note of the edition of 1763.)

It is right to mention that an ardent controversy had since taken place between the ultramontanes and some Gallicans, as to the real signification that ought to be given to the word *quemadmodum*, which is susceptible of two very different interpretations. In one sense, it expresses that the absolute power over the whole church results from the decrees of the councils and the canons; in the other, it means that this power can only be understood, but it is in conformity with these canons and councils. The proof that the first meaning is the true one, is the conduct of the French prelates at the Council of Trent; all the bulls of the popes who have raised their power above that of general councils; and in particular that of Leo X., confirmed by the fifth general Council of the Lateran, where the *pragmatic* was condemned.

‡ The bull excommunicated, besides all heretics, their defenders and fautors, all pirates, violations of the immunities of the church, laymen who gave judgment in ecclesiastical causes, or those of

priests, such persons as made the members of the clergy contribute, in the smallest matter, to the charges of the state, or who accepted their voluntary gifts, those who gave such gifts, the princes who treated with heretics, and, in fact, all who imposed new tributes in their states, without the consent of the Holy See. All such persons could only be absolved by the pope.

* This bull anathematized all persons appealing from the pope to the general council.

† The appeal to the king was not named *appel comme d'abus* until Louis XII.'s time. The thing existed for two centuries, though without the name.

dogma, of the superiority of a general council over the pope;[*] and when, in 1682,[†] after so many vicissitudes, the French clergy again published a celebrated act of independence, it was these same decrees of Constance that furnished them with arms.

The Church, however, continued, on both sides of the Alps, in France and in Italy, to call itself one and infallible; but there were two opinions, as to the supreme power in which this infallibility resided, and its adversaries then inquired how it reconciled the necessary and uninterrupted existence of an extreme infallible power, with the absence of an evident manifestation—the obligation on all to acknowledge it, with the utter impossibility to discern it.

Thus the decrees of Constance and Basle, which in France were the palladium of the Gallican church against the Holy See, and which were held in execration at Rome, were the cause of several popes rendering decisions, in which the reformers found so many arguments against catholicism.

But, amongst all the acts of the Council of Constance, that which, at first, produced the most formidable effects, and which called forth a sudden and terrible reaction, was the sentence of John Huss and Jerome of Prague.

In the religious history of nations, according as a religion is gaining ground or declining, the severities decreed against its adversaries fortify or complete its distraction—excite in the multitude apprehension or en-thusiasm—and, in their opinion, inflict chastisement or martyrdom. This truth was never more evident than after the execution of John Huss and his disciple. In the most Catholic countries of Europe their death was hailed with applause, but the flame of their funeral pile lit up in Bohemia a fire, which all the united forces of the empire could not extinguish in twenty years, and a century had scarcely glided away, when, already, for the half of Europe, Huss and Jerome were martyrs and saints.

Several circumstances concurred to give an immense importance to the double sentence passed by the council. Previously to the funeral piles of Constance, many others had been kindled: popes, kings, ecclesiastical tribunals, and common courts of law, had delivered up to death, for difference of opinion, innumerable victims. But here, to accomplish atrocious acts, there was a frightful accord of all the representatives of the Christian world—here the crime expanded in importance, from the grandeur of the tribunal, and the infallibility which it arrogated to itself. Never did a more imposing authority order a human sacrifice, and never did an assembly, reputed infallible, render itself guilty of that grand heresy which transforms a religion of peace and love into a sanguinary worship—which turns sincerity into a crime, and the priest into an executioner.

The same facts, which concurred to render the persecution so striking, have immortalized the resistance. A grand and terrible spectacle! by which the world was made to feel that there is, in the tribunal of a man's conscience, something against which all that outward force and material power can display falls to the ground and breaks in pieces! Perhaps it was necessary, that there should be ever seen concentrated, on a single point, for the same object, the whole influence of all human authorities—the priesthood and the empire,—the spiritual and temporal power, in order that it might be known, that what is grandest and most powerful on earth is the conviction of the just man, and that the most inviolable asylum is the conscience of the believer.

If we now take in, with a single glance, this period of nearly half a century, to which the great schism has given its name, we shall perceive that what characterizes its tendencies and its results, is the weakening of the monarchical principle of Gregory VII. and Innocent III.

The effect of the schism, with respect to the authority of popes, was, what is at all times disastrous to every power, and particularly to that which has its roots and strength in the opinion of mankind, in the belief of nations—it taught them to despise that authority, to form

---

[*] It has been pretended that the Council of Constance, in issuing the decrees of the fifth session, had not any intention of making them articles of faith; it has also been said that they were not considered as such by the authors of the declaration of 1682. We shall reply to this by the very words of the intrepid champion of the prerogatives of the court of Rome, M. de Maistre, who thus expresses himself: "Who can believe that *nothing which relates to the faith is decided*, when arbitrary limits are affixed to the pontifical authority, when the veritable seat of the spiritual authority is legislated on, when it is declared that *the council is above the pope*—a proposition which overturns catholicism?"—(*De l' Eglise Gallicane*, book ii. chap. viii.) Catholicism, whatever M. de Maistre may say, was less shaken by this proposition, than by the subsequent acts of the popes and the councils that have attempted to annul it, because all contradiction that is acknowledged in the acts of a power declaring itself to be infallible, tells against its infallibility.

[†] This refers to the four famous articles of the declaration of March 13, 1682, when the French clergy, with Bossuet at their head, asserted, in the most positive terms, the independence of the Gallican church. The origin of this determined step was the refusal of Pope Innocent XI. to recognise the right of Louis XIV. to exercise the *Régale*, or the privilege which the French kings, to the exclusion of all other sovereigns, had always enjoyed, of receiving the revenues and exercising the patronage of the ancient bishoprics in their dominions, until the oaths of the new bishops were formally registered.—(*Note of Translator.*)

a judgment on it, to vanquish it, nay, it even did more for it—taught them to do without it. It gave, of necessity, a new and uncounterpoised strength to the great ecclesiastical bodies of the larger states, to the private assemblies of the church of France, and to the general assemblies of the universal Church. There, in presence of the pontifical throne, degraded, divided, or vacant, the high aristocracy of the clergy, the episcopacy, were led, by mere force of circumstances, to pronounce words of contempt, of examination, of independence, and of authority, which, at a later period, were responded to most powerfully from the ranks of the inferior clergy, and which found loud and formidable echoes in the bosom of the oppressed and suffering populations. Thus the clergy, who during this long schism had not accomplished the reforms which it undertook, prepared others, still more important, which they had never contemplated, and were *reformers* without intending it. The revolution was not immediate; and on the very eve of the shock, which so powerfully caused the theocratic monarchy to totter on its throne, the power of the church appeared to settle itself more firmly on its basis: but in religion, as in politics, reforms require many generations before they pass from the intelligence which conceives to the act which accomplishes them: ideas, like subterranean waters, work their way slowly, and their progress is so much the more formidable in proportion as it is the longer secret. The pretensions of the kings of France to Italy rendered the support of the popes necessary to them in the fifteenth century; and the latter skilfully took advantage of their aid being required, and resumed a language of which the Holy See, during the schism, had lost the habit, rather than the remembrance. But the acts which seemed to announce the theocratic despotism was again obtaining strength, were fallacious signs of the spirit of the time: for this pontifical authority, which formerly had risen against the kings, because it drew its strength from itself, at present supported itself only by their aid, because its encroachments were no longer to be dreaded by them;—in fact, it might be truly asserted that its weakness constituted its strength.

The popes no longer resisted the kings, without immediately beholding themselves threatened in their double power:—in the midst of the contests for the duchy of Milan, Machiavel, sent to France by its republic as its representative, wrote: "Nothing is talked of but to assemble a council, and ruin the pope in his temporal and in his *spiritual* power,"* and

* Letter to the government of Florence.—Matter. *Hist. des doctrines morales et politiques des trois derniers siècles.* First period, chap. xvi.

it was a pious and Catholic prince who had this famous exergue struck: *Perdam Babylonis nomen.**

The prestige was destroyed, and this was clearly perceived when scandalous acts had anew raised up, against Rome, a part of Europe, and when opinions, so many times condemned, appeared illuminated by the double light of the revival of learning and of printing. Already, with the greater number of princes, the religious interest had descended to a secondary rank; religion, in their eyes, was no longer an end, but a means; the unity of the church occupied their attention less than the balance of the political power, and almost all declared for or against the doctrines of the new reformers, not according as they appeared in conformity with, or opposed to, the principles of Christianity, but according as they were advantageous or injurious to their temporal interests.

It was necessary that it should be so, in order that the Reformation should gain strength and not be nipped in the bud in the midst of the storms that were raging around it.

Thus, therefore, the principal results of the grand schism were, in the first place, the weakening of the principle of authority in the Church, and in the second, a strong impulsion given to two very opposite tendencies of freedom: one led, as has been seen, to the reform of the clergy by the clergy, and to the substitution of the aristocratical principle for the monarchical one; its great acts were the decrees of Constance and Basle, the Pragmatic of Charles VII., and the declaration of 1682; its principal sphere of action was France, and its most illustrious representatives in the fifteenth century were Gerson and D'Ailly, and in the seventeenth, Bossuet.

The second tendency was that which substituted the authority of the Bible, interpreted by individual judgment, for the authority of the priesthood: it brought on the great war of Bohemia in the fifteenth century and the reformation in the sixteenth, of which the principal centres were Germany and England—a revolution, until then, unexampled, which had Wycliffe for parent, John Huss for precursor, and to which Luther attached his name, after having accomplished it.

* The prince here alluded to is Louis XII. of France, surnamed the "Father of his People," who, in 1512, when at war with Pope Jules XII., relative to the duchy of Milan, had a medal struck and distributed in great profusion, in Italy, bearing the inscription *Perdam Babylonis nomen,* expressive of his intention to destroy even the name of the popedom. It must be borne in mind that the formidable army which he was at the time sending into Italy, left no doubt of his determination to carry the threat into execution. (*Note of Translator.*)

BOOK V.

CHAPTER I.

CONTINUATION AND END OF THE SCHISM.

This work, the principal object of which is to give an account of the doctrines produced during the schism, and of the great events accomplished at the Council of Constance, could have been terminated at the close of that celebrated assembly. Yet, in order to give the complete picture of a period, the history of the personages who occupied the chief places in it ought to be brought to a conclusion. We shall, therefore, before we treat of the end of the schism, give an account of the closing years of the two last pontiffs, who had contributed to maintain it; we shall refer to the many different destinies of the most eminent of their adversaries; we shall follow the emperor to the battle-fields, where he wore away his life, and accompany Gerson to the retreat where he sanctified his; and we shall, last of all, give an account of those terrible men who exacted a dreadful vengeance for those whom the council immolated.

The schism, as has been seen, was not entirely extinguished at Constance. Peter de Luna, under the protection of Alphonso V., was still protesting at Peniscola; and Balthazar Cossa, held captive at Heidelberg* under the

guard of the Elector Palatine, still gave cause for apprehension. He possessed in his vast wealth a powerful auxiliary, which he made use of to procure his liberty: he gave the Elector, it is said, thirty thousand golden crowns to let him escape, and he immediately repaired to Italy.

Several petty tyrants who had seized on church lands in the marches of Bologna, in the duchy of Spoleto, and the marches of Ancona, stimulated him to resume the tiara, offering to assure it to him with their troops, in order that they might thereby strengthen themselves in their usurped possessions. Their support, against the united forces of the church and the empire, inspired Balthazar with less confidence than apprehension; and he proceeded, of his own suggestion, to Florence, where Martin V. was keeping his court.

There, one day, in an assembly at which the pope happened to be present, a man suddenly appeared without any attendants, and advancing towards him, fell at his feet, and acknowledged him as the vicar of Christ. That man was Balthazar Cossa, and had been John XXIII. The pope felt grateful to him for this voluntary step, and as a recompense, created him cardinal, Bishop of Frascati, and kept him about his own person; whether through a kind feeling or through calculation, in order to be the surer of him, or to exalt himself the more, by loading with benefits the sovereign whose place he held. Balthazar died a few months after at Florence, and his tomb may be still seen in St. John's church.

---

* He had been transferred, by the emperor's order, from Gotleben to Heidelberg, where he was honourably treated. (Theod. Niem, *de Vita Joh.*)

In an old chronicle, John XXIII. thus deplores his misfortune:

Qui modo summus eram, gaudens de nomine,
    Præsul,
Tristis et abjectus nunc fata gemo.
Excelsus solio nuper versabar in alto,
Cunctaque gens pedibus oscula prona dabat;
Nunc ego ponarum fundo devolvor in imo,
Et me deformem quemque videre piget.
Omnibus ex terris aurum mihi sponte ferebant;
Sed nec gaza juvat, nec quis amicus adest.
Cedat in exemplum cunctis quos gloria tollit,
    Vertice de summo quando ego papa cado.
        Engelhus, *Chronic.* p. 296, 297.

" I, who lately held the highest place and bore the proud title of supreme chief, now, sad and borne to the earth, bewail my destiny. Seated on my lofty throne, I beheld all nations emulous to kiss my feet—now that I am fallen to the lowest abyss of misfortune, every one disdains to look at me in my disgrace. From every land they brought me gold, as their spontaneous offering, but now no treasures delight my eye, nor is any friend near me. Let this serve as an example to all whom glory exalts, that I, who was pope, have fallen from the loftiest pinnacle of grandeur."

Peter de Luna was for the church an object of more serious apprehension. Martin V. had ordered a crusade against him, but the King of Aragon would not allow him to be disquieted. Alphonso pretended to the throne of Naples, which Joan, the daughter of Charles de Jura, had inherited in 1414, at the death of her brother Ladislaus. This princess, who was the representative of the elder branch of the house of Anjou, needed a support against young Louis III., head of the younger line, and with that object adopted, as heir to her kingdom, Alphonso V. of Aragon. The great value of this rich inheritance removed all moderation or discretion from those who coveted it, and Alphonso, who was too ambitious to wait, attempted to seize, as a prey, the property which was offered him as a heritage, and endeavoured to force the pope to adjudge it to him without delay.* On Martin V. refusing to comply, Benedict XIII. was again proclaimed pope in Aragon, and fears were entertained that the whole of Spain might follow this example; but before the schism had time to make further progress, the untameable old man died at Peniscola.†

This most extraordinary person, whose obstinacy was so fatal to the church, had at least this excuse for his conduct, that he was firmly convinced of the justice of his cause, and in this conviction death itself did not cause him to waver. " He died with the same intrepidity that he had lived," says Maimbourg,‡ " perfectly composed, and so strongly persuaded that he was the true pope, that he bound, under pain of God's malediction, the two cardinals who had remained with him to give him a successor."

Nothing can be compared to the energy of his mind, unless, perhaps, the vigour of his body. Although he was not far from being a hundred years old, it was not believed that he died of old age, but was supposed to be poisoned by a monk,§ at the instigation of the cardinal legate in Aragon.|| The opinion was very generally spread abroad, that this man, who had struggled without quailing against the whole of Christendom, triumphed even over death itself. It is positively asserted that his body, when removed six years later to Illucca, to the family vault, exhaled an agreeable odour, and that it has remained in a state of preservation to the present day.*

Benedict was obeyed after his death; for his two cardinals chose as his successor an honest canon of Barcelona, a doctor of canon law, named Gilles Mugnos. This poor man appeared as much overwhelmed with this unexpected honour as embarrassed how to get rid of it. The anger of Alphonso, who ordered him to accept it, appeared to him more formidable than the distant fulminations of Martin V., and Gilles Mugnos in consequence assumed the title of pope, and, from the moment he did so, looked at the matter with perfect seriousness, and thought himself really the sovereign pontiff. He publicly exercised, under the name of Clement VIII., all the functions of pontificate; he appointed a consistory, excommunicated Martin V., made a promotion of cardinals, and took care to include his nephew in it, " in order not to forget any thing," as Maimbourg again remarks, " of what the popes were accustomed to do on such occasions."†

The states of Alphonso then comprised the kingdoms of Aragon, Valencia, Sardinia, and Sicily; the authority of the new pope extended therefore over these countries, and the schism appeared to revive. But after five years' struggle, Alphonso, either from repentance or weariness, abandoned his pope Clement VIII., and acknowledged Martin V.‡ Gilles Mugnos, who had assumed the tiara solely through obedience, exhibited the same readiness to comply by laying it down. He showed by this facile submission, that he had been pope only in name: also having determined to follow in the form of his abdication the imposing example which Gregory XII. had given him, he surrounded himself with so much ceremony and such misplaced pomp, that he attracted less respect than contempt, and rendered ridiculous, from the number of solemnities, a scene which, if made more sim-

* Irritated at the ingratitude of Alphonso, Queen Joan revoked her will, and adopted Louis III. of Anjou. Martin V. confirmed this new adoption, and from thence arose a long war between the partisans of the house of Anjou and the Aragonese.
† In 1424.
‡ Hist. du Grand Schisme d' Occident, book vi. p. 535.
§ Marian. Ciacon, in Benedict.
|| The person here alluded to was the Cardinal of Pisa, but an author worthy of credit declares that he had died before Benedict. See Bzovius, Annal. Ecclesiast. post Baron.

* A phenomenon which must not be considered, as the continuator of Fleury prudently remarks, a proof of his sanctity. Hist. Eccles. book civ. ann. 1424.
† Hist. du Grand Schisme, book vi. p. 539.
‡ Several authors have considered this conduct of King Alphonso, as the effect of a miraculous conversion. They seem to have forgotten that the pope had at last accorded him all his demands, except one, namely, to give his approbation to all that he had done during the schism, a demand which Martin V. could not have agreed to without dishonouring himself. See the Continuator of Fleury, Hist. Eccles. book v. ann. 1429.

ple, would have possessed some grandeur. He recalled, from his throne, all the censures that he had pronounced against Martin V., declaring him fit to receive all dignities, including the pontificate, and then, descending from his throne, he handed his act of renunciation to the commissioners of Alphonso, and taking off his ensigns of dignity, requested the cardinals to make choice of a good pastor in his place.

A pretended conclave was opened, at which all the precautions usually adopted at Rome were observed. Three cardinals entered it, representing, as they declared, the whole sacred college, and then came out again, proclaiming with a unanimous voice, as if by the inspiration of the Holy Ghost, OTHO DE COLONNA to be pope under the name of Martin V.

Thus finished the great schism of the west, on July 26, 1429. It had lasted for half a century, and it left behind it the germs of still greater troubles than those which it had given birth to.

CHAPTER II.

FRANCE AND GERSON.

GERSON, who devoted his life to the extinction of the schism, expired the very year in which it was brought to a conclusion. This great man had beheld all his illusions vanish one by one, and all his hopes remain unaccomplished—he had seen the council abandon the great cause of reform, and the pope render himself independent of the council; his country, torn by civil contentions and foreign war, offered him no consolation; for he beheld there the illustrious body to which he belonged, the University of Paris, erring, as Pasquier expresses it, *from its ancient virtue,*[*] and support the pretensions of the pope against the liberties of that Gallican church, of which it had in part constituted the strength and glory.

The bishops, in distributing the benefices, had preferred their creatures to the graduates of the university. The latter complained to the pope, and Martin V. rendered the learned body favourable to him, in granting it a share in the advowsons, by his concordate with the French nation.[†] This concordate was injurious to the Gallican church in what concerned advowsons, appeals to the pope, and annats.[‡] It was not at first accepted in France, where the dauphin and the Armanacs exercised sway: the election of the pope was even contested there, and when the University of Paris made an appeal to Martin V. before this pontiff had been recognised in the kingdom, its rector and several of its members were thrown into prison.[*] Treason soon after delivered the capital to the Burgundians, and there was then a revolution in the church, as in the government. John-Sans-Peur, grateful to the pope, for not having condemned his apologist, notwithstanding the strong opposition of the parliament of Paris, sacrificed to him the liberties of the Church of France. Gerson beheld with affliction the abrogation of the celebrated edict of 1407, which established them; he saw the university constrained to disavow, respecting the doctrine of John Petit, the opinion which it had so long thought it a point of honour to uphold; he beheld the sentence, rendered four years before by the Bishop of Paris, against the apology of murder, broken with a solemnity which was an additional scandal; and in fine, he beheld his unfortunate king betrayed by his relations and abandoned, the dauphin a fugitive, his friends slaughtered, and the greatest part of the kingdom in the power of foreigners, and of that same John Petit whom he had made his mortal enemy.

France, open to all her enemies, was closed for her noblest son. The illustrious chancellor could only make a choice on one point—the place of his exile; and about the middle of the year 1418, when already upwards of sixty years of age, he quitted Constance like a banished man and repaired to Bavaria,

---

* *Recherches de la France,* ed. 1633, p. 253.
† *Concord. Mart. pap. cum Gallis.* Ex Msc. Parisiens. Bib. S. Victor. Ap. Von der Hardt, vol. iv, p. 1576.
‡ The pope, as has been already mentioned (b. iv. c. iii.), maintained by his concordate the principal dispositions of his plan of reform, he preserved his annats, but he pledged himself not to require more than the half of them during five years, in consideration of the state of the kingdom.

* The king's council having afterwards learned that Martin V. had been canonically elected, caused this pontiff to be acknowledged in France, but it maintained at the same time the ordinance of 1407, relative to the liberties of the church.

crossing the mountains of the Tyrol, in a pilgrim's dress. He at last arrived at Rattenburg on the banks of the Inn, where Duke Albert had offered him an asylum. There he took up his residence, though with a most desolate heart. He called to mind with bitterness the closing acts of the Council of Constance; the perils that surrounded him after a long life of fatigue and trial; and he strengthened his soul by religious meditation,—he forgot the actions of mankind as he drew closer to his God. It was there that he wrote, after the example of Boetius, his four books of the *Consolation théologique*. " He had seen," he says, " discord and iniquity bearing sway in the midst of his people: from all sides snares were laid for him, and as the bird escapes from the nets of the fowler, so he had withdrawn from the storm that was raging, bearing with him at least hope."[*]

In this same retreat his indefatigable mind, by way of relaxation, exalted itself with other labours[†] in which he engaged as an exercise which he believed could be of service to himself alone. " Alas !" cried he, " in this unfortunate age, who will read these things ? who will study them ?" He pursued his labours nevertheless with ardour: no obstacle turned him aside from his holy occupations, because in his case, from infancy, to study, to meditate, and to strive, was to live.[‡]

The benefits of the archduke Frederick sought him out in this obscure retreat. Frederick desired ardently to have so brilliant a light, to illuminate his University of Vienna; he invited Gerson to proceed there, and, on his arrival, gave him the most cordial reception.

But Gerson, though distant from France, did not forget her. " O France !" he says, in a copy of Latin verse still extant, " What is become of thy piety and ancient faith ? Thy children are forced to undergo exile and death.

O powerful God ! how many theologians, how many pontiffs have perished for thy law, imprinted on their hearts ! How many men bewail their fate, imprisoned by a cruel rage ! others have fled and inhabit distant lands, protected by exile, but stripped of all things; and amongst them is the chancellor of the pleasing studies of Paris—he has gone to a distant country—he has become a wanderer on the face of the earth !"[*]

However, he uttered no accusations either against destiny or mankind for his misfortunes: his grief resembled those streams which glide in the shade without a murmur: and in the very pages where not a complaint is uttered, may be recognised the impress of his affliction,—the trace of his tears.

After some months' residence at Vienna, Gerson learned the assassination of the Duke of Burgundy at Montereau. His enemy being no more, France was again open to him, and he at once turned his footsteps towards her. He did not however proceed to Paris, for that city, then the theatre of sanguinary struggles, held out to him no prospect of that repose to which he aspired ; besides, the English were masters there, and Paris, in that case, could not be considered by a Frenchman as France. He repaired to Lyons, where the dauphin was in command, and where he had himself two brothers residing, one of whom was prior of the Celestine Convent. He arrived there towards the end of the year 1419, old and indigent, and there he finished his exile and earthly pilgrimage.

From that time forward, Gerson gave up holding a position in the midst of men—in the stormy sphere of the world : he directed all his attention to his soul, the greatest treasure that man possesses on earth.[†] The trials and tempests of the world had purified his own, for they had forced him to turn his thoughts inwards, and to intrench himself there, as if in a fortress, where no intruding fools were allowed to follow him.[‡] In place of eloquent bursts of passionate indignation, and biting invectives against error, there now were heard from his lips only the accents of a mild and infinite compassion. In the humble cell of the cloister of St. Paul, to which the great orator of Constance had retired, one

---

[*] *De Consolatione Theologiæ, Gers. oper.* vol. i. page 130.—This work is a dialogue between a person named Volucer, sent by Gerson to his brother, and this brother himself, whom he designates by the name of Monicus. " O Volucer," says the latter, " does not the friend of my soul bewail his being thus banished to a foreign and distant land, where he hears the language that is not familiar to him ?" " He glorifies God," replies Volucer; " he raises his hand to that God who is his salvation, and, like another Jeremiah, laments over the woes of his unhappy country." (*Ibid.*)

[†] He wrote at this period the *Monotessaron*, or the only Gospel, formed of extracts from the four evangelists.

[‡] Ab infantia enim sacras literas novit, neque furor hostilis, neque terror persistere potuit quin persequeretur iter suum. (*De Consol. Theol.* p. 131.)

[*] Heu pietas, heu prisca fides ! Coguntur alumni Francigenæ mortes exiliumque pati, &c. &c. (*Carm. in laud. ducis Austriæ*, vol. iv. p. 787.

[†] Non habet homo cariorem thesaurum super terram quam animam suam. (*Epist. script. ad divers.* vol. iii. p. 750.)

[‡] Securo munitus vallo, quo grassanti stultitiæ aspirare fas non est. (*Epist. frat. Joan. Gerson.* vol. i. p. clxxvii.)

thought was ever present to his mind, and that was his country.

"It is impossible to believe," says his brother, "what torrents of tears gush forth, from the depths of his soul, at the spectacle of the frightful woes which affect the lovely kingdom of France, so cruelly torn to pieces by civil discord, and held by foreigners. . . . . It is on that account, that, when offering the holy sacrifice at the altar, he supplicated the Lord to accord some respite to his people, worn out by so many griefs."[*]

Amongst his numerous subjects of affliction, ought we to assign a place to repentance for his severity against those whom the council condemned? It would be difficult to reply positively in the affirmative, for in an age when heresy was branded as the most heinous of crimes, intolerance was honoured as a virtue. Yet when Gerson had discovered, that the design which he pictured to himself of the spiritual government of Christian society by the episcopacy, of the reform of the church by the church, was impracticable,—when, above all, he found the great assembly which he reputed infallible, refuse to censure men more culpable than they whom it had burnt to death[†]—in proportion, in fact, as, weaned more from the world, he rose above human disputes to cling to that gospel which was the vivifying source of John Huss's doctrines and his supreme law, it may be supposed, that, in the bottom of his soul, a secret voice protested silently in favour of that Christian who died confessing his Saviour. "Every man," says Gerson, "who is put to death in hatred of justice and of truth, which he honours and defends, is worthy in the sight of God of the title of martyr, whatever may be the judgment of men."[‡] It is impossible that, in tracing these words in the solitude of his exile, Gerson could have forgotten that just man whom he had beheld preferring death to perjury; and when his brother asked him,[§] if, in going over in his memory all that he had done at the council, he felt neither remorse nor scruple, he replied: "Who will boast of possessing a spotless heart? Who can say, I am innocent and pure? Who will not fear the judgments of the terrible God?" Perhaps, then, John Huss occurred to his thoughts, and perhaps, too, this was what contributed, as much as the miscarriage

of his designs and the ruin of his dearest hopes, to withdraw him from the world. "Many are astonished," said the prior, his brother, " that he holds himself thus apart and leads a solitary life. You would deem him an anchorite, if he sought out a wilderness, but he lives amongst his people, and hence it is that so many inquire: Why does he not appear more in public? Why goes he no more to appease the quarrels of the men who rage against each other with so much fury?"[*] He no longer interfered in these fiery discussions, because too often charity suffered from them and disappeared; but his life, although tranquil, was not unoccupied, and what he did, his brother informs us, he commenced with wisdom, to which, as his companion, he had devoted his life from his tenderest years: she visited him early in the morning; and, if he was sad or disquieted, she did not leave him until she had afforded him consolation.[†] His conversation manifested no sorrow or bitterness; the whole day scarcely was sufficient for him to accomplish all that his noble mind suggested; he meditated, he wrote, he exhorted. When consulted, as he frequently was, by men living in the world, he freely gave them his sage counsel; and if he mingled with them, it was not, as formerly, to dispute, but to instruct; not to condemn, but to save.

The profound thinker, who had sounded and examined every thing, though not without fear, no longer sought for the solution of the problems which had disturbed him;[‡] two great necessities, to reflect and to love, had divided his existence between them, but now reflection yielded the place to faith, to love, to intimate and mystical contemplation.[§] Yet, although he edged the profound abyss of mysticism, in which so many eminent men had lost themselves, his strong sense and upright feeling guarded him from falling into it.[||] He had besides a sure guide in the gospel, to which he became more and more attached; all that he did or wrote was imbued with that divine spirit, with which he each

* Non crederes quantis lachrymarum proluviis ab intimo cordis proruentibus deflet miserabilem cladem nunquam dignis planctibus adequandam, præclarissimi Franciæ regni, etc. (Ibid.)

† See book iii. ch. viii.

‡ De Consol. Theol. vol. i. p. 183.

§ Ibid. p. 169.

* Cur ad publicum non procedit? cur non it sedatum hominum jurgia, quæ tum acriter ubique debacchantar? (Epist. fratr. Joan. Gers. ad Anselm.)

† Quæ si viderit eum vel ad modicum tristem et anxium, non cessat blanditiis, donec consolatum relinquat. (Ibid.)

‡ Cur fuit prima dæmonis vox et interrogatio. (Tract. viii. sup. Magnif.)

§ It was at this period of his life that Gerson composed his commentary on the song of Solomon, and his twelve treatises on the Magnificat.

|| See on this subject some excellent remarks in an admirable work published on Gerson by M. Charles Schmidt, Strasburg, 1839.

day became more and more inspired.* He had formerly feared to place the Scriptures written in the vulgar tongue† in the hands of the multitude, but now he invited all souls to this life-bestowing fountain, and he instituted schools in which he himself taught the word of God to the children of the people.‡ What a touching spectacle was given by this illustrious man, whose eloquence had enlightened the kings of Europe! When retiring from the honours and storms of the world, he collected around him, in the temple of God, the young and feeble infants of the place, and with delight formed their young minds to the knowledge of things divine. Such were the relaxations of his latter days. Even when he felt the approach of death, he once more had his little pupils, whom he loved so well, brought around him, and made them pray for him in their native language, telling them to repeat after him, in French,§ these words, affecting from their very simplicity: *My God, my Creator, have pity on your poor servant, Gerson.*

On July 12, 1429, this great man rendered up his spirit unto God. He was interred in the church of St. Paul, where he was accustomed to teach, and his pilgrim's ensigns were hung up near the tomb of him who had looked on his sojourn on earth only as a laborious pilgrimage.‖

Rome, whose haughty pretensions he had unceasingly combated, did not place this man of God among the catalogue of her saints. The voice of the people was more just, for it attributed miraculous virtues to his relics, and for a great length of years crowds came with great devotion to his tomb. A chapel was raised to his memory, and Gerson there received the same kind of worship as is paid to saints in the Roman Church. A catholic historian, a celebrated doctor of the Sorbonne, has made on this subject the following reflec-

tion: "I have the utmost difficulty in conceiving that this honour should not be rendered to Gerson with as much reason as to all those to whom Rome has awarded it for the last three centuries, none of them having better deserved it."*

If we now cast a glance over a life so full of occupation, and so agitated, we shall recognise in person the moralist, the reformer, and the thinker that founds and constitutes.

As a moralist, Gerson is worthy of all our admiration. In a barbarous age, when the precepts of morality were reduced to the subtleties of the schools, and when the observance of vain practical ceremonials supplied the place of the practice of virtue itself, Gerson preached to men the pure morality of the gospel, and showed them, in the revealed word, at the same time a mirror to recognise their wanderings and a bright light to guide them and conduct them to good.

As a reformer of the clergy, he failed, because he wanted to reform the church itself; but the evil was too profound to admit of that course of proceeding. The clergy, in order to give up a vast number of abuses, ought first to have given up what nourished their vices—the sources of wealth which these same abuses had laid open. But that was in truth a thing altogether impossible; ecclesiastical society could not be restrained within narrow limits, but by the civil power, as it was in France, or by those who established it on new bases in the countries where the Reformation triumphed.†

As a constituent mind, regulating the action of the religious powers, and indicating the sources of ecclesiastical authority and the hands in which God had placed it, Gerson exercised great influence, and his undertaking is not without a certain grandeur. Its object was to institute in the church the authority of several for that of one; the supreme government of the episcopacy for that of the popedom. Gerson, however, did not succeed: but if all his efforts did not obtain a general and durable success, they left at least in the religious world profound traces, and produced results which it was impossible to foresee. We have shown by facts‡ all the importance of the fa-

---

* The noblest title of Gerson as a writer would undoubtedly be the *Imitation of Jesus Christ*, if it were certain that he was the author of it. The question does not appear to us yet absolutely decided, notwithstanding the excellent book of M. Onésime Leroy (*Études sur les Mystères*) : the strongest objection, in our opinion, is found in the style. But it is sufficient for Gerson's glory, that this inimitable work has been attributed to him, and that he has been deemed worthy of having written it.

† See the Historical Introduction, p. 96.

‡ *De Parvulis ad Christum trahendis.* Gers. Oper. vol. iii.

§ In verbis Gallicis.

‖ Gersonem seu peregrinum aut advenam se meminerat in hoc orbe, in quo hospes spectaret quid facerent alii, suamque personam virtutibus decoratam decenter, ageret mox brevem hanc migrationem, tanquam per somnium, absoluturus. (*Vita Joh. Gers. ap. Von der Hardt*, vol. i. part iv. p. 50.)

* J. Launoii Erv. Navar. Gymnas. Paris. hister. p. 475. See also Lecuy's Life of Gerson, vol. ii. p. 252, &c.

† To this assertion will be opposed the reforms decreed by the Council of Trent; but these, in addition to being exceedingly incomplete, were above all the effect of a salutary fear, and of an imperious necessity, in presence of the progress made by a rival church.

‡ Book iv. chap. v.

mous decrees of the fifth session of the Council of Constance: these decrees, completed by those of the thirty-ninth session, and which Gerson more than any one contributed to draw up, established the regular and supreme government of general councils: yet, in order that this government should be real and durable, it was necessary that the permanency of these councils, or at least their regular and periodical convocation, were possible. But the world was no longer at that time, as in the fourth century, in the hands of one man, who was himself interested in convoking and maintaining these grand congresses of Christendom. In Europe, such as the fall of the Roman Empire had made it; in the states parcelled out after that event, for which peace was so long the exceptional condition, and war the nominal one, the existence of general councils was itself only an exception, and their periodical recurrence a chimera. It was therefore inevitable that the government of the Catholic church, the principle of which is authority, should become monarchical; it followed from the natural course of things, that a single and central power should place itself in competition with that of the councils, and rapidly rise above them; for between two rival powers, one of which is perpetual and the other accidental, the equilibrium will never be of any long duration.

The decrees of Constance, besides, did not fortify the power of the bishops and render them independent in some respects of the court of Rome, but inasmuch as they consented to be so, they gave them arms against the Holy See, but only on condition that they should be willing to use them. They did make use of them in France with the support of the kings. The latter very skilfully took advantage of the liberties of the Gallican church, in their foreign relations with Rome, to render it subject to themselves at home,* and they substituted in part, over the ecclesiastical society, their authority, or that of their parliaments, for the authority of the pope and the councils.† The consequence was, that in France two things altogether peculiar and of immense importance took place. On the one hand, the kings, masters of their clergy, were interested in maintaining the religious establishment, such as it existed in the kingdom: and on the other, from the French clergy being more restrained, their conduct was more pure, their abuses less trying, and,

notwithstanding the strange effects of the intrusion of the civil power in the spiritual domain,* a radical reform of the institutions of the church appeared to the people less desirable. The decrees of Constance, confirmed at Basil, and which were in a great part the work of Gerson, powerfully contributed to this double result; and if they preserved France from the tribunal of the Inquisition, and from the usurpation of the Roman court, they also rendered her more difficult of conquest for the reformers of the sixteenth century.†

And yet Gerson and the reformers had several points in common, not only relative to outward discipline, but even to questions of doctrine. In what relates to absolution of sins,‡ good works, and predestination, Gerson was almost of the same opinion as Wycliffe and his successors.§ What separated him most from the grand reformer of England, was his doctrine on the authority of general councils, which Gerson recognised as sovereign, infallible, and without appeal: the points which brought him most closely to Wycliffe, were his resistance to the ambitious pretensions of the Holy See, his unbounded veneration for the *revealed word*, which, in the eyes of the great Gallican doctors of this period, as in Wycliffe's, is the

---

* See note Q at the end of the volume.

† However, the time was sure to arrive, when the immutable dogmas of the church would cease to be in perfect harmony with the ideas in progress, and with the new forms of political and civil society; when the enlightened part of the most intelligent people would not cling to doctrines which spoke nothing to its intelligence; when the clergy would necessarily lose those advantages which they held only from a blind faith or a confidence without bounds: viz., their temporal authority and riches. Whenever this time should arrive, it was easy to foresee that the French episcopacy, for want of the sword of the kings and the thunders of the councils, to bring back men's minds and regain its losses, would seek to regain its strength at the grand focus of catholicism, Rome, and in these same ultramontane doctrines so long combated by themselves. If Gerson could have glanced into futurity, he would perhaps have seen the time when the liberties of the church of France would be abandoned by the successors of those who had defended them, and when the Gallican church would cease to exist, because there would be no longer a Gallican clergy.

‡ The celebrated treatise *De l'Union et de la Réformation de l'Eglise*, is the only one of Gerson's writings, in which we have perceived a very marked difference between his opinion and the sentiment of the church relative to the power of the priest in absolution: his doctrine, besides, differs but little from that condemned under the name of Jansenism.

§ See the Historical Introduction; see also *Gers. Oper.* vol. i. p. 139; ii. p. 56; iii. pp. 1239, 1273, 1274.

---

* Book iv. chap. v.

† See the concordats between Francis I. and Leo X.

veritable rock on which Jesus Christ founded his church; [*] and lastly, this simple creed, this phrase so essentially Christian, which Ger- son was always repeating, and which was inscribed on his tomb—REPENT AND BELIEVE THE GOSPEL.[*]

CHAPTER III.

BOHEMIA AND THE HUSSITES TO THE DEATH OF ZISKA.

IT has been seen that the doctrines of John Huss were not without influence in preparing men's minds in Europe for the grand reformation of the succeeding century. It remains to show what fruits they bore in his native country; to tell what became of his disciples after their master's death, and what the Hussites did after John Huss.

Shortly before the troubles which agitated Bohemia, the most illustrious of the sovereigns of that kingdom, the Emperor Charles IV., visiting one day the citadel of Prague, approached a window, and as he looked forth over the city, his eyes filled with tears. His courtiers having asked the reason, he replied: "I weep, because my sons will be the enemies of my kingdom; I foresee that one of them will ruin this city, and if I knew which, I would kill him with my own hands."[†]

Subsequent events confirmed this saying, which they had perhaps dictated. Wenceslaus and Sigismund were born for the misfortune of Bohemia, and the better one of the two was the more fatal to it.

Severe trials had modified in Sigismund an irascible and cruel temperament: he had acquired a certain mastery over himself, but at times his natural character prevailed, and he then drew his inspirations from passion rather than prudence. He gave a fresh proof of this a little after the execution of John Huss, when the first intelligence reached him of the agitation of the Bohemians. He wrote to them several angry letters, and his threats Bohemia looked on as an insult. "Sigismund forgot," as Balbinus remarks, "that he was not yet king of that country: he forgot that, in order to master an unbroken horse, it is necessary first to soothe him with the hand, and that the rider must wait until he is firmly seated in the saddle before he uses bit and spur."[†]

He discovered this at a later period, and wrote in the year 1417 to appease the Bohemians, and to induce them to pardon his conduct towards John Huss, alleging as his excuse the violence which was exercised on himself;[‡] but his last letters did not efface the impression which his first had produced.

The death of Jerome raised the irritation of the Bohemians to the highest pitch. Until then, however, the agitation appeared to manifest itself much more by acts of mourning and popular superstition than by actual violence. Then, however, the university, by a decree signed by its rector, John Cardinal, established the communion in the two kinds; the churches resounded with lamentations; a solemn feast day was consecrated to John Huss and Jerome; medals were struck with their effigy; the people wept and honoured, before they avenged them: altars were raised to them, but no victims were yet immolated.

The headstrong rigours of the council swelled the storm, and the twenty-four articles, fulminated against the Hussites, hastened the explosion. These articles, says an old author, *cast oil on the fire.*§ They struck at the same time the citizens of all classes and orders in the kingdom—the members of the university, by annulling its decrees—the Hussite clergy, by citing to Rome the principal members, John Jessenitz, Jacobel, Rockizawe, John Cardinal, and several others—the nobles of the kingdom, by ordering the restitution of all the ecclesiastical property—and the mass of the people, by prescribing the individual abjuration of the doctrine of Wycliffe and Huss. Then there burst forth throughout the whole of Bohemia a cry of horror: a vague, general, and im-

---

[*] Non tamen videtur quod in petra Petrus sit intelligendus. . . . . . Secundum spiritualem intellectum, per hanc petram divinam scripturam et sacram Christi doctrinam signare possumus, quæ tam firmæ soliditatis et tam solidæ firmiditatis existit ut non immerito super eam Christi ecclesia fundata sit. (Petr. de Alliac. *Recomm. Sacra Script.*; *Gers. Oper.* vol. i. page 604.
[†] Theobald. *Bell. Huss.*, according to the chronicle of Hagec.

[*] Pœnitemini et credite evangelico.
[†] Balbinus, *Epit. rer. Bohem.* p. 424.
[‡] See page 67.
§ Sigfried.

mense clamour gave the reply to the decrees of the council. In every quarter fire and sword were prepared. Wenceslaus trembled and awaited events, withdrawn or rather concealed in one of his castles outside Prague.

However the nobles of the kingdom assembled and held council on the course to be pursued. They came to the determination of sending a deputation to the king, to invite him to conjure away the storm by his presence in the capital—to give the Hussites the churches which they had need of—and to act with rigour against the robbers who infested the city and surrounding country. They chose for chief of the deputation Nicholas de Hussinetz, lord of the village where John Huss was born, his faithful friend and fervent disciple.

The desire to put down so menacing an agitation prevailed in Wenceslaus' mind over his resentment at the proceedings of the council of the emperor. He feared both one and the other, and, besides, as monarch, and slave to his passions, he equally dreaded those innumerable sectarians, amongst whom there already appeared audacious levellers, who spoke of changing Bohemia into a republic, and ardent apostles, who quoted in opposition to his vices the austere morality of the gospel. But, sunk in effeminacy, worn out with debauchery, and incapable of a strong resolution, he had every desire to repress, but wanted force to act with vigour. He therefore promised to attend to certain demands made by the deputies, taking care to warn the spokesman, Hussinetz, that *he was spinning a cord which would serve to hang him.*

He proceeded to Prague, and manifested an inclination to give the Hussites the churches which they demanded: he hesitated, however, because they asked for them with menaces. "Let them come to the palace," said he, "and bringing their arms, let them lay them down in my presence."

The chiefs deliberated on the reply, disquieted and uncertain how to act. "How silly you are," said one of them; "I have lived at court, and I know our king: appear before him clad in your warlike attire and with your arms, and be satisfied that he will leave them to you." He who spoke thus, was John Ziska. His advice was followed: the Hussites took up arms in ancient and modern Prague, and, led on by Ziska, appeared before the king in this formidable array. "Very illustrious and most excellent prince," said Ziska, "behold us here in obedience to your orders; point out to us your enemies,

and we will fight to our last breath for your life and your glory." "Thou hast spoken well," replied the king, "but return and take with thee thy companions."[*]

Ziska by this conduct, as well imagined as intrepid, won the hearts and confidence of the Bohemians. The indolent Wenceslaus remained inactive, divided between fear and anger:[†] the nobles preserved an irritated silence :[‡] the multitude still waited on for some time, a prey to gloomy and restrained indignation, which at intervals manifested itself in ill-boding outbreaks.

Such was the state of things in Bohemia up to the arrival of Cardinal Jean-Dominique, legate of Martin V., charged with the execution of the twenty-four articles of the council and of the pope's bull.

This inquisitor had recourse to the stake to reduce a people much more likely at the time to inspire dread than to experience it themselves. Loaded with maledictions and insults, and pursued with cries of death, the legate, in the utmost dismay, fled to the emperor, calling for fire and sword against Bohemia, which he declared was in insurrection. Then the anger of the people burst forth on all sides, and the avenger, the man of blood, appeared in all his strength—Ziska drew his invincible sword, and never again returned it to the scabbard.

Never did any man unite in his own person to a higher degree all the qualities requisite for the leader of an army and the head of a party. No one on the field of battle had more genius for conceiving a plan, or more determination and promptitude in carrying it into execution: none also better knew the art of gaining mastery over men, of striking their imagination, of attaining his object by popular resolutions and sudden and decisive movements. Bohemia was in arms for the communion with the cup. Ziska exhibits a sacramental cup to his army, and tells them that they behold their standard. He has no troops but infantry; by an unexpected attempt he carries off a thousand horses from the emperor, and is at once supplied with cavalry. He possesses no fortresses; he ascends a lofty mountain with his soldiers. "Do you want houses?" says he to them, "dress your tents here, and let this camp be speedily converted into a town." Such was his fortress, and thus was founded the im-

---

[*] Theobald. *Bell. Huss.* p. 68.
[†] Several authors pretend that he had a Hussite shoemaker burnt for having administered the Eucharist, but this fact does not appear sufficiently proved.
[‡] Balbinus, *Epit. rer. Bohem.* p. 420.

O

pregnable Tabor.* In his proclamations and letters, Ziska showed himself, as Cromwell did afterwards, a warrior using the glowing language of the Bible, whom nothing could stop, and who provided for every case. He wrote thus to the inhabitants of Tausch: "May God grant, dearest brethren, that performing good works, like the true children of your heavenly Father, you may remain steadfast in His fear; if He has visited you, let not affliction abate your courage: think of those who labour for the faith, and who suffer on account of Jesus Christ's name. Imitate the old Bohemians, your ancestors, always ready to defend the cause of God and their own. Let us constantly have before our eyes the divine law, and the good of the common weal; let us be vigilant; and let whoever knows how to handle a knife, or to throw a stone, or brandish a club, be ready to march. . . . Let your preachers encourage your people to the war against antichrist—let every one, young or old, prepare for it. When I shall arrive amongst you, let there be no want of bread, or beer, or forage: lay up a store also of good works. Behold the time is now come to arm yourselves, not only against your outward enemies, but also against those that you have within yourselves. Remember your first combat, where you were few in number against many, and without arms against those that were well provided. The hand of God is not shortened—courage, therefore, and be ready.

"ZISKA *of the cup*."

The popular tide, directed by such a man, was certain to bear down all before it, and was the more destructive that it had been the longer restrained. Bohemia, from one extremity to the other, soon became one vast field of carnage; everywhere conflagrations displayed to view dreadful massacres: wo to the towns, castles, and above all, the monasteries, that closed their gates—all passed by the edge of the sword. The sight of a monk or a priest filled Ziska with a gloomy rage—they recalled to his memory the image of his sister outraged, and his friend at the funeral stake. He smote, burned, and exterminated, coldly glutting his vengeance in the shock of combatants, the gleam of flames, the shrieks of victims, "punishing," as Balbinus expresses it, "*one sacrilege by a thousand!*"†

Bohemia, Germany, and Europe, were soon filled with the name of this terrible man. Wenceslaus awoke from his shameful slumber, at the noise of his falling palaces, of his churches in ashes, of his senate massacred—he started up in a frightful fit of passion, which was injurious to himself alone, for his fury suffocated him, and this king, who had lived like a brute, died roaring like a lion.*

Bohemia was then divided into various parties, and these divisions became more profound after the death of Wenceslaus, for to the religious interests were joined the political ones—the latter, however, being subordinate to the former. The three principal parties were the Catholics, the Calixtines, and the Taborites. The Catholics had lost all their influence: the most zealous remained quiet and waited, whilst the others joined the Calixtines and made common cause with them. The latter were surnamed the *limping Hussites*, by the men who went farther than they into reforms; and although accused of being unfaithful to the doctrines of their master, they, on the contrary, brought them forward in a very concise formulary, composed of only the four following articles:

1°. The communion in the two kinds, whence they received their name of partisans of the chalice, or Calixtines.†

2°. The free preaching of the word of God.

3°. The punishment of public sins, without privilege of clergy.

4°. The non-possession of temporal pro-

---

* " Ut quisque tentoria fixerat, ita ædificare sibi domos imperavit." *Æneæ Sylvii Hist. Bohem.* chap. xl.

† *Epit. rer. Bohem.* p. 424.

* This roaring of Wenceslaus has been mentioned by several historians : the greater number represent this prince as a monster of cruelty, and narrate some acts of his, of an incredible ferocity. It is however possible that party spirit has caused them to represent him as more criminal than he was in reality. No one contests either his shameful indolence or his depraved tastes ; and his effeminate character is well depicted in these words, addressed, at the commencement of the disturbances, by the priest Coranda to those who wanted to dethrone Wenceslaus: "We have," said he, " a king, and we have not, for he is king in name only—he is, in fact, like a painting on a wall. What can a king, who is dead whilst alive, do against us? I think, therefore, that we ought to pray to God to preserve him to us, for his indolence constitutes our safety." (Dubrav. p. 624 ; Æneas Sylvius, p. 75.) When the intelligence of the massacre of the magistrates of Prague was brought to the king, the grand cup-bearer, who was present, remarked that "he had always foreseen all this evil." At this word, which might be construed into a reproach, Wenceslaus fell on the cup-bearer, seized him by the hair, threw him down, and drawing his dagger, would have stabbed him to the heart, if his arm had not been held. He was immediately struck with apoplexy and died a few days after. (See Lenfant, *Guerre des Hussites*, vol. i. p. 109.)

† They admitted the real presence and transubstantiation.

party by priests or monks, with civil administration, and with a title to independent property.

Most of the influential men in Bohemia adopted these four articles, and, in the end, Archbishop Conrad joined them, declaring himself a Calixtine.

The Taborites were so called, because they composed the greater part of the army which founded the city of Tabor, and remained sole masters of that place to the end of the religious troubles. They admitted in the church neither a hierarchy of the priesthood, nor such practices as were purely ceremonial, nor exterior ornaments: they maintained the communion of the cup, like the Calixtines, but a great number of them rejected the dogma of the real presence.* The doctrine of the latter parties was purely that of the Waldenses, such as it has been preserved in the greater number of Protestant countries. The common name of Hussites was given, without distinction, to the Calixtines and the Taborites: the former prevailed in old Prague, and the latter in the new town, and, in consequence, for twenty years a permanent state of war or rivalry existed between the two parts of the city of Prague.†

The great majority of the Taborites belonged to the lower classes. A part of them, who rejected all sacerdotal authority, were guilty of great disorders, and it could not be otherwise, at a period when the excesses and violence of the priesthood had called forth a terrible reaction, and when civil and foreign war kept up in men's minds a burning effervescence. In such circumstances, religious enthusiasm ought necessarily to degenerate with a great number into raging delirium—in wild and sanguinary acts of madness. These men, at first, contributed powerfully to the successes of the Hussites, but at a later period, they compromised it: it was they, in particular, who composed that ill-defined and indifferently understood portion of the Taborites, called *Picards*.

At first, however, a great number of those persons so designated, spent an exemplary life, and were not distinguished from the Waldenses, either by doctrine or mode of living; but some of them renewed the criminal extravagances of the *Adamites*,* and were in part exterminated by Ziska. It is therefore perhaps erroneously, that most of the historians of the war of the Hussites have applied the name of *Picards* to the men, the most enthusiastic of the Taborite party.†

Immediately after the death of Wenceslaus, the first question to be decided was the form to be given to the new government. The nobility of the kingdom inclined towards the Emperor Sigismund, brother of Wenceslaus: they did not however intend accepting him without certain conditions, the first of which was the recognition and maintenance of the four articles. They would have succeeded, had not the emperor, at the diet of Braun, in 1420, rejected all their demands, and announced that he should govern Bohemia like his father, Charles IV.—in other words, that he should enter into no terms with heresy.

The majority of the Calixtines were anxious for some other king than the emperor, and were in favour of offering the throne to Wladislaus IV., king of Poland, on the single condition of maintaining in Bohemia the four articles of their creed. The Taborites, and Ziska at their head, were opposed to choosing any king at all, and demanded to have Bohemia constituted a republic. Many of them, however, proposed to confer the crown on Nicholas de Hussinetz, who still enjoyed a great credit amongst the Hussites, and remained their nominal chief until his death.

These various parties made war on each

---

* A celebrated writer, who published in the *Revue Indépendante* (April and May, 1843) some admirable articles on the war of the Hussites, attributes to this question of the cup, in Bohemia, an importance which we consider exaggerated. The language used is this: "The re-establishment or suppression of the cup was the vital question of the church, constituted as a political power. . . . It was a vital question of the population, constituted as members of humanity, as thinking beings, civilized by Christianity, as an ascendant force towards the conquests of social truths, which the gospel had, to a certain point, made apparent." (Vol. viii. page 36.) In our opinion, the people of Bohemia did not see so far. Nourished by the Scriptures, they protested against the suppression of the cup, simply because they found in the gospel the contrary practice, supported by the authority of Jesus Christ. The question of the cup, besides, possesses importance in the order of ideas, only when connected with the denial of the real presence. But the great majority of the people of Bohemia, converted to Christianity by Greek monks, professed the doctrine of the Eastern Church on the communion—they admitted *transubstantiation*, and the principal authors of the religious revolution, John Huss and Jerome of Prague, had done the same.

† The capital of Bohemia, as is well known, is composed of two towns, the old and modern Prague.

---

* They were called Adamites, because it was supposed that they remained naked in their meetings,—in order, thereby, to imitate the innocence of Adam.—(*Note of Translator.*)

† See the Dissertation of Lenfant on the Picards in the *Histoire du Concile de Bâle et de la Guerre des Hussites*, book v., and the learned notice of M. de Beausobre on the Adamites of Bohemia, inserted at the end of the same work.

other, but the four articles of the Calixtines were the common creed which united them against all foreign enemies; and in the latter struggle the principal influence at first belonged to the most ardent, as always happens, when a people in revolution are called on to resist, by the energy of enthusiasm, the double ascendancy of numbers and discipline. The Taborites, of whom Ziska was the chief, were, on this account, for a length of time, the predominating party in Bohemia.

The emperor had at first been diverted from the war against the Hussites, by the invasion of the Turks into Hungary. If, after the diet of Braun, he had at once marched on Prague, he might perhaps have succeeded in becoming master of it: but whilst he gained time to multiply his means of attack, he afforded the enemy the opportunity of preparing for their defence. At last the storm burst—Pope Martin V. had ordered a crusade to be preached against Bohemia, and a powerful army, drawn from the various countries of Germany, was directed towards Prague. Sigismund determined that terror should herald his approach; he gave way to his instincts of cruelty, and punished a sedition at Breslaw with frightful executions. Amongst the victims was a disciple of John Huss, named John Crasa, guilty only of having honoured his master, and of having blamed those who had caused his death—John Crasa was quartered alive.

At the news of these executions, Prague, until then divided, rose in arms: a Premonstrante* monk, named John, animated the popular indignation, and in the figurative language of the Taborite enthusiasts, their enemies were the Philistines, the Moabites, the Ammonites: Sigismund was the red horse of the Apocalypse: Bohemia was the land of promise. The mountains adjoining Prague received the biblical name of Horeb: their fierce inhabitants descended from them at the call of Ziska, and hurried to his standard: the people, the university, the Taborites, the Calixtines, all bound themselves together by oaths; one hundred and forty thousand men were advancing against Bohemia, but Bohemia was up in arms, and on both sides commenced a war of extermination.

Never were there witnessed, on a narrow space, so many acts of cruelty and sacrilege. There, it was the tombs of the kings which Sigismund violated, and, with the golden plates on the coffins, which no longer protected the mortal remains of the dead, paid the army which profaned them :* here, it was the pavement of the churches, and the marble of the altars, that charged the catapults; in other places, it was putrid corpses, flung by pieces, into the besieged towns, to add pestilence to famine; everywhere the conquered were massacred by the victors, to whichever party they belonged, imperialists or Hussites. After the soldiers came the executioners, and they who had escaped the sword envied the fate of those whom it had mowed down—on the two sides fell innumerable victims and glorious martyrs.† Dreadful traditions have perpetuated the memory of so many frightful scenes : near Toplitz may be seen, it is said, a pear tree which blossoms every year, and never yields fruit—a tree accursed, from the streams of blood which saturated its roots :‡ at Commotau, near a church where thousands of victims perished, slaughtered by Ziska, it is asserted that the soil is formed of the remains of their bones, and that at whatever depth search is made, nothing is found, to this day, but human teeth.§

Sigismund, at the beginning of the war, after the revolt of Prague, was still in possession of the two strong fortresses of the capital,—the castle of Wenceslaus, situated in the old town, and the celebrated citadel of Wishrade, which commanded the modern part. The two forts were attacked by the Hussites, and they still held out for the emperor, when Sigismund invested Prague the first time. He penetrated into the fort Wenceslaus and had himself crowned king of Bohemia, by Archbishop Conrad : but, pressed on all sides, and surrounded, with his army, by the Bohemians, he soon was forced to quit, as a fugitive, the kingdom which he had come to as an irritated master.

The retreat of the emperor was followed by the capture of the castle of Wenceslaus. The garrison of the fort of Wishrade long resisted, but, at length, when reduced to the last extremity, promised to surrender. It then learned that the emperor, at the head of a new army, levied in Hungary and Moravia,

---

* The Premonstrants were a religious order founded in 1120 by St. Norbert, under the rules of St. Augustine. They derive their name from the Abbey of Prémontré, in the department of the Aisne, in France, which was considered the chief house of the order. A century after their foundation had scarcely elapsed, when they were already exceedingly powerful.—(*Note of Translator*.)

* The pillage of the churches and convents was the resource of both parties.
† Many monks and nuns affronted death and tortures for their faith. Historians reckon at five hundred the number of monasteries destroyed by Ziska.
‡ Theob. *Bell. Huss.* p. 120.
§ Balbin. *Miscellan.*

was returning to Prague. The city was invested a second time, whilst the Hussites, under cover of their formidable retrenchments, still blockaded the citadel. Sigismund, from the top of a hill, showed himself to the imperial garrison of Wishrade, and made a sign to them to attack the enemy, whilst he, on his side, also assaulted them. The garrison, which had capitulated the evening before, remained motionless, and the emperor received a recommendation to retire. Then, casting a look of contempt on the Hussite army, in which the inhabitants of Prague were mingled with the Taborites of Ziska and undisciplined peasants, armed with long flails, loaded with iron, in place of swords and lances—" I want to come to blows," said he, " with those flail-bearers." "Sire," rejoined a nobleman of Moravia, named Plumlovjsc, " I fear that we shall all perish; these iron flails are exceedingly formidable." " Oh! you Moravians!" replied Sigismund, " I know you—you are afraid."

At this rash declaration, the chiefs flung themselves off their horses. " You shall find, sire, that we are not afraid," said Plumlovjsc; " behold us ready to obey your orders, and we shall go where your Majesty will not venture." The Imperialists all alighted like their leaders, and precipitated themselves with fury on the retrenchments of the Taborites. Their coming was expected, and they were unable to force the enemy. The defenders of Prague then sallied forth from the city, in several columns, and fell on the besiegers, who gave way and fled; but, pursued on all sides, they fell in thousands, by the sword of the Taborites, and by those same flails which the emperor had so much disdained.* A great part of the nobility of Moravia remained on the field of battle; Sigismund was hurried away by the rout of his troops, and the same day the fortress of Wishrade opened its gates to the victors.

Ziska, however, had received a wound which would have arrested any other man in his sanguinary career; for an arrow, at the siege of Raby, had deprived him of the sight of the eye that remained. But, in becoming blind, he became still more terrible—his wound was a fresh stimulus to his rage as to his genius, and revealed in him faculties really almost incredible. His memory of localities was prodigious: it was quite sufficient for him to have once passed through a country to remain for ever perfect master of all its slightest incidents. Bohemia, with her

waters, woods, valleys, and plains, was now as present to his thought as the reality had ever been to his sight. A spirit of fire in a body of iron, his activity knew no fatigue, and became exasperated at rest. " All seasons and weather are alike to this blind man," his soldiers used to mutter; " he goes by night as by day." Wherever there was a monastery to burn, or a town to take, or any army to combat, he hurried to the spot, and was soon accomplishing the deed of blood with a superhuman force, and as if urged to the work by an exterminating God. It was in this way that he overcame the various factions, several times delivered Prague and Bohemia, and put to flight all the armies of the empire.

The diet of Czaslau opened in July, 1421, after unheard-of successes. All the states of the kingdom of Bohemia and of the Marquisate of Moravia had sent their representatives. They appointed a regency of twenty members, taken from the different orders of the nation. Ziska appeared in it, in the first rank of the nobles. The deposition of Sigismund was solemnly pronounced, and the maintenance of the four articles of the Bohemian formulary was again solemnly sworn to.

Sigismund, tamed by his reverses, once more changed his style of language. He wrote to the diet to justify himself, promising every reasonable concession, and assigned as a motive of the inaction in which he remained, not fear, but a merciful compassion for his people.

The Bohemians and Moravians replied haughtily to the emperor: " Very illustrious prince and king: since your majesty assures us that if you have caused any disorder in the kingdom of Bohemia, you are inclined to afford a remedy, these are our grievances; you have permitted Master John Huss to be burnt, notwithstanding your safe-conduct, which was a great affront to the people of Bohemia. Liberty was given to all, who departed from the Catholic doctrine, to explain themselves freely, before the Council of Constance, except to our illustrious citizens; and to add to the contempt evinced towards Bohemia, you have suffered Master Jerome, whose merit was so great, to be, in like manner, put to death. You also have permitted, in the council, the kingdom of Bohemia to be devoted to extermination: you have excited the neighbouring nations to destroy us as accursed heretics. The foreign princes whom you have drawn into our country have ravaged Bohemia with fire and sword, sparing nothing, either profane or sacred, and inflict-

* Theob. Bell. Huss. p. 88.
21   o 2

ing, on our wives and daughters, the most cruel outrages." After these grievances, the Bohemians enumerated others, chiefly relating to the treasures which had been taken away by Sigismund, and to the provinces which he had alienated from the crown. "Put an end," said they, " to the invasions of the neighbouring nations, restore what you have taken away or misapplied, swear to maintain the observance of the four articles, and preserve to the kingdom of Bohemia and the Marquisate of Moravia their institutions and their privileges."*

The emperor, having returned an evasive reply to these demands, the Calixtines, on the refusal of Wladislaus, king of Poland, sent a deputation to his brother Witold, grand-duke of Lithuania, and offered the crown of Bohemia to Sigismund Coribut, son of the grand-duke, who accepted it.

However, as always happens in a state delivered to itself, in which so many elements of agitation are fomenting at the same time, when there was a truce abroad, there was war at home. Certain Picards, wild enthusiasts, having committed grave excesses, Ziska smote them as he had smitten their enemies, without delay or pity.†

The noise of these severities arrived at Prague, at a time when men, equally excited, and directed by John, called the Premonstrant, had acquired a formidable ascendency. These ran through the modern town, of which they were master, rang the bells, and called the multitude to arms. The Premonstrant attacked Old Prague at the head of an eager and irritated multitude: he hastened to the Hotel-de-Ville, dismissed the magistrates, and replaced them by others, chosen amongst the Picards, who declared against Ziska himself, and, for some time, held both the one and the other Prague obedient to them, through terror.

These intestine discords concurred, with the approach of a numerous army levied in Silesia, to render courage to Sigismund ; and at the moment he was entering Bohemia to reduce it, Ziska was called to Prague by his own enemies, to defend the city. He hastened there, the Moravians joined the Bohemians, and Coributi, whom the Calixtines desired to have for king, advanced to the aid of the capital with five thousand horse.

The most dangerous adversary of Ziska, in this rapid campaign, was that same bishop of Litomissel, who, after having persecuted Huss and Jerome, at Constance, with such implacable language, showed himself athirst for the blood of their disciples. He had been promoted to the bishopric of Olmutz, and when Archbishop Conrad declared himself Calixtine, Bishop John was named as his successor at Prague. But this prelate was a warrior, rather than a churchman, and in his efforts to reclaim his flock, the crozier he used was his sword. After saying mass, he used to mount on horseback, helm on head, and armour on his body, and, in consequence, had acquired the name of the Iron Bishop. His rage against the Hussites had in it something fiendish, and he boasted of having killed two hundred of them with his own hand. But iron as he was, he gave way before Ziska, and the new invasion of the imperialists had the same result as the preceding one. Worsted in all the encounters, they were at last cut to pieces, in the neighbourhood of Broda. Ziska shared an immense booty amongst the Taborites, and seated on the colours taken from the enemy, he knighted the bravest among the victors.

Sigismund withdrew into Hungary, and his retreat was followed by a revolution in Prague. The Calixtine party recovered their ascendency, more moderate magistrates were elected, and they cited before them the formidable John the Premonstrant, whom they accused of tyranny and sanguinary acts. The Premonstrant boldly presented himself with ten of his followers, but they were immediately seized and beheaded. At the sight of their blood flowing through the streets, the populace rose in tumult. Jacobel inflamed them, exhibiting the head of him whom he named a martyr, and the bodies of his companions. The multitude avenged their deaths by massacreing those who had ordered their execution.

However, notwithstanding this sedition, the Picard party did not recover the ascendency, and the entrance of Coributi into Prague, with his Lithuanian and Polish troops, still more strengthened the Calixtines. In the midst of the military operations carried on against the fortified places, which held out for Sigismund, the civil war continued in Prague.

---

* Theob. Bell. Huss. p. 100.

† Amongst the fanatics exterminated by Ziska, historians mention the pretended Adamites of the river of Lusinitz, who committed all sorts of abominations, under the cloak of religious zeal. They also speak of a Taborite priest, Martin Loquis, who denied the doctrine of the real presence, and declaimed most violently against the open profession which Ziska made of the contrary doctrine. Ziska had him put to death in a barrel of boiling pitch, which he never would have ventured to do, notwithstanding his daring, if the greater part of the Taborite army had then professed the opinions of the priest, as they professed them afterwards, and denied transubstantiation.

The greatest number of the nobles again declared for the emperor, whilst a strong majority of the Calixtine party persisted in wishing to have for king, Coribut, whom the Taborites rejected. The latter, too weak to succeed in Prague, by open force, attempted to seize on the town by a nocturnal surprise; but they were vanquished, after a sanguinary combat, and a great number perished in the Moldau.

Ziska was in the field preparing to pass into Moldavia, at the beginning of the year 1423, when he heard of the culpable attempt of the Taborites, and the triumph of the Calixtines. He immediately sent to the city to deny all participation in the seditious movement which had turned out so fatally, and at the same time he exhorted Prague not to elect Coribut for king. "I have defended Bohemia," said he, "with my army, against all the forces of the empire: a free people have no need of a king." The citizens of Prague, in their turn, sent a deputation to Ziska. "The nation must have a head," said they, and insisted on having Coribut crowned. Then, torn with passion, the terrible blind man struck the ground three times with his commander's staff,[*] and replied: "I have twice saved Prague from the hands of the emperor; I will now destroy it. I will prove that I am equally able to save and destroy my country."[†]

The nobles of Bohemia who were in favour of Sigismund, made common cause with the party which preferred Coribut; the Catholics and the Calixtines took up arms against Ziska, and a numerous army went out of Prague to engage him. It was beaten in three battles, and Ziska, wild with passion and the thirst of vengeance, marched his victorious Taborites to Prague. At the sight of this city, which they called their mother country, these men, who had, without scruple, shed so much blood, stopped short; their hardened hearts were affected, and murmurs rose in the ranks. Ziska harangued them with his powerful and warlike voice, standing on a cask, whence he could be viewed by those whom he no longer saw. "Companions," said he, "why do you murmur? I am not your enemy, but your general. It is by me that you have gained so many victories—by me that you are illustrious and rich. And yet, for you, I have lost my sight—I am con-

demned to eternal darkness. . . . ; For all the labours that I have achieved, what has been my reward? Nothing but a name. It is, then, for you that I have acted—that I have conquered; and it is not my own interest that arms me against this city. It is not the blood of a blind old man that it thirsts after, but it dreads your intrepid hearts and your invincible arms. When they shall have taken me in their nets, they will lay snares for you, which you will with difficulty escape from. Let us therefore take Prague: let us crush the sedition before Sigismund is informed of it. A few men, well united, will do more against the emperor, than a vast multitude, divided. Let no person, therefore, accuse me; for I act in your interest. Now, make your choice. Will you have peace? Take care that it does not cover some ambush. Will you have war? Here I am!"

These words reanimated the army: the Taborites invested the city, and prepared for the assault. Terror then seized on Prague: the citizens met to deliberate, and determined to send a deputation to Ziska, to beseech him to relent. At the head of the persons sent, was a Calixtine priest, of great credit, and who afterwards acquired a great celebrity—John de Rockizane. This priest represented, to the new Coriolanus, his country suppliant at his feet; the city which he had saved and loved, ready to perish by his hands. Ziska consented to pardon: he, for once, and only for once, gave up his vengeance: he granted peace; and in his camp, on the very spot where it was signed, a pile of stones was heaped up, according to ancient custom, as a monument of the alliance, that whoever violated it should perish under the stones which formed that rude altar. Ziska then made a public entry into Prague, where he received the greatest honours and exercised a sovereign authority.

The emperor, seeing the Bohemians again united under this invincible chief, comprehended that he should never reign in Bohemia, as long as Ziska was his enemy. He therefore endeavoured to gain him over by magnificent offers: "It was sufficient for him," he observed, "to be merely proclaimed king in Bohemia; Ziska should govern the kingdom:" and, to the promise of great honours, Sigismund joined that of immense wealth.

Æneas Sylvius manifests great indignation in relating this fact, and the very violence of his expressions against Ziska gives the highest idea of the influence and power of the

---

[*] Balbinus, *Epit. rer. Boh.* p. 453.
[†] Patriamque meam a me et conservari et opprimi posse re ipsa ostendam. (Theob. *Bell. Huss.* p. 112.)

man.* The same author declares, although without proof, that Ziska did not remain indifferent to the emperor's offers. It is not unlikely that the leader of the Taborites may have had, in fact, some idea of reigning, under the name of the prince whom he had conquered, and he probably thought no hand was more worthy to direct Bohemia than that which had liberated it. He carried his secret with him to the tomb, and after having lived to ruin the emperor's plans, he died too soon to serve them. The plague, which ravaged Bohemia, struck him at the siege of a little town on the confines of Bohemia and Moravia.† He expired on Oct. 11, 1424, ordering his soldiers to abandon his body to birds of prey, and to have his skin made into a drum, the mere noise of which would cast terror into his enemies.‡

Thus fell the warrior, whose equal will be sought in vain among the most famous—this blind man, who executed against the enemy as great things as they whose sight was the most rapid and penetrating.§ He withstood the forces of all Germany, delivered his country, put down factions, and conquered eleven times in pitched battles.‖ He was not indebted for his success to religious and personal enthusiasm: making his religion subordinate to his policy, he declared himself a Taborite, because the popular strength was in that party, and because they were opposed to having a king; but perhaps he was the only man, who, in a religious war, dared to show himself the implacable enemy of fanaticism, although leading fanatics to battle.¶

His ascendency proceeded from his genius, his intrepidity, and the incredible resources which he was master of. Ziska, according to the writings of historians, was not less remarkable for prudence, and for craftiness, than for courage and activity; and his stratagems are as celebrated as his deeds of arms. It was his inventive and abundant mind, which gave to the Hussites the long shield, and the spear, armed with a hook near the end, by which they unhorsed the cavalry: he invented movable redoubts, formed of cars,* bound together with iron chains; and he taught the art of throwing up retrenchments in earth, against the artillery, then lately introduced into armies. Carrying ideas of order and organization into the midst of the most tumultuous scenes, Ziska drew up a military code, embracing all matters relating to discipline, encampments, marches, and regulating even pillage. In it, all infractions of orders were punished with death.† Affable, in common life, with his soldiers, he used to call them his brothers, and always generously abandoned to them the booty, of which he reserved nothing to himself. He was undoubtedly ambitious, but the predominating trait in his character was his love of vengeance, and although born in a cruel age, his cruelty causes one to shudder: he found in it a cold and execrable voluptuousness, and showed himself so much the more pitiless, that he did not behold what affected the most hardened. He beheld neither the tears of the suppliants falling, nor the blood of his victims flowing; and when once he had given the fatal word—strike!—his word was as inexorable as destiny.

Ziska was of middle stature, exceedingly wide and strong in the shoulders and chest. His head was large, round, and shaved close, his nose aquiline, and his mustaches long. His complexion was exceedingly dark and bilious, and his forehead presented that indenture, falling perpendicularly down the forehead, which has been remarked in several famous warriors, and which is, in consequence, called the *martial line.*‡ This man

* O disgrace! O humiliation of royal majesty, of the glory of the empire, and of the Christian world! This Sigismund, possessor of several kingdoms, the descendant of emperors, an emperor himself, revered in Italy, in France, in Germany, dreaded by barbarous nations, has been seen, in our age, supplicating a man, scarcely noble by birth, old, blind, sacrilegious, ready to commit all kinds of crime, and a heretic: he has offered him treasures and the highest honours, to induce him to favour his cause! (Æneas Sylvius, *Hist. Boh.* p. 98.)
† Przibislau, according to Theobald, *Bell. Huss.* p. 115; Preslovic, according to Æneas Sylvius, *Hist. Boh.* p. 98.
‡ Same authors, same pages.
§ Cochlæus, an historian, the most prepossessed against Ziska, has declared that he might not only be equalled, but even preferred to the greatest captains. (*Hist. Huss.* p. 217.)
‖ In his battles, he had himself carried in his chariot, near the principal standard, and there, from the reports made to him, he drew out his army, gave the signal of attack, and fulfilled all the other duties of a general. (*Balbinus,* p. 456.)
¶ Ziska used to hear mass, in his camp, according to the old ritual, and would have the priest officiate, clad in his surplice and ornaments, which, in the eyes of the Taborite soldiers, were the

pomps of the devil: however, as long as he lived, the greater part of his army admitted the doctrine of the real presence. See Beaussobre, *Suppl. de la prem. partie de la dissertation sur les Adamites.*
* These cars, filled with soldiers, were so arranged, as to present, outside, a wall of defence, and, within, winding streets, traced out on the model of letters of the alphabet, or ciphers, which were known to the defenders, but not to the enemy.
† Præcepta severe et serio sub capitali pœna inculcantur. (Balbinus, *Epit. rer. Boh.* p. 465.)
‡ Balbinus. (*Ibid.*)

was never conquered: for four years he appeared in Germany, as the living image of God's wrath, and merited but too well this inscription engraved near his tomb:* "O Huss! here reposes John Ziska, thy avenger, and the emperor himself has quailed before him!"*

CHAPTER IV.

THE HUSSITES AFTER ZISKA.

The noblest funeral eulogium of a general is the mourning of his army, and nothing does more honour to the memory of John Ziska than the name, which a great number of his soldiers insisted on being called, when they had lost him—they called themselves the *orphans;* and they, at first, refused to elect another chief, none being worthy to command them, after Ziska. When the enemy re-appeared, the Bohemian army was divided into three bodies, the Taborites, the Horebites, and the Orphans, of whom the principal chiefs were two men who afterwards became celebrated under the names of Procopius the Great, and Procopius the Little. The first of these leaders, who was also called Procopius the Shaven, because he had worn the tonsure, had quitted the monkish dress for the cuirass, at the beginning of the war of the Hussites: he had been the companion of Ziska in all his battles and dangers: and had received from that chief the title of the *Hercules of his country.*† Ziska, it is said, intended him to be his successor,‡ and Procopius in fact became so by his talents and his victories.

This rapid sketch of the wars of Bohemia, after John Huss, does not allow of any details: it is sufficient to say that the death of Ziska revived, in this unfortunate country, the civil disorders which had been a moment put down and restrained, and again restored hope to Sigismund. Pope Martin V. then had a second crusade preached against the Hussites, and they, under Bozkode Podiebrad and Procopius the Great, put to flight, the first time, an army of one hundred thousand Imperialists, in a dreadful battle fought in 1426, near the town of Aust.§ The following year, a second army, still more formidable, marched on Bohemia, under the direction of the Cardinal of Winchester, to whom the pope had intrusted the chief command of the crusade. This army engaged the Hussites before Mise, and was again cut to pieces; ten thousand men fell afterwards in the woods, under the iron flails of the Horebites.

The Bohemians, at this period, imprisoned Coribut, whom a party amongst them had proclaimed, and whom they accused of complicity with the emperor and pope. They afterwards turned him disgracefully out of the kingdom, and, after his departure, they again divided against each other, and furious combats took place in the two parts of Prague, still divided amongst the Calixtines, the Orphans, and the Taborites. Amidst these sanguinary scenes a man is mentioned whose name is inseparable from those of Huss and Jerome: it is the prince's notary, Peter Maldoniewitz, who, after having at first opposed the excesses of the Taborites, declared, at a later period, against the Calixtines of Old Prague, who leaned towards Sigismund. They made him prisoner, with the celebrated Doctor Prailiram, and both, when restored to liberty, rejoined the Orphans in their camp.†

---

* The body of Ziska was interred with honours, at Czaslau, in the cathedral church, and his iron mace was suspended near his tomb, on which the following epitaph may be still read: "Here lies John Ziska, inferior to no other general in military science, the rigorous punisher of the pride and avarice of the priesthood, and the zealous defender of his country. What the blind Appius Claudius did for the Romans by his counsel, and Curius Camillus, by his actions, I accomplished for the Bohemians.—I never failed fortune, nor she me; and, although blind, I always perceived what ought to be done. I have fought eleven times, with standard displayed, and I have always been conqueror. I was unceasingly seen defending the cause of the unfortunate and the poor, against sensual and bloated priests, and therefore did God sustain me. If their hatred did not oppose it, I should be reckoned amongst the most illustrious: and yet, in spite of the pope, my bones repose in this holy place."—(Theob. *Bell. Hussit.* p. 116.)

† Maldoniewitz afterwards became a priest, and preached at the Church of St. Michael at Prague. He had succeeded in this charge another friend of Huss, Christian de Praschatitz, who died of the plague in 1439. Maldoniewitz lived to 1451. He is the author of a *Life of John Huss,* which used to be read in the churches of Prague.

---

* On an altar, where John Huss and John Ziska are represented together.
† Balbinus, *Epit. rer. Boh.* p. 457.
‡ Theobald, *Bell. Hussit.* p. 117.
§ This town is also called Aussig.

These frightful disorders agitated Prague, as might. be expected, particularly in the years when she had no foreign invasions to repel; on the return of the enemy, all parties united again. The Taborites, so dreaded by the Calixtines of Prague, were, however, always appealed to by them in the moment of peril, as the guardian angels of the country, and these invasions, which brought desolation on the kingdom, also constituted its strength.

No person exhibited more ardour to conciliate parties than Procopius the Great, who, according to the occasion, appeared, by turns, as theologian, negotiator, and general. He believed that Sigismund could, better than any other, re-establish peace in Bohemia; but he comprehended, at the same time, that this peace could not be lasting, unless with the maintenance of the evangelical doctrines, which had become those of the nation. It was necessary, therefore, that the emperor should give pledges of insuring this, by agreeing to the wishes of the states of the kingdom, and by taking the sacrament himself in the two kinds. Procopius proposed, in an assembly of the states, held at Prague, in 1428, to receive the emperor on these conditions, whether it was that he really had hopes of succeeding, or that he only wished to gain time. He obtained the assent of the states, and named several nobles to go and confer with Sigismund, whilst he proceeded himself to Presburg, where the Diet was sitting. He appeared there, with the other deputies, chosen amongst the most noble persons in the kingdom,* but he negotiated without success, and returned to Prague, convinced that the Bohemians ought not to reckon on any but themselves.

His efforts again effected a union of all the parties; a solemn reconciliation took place at Prague, before the altar, in the Church of St. Ambrose; an enormous fine was named as the punishment to which those infringing it should be liable, and Procopius, the principal author of this compact, was elected generalissimo. He knew that, when once the peace was sworn to, the means of insuring it within the kingdom, was to keep employed, outside, an army accustomed to conquer. Therefore, addressing his Taborites, he said: " Brethren, you have not forgotten how the Misnians† fell on our towns and would have extermi-

nated us, if they could. Thanks to our valour, the flower of their nation is buried in the plains of Bohemia. They have now a young and inexperienced prince: they tremble at the thought of falling into our hands: this is the moment to act: the hour of great things has arrived."*

Loud acclamations greeted these words. Procopius led the army forth, crossed the Elbe, and fell on Misnia, whilst other bodies penetrated * into Silesia, Brandenburg, and Saxony. Dreadful ravages marked the progress of the Hussites: in every direction churches and monasteries were destroyed: many towns were reduced to ashes with their defenders, and the conquerors shouted over their smoking ruins: " Behold the funeral obsequies of John Huss !"

Such were the frightful acts of the Hussites in Germany, when Martin V., who had resolved to exterminate them, died; he expired in 1431, after having, to no purpose, published two crusades against them. This pontiff opened, without result, the councils of Pavia and Sienna, and convoked that of Basil, which did not assemble until after his death. His successor, Gabriel Condulmer, took the name of Eugenius IV., and of all the decrees of Martin V., he really began with greater ardour than that which struck at heresy. A third crusade, with promise of indulgences, was, in 1421, preached up against the Hussites.

At the noise of the new peril which menaced Bohemia, Procopius led back his army to meet the storm. The whole of Germany had risen at the appeal of the pope, and all her states had furnished their contingent; the supreme command was given to the Cardinal legate, Julian Cesarini, and eighty thousand infantry, forty thousand cavalry, and a formidable artillery, advanced under his orders, the heads of the several divisions being the Archduke Albert of Austria, the Elector Frederick of Brandenburg, the Elector Frederick the Warlike of Saxony, and the Duke of Bavaria.

This immense army divided itself, and attacked in different quarters: the Archduke reduced Moravia, the Elector of Saxony invested Tachau: and the other corps proceeded towards Bohemia by Ratisbon. When the Imperialists arrived at the entrance of the Black Forest, they halted: a council was held, and scouts were sent out to explore. Deceived by false rumours circulated by Procopius, they took confidence, and thinking the Hussites to be divided, they accordingly

---

* The negotiations failed, because the emperor declared that to separate from the Roman church, was to renounce Christianity. (Theobald, Bell. Hussit. p. 135.)

† Inhabitants of Misnia, a province of Saxony, adjoining Bohemia.

* Theob. Bell. Hussit. p. 136.

entered the forest, between Tausch and Frauemberg. All of a sudden they learned that the Hussites were in arms, were united, and approaching rapidly. A sudden terror seized on the leaders and the army: the Duke of Bavaria raised his camp in the night, and gave the example of desertion; and the vanguard, commanded by the Elector of Brandenburg, tore their colours into pieces in the morning, and dispersed: Cardinal Julian rushed into the midst of the runaways, and recalled them. "Your pagan ancestors," said he, "have fought better for mute idols than you for the glory of Christ. Remember your oaths and be men." His words restored courage to the troops: they plunged into the defiles of the forest and pitched their camp on the Giant's Mount, in the neighbourhood of Tausch. There Procopius and the Taborites soon appeared: at their aspect, another panic seized on the Imperialists: they fled, without striking a blow, and, in the utmost terror, sought for refuge in the depths of the woods and wastes. A spectacle of horror was then seen in that ancient forest,* so often witness of the disasters of Germany: one hundred thousand men, overwhelmed, one on the other, were flying pell-mell with eight thousand chariots and one hundred and fifty pieces of heavy artillery, before Procopius and his Hussite destroyers. The whole night might be heard, to a considerable distance, confused and frightful noises of shouts and cries, intermingled with shocks of steel, the crash of breaking cars, and the loud intonations of powder caissons. blowing up. Eleven thousand men were slaughtered during the night, and the provision magazines, the strong chest of the Imperial army, and all the artillery, became the prey of the Hussites: the insignia of the cardinal legate and the pope's bull also fell into their hands. This bull, which had raised all Germany against the Bohemians, was, for a long time, preserved at Tausch, as the most glorious trophy of their victory. The Hussites then passed their frontiers, fell on the natives which had leagued against them, drove the Teutonic knights from the marches of Brandenburg, and paid back to Hungary, Austria, and Silesia the ravages they had inflicted on Bohemia.

So many incredible successes on the part of the Bohemians caused their enemies to alter their language. They were invited by the cardinal legate to go with full freedom and discuss their doctrines at the Council of Basil, which opened in December, 1431, under his presidentship. The council renewed the invitation, and they received a safe-conduct, the principal articles of which declared that they should have entire liberty to remain at Basil, to act, decide, judge, treat, and enter into arrangements with the council; that they should celebrate with perfect liberty their sacred worship in their own houses; according to their custom; that they should be permitted, in private and in public, to establish and prove their four articles, by the testimony of the Scripture and of the holy doctors;— that the council would punish, most severely, any attempt to violate the safe-conduct;* that it should not be allowable for the Catholics to preach against the four articles, during the sojourn of the Bohemians at Basil, and that on their return a safe escort should be given them to the frontier.†

Notwithstanding such favourable conditions and the reiterated promises of the pope, the emperor, and the council, the Bohemians hesitated, held back by the remembrance of John Huss and Jerome of Prague; and whilst they were deliberating, a new schism was in preparation.

Eugenius IV., as on a former occasion John XXIII., had beheld, with uneasiness, the convocation of the council in a city which was not within his own jurisdiction, and it had been scarcely assembled, when the pope pronounced its dissolution, in spite of the emperor, and convoked it anew at Bologna. The fathers at Basil opposed this translation, and adopted vigorous measures against Eugenius. The decrees of the fourth and the fifth sessions of Constance, relative to the superiority of general councils, were confirmed; all decisions on the part of Eugenius against the rights of the assembly were declared null; it was decided that in case of the Holy See becoming vacant, the election should take place at Basil and nowhere else; all nomination of cardinals was forbidden, during the duration of the council; and the pope himself was summoned to appear within the space of three months.

The council, on the demand of the emperor, accorded several successive delays to the pope; but its acts, in other matters which related to Eugenius, were neither less firm nor less rigorous. In its eleventh session, held on April 27, 1432, it confirmed the decrees of Constance, touching the periodical convocation of general councils; it decreed that the pope was bound to appear in the

---

* The Black Forest, (*Hercynia Sylva*.)

* Theobald, *Bell. Hussit.* p. 151.
† Labbæi, *Sacr. Sanct. Concil.* vol. xii. p. 483, 484.

council, in person, or by his legates; that if he did not come forward within the space of four months, he should be deposed from the pontificate; that general councils should not be dissolved without the consent of two-thirds of their members: and that the observance of this decree should be sworn to by the sovereign pontiff.

Sigismund again interposed between the pope and the council, and obtained from Eugenius the positive confirmation of the decrees of Basil. The pontiff promised, besides, to proceed to the council or to appear there by his legates, as soon as the resolutions already entered into against him should be annulled. In the month of November the emperor came, and gave, by his presence at Basil, a new force to the council. This prince remembered the evils of the grand schism, and the infinite pains he had been obliged to take to extinguish it, and, already too feeble against Turks in Hungary and against the Hussites in Bohemia, he spared nothing to prevent a rupture between the council and the pope; the consequences of which he had learned by experience to dread. He succeeded in suspending all hostile demonstrations, and the two grand powers of the church finished the year 1432 in an apparent reconciliation, which on both sides cloaked a profound irritation and violent designs.[*]

The Bohemians, however, had come to the determination to accept the safe-conduct:

they set out on their journey, and in the beginning of the year 1433, Basil beheld a new and most curious spectacle; the Hussites made their entry into the city, to the number of three hundred; chosen from the most noble in the land.[*] Their haughty bearing afforded a curious contrast with the humble situation of their master at Constance. John Huss had come, strong only in the uprightness of his soul, his sincere piety and his fervent faith, which was attributed to him as a crime, disdained besides by a proud assembly, and on all sides a mark for insult and violence. His disciples now arrived, preceded by their reputation of invincible, after having made Germany and the empire tremble; they had avenged their master, and came boldly to maintain his doctrines, and treating, as power with power, with many of those who had condemned him.

The council sent to meet them, and received them with great honour. Amongst the heads of the deputation was the Calixtine priest, John de Rockizane, who administered the archbishopric of Prague, and Procopius the Great, the general of the Taborites. "The crowd, and with it a great part of the members of the council," writes Æneas Sylvius, himself an eye-witness, "had dispersed themselves outside the walls, waiting for the sight of these men, so intrepid and so famous.[†] The public places and streets along their passage were thronged with spectators; women, children, and young girls filled the windows and even occupied the roofs of houses; the lookers-on pointed out to each other these foreign costumes which had never before been seen there; they gazed with surprise at these visages, marked with scars, and these terrible eyes; and in beholding men of so stern an appearance, they were the less astonished at the things which fame related of them."[‡] Procopius, in particular, attracted attention.[§] That is he, said they, who has conquered so many armies, destroyed so many towns, massacred so many thousands of

---

[*] After some new disputes, the pope again solemnly adhered to the Council of Basil, by a bull published in April, 1434, and declared that this council had been legitimately opened and continued, until then; but soon after, the division recommenced. The emperor and the patriarch of Constantinople demanded to be heard in a general assembly, to unite the Eastern Church to the Latin Church, and the Greeks wished to have a council in Italy. The pope indicated Ferrara for the purpose, and invited to that place the fathers at Basil, who looked on this translation as a pretext to dissolve their council. This was afterwards, in 1439, transferred by Eugenius from Ferrara to Florence. A part of the fathers proceeded there, but several remained at Basil, where they still declared themselves to be the universal council. There, following the example given at Pisa and at Constance, they deposed Eugenius IV., and elected in his place, as sovereign pontiff, Amadeus VIII., duke of Savoy, who accepted this dangerous honour and took the name of Felix V. The Council of Basil held twenty more sessions until 1443; France presented, in 1438, and got authorized, the edict issued by the clergy assembled at Bourges, and celebrated under the name of the *pragmatic sanction.* However, this council, according to Fleury, ought not to be recognised after its twenty-fifth session, held on the 7th May, 1437. Felix V. abdicated in 1448, at the solicitation of Charles VII., king of France, and the Catholic Church was again united under a single pontiff, although divided on the very principle which constitutes its sovereign authority.

[*] Trecenti equites Bohemi nobilissimi.—(Balbinus, p. 481.)

[†] Ad eos videndos velut mivacula belli universa civitas concurrit.—(Balbinus, *Epit. rer. Bohem.* p. 481.)

[‡] It was a proverb in Germany that in the body of one Bohemian soldier there were a hundred devils.—(*Ubi supra,* p. 187.)

[§] Procopius, whose statue was long seen on the bridge of Basil, bore a great resemblance to Ziska, his master. He was of middle stature, with powerfully athletic limbs; his head was large and close shaved, like those of priests; his nose was aquiline, and his complexion exceedingly dark; his eyes, which were of uncommon brightness, darted terrible glances.—(Balbinus, p. 481.)

men—as much an object of terror to his own people as to the enemy—the daring and invincible chief, who has never yielded either to fatigue or fear.[*]

The Hussites were heard in several public and private conferences, and contented themselves with defending their four famous articles by the eloquent mouth of John de Rockizane. They declared that they could not listen to any arrangement until they had obtained for Bohemia the maintenance of these articles. Nothing was concluded, and the Hussites quitted Basil; they were speedily followed by a deputation of the council, with Philibert, bishop of Constance, at its head, charged to bear the propositions of the fathers of Basil to the people of Bohemia.

These propositions were relative to the four articles of the Bohemian creed, viz.: the free preaching of the gospel—the punishment of public offences without privilege of clergy—the secular administration of the property of the church—and the communion in the two kinds. The council admitted the three first articles, but in interpreting and modifying them in such a way as to render them nearly illusory; as to the fourth, it granted, for a time, to the Bohemian clergy, permission to administer the communion in the two kinds, but the communicants were to be warned to believe, that the body of Jesus Christ was not merely in the bread, and that His blood was not merely in the wine, but that Jesus Christ was altogether in one and the other kind.

The formulary proposed by the council was drawn up with great art, and in such a manner as to satisfy those who only sought to finish the war and put an end to the violent state of the country. Of this number was Rockizane, whose ambition the deputies flattered with the hope of preserving the archbishopric of Prague. The peace party gained the advantage in this city, and sent deputies to the council to draw up the definitive conditions, which were signed the following year, and which are celebrated in history under the name of *Compactata*.

On the occasion of the proposed agreement, the civil war broke out in the kingdom, more furiously than before. The Catholics united with the nobles, and the old utraquist or Calixtine party,[*] directed by Rockizane, and by the Barons de Neuhauss, and de Rosemberg, were anxious for peace: the Taborites, the Orphans, and the Horebites, under the two leaders Procopius, wished for war, and showed how much the concessions of the council were insufficient and illusory, to guarantee the observance of the four articles. Their judgment on this point was correct, but the remembrance of their innumerable violences rose against them—their savage fury, so formidable to their enemies, had not been less terrible in Bohemia; and, at last, the country revolted against such dangerous defenders.

Old Prague, in which the Calixtine party had the predominance, rose against the new town, which was in the power of the Orphans and Taborites, under the lesser Procopius: a bloody battle was fought, and the Taborites were conquered, leaving twenty thousand men on the field; and the survivors joined Procopius the Great, before Pilsen, which he was besieging.

The siege was immediately raised, and Procopius marched on Prague, as Ziska had formerly done: but all the nobility of Bohemia had joined the Catholics and the Calixtines, against the Taborites, and a formidable army left the city and marched out to meet them under Rosemberg, Neuhauss, and Koska. The two armies met in a vast plain, four miles and a half from Prague, between Broda and Kursin.

Procopius had forbidden his troops to deliver battle, unless an opportunity of victory presented itself, his intention being to appear before Prague, convinced that the modern town would open its gates to him.[†] The action, however, commenced, by accident, from some war-chariots being dashed against others with insulting challenges: the nobles, by a pretended flight, drew after them the Taborites, of whom a great number quitted their chariots and mounted their horses to pursue with greater speed: suddenly, the nobles stopped, and being collected, under the banner of Rosemberg, turned round and fell on the Taborites, before the latter could re-establish their formidable retrenchment of chariots. The cavalry rushed into the openings, and for the first time broke through and carried, at a gallop, those lines which had hitherto been impenetrable. Procopius beheld the peril, and he called with loud cries his Taborites into the plain. His orders

---

[*] In unum tamen cuncti Procopium defigere lumina; illum esse qui toties fidelium fudisset exercitus, qui tot oppida subvertisset, tot huminum millia neci dedisset, quem sui pariter atque hostes metuerent: invictam ducem, audacem, intrepidum, neque labore neque timore superandum.—(Æneas Sylvius, *Hist. Bohem.* cap. xlix.)

[*] The Calixtines were called *utraquists*, because they took the communion in both kinds.

[†] Æneas Sylvius, *Hist. Bohem.* p. 114.

were but indifferently understood; the unexpected capture of the chariots had thrown his
men into confusion, and Czapeck, the leader
of his cavalry, fled from the field of battle.[*]
Then Procopius, with his bravest men, to
whom he had given the name of the fraternal
cohort, threw themselves into the very thick
of the squadrons of the enemy, and beat
them back: but surrounded at last on all
sides, overwhelmed by an unceasing shower
of darts, he fell, pierced by an unknown
hand, tired of conquering, rather than vanquished. The other Procopius also perished
in this famous battle, in which the word of
the emperor was accomplished :—"The Bohemians will be conquered only by themselves."[†]

The Taborites never recovered from this
defeat; the civil discords were, it is true,
quenched in their blood; but these terrible
men, who so often agitated Bohemia, were
also they, who, for twenty years, had enabled
it to resist the council, the pope, and the emperor. From that fatal day, in which Bohemia tore herself to pieces with her own
hands, she never ceased decreasing in power
and liberty.

The *Compactata* [‡] or articles of agreement
between the council and states of Bohemia,
were approved of by the emperor and signed
at Iglau on July 12, 1436, and, in addition,
particular concessions were made by Sigismund to the Bohemians. The kingdom was
still heaving under his fief and casting forth
flames; impatient to reign, Sigismund treated rather through necessity, than as his inclination would have led him. "He desired, at
any price," says Æneas Sylvius, "to regain
possession of his kingdom, and then to bring
back his subjects to the true religion of Jesus
Christ."[§] He therefore accorded great privileges to the town of Tabor, leaving the
Taborites, for five years, full and entire liberty
of conscience.[‖] He promised not to recall to
their monasteries the banished monks, to
leave unmolested the possessors of ecclesiastical property, and to confirm the gift of the

archbishopric of Prague to Rockizane; but
he afterwards violated the greater number of
the articles, or eluded the observance of them:
he interpreted the *Compactata* as the pope
would have done, and he re-established, with
all his authority, the Roman worship in the
kingdom: he forced the churches from the
Hussites, to restore them to the Catholics,
re-opened the monasteries, recalled the monks,
and refused to keep his word with Rockizane,
unless he abjured. Threats escaped from the
archbishop, and when they were related to
Sigismund, he exclaimed, "I should joyfully
shed Rockizane's blood on the altar." The
emperor was afterwards punished for his culpable deference to the Holy See,[*] and nar-
rowly escaped again losing this hereditary
throne, so dearly recovered, and on which he
was scarcely seated. He was growing old,
and not having a son, he destined his rich inheritance to Albert, Archduke of Austria, his
son-in-law, whose aid he, for a long time, had
availed himself of, in his enterprises against
Bohemia. His designs were opposed and
frustrated by the culpable intrigues of his
second wife, Barbara de Cilly. This princess,
famous by her adulteries, in expectation of a
speedy widowhood, conceived the design of
inflaming the ambition of Wladislaus, King
of Poland, by offering him, with her hand,
the rich inheritance of the emperor; she, at
the same time, turned to account the just resentment of the Bohemians, and pointed out
to them Albert of Austria as an ardent Catholic, who would infallibly put down all religious liberty. Many pledged themselves
to second her views, and to proclaim Wladislaus King of Bohemia, after the death of
Sigismund.

The emperor was at Prague, dangerously
ill, and almost alone, in the midst of an irritated people, when he learned that a conspi-
racy was formed against him, and that the
empress was amongst those engaged in it.
He saw the danger, and immediately called
around him some Hungarian noblemen, then
at Prague, and whose fidelity he had proved,
and who, on that account, were, like him, objects of popular hatred. "The close of my
life," he said to them, "is approaching:

---

[*] The opinion of the Catholics themselves is,
that without the flight of Czapeck, Procopius
would have conquered. (Balbinus, p. 468.)
[†] Æneas Sylvius, *ubi supra.*
[‡] See Cochlœus, *Hist. des Huss.* p. 271, and
the following; and Lenfant, *Hist. du Conc. de
Bâle.* vol. i. p. 449, and the following.
[§] Quibus ex rebus liquet imperatorem quæ fœ-
dera cum hæreticis percussit, necessitate magis
admississe quam voluntati, &c. (Æneas Sylvius,
p. 120.)
[‖] See in Note 8 the confession of faith of the
Taborites, very little different from that of the
Waldensian churches, and the most part of the
Protestant churches of the following century.

[*] Sigismund had recently given the church a
new proof of his submission. He possessed, for
twenty years, as King of the Romans, the rank
and authority of emperor, when he determined to
get the pope to confer the title on him : he underwent, at Rome, for this purpose, the humiliations
attendant on a coronation (in 1433), and, prostrate
on the ground, suffered the foot of the pope to
straighten the crown on his brow. (See Wendek,
Hist. imperat. Sigism. in Script. rer. Germ. von
Menck. Pfister, *Hist. d'Allem.* book iii.)

should I die, the Bohemians, now in such irritation, will deprive you of life; they thirst after your blood, and I wish to remove you, with myself, from their fury." He then got a report circulated, that he was going to meet his daughter, whom he desired to embrace, before he died.* Resuming then all his dignity, he wreathed his brow with laurel leaves, as on solemn feast days, invested himself with all his imperial robes and ensigns, and, decorated still more with his long white hair, which flowed freely on his shoulders, with his long majestic beard, and the nobility stamped on his pale visage, he had himself borne through the city, in an open litter, in the sight of all, followed by his wife and his faithful Hungarians. It is said that he shed tears in regarding this city, where his ancestors had so gloriously reigned, and which he was looking on for the last time; the people themselves, affected at this unexpected and imposing spectacle, forgot their vengeance, and saluted with their adieu their aged emperor.†

Sigismund proceeded towards Hungary, but overwhelmed with fatigue and illness, he with difficulty reached Znoima in Moravia, and went no further. There he had the empress arrested, whom he ordered to be kept prisoner, and held a long secret conference with the archduke, his son-in-law. Then, finding his death approaching, he ordered to his bedside the Moravian, Bohemian, and Hungarian noblemen who flocked to Znoima: he represented to them how important it was for Hungary and for Bohemia to remain united under an able prince, and pointed out to them the Archduke Albert, as more in a position than any other, from his personal resources and talents, to defend these two kingdoms. "He would be the most worthy to succeed me," said he to them, "even were he not my son-in-law."‡ Having obtained the assent of all, Sigismund named deputies, whom he charged to get the Archduke of Austria recognised as his successor to the throne. He added to their number Gaspard Schleick, his able chancellor, and almost immediately expired.§ With him ended the house of Luxembourg, which Henry VII. had seated on the imperial throne in 1308, and which had given four kings to Bohemia.

Sigismund had several noble qualities, and

he was endowed with a certain grandeur of soul, which, however, was but too often neutralized by a narrow and blind devotion. He paid dearly for all the infractions which he committed against sworn faith, and the law engraved on the conscience by God himself, in order to servilely obey the voice of the priesthood. The first violation of his word, by causing the death of John Huss, produced a revolt of twenty-two years' duration, and lit up a frightful war. To put it down, he exhausted his finances, alienated numerous domains, and abandoned whole provinces; he was forced to elevate that same house of Austria which his ancestors had humiliated, and he wore out his life in the labours of war, without even tasting either the joys of victory, or the sweets of repose. His efforts were constantly ineffective: he put down rebellion only by swearing to maintain and respect what he could not have destroyed by arms, and in violating his new oaths, he prepared other disgraces for his old age. His grandfather, Henry VII., had raised to a great height the fortunes of his house, and of the imperial power, by opposing a check to the pretensions of the Holy See. Sigismund, on the contrary, making all his wishes subordinate to those of the church, sacrificing all interest, all duty, to the destruction of heretics and the extirpation of heresy, himself stood in the way of his fortune, did irreparable wrong to his reputation, and loosened all the ties which united the vast body of the empire to its head. During his whole lifetime, he met with nothing but crosses and perils; but he escaped, at least, a tragical and premature death.*

The Archduke Albert, who became King of Hungary, and emperor, met with much opposition at Prague, where the Hussites set up against him the young Casimir, brother of Wladislaus, king of Poland. Albert was not yet peaceably established in Bohemia, when he died, leaving his widow, Elizabeth, the daughter of Sigismund, pregnant. This princess was delivered of a son, named Ladis-

* Balbinus. *Epit. rer. Boh.* p. 496.
† Dubrav. *Hist. Bohem.* p. 312.—Pfister, *Hist. d'Allem.* book iii.—Æn. Sylv. *Hist. Boh.* cap. liii.
‡ Dubrav. *Hist. Bohem.* book xxvii.
§ Sigismund died Dec. 9, 1437, in his seventy-second year.

* The death of the Emperor Henry VII. was caused, according to the German historians, by poison, which a Dominican monk, named Bernard de Monte-Pulciano, administered to him during supper. See the contemporary writers, Alb. argent, Volcmar, John Vitoduramus, and, above all, *Gest. Baldzini,* the author of which had obtained his information from the emperor's brothers. Two Dominicans acknowledged the poisoning. Æneas Sylvius, who became pope, under the name of Pius II., also states, in his *Hist. de Bohême,* (p. 59): *Henricus VII. hostili fraude veneno extinctus fertur.* Similar reports, although not so well substantiated, were circulated, relative to the deaths of the Emperors Frederick II. and Conrad IV. Pfister, *Hist. d'Allem.* book iii.

laus, who became king of Bohemia; but he reigned only in name, having only lived to his sixteenth year. During this reign, which was only a stormy minority, the Calixtines regained the ascendency, and the real masters of Bohemia were Rockizane. in spiritual matters, and in temporal affairs two nobles of the country, Ptaezeck and George de Podiebrad; the latter of whom, after the death of Ladislaus, was elected king.

Podiebrad joined to the talents of an administrator those of a captain: he made himself respected, and restored tranquillity to the kingdom. Head of the Calixtine party, he maintained, through motives of honour, and through conviction, the concordate of Iglau, but, at the same time, his severity fell heavy on the remnants of the Picard and Taborite party. From the purest remains of this vanquished party, several churches had been formed, the members of which took the name of the *United Brethren*, their doctrine differing but little from that of the Waldenses.* The fierce and sanguinary spirit of the Taborite warriors did not manifest itself in the midst of this chosen and truly Christian society. Distinguished amongst all other sects by the purity of their morals, and by their simple and pious life, the *United Brethren* beheld themselves the object of the hatred of the Catholics and Calixtines, but the only arms which they opposed to their enemies were resignation, faith, and hope.

George de Podiebrad, a zealous Calixtine, thought to appease the Catholics and the pope, by sacrificing the *Brethren*, and in concert with Rockizane, he ordered a cruel persecution against them: but this culpable sacrifice did not save himself, and the persecutor was, in his turn, persecuted. In maintaining the concordate of Iglau, he drew on himself the anger of Pope Pius II.† This pontiff again lit up the civil war in Bohemia; he demanded that the *Compactata*, or con-

cordate, should be abolished, under pretext that no pope had signed them: he armed the Catholics against the Calixtines, and excommunicated Podiebrad. His successor, Paul II., did still more; for, to the civil war, which he kept up in Bohemia, he added a foreign invasion, in the crusade which he published against the kingdom and its king. Matthias Corvinus, king of Hungary, became the minister of pontifical wrath; he attacked Podiebrad, who had been his friend and benefactor, and he again covered the unfortunate kingdom of Bohemia with blood and ruin.

Podiebrad died dethroned, leaving to his successor Wladislaus, son of Casimir IV., king of Poland, the double burden of a mutilated crown, and the hostility of the Holy See. The reigns of Wladislaus and his son Louis were the last moments of the political and religious independence of Bohemia. The Princess Anne, sister of King Louis, heiress of the crowns of Bohemia and Hungary, transferred them to the house of Hapsburg, by her marriage with Ferdinand of Austria, grandson of the Emperor Maximilian. Since then, Bohemia scarcely reckons in the history of Europe, but by her misfortunes; and this kingdom, in which Austria had been formerly several times placed in jeopardy, thenceforward formed part of the Austrian states.

Fire and sword had not been able to extirpate, in this unfortunate country, the opinions condemned at Rome. The Calixtines formed there a considerable part of the population, and the *United Brethren* reckoned about two hundred churches in Bohemia and Moravia at the end of the fifteenth century. This latter community always evinced a fervent desire to join all Christians who recognised the revealed word as their supreme law; and twice sent some of their people to seek, throughout the different countries of Europe, a people whose opinions were like their own. Their emissaries found, with the exception of a small number of Waldenses, only a few isolated believers, several of whom perished in the flames before their eyes. The *Brethren* then waited with resignation until God should come to the succour of his church and his people; and in a memorable synod, which they held in 1489, they decided that *if God should any where raise up faithful doctors and reformers of the church, they would make common cause with them.* When, at last, Luther appeared, a century after the death of John Huss, the Bohemians remembered the words pronounced by the glorious martyr, in presence of his judges and executioners: "*In one hun-*

* The *United Brethren*, like the Waldenses, had bishops, who, under the name of ancients or presbyters, were placed above the priests of their united churches. For this object, they elected three of their pastors, and sent them to demand their spiritual authority from the Waldensian bishop "Stephen:—he exposed to the three envoys, in the presence of his colleagues, the origin, history, and rude persecution, which the church, to which he belonged, had endured, as well as the uninterrupted succession of their bishops, and then, assisted by his brother bishop and other ecclesiastics, he conferred on the three pastors of Bohemia the consecration which they desired." (Bost, *Histoire de l'Eglise de Frères de Bohème et de Moravie*, book iii. ann. 1467.)

† Æneas Sylvius, pope, under the name of Pius II., decreed and executed, as pontiff, the very opposite of what he had voted and done at Basil.

dred years you shall answer before God and before me." This people, who might have been supposed subdued by so many persecutions and sufferings, rose for the sake of religious liberty, and joined the confederates of Smalcalde against the emperor, Ferdinand I., head of the Catholic league.

In 1547, after the disastrous day of Muhlberg, a hostile tribunal, the *diet of blood*, renewed against the conquered the severities decreed against their fathers at Constance.

Once more, in 1619, at the commencement of the Thirty Years' War, and the accession of the fanatical Ferdinand II., Bohemia performed an act of independence: she dared to withdraw herself from the yoke of the House of Austria, in decreeing the crown to the unfortunate Frederick, the Elector Palatine, son-in-law of James I., king of Great Britain. The issue of the great battle fought in 1620, on the White Mountain, delivered up the Bohemians, without a chance of deliverance, to their conquerors. Ferdinand had to chastise in them, at the same time, rebels to the empire and rebels to the church; his severities were atrocious; a new tribunal of blood was established, and its decrees made more victims than a century of civil discords and foreign war had done.

Ferdinand II. prided himself on having brought back Bohemia, pacified and united, under the authority of the Holy See. With him the Roman church triumphed in that kingdom, but at what a price! Thirty thousand families were proscribed; an immense multitude emigrated, *en masse*, to preserve a faith which they held more dear than the joys of their country; the number of cities diminished by half; and from a population of three millions of souls, only one million remained in its ruined towers and devastated districts. An execrable description of glory!—and which renders applicable to the two Ferdinands this terrible observation of the great historian of ancient Rome:—They make a desert and they call it peace!*

CHAPTER V.

THE MORAVIANS, OR THE UNITED BRETHREN OF BOHEMIA.

THE liberty of conscience, so ardently demanded and so valiantly defended in Bohemia, has not produced, save at rare intervals, much fruit in that unfortunate country. The tree watered with so much blood has disappeared, but the tempests have borne its seeds to distant shores.

It has been seen how much the commotion produced in Europe by the grand schism had contributed to prepare men's minds for the reformation of the following century. The emigration of so many thousands of Bohemian families diffused the knowledge of the Bible through foreign countries, and the habit of reading it and meditating on it—the foundation of all serious reaction against the abuse of sacerdotal authority.

Six years, from 1621 to 1627, had sufficed to destroy in Bohemia the last vestiges of all external observance of the evangelical religion. The Protestants of this country were abandoned by those for whom they had opened the way and given so many heroic examples; they reaped no advantage from the treaties, which, after the Thirty Years' War, insured to the reformers of Germany liberty of conscience and the exercise of their religious worship. The reformers of Bohemia, and particularly the United Brethren, continued to live under the severest oppression; one of their pastors, the Bishop Commenius, thus bewailed his afflicted church: "Alas! what remains there to this poor people, who, for having faithfully followed the doctrine of the apostles, and the example of the primitive church, find themselves persecuted and abandoned by their friends! There only remains to them the aid of the God of mercy; they are reduced to exclaim, like the prophet of old, 'I called on my friends, but they did not listen to me! O Eternal God, regard and consider our disgrace, we are become like orphans, who are without a father. We have suffered persecution, we have laboured and we have had no rest. Our feasts are changed into mourning. O Eternal, wouldst thou forget us for ever?'"

Commenius retired to Poland with a part of his flock. When about to quit his country for ever, he stopped on a high mountain, on the frontier, whence his looks could take in Bohemia and Moravia. There he fell on his knees with his brethren, and in the midst

* "Ubi solitudinem faciunt, pacem appellant." —Tacitus.

of his tears and sobs, he cried, "O God, abandon not this country, deprive it not of thy word, and preserve in it always a holy seed." His prayer was granted, for the pure worship of the gospel, in spirit and truth, did not entirely disappear from these countries. The churches of the Brethren were fallen, but God preserved there, in noble hearts, his living temples. There took place there, in the beginning of the eighteenth century, a revival of evangelical faith, and from that period dates a new era in the history of the United Brethren. Touching relations were entered into between the descendants of the ancient emigrants, at liberty in a foreign country, and those who were united to them in Bohemia by the bond of the same faith, and by the traditional reminiscences of a common worship.

New emigrations then took place. Several poor families were kindly received in Upper Lusatia, by a pious and charitable man, Count de Zinzendorf, and found a hospitable refuge in his domains; they founded there the town of Herrnhut, where there was formed the principal establishment of one of the most respectable branches of the great Christian family. This society, which extended its ramifications far, preserved the name of *Evangelical Unity*, and its members are still, in our days, generally known by that of MORAVIANS or UNITED BRETHREN.[*]

In a work, of which the principal object is to assert the rights of conscience—to manifest, in the sincere manifestation of one's convictions, the first duty of a Christian, it is highly becoming to study one of the distinctive marks of a society, loved and admired by all who have been well acquainted with it.

The following are the remarks made thirty years back, of the United Brethren, by a man who was in a position to appreciate their worth:[†]

"Their establishment prospered, by the blessing of the Lord, though not without ex-periencing many crosses. They were calumniated and defamed by several ecclesiastics and learned men of Germany, and treated as innovators. Obliged to refute what had been published against them, they showed that their church was anterior, by a whole century, to Luther's reformation; that their faith was in conformity with that of the Protestants, and they laid before the world the regulations of their discipline. These writings attracted the attention of many persons to the little town of Herrnhut; several even proceeded there to see, with their own eyes, if regulations so peculiar and so wise were really in force, and they were exceedingly edified by the good order, simplicity of faith, purity of morals, and charity, which they there perceived. Then, in several parts of Germany it was desired to form similar establishments. Lutherans and reformed societies adopted the rules of these Moravians, and entered into relations with them. The latter, who had considered them as brothers, did not refuse, and never required that any of them should give up the religion in which he was born. It is worthy of remark, that they have never attempted to establish themselves anywhere, without the consent of the government, and that several sovereigns, after having inquired into their principles and their actions, have favoured them in their states. This religious society was then found to be composed of three branches, perfectly united together by charity, the same discipline, and the same public worship, although differing in several matters of doctrine. By banishing, from amongst them, all vain disputes, they have happily operated the union of the principal branches of Protestantism; and it is on that account that this society has assumed the name of the *Evangelical Church of the United Brethren*. They do not pretend, in taking this title, to look on themselves as the only good Christians: they love, esteem, and regard, as a brother in Jesus Christ, whoever sincerely loves the Saviour, whatever be the external community to which he belongs. They are persuaded that Jesus Christ is the true *centre of unity*, towards which tend the true believers of all communions, and they have placed themselves under the powerful protection and direction of that eternal and only head of the universal church."[*]

---

[*] No man has been more unworthily calumniated than Count de Zinzendorf. He had, undoubtedly, the misfortune of not preserving himself free from all the errors of mysticism; but these stains disappear before the good which he effected, and he is entitled to the gratitude of all true Christians.

These last emigrations and the foundation of Herrnhut are one of the most interesting episodes in the history of Christianity. An account of them has been given after original documents by the pastor Bost.—(See *Hist. de l'Eglise des Frères de Bohême et de Moravie*, second part, book i.)

[†] The pastor Chabrand.—(See the *Elève de l'Evangile*, by Boniface Laroque, vol. i. book i. chap. iv.)

[*] It is not without interest to compare with this picture, traced by a Protestant author, the testimony which a Catholic writer, whose name is the best guarantee for the authority of his words, has just rendered to the Moravians. "Want," says Mr. Joseph Droz, "is unknown amongst them; they all live peaceably and united; they

It is most pleasing to the historian of John Huss to find, in the descendants of his first disciples, the society which presents one of the finest models of a Christian life, and which, prosper in many points of Europe and America; they have penetrated into Asia, Africa, and distant islands, and everywhere the same spirit animates them. I was anxious to ascertain how they had succeeded in realizing their benevolent views, and I visited them at the village of Zeist, near Utrecht. Their society, in a moral point of view, differs much from ours, and yet its founders have changed nothing in the ordinary bases of social order. Some travellers are of a different opinion, and suppose that each of the brethren labours for all, and that the produce of their industry is thrown into a common stock; but this supposition is erroneous, for each member disposes of the property which he possesses. A well-united family being the model of the society of the Moravians, they love to draw close together, but they do not live in common. It is neither by strange institutions, nor extraordinary costumes, that the society has realized its views. What then is the source of the union, peace, and happiness which these men enjoy, and which is depicted in their serene physiognomy, almost always animated by a gentle gayety? The source of all these blessings is the religious sentiments which pervade their mind. The important matter for the Moravian is his salvation, and he is deeply penetrated with the conviction that he cannot obtain it without practising love towards God and man, with the intercession of Jesus Christ. The Moravians are faithful observers of the laws of every country that admits them. They are at liberty to invoke the protection of these laws, and to have recourse between themselves to the justice of the country, but the elders hasten to prevent the scandal of a brother summoning a brother before the tribunals, and the differences are arranged amicably." One of their pastors, (M. Raillard,) being asked by the writer of these lines, what his means to preserve peace amongst men, replied: "There are two, faith in Jesus Christ and the practice of his maxims! with these two means every thing is easy, but nothing can supply their place."—*Pensées Chretiennes*, vol. i. 1844.

M. Droz, a Catholic writer, considers the belief of the Moravians to be erroneous, in whatever points it departs from the doctrines of his church; and yet, seeking a model of Christian society, it is amongst Protestants that he finds it, and points it out; a rare impartiality, and which honours him who accords the eulogium, as much as those who are the objects of it.

perhaps, more than any other, has carried into practice the great principle for which John Huss died—a sincere respect for the rights of conscience.* The Moravians, it is true, are only an exceptional society, a feeble fraction of the great Christian community; the uniform and universal application of the ideas on which their institution reposes would be a utopian scheme; but, in our eyes, it is far less important to multiply everywhere certain institutions, reputed excellent, than to have their principle admitted by all great, elevated, and truly Christian minds, leaving them to draw practical consequences suited to times, places, and circumstances. But, the principle which we have showed as forming the distinctive characteristic of the United Brethren, is *respect for religious convictions*, not only in themselves, but in every man who seeks God in the gospel and in his heart—it is liberty of conscience and of worship in its most elevated and general sense, extended to every manifestation that does not offend any of the laws which serve as the guardians of morality and order.† But what! it may be objected, this liberty took its origin in blood! It increased in the midst of frightful convulsions! Can a principle which has turned the world upside down be so pure? If there be sincerity in these reproaches, there are also grave errors. Let us beware of taking effects for causes. If it is true, and no person denies it, that sincerity of heart is the first duty which religion imposes on man—if it is true that each man is bound to honour his God according to his conscience, it follows that the right of offering to the Creator the homage, which in the bottom of his heart each deems most worthy to be offered up, is a natural right; and if the negative, if the violation of this right produces frightful results, to whom are they to be imputed? Who is to be responsible—they who lay claim to it, or they who deny and violate it? If the tree crushes in its fall those who hastened its destruction, does the fault rest with the hand which cultivated it, or with that which rashly applied fire and sword to its roots? When John Huss defended, with so much intrepidity before his judges, the rights of conscience, who was it pleaded the cause of eternal justice, the accusers or the accused? When the pope issued at Constance the terrible edict, which placed an entire nation between perjury or revolt, who prepared

---

* An interesting account of the Moravian settlements in the United States is given in Baird's *Religion in America*, already alluded to. That work states that Count Zinzendorf, who had eventually become one of their bishops, when on a visit to America, in 1741, took part in founding a mission amongst the Indians, and established several settlements of the United Brethren. Such was the origin of the pleasant villages of Bethlehem, Nazareth, and Litiz, in Pennsylvania, and Salem, in North Carolina. Moravian families settled also and formed societies in Philadelphia, New York and several other places. "The peculiar economy of the United Brethren," says Mr. Baird, "is too widely known to require any notice of it here. Their settlements in America are the same abodes of order, provident regard for the morals of the young, and for the comfort of the aged, of cheerful industry, and pleasant social life, enlivened by the sweet strains of music, and withal, of that deep interest in missions, which characterize their settlements in the Old World." The number of their churches and congregations in the United States is stated to be 23; of their ministers, 27; of their communicants, about 3000; and the entire population under their instruction is about 12,000 souls. An interesting account of their missions is given in Latrobe's "Rambles in North America." (*Note of Translator.*)

* See Note T.
† It does not follow, however, that all conscientious interpretations of the divine word are to possess an equal value in our eyes; but in all, the rights of conscience ought to be respected.

the work of blood, the pontiff or the people? Christian perfection would, perhaps, have consisted in letting themselves be slaughtered in silence; but who, nevertheless, would dare assert that a whole people, to whom falsehood was enjoined under pain of death, ought to resolve to perjure themselves or to die? War was, therefore, inevitable. But when the best men fell in defending their principles, or died before they could insure their peaceful triumph, war burst out; with it, violent men were sure to show themselves. Then were seen to appear, those who thought they had rekindled the torch of faith, when they had extinguished that of reason,—and those who spoke of reforming, but who knew only how to ravage and destroy. Hence, in the new formularies tumultuously proclaimed, there was often an impure mixture, a deplorable union of evil and good, at which pious and sagacious men were struck with terror, until, with time, in the reforms which were accomplished, the part containing the good and the truth gained the advantage over that of human passions. Such is the spectacle that was offered to Europe after the terrible wars of the fifteenth and sixteenth centuries.

Hitherto too much stress has been laid on the arguments brought forward against the partisans of liberty of conscience, from the differences existing between various sects, and from their number. "The storms of the atmosphere," says an eloquent religious writer,[*] "are not more necessary to the economy of our globe, than are the tempests of thought to human society. There, as every where, it is movement which preserves and rest which destroys. To take away from the life of nations firmness of thought and obstinacy of conscience, is to refuse to society its morrow—to open to civilization a deep and silent tomb. . . . They who deem silence peace, and for whom death is order, ought to be told, that the true protectors of society are those very persons to whose names are attached in history remembrances of struggles, persecution, and martyrdom. Each of their sacrifices has been worth to us one of our blessings of civilization; each of their combats one of our pledges of peace."[†]   "In

Christianity we must trust," says the same author, farther on, " to the secret and powerful principle of unity."[*]

In judging the various Christian communities on the apparent points which divide them, sufficient attention has not been paid, nor a sufficient allowance made, to the grand principles which serve as a bond of union, and of which the first of all ought to be respect for the rights of conscience in the interpretation of the divine word; this principle forms, as it were, an invisible and sacred tie between martyrs of all Christian creeds, and it had at Constance its most striking manifestation. The cause of John Huss is that of all with whom religion is less an affair of form and habit than of conscience and conviction. John Huss defended this noble cause at Constance—he gave up his life for it, and on that account is he great.

The traveller in visiting this celebrated city finds everywhere the living remembrance of this immortal drama—John Huss and Jerome present themselves to his memory in every part—he inquires and seeks out where they protested, where they suffered, where they died. Amongst the famous relics of the grand council which the city still preserves, it is not those which are the most costly, or which belonged to the powerful, that attract all eyes: the chair of state which served as the emperor's throne—the altar at which John XXIII. officiated—and the mitre which he disgraced before he lost it, are rapidly passed by; but the stranger pauses before John Huss's Bible—a precious volume, noted with his own hand, and from which he derived the hope that sustained his courage; he examines with a mixture of admiration and horror the faithful image of the narrow and gloomy cell, where the love of the truth gained the victory, in a heroic soul, over the rigours of the most frightful imprisonment and the terrors of death; and he interrogates, in fine, that rude brick on which the hand of the great martyr traced, in the dark, characters now illegible for the eyes of the flesh, but where the eyes of the soul will always read an eloquent protest against the oppressors of conscience. At Constance, a Catholic city, no monument is found raised to John Huss and his friend; but the whole place, the theatre of their sufferings, is filled with their memory—is an imperishable monument of their glory.

---

* Vinet, *Essai sur la manifestation des convictions religieuses*, p. 63.

† What country in modern times has rendered a stronger testimony to this truth than Scotland? The most magnificent triumphs of ancient Rome offer nothing comparable in grandeur to that simple and pious procession of Presbyterian ministers, who, in 1843, peaceably passed through Edinburgh, placing all their confidence in God, after having sacrificed their position, their welfare, and that of their families to their conscience. I, as a

foreigner, do not decide on the intrinsic merits of the question, nor do I examine whether the separation was a duty. It is sufficient that Christians have considered it so, to be bound to accomplish it.   * Vinet, *ubi supra*, p. 369.

CONCLUSION.

Four centuries have elapsed since John Huss and Jerome were called on to bear testimony. If we consider the religious state of Europe during that long period, in its principal phases, we shall find the great principles of subjection to the priesthood, and the free and individual interpretation of the Scriptures, always in opposition.

Four hundred years ago, crusades unceasingly renewed, and funeral piles without number kept down every independent manifestation; the Bible was mutilated or concealed; the priesthood, notwithstanding most crying scandals and numerous disgraces, were still the masters of the world: and in that formidable body, the very best and most worthy forbade the reading of the holy word. Some few courageous voices protested, but to protest was to brave death.

A century later, and half of Europe was throwing off the sacerdotal yoke, and recognised Jesus Christ as the only mediator between God and man, and his word as the supreme rule of faith and life.

The Roman religion, at first shaken to its centre, and on the point of being overturned in the greater number of European states by the revolution of the sixteenth century, nevertheless, a few years after the *Reformation*, recovered an unhoped-for vigour: it maintained itself on the ground which it had preserved; and, in some countries, it even took deeper root, whilst Protestantism ceased to progress.

Two great facts explain this state of things, which has excited the astonishment of most able and excellent men.

Catholicism fortified itself externally after the Reformation, by returning to its true principle—authority; Protestantism lost its expansive force and became enfeebled, by denying its own—liberty.*

Whem at the voice of Luther, Europe was divided, the clergy, through the influence of a salutary rivality, felt the necessity of purifying their morals, acquiring information, uniting together, and rallying to a common centre under a single direction. At the same time was seen to start into existence a body militant, admirably disciplined, ardent and indefatigable, advancing to its object by every road, over every obstacle, and absolutely devoted to advance the influence and authority, not of the pope but of the popedom. Never was an enterprise prosecuted with greater unanimity, vigour, and tenacity. To annihilate all individuality* to the profit of the order—to strengthen the order, in order to render the popedom more powerful—in fine, to elevate the authority of the Holy See above all other authority, in order to extend and fortify the Catholic principle, was what the Jesuits aimed at; and if the morality of their proceedings may be called in question, it is impossible, at least within certain limits, and in spite of numerous disgraces, to refuse them the merit of success.

And yet the men who claimed for the pope the privilege of infallibility, immediately after the great Councils of Constance and Basil, and who proclaimed the authority of the Holy See superior to that of general councils, had contributed to place the Church in opposition with itself. It has been seen that they weakened it, by compromising, at the same time its unity and its authority.† But the Jesuits did not create that state of things, for it existed before them; they accepted the situation as they found it, and are not responsible for it. They looked on the Catholic Church as divided into two very distinct parts, one representing the Gallican principle, the other the Roman principle,—obliged to choose, their choice was not doubtful. Ambitious of conquests and vowed to obedience, they knew that to conquer whilst obeying, it was necessary that the authority should be one, stable, always visible, always.

---

* Many Protestant churches lay down *gratuitous salvation* as the fundamental principle of the Reformation; but in order to detach one's self on that point, as on so many others, from the Roman church, which admits the merit of works, it has been necessary to have recourse *to free examination*, which St. Paul recommends, and which, with the most entire obedience to the gospel, is the most general *distinctive principle* of dissenting communions.

* The words of Ignatius Loyola, the founder of the Jesuits, were, "Every member of the order shall be, in the hands of his superiors, as a dead body," (*perinde ac cadaver*.)
† See page 146.

influential, and without appeal. Not finding these guarantees of strength and durability in general councils, they turned towards the Holy See, which alone presented them. By their narrow theology, they undoubtedly lowered catholicism in the sphere of ideas, but by their incomparable discipline, they strengthened it for a time in the external world, in the sphere of action.

Protestantism appeared then to stop short, in consequence of the frightful disorders caused by those who, even from the time of Luther, had carried to excess the consequences of the right of examination. The reformed populations were required to give pledges to the temporal governments: they found themselves under an absolute obligation to show that their doctrines were in harmony with the laws and civil order; and they defined them in private and national confessions. A great number of churches soon forgot that these confessions had no canonical character,—that they were testimonies and not decrees—that they were evidences of faith, but not obligatory on the conscience. Many men of eminent merit, who had refused to be constrained, dared to impose constraint on others, and from that error proceeded innumerable evils. On all sides, a coercive authority, which had but just sprung into existence, was substituted for that which at least could boast of ages of existence. From that time a spirit of sectarianism, which divides, in spite of common principles, usurped the place of the spirit of the gospel, which unites, in spite of differences. Protestantism suffered from it, and the spectacle of its intestine struggles multiplied amongst its members the indifferent and the incredulous.

Catholicism profited by it; it gained ground, as is always the case, by the faults of its adversaries, as much as by the strength which it possessed inherently. Its progress, however, was neither general nor constant. The Roman Church had terrible crises to pass through, and its history presents, during this period, numerous alternatives of advancement and reverses.

At present, another epoch is commencing; the Christian world is entering on a new crisis, to which the religious awakening, now declaring itself, is the prelude. Never were the Roman clergy better disciplined; never did they march more unitedly under a single flag and under the command of a single person. Yet they have more cause to fear than to hope; they feel the danger, and their very discipline betrays their alarms.

The priesthood will find it a difficult matter to recover their empire; they are active and noisy in their exertions, it is true, but in the midst of even Catholic countries they act alone

—the lay society almost entirely keeps silence,* for a secret voice tells it that the clergy, in raising their war-cry, are sustaining their own cause more than that of mankind and of the eternal gospel.

In order to sway the present for a length of time, it is necessary to possess an instinct of the future; in order to guide the world, it is requisite to possess, with the power which civilizes, the intelligence that ameliorates. Formerly the priesthood fulfilled this glorious mission, but it has ceased to comprehend the age by which they are no longer understood. There exists, throughout Europe, the feeling of a crushing obligation between them and the men of a past time, which has no future—there is a sort of fatal bond, an irremediable association between their cause and all ruined ones;† in fact the authority on which the Roman Church reposes, achieves but few conquests in our day: if there are discipline and obedience in the ranks of the clergy, there are also everywhere, in men's minds, disorder and anarchy: the Catholic world is itself in travail with a new order of things; it aspires to find a formula of worship, which may put an end to a lamentable antagonism, by conciliating to a greater extent faith and reason.

Already the principle of *liberty of conscience*, which bears within itself the *liberty of examination* and of *worship*, is everywhere taking root and spreading widely. In those countries where superstition most bears sway, where not long since this liberty of conscience was proscribed, as the high road leading to impiety, it is recognised as a right;‡ and is tolerated even in those where the priesthood reigns alone and unquestioned.§ It is feared and hated, but no one dares openly proscribe it; because it is strong, and its most mortal enemies do not avow themselves.

Whilst preaching blind obedience, they pride themselves on respecting liberty; they have a horror of violence; they proclaim loudly that the arm of the flesh is powerless to constrain the spirit; the sons of the crusaders boast of

* "I am alone here, in my opinion," said M. de Montalembert, in a memorable discussion, (on the Secondary Instruction Bill in the Chamber of Peers,) and his words were then the veritable expression of sacerdotal catholicism.

† Let not the sense of our words be misapprehended; to compassionate misfortunes is the duty of the clergy, and to remedy it is their glory; but to lead astray the suffering or the conquered, to nourish hopeless regrets, and to fan the flame of ineffectual resentments, is of all errors the most deplorable.

‡ See the declaration which the Queen of Portugal has just made in reference to the young woman condemned to death in the island of Madeira. (*Archiv. du Christ.* July 13, 1844.)

§ Protestant foreigners are suffered to remain at Rome, and are at liberty to assist at the celebration of their worship in the chapels of the embassies.

the pious ardour of their ancestors, but they hide one side of their sombre coats of armour; they do not acknowledge all the stains that still rest on them ; for near the infidel blood, which serves as their decoration, there is other blood which sullies them—the blood of Christians !

The liberty of conscience has conquered— like an immense sea, which mounts and mounts continually, it has swelled until it has reached the fort of the Vatican, the thunders of which remain powerless before it.

Thus prevails the great principle, for which John Huss offered up his life ! A truly Christian principle, which reproves and brands with reprobation every brutal effort of the flesh over the mind, which admits and sanctions, as a sacred duty, in every thinking being, the resistance of his conscience to all external influence before a conviction is formed—a truth, which constituted the glory of the first Church, and which they, whose fathers died for it, too much neglected—an imperishable truth, on which depends the religious prospects of the world, and the triumph of which recalls this expression of the great martyr of Bohemia: " The pontiff, the priests, and the pharisees formerly condemned the truth and buried it; but it rose from the tomb and vanquished them all !"

NOTES.

NOTE A.

Maxims of Pope Gregory VII.

1°. The church of Rome is the only one founded by God.

2°. The title of Universal belongs to the Roman Pontiff, who alone can take the name of Pope.

3°. He alone can depose and absolve the bishops.

4°. His legate presides over the bishops in all councils, and can depose them.

5°. The pope can depose those absent.

6°. Those who have been excommunicated may not be dwelt with.

7°. He can make new laws, create new churches, divide a bishopric into two, or unite two bishoprics in one.

8°. He alone may assume the attributes of empire and bear the signs of it.

9°. All princes must kiss his feet.

10°. His name is the only one to be pronounced in churches.

11°. It is the only name in the world.

12°. He may depose emperors.

13°. He can, according to his pleasure, transfer bishops from one see to another.

14°. He can in any church ordain a priest.

15°. Those ordained by him can govern other churches, and can receive no superior rank of any other bishop.

16°. No council can be termed a general council, unless the pope have so ordered it.

17°. No chapter, nor any book, can be received as canonical without his authority.

18°. None may annul the sentences of the pope, although he may quash those of all others.

19°. He neither may nor can be judged by any one.

20°. None may dare to condemn those who appeal to the apostolic see.

21°. To that see must be referred all the important causes of all churches.

22°. The Church of Rome has never erred, nor ever can do so.

23°. Every Roman pontiff, canonically ordained, becomes holy.

24°. It is permitted to accuse when he permits or orders it.

26°. He who is not united to the Roman Church is not Catholic.

27°. The pope can release the subjects of bad princes from their oaths of fidelity.

NOTE B.

More favoured by circumstances than the reformers who had preceded him, Wycliffe found a government which protected him, and a nation less prejudiced and less hostile.

England had never completely submitted to the despotism of the Roman clergy, and when Wycliffe appeared she was still resounding with the energetic preaching of the famous bishop of Lincoln, Robert Grosse,—one of the most formidable adversaries of papal omnipotence. The Church of England, during the whole course of the Anglo-Saxon dominion, had preserved, with respect to the Holy See, a certain independence, which had alienated from her sovereign pontiffs, and had determined the celebrated Hildebrand to favour the pretensions of William at the time of the Norman invasion.

From that time are dated the general adhesion of England to the Roman dogma of transubstantiation, and a more complete recognition of the supremacy of the Bishop of Rome, as well as of his right to lay upon it the tribute of St. Peter. However, these doctrines obtained less popularity in England than on the Continent, precisely because they had been implanted there as a result of the conquest. The Norman kings soon made common cause with the people against the temporal authority of the Holy See. The supreme jurisdiction of the pope over all the members of the clergy, and his pretensions to dispose of all ecclesiastical dignities and benefices, were particularly insupportable to the English monarchs, and the celebrated decrees of Clarendon are a remarkable monument of their resistance.

It required all the grovelling baseness and cowardice of King John to determine him to the humiliating act of homage which he made of his kingdom to the Roman pontiff, and the promise of an annual tribute to the Holy See. The nation was not a party to this degrading act of the most despicable of its princes; the popes themselves appeared to doubt for a long time the validity of a title which they held from that act alone, and during a period of thirty-three years the feudal tribute, consented to by John Lackland, had ceased to be acquitted when Urban V. obtained the payment of it.

But the parliament of England had become indignant at this subjection of the kingdom to a foreign sovereign, and the taxes were no longer levied without its consent. A prince (Edward III.) was now on the throne, who, jealous of the rights of his crown, and proud of his victories, felt less than any other a disposition to show respect towards the foreign priest who ruled at Avignon, surrounded by the states of a regal sovereign, and under his immediate influence.

Q

Wycliffe was beginning to appear; and had made a brilliant commencement, by the energy with which he opposed the pretensions of the Roman clergy,—pretensions which he looked upon as subversive of all evangelical discipline. Edward approved of his conduct, and not only refused to acquit the annual tribute of vassalage, but also that of St. Peter. In the course of the year 1374 he named Wycliffe one of the embassy which he was sending to Pope Urban V. to regulate serious differences as to reserved benefices and papal grants. The embassy did not go to Avignon, but stopped at Bruges, where it conferred, without any definitive result, with the Archbishop of Ravenna, representing the sovereign pontiff. On his return, Wycliffe received from the king the prebend of Aust, in the collegiate church of Westburg; and soon afterwards the rectory of Lutterworth.

At the death of Edward, and during the minority of his grandson Richard, Wycliffe, protected by the powerful Duke of Lancaster, opposed with even greater success the exactions of the court of Rome, which by its taxes upon the church property, its reservations and advowsons of benefices, drew immense sums from England: The kingdom was at this time wasted by a ruinous war; parliament found that the treasury was deprived of a part of its resources by the money the pope drew from it, and in consequence contested the right of the sovereign pontiff, not only over the kingdom, but also over the church property in England. In this struggle, which was begun by Wycliffe with ardent and pious zeal, he at once gained the sympathy of the descendants of the old Saxons, as well as that of the parliament, and of the prince: the first were gained by a national feeling, which prompted them to hate every thing that could be traced back to the conquest; the others were favourable from state reasons and through jealousy of a rival and foreign power.

What precedes, explains how it was that Wycliffe, during a space of twenty years, escaped the terrible punishments which were the penalty throughout Europe of all reactions of reason or individual judgment against the authority of the Church of Rome. Among the great reformers, none attacked vice and error more boldly, and none displayed more strength in the struggle. It is only by measuring the number and magnitude of the abuses which, in the fourteenth century, had gradually been substituted for the pure and simple doctrines of Christianity, that any idea can be formed of the moral courage that was necessary to denounce and brand them; it is in sounding the depths of such darkness that the power of that light, which was strong enough to dispel it, can be fully ascertained. Finally, to judge and comprehend Wycliffe, we must not look to the Roman catholic clergy of our times, kept within prudent limits by the manners of society, by the civil power, and by the salutary influence of dissenting communions; we must look upon it as it was in the middle ages, when it considered itself as the sovereign master of all things on earth and in heaven; and when the abuse of such power had in every point been carried to extremes. The bitter complaints of Wycliffe against such scan-

dalous disorder, as in our days appears scarcely credible, may be found in various forms in contemporary writings;—in the lighter productions of the poets, as in the serious pages of the most wise and pious men.

The constant end to Wycliffe's efforts was to recall the clergy to evangelical discipline, and his contemporaries to a purer worship, founded more on inward and spiritual improvement than on vain and useless ceremonies.

To this end, he enforced on the one part the prescriptions of the gospel and the example left by Christ and his apostles; and on the other hand he endeavoured to draw the clergy from whatever might contribute to lead them from the right path, or turn them from their holy mission. He was of opinion that the Jesuits would grow in virtue as they decreased in perishable riches; and that their spiritual authority would have more influence on the soul if they showed themselves indifferent to any other power, and kept distinct and apart from all temporal authority.

To succeed, Wycliffe would not invoke the traditional authority of a church which had sanctioned or tolerated so many abuses; it was to the gospel alone he could turn, and that he did with energy, logic, and perseverance. Painfully struck by the contrast between the spiritual gifts with which the clergy declared themselves endowed, and the disorder of their lives, Wycliffe did not hesitate to attribute the whole to their riches. He thus expresses himself on the subject:—"Men wonder greatly why curates are so unfeeling to the people in taking tithes, since Christ and his apostles took none, as men now take them, neither paid them nor spake of them either in the gospel or in the epistles,—the perfect law of freedom and of grace. But Christ lived on the alms of Mary Magdalene, and other holy women, as the gospel telleth. And the apostles lived sometimes by the labour of their hands, and sometimes accepted a poor livelihood and clothing given by the people, in free will and devotion, without asking or constraining; and to this end, Christ said to his disciples, that they should eat and drink such things as were set before them, and take neither gold nor silver for their preaching, or their giving of sacraments. And Paul, giving a general rule for priests, saith thus: ' We having food and clothing, with these things be we content in Christ Jesus.'"

Wycliffe has again, on the same subject, the following admirable language:—"Those who despise the will of the dead are said to be 'cursed solemnly of God and man.' But Jesus Christ, in his testament, bequeathed to his disciples and their successors, peace in themselves, and in this world tribulation and persecution for his word. But worldly clerks have foully broken this good testament of Jesus Christ. For they seek the peace and prosperity of this world; peace with the fiend and with the flesh, and will endure no labour in keeping or teaching the truth of God; but rather persecute good men who would teach it, and so make war upon Christ in his people, to obtain the worldly things which Christ forbid to their order. In the life of Christ in his gospel, which is his testament; in the life also and teaching of his apostles, our clerks may find nothing but poverty, meekness, ghostly toil, and contempt from worldly men, on account of reproving their sin; their reward being in heaven, through their pure life, and true teaching; and cheerful suffering of death. Hence Jesus Christ was so poor in this life, that by worldly title he had no house to rest his head, as he himself saith in the gospel. And St. Peter was so poor, that he had neither gold nor silver to give a poor crippled man, as is witnessed in the book of the apostles' deeds. St. Paul, also, was so poor in this world's goods, that he laboured with his hands for a livelihood, and that of his fellows, and suffered much persecution and watchfulness, and great thought for all the churches, as he himself saith in many places of Holy Writ. And St. Bernard writeth to the pope, that in his worldly array, and plenty of gold and silver, and lands, he is a successor of Constantine the emperor, and not of Jesus Christ and his disciples. Jesus also saith, on confirming this testament, after rising from the dead, 'As my Father hath sent me, so I send you,' that is, to labour, and persecution, and poverty, and hunger, and martyrdom.'"[*]

But it was not enough to point out the abuse made of riches, if the means could not be found of hindering their increase. Wycliffe therefore went on unhesitatingly to examine the lawfulness of the means by which the clergy was thus enriched; these means were, first, the arbitrary disposal of spiritual gifts, and next the dominion they held over things temporal. We may suppose with what burning energy such a man would stigmatize the sale and traffic of holy things. "Wicked prelates," says he, "sell the souls of Christian men to Satan for money, souls for which Christ shed his precious heart's blood upon the cross!"[†] . . . . "If pardon be a spiritual and heavenly gift, it should be given freely as Christ teaches in the gospel, and not for money, nor worldly goods, nor fleshly favour. But if a rich man will dearly buy it, he shall have a pardon extending to a thousand years, though he be really accused of God for his sinful life. While the poor bed-ridden man, who may not travel to Rome, nor to such another place, shall have no pardon of the pope, though he be holy and full of charity. Since then, this pardon, if there be any such, should be freely given, it is theft and robbery to take thus much gold for it."

When we reflect on the power of the clergy in that age, we are astounded by the daring of Wycliffe's writings; and if we consider the numerous abuses which sprung from this excess of power, and of which all classes were victims, we may suppose the immense reach of his searching words. Wycliffe said, in the hierarchy of the Roman clergy was the chief difficulty he had to overcome. The ecclesiastical dignitaries were those who, by their riches, caused the greatest scandal in the church; and so long as all power was centred in their hands, it might be feared that any reform might be impossible. He therefore attacked this hierarchy in all its degrees.

"By the ordinances of Christ, priests and bishops

were all one. But afterwards, the emperor divided them; and made bishops lords, and priests their servants; and this was the cause of envy, and quenched much charity. For the ordinances of Christ are founded in meekness, in unity, and charity, and in contempt of riches and high estate."[*]

The unhappy celebrity which was at this time attached to many of the principal religious orders is well known; the attacks made on the secular clergy by the mendicant orders, who were the constant defenders of the pretensions of the Roman pontiff—pretensions which Wycliffe combated, are also known.

He looked upon the monks as possessors of immense wealth, which was turned from its proper purpose and employed in a manner that was frequently profane, too often criminal. It was impossible for him to remain at peace with them; he therefore signalized the institution of such orders, and particularly those of the mendicants, as wanting the spirit of Christianity; his whole life was spent in opposing them, and they were his most dangerous enemies.

Wycliffe admitted the seven sacraments of the Roman Church, but differed from it upon several essential points as to the explanation given of them. This difference was above all remarkable with respect to the sacraments of ordination and the eucharist. He considered the priest as in a manner partaking of two characters: one of a nature more external than internal, and which he received from the consecrating bishop; the other entirely spiritual, given by the invisible bishop of souls through the infusion of the Holy Ghost, and bestowed only on such as were worthy to receive it.

In the eucharist he denied the real presence, the doctrine of transubstantiation; and looked on it as more impious and more contrary to common sense than any belief into which man had at any time fallen.

Wycliffe during his whole life kept two things in view, one with respect to the clergy, the other relating to the people. His endeavour was to bring the former back to the discipline of the early church, and to good morals; and to develope Christianity in the others by the free and constant use of their most noble faculties, those which constitute man, conscience and reason.

To attain this double end it was necessary to do away with the authority of the priests, and make an appeal to a higher authority, to that of God revealed in the Scriptures. And this Wycliffe did with a perseverance equal to his courage. No prescription, he says, no doctrine is of value, but so far as it is in conformity with the Holy Scripture, and derived from it; a Christian must, however, be upon his guard against the dangers of individual interpretation; and must not lightly reject received opinions. An attentive and patient inquiry, aided by fervent prayer, is indispensable, he says, to study the Scriptures in such a way as to understand them. Wycliffe therefore looked upon it as his duty to spread them abroad; and to this end he translated them into the vulgar

---

[*] Vaughan's Life and Opinions of Wycliffe, vol. ii. chap. viii.

[†] MS. on Prelates. Vaughan.

[*] MS. on the seven deadly sins.—Vaughan, vol. ii. chap. viii. p. 233—275.

tongue, that they might be familiar to all. The clergy, in his opinion, were most guilty in withdrawing from the people the possession of the holy word, and in putting the decisions of popes and councils over those of the Bible. He protests with great energy against this scandal:

"All those who falsify the pope's bulls, or a bishop's letter, are cursed grievously in all churches, four times in the year. Lord, why was not the gospel of Christ admitted by our worldly clerks into this sentence? Hence it appeareth, that they magnify the bull of a pope more than the gospel; and in proof of this, they punish men who trespass against the bulls of the pope more than those who trespass against the gospel of Christ.

"Accordingly, the men of this world fear the pope's lead, and his commandments, more than the gospel of Christ, or the commands of God. It is thus that the wretched beings of this world are estranged from faith, and hope, and charity, and become corrupt in heresy and blasphemy, even worse than heathens."[*] "True teaching is the debt most due to holy church, and is most charged of God, and most profitable to Christian souls. As much, therefore, as God's word, and the bliss of heaven in the souls of men, are better than earthly goods; so much are these worldly prelates, who withdraw the great debt of holy teaching, worse than thieves, more accursedly sacrilegious than ordinary plunderers, who break into churches and steal thence chalices and vestments, or ever so much gold. The greatest of all sins is to deprive men of faith, and of the mirror of Christ's life, which is the ground of all well-being hereafter."[†]

Wycliffe, after having by his word and his writings shaken the authority of the priests, dealt it a still more fatal blow by his own example and that of his disciples. To take from the dignitaries of the church the disposal of temporal benefices, in order to give it to the laity and civil magistrates, was merely rendering simony less shameful, and the clergy less powerful. Wycliffe knew that the church property would not fall into hands more pure; he distrusted the corruption of all men high in authority, whether ecclesiastics or laymen, and he feared above all the corruption which riches bring in their train; therefore he advised his disciples to imitate the life of Christ, of his apostles, to renounce the goods of the world, and he himself lived and died in voluntary poverty. He exhorted them not to seek the favour and patronage of the great; to prefer the poor and wandering life of the missionary to the tranquil and well-paid existence of a parish priest. He sent his disciples from town to town, from county to county, under the name of *poor priests* and under a costume of remarkable simplicity. He engaged them to preach the gospel without fear, in the churches, cemeteries, markets, fairs,—everywhere that multitudes assembled; and they preached without caring about the prohibition of bishops, braving threats and persecutions, captivating men's hearts and persuading the crowd. Wycliffe proved thus that the influence of priests was entirely independent of their external power, and this last blow given by him to the ecclesiasti-

cal authority was not that which was least felt by the clergy, whose resentment he raised to the highest pitch. Wycliffe braved their anger, agitated the whole kingdom, made an immense number of proselytes, known by the name of *Lollards*, and remained unpunished under the royal protection. Chaplain of Edward I., he was supported after the death of that prince by the celebrated John of Gaunt, Duke of Lancaster, and when brought before his ecclesiastical superiors at St. Paul and Lambeth, he twice escaped the vengeance of his order. But at last, in the storms which marked the reign of Richard II., the clergy became formidable at court: Lancaster became alarmed at the boldness of the reformer, and partly withdrew his support. The doctrine of Wycliffe was publicly condemned at Oxford, and he himself expelled from the University. He lived a year longer, persevering in the same path, consecrating his last days to the great cause to which he had devoted his whole life, and less cast down by the triumph of his enemies than by the progress of the illness which carried him off in the sixtieth year of his age, and which saved his body from the sufferings of an execution, though not from the scaffold.[*]

NOTE C.

For such persons, as voluntarily shut their eyes on the errors of a church which they hold to be infallible, the bull of John XXIII. proves nothing. There is nothing, they will say, to be concluded from this exceptional act of an unworthy pontiff. Yet the spirit and style of the bull are repeated in the acts of many councils and popes. The following, amongst so many examples, is an extract of the bull of Pope Innocent VIII. against the Waldensian population. We compare it, intentionally, with the bull of John XXIII., as a proof that all power which deems itself infallible, places itself easily, and according to the circumstances, above all law. The bull institutes Albert de Capitaneis archdeacon of the church of Cremona, nuncio and commissioner of the Apostolic See in the states of the Duke of Savoy, and prescribes to him to labour in the extirpation of the very pernicious and abominable sect of men called the Poor of Lyons or the Waldenses, in concert with the Inquisitor-General Blasius, of the order of the Preaching-Brotherhood. The pope gives him, for that object, full authority over all archbishops, bishops, their vicars and chief officers; "in order," says he, "that they may have, together with you and the said inquisitor, to take up arms against the said Waldenses and other heretics, and to come to an understanding to crush them like venomous asps, and to contribute all their care to *so holy and so necessary* an extermination. . . . We give you power to have the crusade preached up by fit men: to grant that such persons as shall enter on the crusade and fight against these same heretics, and shall contribute to it, may gain plenary indulgence and remission of all their sins once in their life, and also at their death; to command, in vir-

---

[*] Vaughan, chap. viii. p. 202. [†] Ibid.

[*] See, on the opinions and errors of Wycliffe, and on the sentence passed against him after his death, Book II. chap. vi. page 69—72.

tee of their holy obedience, and under penalty of excommunication, all preachers of God's word to *animate* and *incite* the same believers to exterminate the pestilence, without sparing, by force and by arms. We further give you power to absolve those who enter on the crusade, fight, or contribute to it, from all sentences, censures, and ecclesiastical penalties, general or particular, by which they may be bound, as also to give them dispensation for any *irregularity* contracted in divine matters, or for any apostasy, and to enter some *terms of composition* with them for the *goods* which they may have *secretly amassed, badly acquired*, or held doubtfully, applying them to the expenses attendant on this extirpation of heretics; . . . to *concede*, to each, permission to *lawfully seize on the property*, real or personal, of heretics; also to command all being in the service of these same heretics, in whatsoever place they may be, to withdraw from it, under whatever penalty you may deem fit; and by the same authority to declare that they and all others, who may be *held* and *obliged by contract*, or other manner, to pay them any thing, are not for the future *in any way obliged* to do so; and to deprive all those refusing to obey your admonitions and commands, of whatever dignity, state, order, and pre-eminence they may possess, to wit, the ecclesiastics of their dignities, offices, and benefices; and the laity of their *honours, titles, fiefs, and privileges*, if they persist in their disobedience and rebellion; . . . and to fulminate all kinds of censures, according as the case in your judgment may demand; . . . . to absolve and re-establish such as may wish to return to the lap of the church, although they may have sworn *to favour the heretics*, provided, *taking the contrary oath*, they promise to abstain most carefully from doing so. . . . You therefore, beloved son, receiving with a devout spirit the charge of so praiseworthy an affair, must show yourself diligent and careful of word and deed in its execution. Act so that, by your acts, accompanied by the divine grace, all may succeed in conformity with our expectation, and that by your solicitude you may merit not only the glory which falls to the lot of those engaged in *works of piety*, but that you may also be in far greater favour with us and the Apostolic See, on account of your very exact diligence and faithful integrity.

. . . "Given at Rome, at St. Peters, the year of the incarnation of our Lord, 1487, 5th of the Calends of May, and the thirteenth year of our pontificate."[a]

In reading such a bull, published only a few years before the Reformation, we are obliged to ask what abuse of the principle of free examination would be worse than that of the principles of authority.

Let us now see how the fourth of the Council of the Lateran, the twelfth œcumenical, held in 1215, under Innocent III., expresses itself on the subject of heretics.

"Let all the secular powers be led, and if ne-

cessary forced by ecclesiastical censure, to take an oath in public for the defence of the faith, swearing to exert themselves to exterminate from the countries subject to their jurisdiction all the heretics designated by the church. Each person, when he has received any authority, whether spiritual or temporal, shall be bound to take this oath. Should any temporal lord, when warned by the church, neglect to purge his country of the stain of heresy, let him be excommunicated by the archbishop and the provincial bishops; and should he refuse to give satisfaction within the year, let advice be given of it to the sovereign pontiff, in order that he may free the said lord's vassals from their oath of fidelity, and give his lands to Catholics, in order that they may possess them without any contradiction, and maintain them in the purity of the faith, after having exterminated the heretics. Catholics who shall take the cross to exterminate heretics shall enjoy the same indulgences and the same holy privilege as they who fight the infidels. He who listens to unbelievers, receives, defends, and aids them, is excommunicated like them, and after a year has revolved becomes infamous *ipso jure*; he cannot from that moment be called to public employments or councils; he cannot vote for the election of inquisitors or councillors; he cannot even be admitted as a witness; he loses all faculty of acting as witness to a will, or of accepting an inheritance or legacy. No person shall be bound to appear before a court of law at his suit, for any affair whatever; but he shall be forced to appear at the demand of every one. Should he be a judge, his sentences shall not have any force, and no suit can legally be brought before his tribunal; if an advocate, he shall not be permitted to defend; if a notary, the acts which he passes shall be of no value, and they shall be condemned with him who drew them. . . . . All that shall not fly those whom the church shall have thus noted, shall be also excommunicated; priests are not to administer to them the holy sacraments, or give them ecclesiastical burial, or receive their gifts and offerings, under pain of deposition."[b] This decree of an œcumenical council, sanctioned by a pope, has never been revoked.

The individual inspirations of the heart or conscience are often worth more than the most logical deductions, and it would be to offer an insult to the clergy to attribute to its members doctrines in conformity with the proscriptions just quoted. We have not the slightest doubt that the greatest number of them individually protest with horror against all participation in such cruel acts, were it possible to put them into execution. It must, however, be also declared that the Roman Church, acting with authority by its popes and councils, has never hesitated to employ violence, when it had the power of using it, and that it never visited with any condemnation those who, not being able to convert the heretics, have attempted to exterminate them.

NOTE D.

The Abbé Frayssinous has attempted to establish on what touches the question of *men's sal-*

---

[a] The original of the bull of Pope Innocent VIII. is preserved in the library of the famous university of Cambridge.—(Leger, *Hist. des egl. Vaudoises*, vol. ii. chap. ii. p. 5.)

[b] *Sacror. concil. collect.* Mansi, Venice, 1782.—Labbe, vol. xi. part i. p. 146.

influential, and without appeal. Not finding these guarantees of strength and durability in general councils, they turned towards the Holy See, which alone presented them. By their narrow theology, they undoubtedly lowered catholicism in the sphere of ideas, but by their incomparable discipline, they strengthened it for a time in the external world, in the sphere of action.

Protestantism appeared then to stop short, in consequence of the frightful disorders caused by those who, even from the time of Luther, had carried to excess the consequences of the right of examination. The reformed populations were required to give pledges to the temporal governments: they found themselves under an absolute obligation to show that their doctrines were in harmony with the laws and civil order; and they defined them in private and national confessions. A great number of churches soon forgot that these confessions had no canonical character,—that they were testimonies and not decrees—that they were evidences of faith, but not obligatory on the conscience. Many men of eminent merit, who had refused to be constrained, dared to impose constraint on others, and from that error proceeded innumerable evils. On all sides, a coercive authority, which had but just sprung into existence, was substituted for that which at least could boast of ages of existence. From that time a spirit of sectarianism, which divides, in spite of common principles, usurped the place of the spirit of the gospel, which unites, in spite of differences. Protestantism suffered from it, and the spectacle of its intestine struggles multiplied amongst its members the indifferent and the incredulous.

Catholicism profited by it; it gained ground, as is always the case, by the faults of its adversaries, as much as by the strength which it possessed inherently. Its progress, however, was neither general nor constant. The Roman Church had terrible crises to pass through, and its history presents, during this period, numerous alternatives of advancement and reverses.

At present, another epoch is commencing; the Christian world is entering on a new crisis, to which the religious awakening, now declaring itself, is the prelude. Never were the Roman clergy better disciplined; never did they march more unitedly under a single flag and under the command of a single person. Yet they have more cause to fear than to hope; they feel the danger, and their very discipline betrays their alarms.

The priesthood will find it a difficult matter to recover their empire; they are active and noisy in their exertions, it is true, but in the midst of even Catholic countries they act alone —the lay society almost entirely keeps silence,[*] for a secret voice tells it that the clergy, in raising their war-cry, are sustaining their own cause more than that of mankind and of the eternal gospel.

In order to sway the present for a length of time, it is necessary to possess an instinct of the future; in order to guide the world, it is requisite to possess, with the power which civilizes, the intelligence that ameliorates. Formerly the priesthood fulfilled this glorious mission, but it has ceased to comprehend the age by which they are no longer understood. There exists, throughout Europe, the feeling of a crushing obligation between them and the men of a past time, which has no future—there is a sort of fatal bond, an irremediable association between their cause and all ruined ones;[†] in fact the authority on which the Roman Church reposes, achieves but few conquests in our day: if there are discipline and obedience in the ranks of the clergy, there are also everywhere, in men's minds, disorder and anarchy: the Catholic world is itself in travail with a new order of things; it aspires to find a formula of worship, which may put an end to a lamentable antagonism, by conciliating to a greater extent faith and reason.

Already the principle of *liberty of conscience*, which bears within itself the *liberty of examination* and of *worship*, is everywhere taking root and spreading widely. In those countries where superstition most bears sway, where not long since this liberty of conscience was proscribed, as the high road leading to impiety, it is recognised as a right;[‡] and is tolerated even in those where the priesthood reigns alone and unquestioned.[§] It is feared and hated, but no one dares openly proscribe it; because it is strong, and its most mortal enemies do not avow themselves.

Whilst preaching blind obedience, they pride themselves on respecting liberty; they have a horror of violence; they proclaim loudly that the arm of the flesh is powerless to constrain the spirit; the sons of the crusaders boast of

* "I am alone here, in my opinion," said M. de Montalembert, in a memorable discussion, (on the Secondary Instruction Bill in the Chamber of Peers,) and his words were then the veritable expression of sacerdotal catholicism.

† Let not the sense of our words be misapprehended; to compassionate misfortunes is the duty of the clergy, and to remedy it is their glory; but to lead astray the suffering or the conquered, to nourish hopeless regrets, and to fan the flame of ineffectual resentments, is of all errors the most deplorable.

‡ See the declaration which the Queen of Portugal has just made in reference to the young woman condemned to death in the island of Madeira. (*Archiv. du Christ.* July 13, 1844.)

§ Protestant foreigners are suffered to remain at Rome, and are at liberty to assist at the celebration of their worship in the chapels of the embassies.

the pious ardour of their ancestors, but they hide one side of their sombre coats of armour; they do not acknowledge all the stains that still rest on them; for near the infidel blood, which serves as their decoration, there is other blood which sullies them—the blood of Christians!

The liberty of conscience has conquered—like an immense sea, which mounts and mounts continually, it has swelled until it has reached the fort of the Vatican, the thunders of which remain powerless before it.

Thus prevails the great principle, for which John Huss offered up his life! A truly Christian principle, which reproves and brands with reprobation every brutal effort of the flesh over the mind, which admits and sanctions, as a sacred duty, in every thinking being, the resistance of his conscience to all external influence before a conviction is formed—a truth, which constituted the glory of the first Church, and which they, whose fathers died for it, too much neglected—an imperishable truth, on which depends the religious prospects of the world, and the triumph of which recalls this expression of the great martyr of Bohemia: "The pontiff, the priests, and the pharisees formerly condemned the truth and buried it; but it rose from the tomb and vanquished them all!"

NOTES.

NOTE A.
Maxims of Pope Gregory VII.

1°. The church of Rome is the only one founded by God.

2°. The title of Universal belongs to the Roman Pontiff, who alone can take the name of Pope.

3°. He alone can depose and absolve the bishops.

4°. His legate presides over the bishops in all councils, and can depose them.

5°. The pope can depose those absent.

6°. Those who have been excommunicated may not be dwelt with.

7°. He can make new laws, create new churches, divide a bishopric into two, or unite two bishoprics in one.

8°. He alone may assume the attributes of empire and bear the signs of it.

9°. All princes must kiss his feet.

10°. His name is the only one to be pronounced in churches.

11°. It is the only name in the world.

12°. He may depose emperors.

13°. He can, according to his pleasure, transfer bishops from one see to another.

14°. He can in any church ordain a priest.

15°. Those ordained by him can govern other churches, and can receive no superior rank of any other bishop.

16°. No council can be termed a general council, unless the pope have so ordered it.

17°. No chapter, nor any book, can be received as canonical without his authority.

18°. None may annul the sentences of the pope, although he may quash those of all others.

19°. He neither may nor can be judged by any one.

20°. None may dare to condemn those who appeal to the apostolic see.

21°. To that see must be referred all the important causes of all churches.

22°. The Church of Rome has never erred, nor ever can do so.

23°. Every Roman pontiff, canonically ordained, becomes holy.

24°. It is permitted to accuse when he permits or orders it.

26°. He who is not united to the Roman Church is not Catholic.

27°. The pope can release the subjects of bad princes from their oaths of fidelity.

NOTE B.

More favoured by circumstances than the reformers who had preceded him, Wycliffe found a government which protected him, and a nation less prejudiced and less hostile.

England had never completely submitted to the despotism of the Roman clergy, and when Wycliffe appeared she was still resounding with the energetic preaching of the famous bishop of Lincoln, Robert Grosse,—one of the most formidable adversaries of papal omnipotence. The Church of England, during the whole course of the Anglo-Saxon dominion, had preserved, with respect to the Holy See, a certain independence, which had alienated from her the sovereign pontiffs, and had determined the celebrated Hildebrand to favour the pretensions of William at the time of the Norman invasion.

From that time are dated the general adhesion of England to the Roman dogma of transubstantiation, and a more complete recognition of the supremacy of the Bishop of Rome, as well as of his right to lay upon it the tribute of St. Peter. However, these doctrines obtained less popularity in England than on the Continent, precisely because they had been implanted there as a result of the conquest. The Norman kings soon made common cause with the people against the temporal authority of the Holy See. The supreme jurisdiction of the pope over all the members of the clergy, and his pretensions to dispose of all ecclesiastical dignities and benefices, were particularly insupportable to the English monarchs, and the celebrated decrees of Clarendon are a remarkable monument of their resistance.

It required all the grovelling baseness and cowardice of King John to determine him to the humiliating act of homage which he made of his kingdom to the Roman pontiff, and the promise of an annual tribute to the Holy See. The nation was not a party to this degrading act of the most despicable of its princes; the popes themselves appeared to doubt for a long time the validity of a title which they held from that act alone, and during a period of thirty-three years the feudal tribute, consented to by John Lackland, had ceased to be acquitted when Urban V. obtained the payment of it.

But the parliament of England had become indignant at this subjection of the kingdom to a foreign sovereign, and the taxes were no longer levied without its consent. A prince (Edward III.) was now on the throne, who, jealous of the rights of his crown, and proud of his victories, felt less than any other a disposition to show respect towards the foreign priest who ruled at Avignon, surrounded by the states of a regal sovereign, and under his immediate influence.

Wycliffe was beginning to appear; and had made a brilliant commencement, by the energy with which he opposed the pretensions of the Roman clergy,—pretensions which he looked upon as subversive of all evangelical discipline. Edward approved of his conduct, and not only refused to acquit the annual tribute of vassalage, but also that of St. Peter. In the course of the year 1374 he named Wycliffe one of the embassy which he was sending to Pope Urban V. to regulate serious differences as to reserved benefices and papal grants. The embassy did not go to Avignon, but stopped at Bruges, where it concluded; without any definitive result, with the Archbishop of Ravenna, representing the sovereign pontiff. On his return, Wycliffe received from the king the prebend of Aust, in the collegiate church of Westbury, and soon afterwards the rectory of Lutterworth.

At the death of Edward, and during the minority of his grandson Richard, Wycliffe, protected by the powerful Duke of Lancaster, opposed with even greater success the exactions of the court of Rome, which by its taxes upon the church property, its reservations and advowsons of benefices, drew immense sums from England. The kingdom was at this time wasted by a ruinous war; parliament found that the treasury was deprived of a part of its resources by the money the pope drew from it, and in consequence contested the right of the sovereign pontiff, not only over the kingdom, but also over the church property in England. In this struggle, which was begun by Wycliffe with ardent and pious zeal, he at once gained the sympathy of the descendants of the old Saxons, as well as that of the parliament, and of the prince: the first were gained by a national feeling, which prompted them to hate every thing that could be traced back to the conquest; the others were favourable from state reasons and through jealousy of a rival and foreign power.

What precedes, explains how it was that Wycliffe, during a space of twenty years, escaped the terrible punishments which were the penalty throughout Europe of all reactions of reason or individual judgment against the authority of the Church of Rome. Among the great reformers, none attacked vice and error more boldly, and none displayed more strength in the struggle. It is only by measuring the number and magnitude of the abuses which, in the fourteenth century, had gradually been substituted for the pure and simple doctrines of Christianity, that any idea can be formed of the moral courage that was necessary to denounce and brand them; it is in sounding the depths of such darkness that the power of that light, which was strong enough to dispel it, can be fully ascertained. Finally, to judge and comprehend Wycliffe, we must not look to the Roman catholic clergy of our times, kept within prudent limits by the manners of society, by the civil power, and by the salutary influence of dissenting communions; we must look upon it as it was in the middle ages, when it considered itself as the sovereign master of all things on earth and in heaven, and when the abuse of such power had in every point been carried to extremes. The bitter complaints of Wycliffe against such scan-

dalous disorder, as in our days appears scarcely credible, may be found in various forms in contemporary writings;—in the lighter productions of the poets, as in the serious pages of the most wise and pious men.

The constant end to Wycliffe's efforts was to recall the clergy to evangelical discipline, and his contemporaries to a purer worship, founded more on inward and spiritual improvement than on vain and useless ceremonies.

To this end, he enforced on the one part the prescriptions of the gospel and the example left by Christ and his apostles; and on the other hand he endeavoured to draw the clergy from whatever might contribute to lead them from the right path, or turn them from their holy mission. He was of opinion that the Jesuits would grow in virtue as they decreased in perishable riches; and that their spiritual authority would have more influence on the soul if they showed themselves indifferent to any other power, and kept distinct and apart from all temporal authority.

To succeed, Wycliffe would not invoke the traditional authority of a church which had sanctioned or tolerated so many abuses; it was to the gospel alone he could turn, and that he did with energy, logic, and perseverance. Painfully struck by the contrast between the spiritual gifts with which the clergy declared themselves endowed, and the disorder of their lives, Wycliffe did not hesitate to attribute the whole to their riches. He thus expresses himself on the subject:—"Men wonder greatly why curates are so unfeeling to the people in taking tithes, since Christ and his apostles took none, as men now take them, neither paid them nor spake of them either in the gospel or in the epistles,—the perfect law of freedom and of grace. But Christ lived on the alms of Mary Magdalene, and other holy women, as the gospel telleth. And the apostles lived sometimes by the labour of their hands, and sometimes accepted a poor livelihood and clothing given by the people, in free will and devotion, without asking or constraining; and to this end, Christ said to his disciples, that they should eat and drink such things as were set before them, and take neither gold nor silver for their preaching, or their giving of sacraments. And Paul, giving a general rule for priests, saith thus: 'We having food and clothing, with these things be we content in Christ Jesus.'"

Wycliffe has again, on the same subject, the following admirable language:—"Those who despise the will of the dead are said to be 'cursed solemnly of God and man.' But Jesus Christ, in his testament, bequeathed to his disciples and their successors, peace in themselves, and in this world tribulation and persecution for his word. But worldly clerks have foully broken this good testament of Jesus Christ. For they seek the peace and prosperity of this world; peace with the fiend and with the flesh, and will endure no labour in keeping or teaching the truth of God; but rather persecute good men who would teach it, and so make war upon Christ in his people, to obtain the worldly things which Christ forbid to their order. In the life of Christ in his gospel, which is his testament; in the life also and teaching of his apostles, our clerks may find nothing but poverty, meekness, ghostly toil, and contempt from worldly men, on account of reproving their sin, their reward being in heaven, through their pure life, and true teaching, and cheerful suffering of death. Hence Jesus Christ was so poor in this life, that by worldly title he had no house to rest his head, as he himself saith in the gospel. And St. Peter was so poor, that he had neither gold nor silver to give a poor crippled man, as is witnessed in the book of the apostles' deeds. St. Paul, also, was so poor in this world's goods, that he laboured with his hands for a livelihood, and that of his fellows, and suffered much persecution and watchfulness, and great thought for all the churches, as he himself saith in many places of Holy Writ. And St. Bernard writeth to the pope, that in his worldly array, and plenty of gold and silver, and lands, he is a successor of Constantine the emperor, and not of Jesus Christ and his disciples. Jesus also saith, on confirming this testament, after rising from the dead, 'As my Father hath sent me, so I send you,' that is, to labour, and persecution, and poverty, and hunger, and martyrdom."*

But it was not enough to point out the abuse made of riches, if the means could not be found of hindering their increase. Wycliffe therefore went on unhesitatingly to examine the lawfulness of the means by which the clergy was thus enriched; these means were, first, the arbitrary disposal of spiritual gifts, and next the dominion they held over things temporal. We may suppose with what burning energy such a man would stigmatize the sale and traffic of holy things. "Wicked prelates," says he, "sell the souls of Christian men to Satan for money, souls for which Christ shed his precious heart's blood upon the cross!"† . . . . "If pardon be a spiritual and heavenly gift, it should be given freely as Christ teaches in the gospel, and not for money, nor worldly goods, nor fleshly favour. But if a rich man will dearly buy it, he shall have a pardon extending to a thousand years, though he be really accused of God for his sinful life. While the poor bed-ridden man, who may not travel to Rome, nor to such another place, shall have no pardon of the pope, though he be holy and full of charity. Since then, this pardon, if there be any such, should be freely given, it is theft and robbery to take thus much gold for it."

When we reflect on the power of the clergy in that age, we are astounded by the daring of Wycliffe's writings; and if we consider the numerous abuses which sprung from this excess of power, and of which all classes were victims, we may suppose the immense reach of his searching words. Wycliffe said, in the hierarchy of the Roman clergy was the chief difficulty he had to overcome. The ecclesiastical dignitaries were those who, by their riches, caused the greatest scandal in the church; and so long as all power was centred in their hands, it might be feared that any reform might be impossible. He therefore attacked this hierarchy in all its degrees.

"By the ordinances of Christ, priests and bishops

were all one. But afterwards, the emperor divided them, and made bishops lords, and priests their servants; and this was the cause of envy, and quenched much charity. For the ordinances of Christ are founded in meekness, in unity, and charity, and in contempt of riches and high estate."*

The unhappy celebrity which was at this time attached to many of the principal religious orders is well known; the attacks made on the secular clergy by the mendicant orders, who were the constant defenders of the pretensions of the Roman pontiff—pretensions which Wycliffe combated, are also known.

He looked upon the monks as possessors of immense wealth, which was turned from its proper purpose and employed in a manner that was frequently profane, too often criminal. It was impossible for him to remain at peace with them; he therefore signalized the institution of such orders, and particularly those of the mendicants, as wanting the spirit of Christianity; his whole life was spent in opposing them, and they were his most dangerous enemies.

Wycliffe admitted the seven sacraments of the Roman Church, but differed from it upon several essential points as to the explanation given of them. This difference was above all remarkable with respect to the sacraments of ordination and the eucharist. He considered the priest as in a manner partaking of two characters: one of a nature more external than internal, and which he received from the consecrating bishop; the other entirely spiritual, given by the invisible bishop of souls through the infusion of the Holy Ghost, and bestowed only on such as were worthy to receive it.

In the eucharist he denied the real presence, the doctrine of transubstantiation; and looked on it as more impious and more contrary to common sense than any belief into which man had at any time fallen.

Wycliffe during his whole life kept two things in view, one with respect to the clergy, the other relating to the people. His endeavour was to bring the former back to the discipline of the early church, and to good morals; and to develope Christianity in the others by the free and constant use of their most noble faculties, those which constitute man, conscience and reason.

To attain this double end it was necessary to do away with the authority of the priests, and make an appeal to a higher authority, to that of God revealed in the Scriptures. And this Wycliffe did with a perseverance equal to his courage. No prescription, he says, no doctrine is of value, but so far as it is in conformity with the Holy Scripture, and derived from it; a Christian must, however, be upon his guard against the dangers of individual interpretation; and must not lightly reject received opinions. An attentive and patient inquiry, aided by fervent prayer, is indispensable, he says, to study the Scriptures in such a way as to understand them. Wycliffe therefore looked upon it as his duty to spread them abroad; and to this end he translated them into the vulgar

* Vaughan's *Life and Opinions of Wycliffe*, vol. ii. chap. viii.

† MS. on Prelates. Vaughan.

* MS. on the seven deadly sins.—Vaughan, vol. 2, chap. viii. p. 238–275.

tongue, that they might be familiar to all. The clergy, in his opinion, were most guilty in withdrawing from the people the possession of the holy word, and in putting the decisions of popes and councils over those of the Bible. He protests with great energy against this scandal:

"All those who falsify the pope's bulls, or a bishop's letter, are cursed grievously in all churches, four times in the year. Lord, why was not the gospel of Christ admitted by our worldly clerks into this sentence? Hence it appeareth, that they magnify the bull of a pope more than the gospel; and in proof of this, they punish men who trespass against the bulls of the pope more than those who trespass against the gospel of Christ.

"Accordingly, the men of this world fear the pope's lead, and his commandments, more than the gospel of Christ, or the commands of God. It is thus that the wretched beings of this world are estranged from faith, and hope, and charity, and become corrupt in heresy and blasphemy, even worse than heathens."[*] "True teaching is the debt most due to holy church, and is most charged of God, and most profitable to Christian souls. As much, therefore, as God's word, and the bliss of heaven in the souls of men, are better than earthly goods; so much are these worldly prelates, who withdraw the great debt of holy teaching, worse than thieves, more accursedly sacrilegious than ordinary plunderers, who break into churches and steal thence chalices and vestments, or ever so much gold. The greatest of all sins is to deprive men of faith, and of the mirror of Christ's life, which is the ground of all well-being hereafter."[†]

Wycliffe, after having by his word and his writings shaken the authority of the priests, dealt it a still more fatal blow by his own example and that of his disciples. To take from the dignitaries of the church the disposal of temporal benefices, in order to give it to the laity and civil magistrates, was merely rendering simony less shameful, and the clergy less powerful. Wycliffe knew that the church property would not fall into hands more pure; he distrusted the corruption of all men high in authority, whether ecclesiastics or laymen, and he feared above all the corruption which riches bring in their train; therefore he advised his disciples to imitate the life of Christ, of his apostles, to renounce the goods of the world, and he himself lived and died in voluntary poverty. He exhorted them not to seek the favour and patronage of the great; to prefer the poor and wandering life of the missionary to the tranquil and well-paid existence of a parish priest. He sent his disciples from town to town, from county to county, under the name of *poor priests* and under a costume of remarkable simplicity. He engaged them to preach the gospel without fear, in the churches, cemeteries, markets, fairs,—everywhere that multitudes assembled; and they preached without caring about the prohibition of bishops, braving threats and persecutions, captivating men's hearts and persuading the crowd. Wycliffe proved thus that the influence of priests was entirely independent of their external power, and this last blow given by him to the ecclesiastical authority was not that which was least felt by the clergy, whose resentment he raised to the highest pitch. Wycliffe braved their anger, agitated the whole kingdom, made an immense number of proselytes, known by the name of *Lollards*, and remained unpunished under the royal protection. Chaplain of Edward I., he was supported after the death of that prince by the celebrated John of Gaunt, Duke of Lancaster, and when brought before his ecclesiastical superiors at St. Paul and Lambeth, he twice escaped the vengeance of his order. But at last, in the storms which marked the reign of Richard II., the clergy became formidable at court: Lancaster became alarmed at the boldness of the reformer, and partly withdrew his support. The doctrine of Wycliffe was publicly condemned at Oxford, and he himself expelled from the University. He lived a year longer, persevering in the same path, consecrating his last days to the great cause to which he had devoted his whole life, and less cast down by the triumph of his enemies than by the progress of the illness which carried him off in the sixtieth year of his age, and which saved his body from the sufferings of an execution, though not from the scaffold.[*]

NOTE C.

For such persons, as voluntarily shut their eyes on the errors of a church which they hold to be infallible, the bull of John XXIII. proves nothing. There is nothing, they will say, to be concluded from this exceptional act of an unworthy pontiff. Yet the spirit and style of the bull are repeated in the acts of many councils and popes. The following, amongst so many examples, is an extract of the bull of Pope Innocent VIII. against the Waldensian population. We compare it, intentionally, with the bull of John XXIII., as a proof that all power which deems itself infallible, places itself easily, and according to the circumstances, above all law. The bull institutes Albert de Capitaneis archdeacon of the church of Cremona, nuncio and commissioner of the Apostolic See in the states of the Duke of Savoy, and prescribes to him to labour in the extirpation of the very pernicious and abominable sect of men called the Poor of Lyons or the Waldenses, in concert with the Inquisitor-General Blasius, of the order of the Preaching-Brotherhood. The pope gives him, for that object, full authority over all archbishops, bishops, their vicars and chief officers; "in order," says he, "that they may have, together with you and the said inquisitor, to take up arms against the said Waldenses and other heretics, and to come to an understanding to crush them like venomous asps, and to contribute all their care to *so holy and so necessary* an extermination. . . . We give you power to have the crusade preached up by fit men : to grant that such persons as shall enter on the crusade and fight against these same heretics, and shall contribute to it, may gain plenary indulgence and remission of all their sins once in their life, and also at their death ; to command, in vir-

---

[*] Vaughan, chap. viii. p. 202.　　[†] Ibid.

[*] See, on the opinions and errors of Wycliffe, and on the sentence passed against him after his death, Book ii. chap. vi. page 69—72.

tae of their holy obedience, and under penalty of excommunication, all preachers of God's word to *animate* and *incite* the same believers to exterminate the pestilence, without sparing, by force and by arms. We further give you power to absolve those who enter on the crusade, fight, or contribute to it, from all sentences, censures, and ecclesiastical penalties, general or particular, by which they may be bound, as also to give them dispensation for any *irregularity* contracted in divine matters, or for any apostasy, and to enter some *terms of composition* with them for the *goods* which they may have *secretly amassed, badly acquired*, or held doubtfully, applying them to the expenses attendant on this extirpation of heretics; . . . to *concede*, to each, permission to *lawfully seize on the property*, real or personal, of heretics; also to command all being in the service of these same heretics, in whatsoever place they may be, to withdraw from it, under whatever penalty you may deem fit; and by the same authority to declare that they and all others, who may be *held* and *obliged by contract*, or other manner, to pay them any thing, are not for the future *in any way obliged* to do so; and to deprive all those refusing to obey your admonitions and commands, of whatever dignity, state, order, and pre-eminence they may possess, to wit, the ecclesiastics of their dignities, offices, and benefices; and the laity of their *honours, titles, fiefs, and privileges*, if they persist in their disobedience and rebellion; . . . and to fulminate all kinds of censures, according as the case in your judgment may demand; . . . . to absolve and re-establish such as may wish to return to the lap of the church, although they may have sworn to favour the heretics, provided, *taking the contrary oath*, they promise to abstain most carefully from doing so. . . . You therefore, beloved son, receiving with a devout spirit the charge of so praiseworthy an affair, must show yourself diligent and careful of word and deed in its execution. Act so that, by your acts, accompanied by the divine grace, all may succeed in conformity with our expectation, and that by your solicitude you may merit not only the glory which falls to the lot of those engaged in *works of piety*, but that you may also be in far greater favour with us and the Apostolic See, on account of your very exact diligence and faithful integrity.

. . . "Given at Rome, at St. Peters, the year of the incarnation of our Lord, 1487, 5th of the Calends of May, and the thirteenth year of our pontificate."*

In reading such a bull, published only a few years before the Reformation, we are obliged to ask what abuse of the principle of free examination would be worse than that of the principles of authority.

Let us now see how the fourth of the Council of the Lateran, the twelfth œcumenical, held in 1215, under Innocent III., expresses itself on the subject of heretics.

"Let all the secular powers be led, and if ne-

cessary forced by ecclesiastical censure, to take an oath in public for the defence of the faith, swearing to exert themselves to exterminate from the countries subject to their jurisdiction all the heretics designated by the church. Each person, when he has received any authority, whether spiritual or temporal, shall be bound to take this oath. Should any temporal lord, when warned by the church, neglect to purge his country of the stain of heresy, let him be excommunicated by the archbishop and the provincial bishops; and should he refuse to give satisfaction within the year, let advice be given of it to the sovereign pontiff, in order that he may free the said lord's vassals from their oath of fidelity, and give his lands to Catholics, in order that they may possess them without any contradiction, and maintain them in the purity of the faith, after having exterminated the heretics. Catholics who shall take the cross to exterminate heretics shall enjoy the same indulgences and the same holy privilege as they who fight the infidels. He who listens to unbelievers, receives, defends, and aids them, is excommunicated like them, and after a year has revolved becomes infamous *ipso jure;* he cannot from that moment be called to public employments or councils; he cannot vote for the election of inquisitors or councillors; he cannot even be admitted as a witness; he loses all faculty of acting as witness to a will, or of accepting an inheritance or legacy. No person shall be bound to appear before a court of law at his suit, for any affair whatever; but he shall be forced to appear at the demand of every one. Should he be a judge, his sentences shall not have any force, and no suit can legally be brought before his tribunal; if an advocate, he shall not be permitted to defend; if a notary, the acts which he passes shall be of no value, and they shall be condemned with him who drew them. . . . . All that shall not fly those whom the church shall have thus noted, shall be also excommunicated; priests are not to administer to them the holy sacraments, or give them ecclesiastical burial, or receive their gifts and offerings, under pain of deposition."* This decree of an œcumenical council, sanctioned by a pope, has never been revoked.

The individual inspirations of the heart or conscience are often worth more than, the most logical deductions, and it would be to offer an insult to the clergy to attribute to its members doctrines in conformity with the proscriptions just quoted. We have not the slightest doubt that the greatest number of them individually protest with horror against all participation in such cruel acts, were it possible to put them into execution. It must, however, be also declared that the Roman Church, acting with authority by its popes and councils, has never hesitated to employ violence, when it had the power of using it, and that it never visited with any condemnation those who, not being able to convert the heretics, have attempted to exterminate them.

NOTE D.

The Abbé Frayssinous has attempted to establish on what touches the question of *men's sal-*

---

* The original of the bull of Pope Innocent VIII. is preserved in the library of the famous university of Cambridge.—(Leger, *Hist. des egl. Vaudoises*, vol. II. chap. ii. p. 8.)

* *Sacror. concil. collect.* Mansi, Venice, 1782.—Labbe, vol. xi. part i. p. 145.

vation, an opinion which he gives as ancient, and which differs exceedingly from the opinion generally received in the Roman Catholic Church. "The Catholic Church," says he, "professes relative to men's salvation three principal doctrines, which are to its enemies a subject of violent declamations and imaginary triumphs, and which are, to Christians feeble and but little enlightened in the faith, a subject of trouble and scandal. These maxims the Church, far from concealing, professes so loudly and so clearly that they form the first elements of its doctrine: infancy repeats them as well as mature age, so fundamental are they. Here they are in all their simplicity:—Without baptism no one can enter the kingdom of heaven:—Out of the Church there is no safety:—Without the true faith it is impossible to please God. Here imagination becomes troubled, and reason appears at first to justify its alarms. What! it will be said, without baptism, no salvation! What then becomes of that prodigious multitude of children dead without having received it? You devote to eternal flames these innocent creatures; what a barbarous dogma. Out of the Church, no salvation! And what becomes then of all these Christian societies which live separated from the Catholic Church, and which you call schismatics, or which profess a doctrine contrary to its own, and which you call heretics? How do you know if the errors which you attribute to them are not in their eyes the truth itself, and if their good faith does not justify them before God? What intolerance on your part! Again, without the true faith there is no salvation! What then is to be the destiny of these nations that have never known revelation! Is it the fault of the negro of Guinea, or the savages of Canada, if the light of the gospel does not shine for him? Must their birth be attributed as a crime to men; must one be sent to heaven because he has been born at Rome, and the other to hell because he comes from Constantinople? 'Were there a religion on earth,' says Jean Jacques Rousseau, 'out of which there would only be eternal punishment, and if on some point of the world a single man who was not struck with its evidence, the God of that religion would be the most unjust and cruel of tyrants, and the priests who teach these abominable maxims would deserve to be prosecuted as the enemies and executioners of the human race. This is perhaps what you have heard. . . . . But what will you say if I show you that these are only lying declamations, which originate in false ideas of the Catholic doctrine, and that in order to do away with the difficulty, it is sufficient to re-establish correct notions of the things in question, to present the dogma such as it really is, and not such as its enemies think fit to forge it?'"[*]

The illustrious prelate who has written these lines develops his opinion with great talent, and arrives at the following conclusions: He allows that, according to the Church, children dying without baptism descend into hell, that they are damned, that there is no middle region for them

between heaven and hell, that they are for ever deprived of the possession of God, which forms the happiness of the elect in the heavenly kingdom; but he adds that there are many mansions in hell as in heaven; he thinks that they do not suffer the punishment of fire, though many Fathers have supposed they do. His opinion is established on the laws of the Church, on the interpretation given by the catechisms of the decrees of the general councils, on the opinion of several Fathers and doctors, and, amongst others, on the passage of St. Augustine: "I do not say," writes he, "that children dying without being baptized ought to undergo so great a punishment that it would be better for them never to have been born."[*]

Thus, according to the Abbé Frayssinous, children dying without baptism will go to hell; but although damned, it was to be supposed that their state was preferable to non-existence. It could be easily proved by stronger and more numerous reasons that the doctrine, already so severe, is much less so than what is generally admitted in the Roman Church. St. Augustine, in the passage quoted, expresses a doubt rather than a conviction that the Catholic catechisms, in the interpretation of the decree of the Church, abstain, it is true, from deciding this last point; but they agree in saying that children dying without baptism shall be for ever deprived of the sight of God, and they teach that of all the punishments of a creature made for God, this will be the most terrible.[†] The book which ought to give the law to the Catholics on this matter, is the Roman catechism, drawn up by Pope Pius V., according to the decrees of the council of Trent: it thus expresses itself: Men, unless they be regenerated in God, by the grace of baptism, are not procreated by their parents, whether believers or disbelievers, but for endless misery and eternal death.[‡]

The Church, says again Abbé Frayssinous, does not exclude the salvation of baptized adults, who live separated from her, in absolute ignorance of its doctrines, and heretics and schismatics who are deceived from conviction; they, he says, have not ceased to appertain to the Church; they are only responsible for bad faith or their bad actions, heresy being less in error than in stubbornness in maintaining it.[§] The disbelievers, in fine, who have not been able to know the gospel shall not be judged but after the law of the conscience, and shall only be punished for faults which they could avoid. They shall be excluded from beatitude in heaven: but according to their conduct, they shall be more or less approximated in their fate to children dying without baptism.[‖]

In this, also, we do not find the doctrine of the

* Frayssinous, Défense du Christian.—Maximes de l'Eglise sur le salut des hommes.

* Frayssinous. Défense du Christian.—Maximes de l'Eglise sur le salut des hommes, p. 182.

† The pains of purgatory exceed all the most dreadful tortures that can be imagined on earth. The greatest of these pains is not to enjoy the sight of God.—(Catech. of Versailles, adopted by Mgr. Blanquart de Bailleul.)

The eternal punishment of not beholding God is the greatest penalty of a creature made for God.—(Catech. of Montpellier, 1758, vol. i. p. 375, &c.)

‡ Cat. ad Paroch. ex decret. concil. Trident. et papa Pio V. jussu edit. Rome 1567.

§ Frayssinous, ubi supra.

‖ Frayssinous, ibid.

Church, for it does not recognise for its own; sincere heretics; and nothing proves it more clearly than the decrees passed of general councils of popes to strike in a mass the heretics of a country.[*]

The courage which defies the executioner has been always considered the most powerful guarantee of an unalterable conviction, whether in the orthodox or in heretics; and if heresy was excused in the eyes of the Church by sincerity, how could it have desired the punishment of all those, who, in braving death for their opinions, have at least proved that they were sincere? Far from condemning them as stubborn for this courageous perseverance, the Church ought to have esteemed them for that very reason above all those who have not proved their sincerity by such a testimony: the Church has, however, always sanctioned the contrary practice, and the history of the councils and popes is a perpetual contradiction given to the assertions of Abbé Frayssinous. In their eyes, the more the heretic shows himself convinced and proves his sincerity by his firmness, in presence of death, the more he merits to be consumed by terrestrial fire—feeble emblem of the eternal fire which awaits him.

The doctrine of the Church on penance would be quite sufficient to overthrow that which the Abbé Frayssinous has attempted to establish on the question of the salvation of heretical or infidel adults. According to this doctrine, one mortal sin is sufficient for the soul of the sinner to be devoted to the utmost torture during eternity, if the sin is not blotted out by the absolution of the priest, or the firm determination to receive it.[†] If that is the case, how will such adults or misbelievers be able to redeem themselves from the eternal penalty, as do not participate in the sacrament of penance and are not inclined to have recourse to it? I will say more; if, in their case, the mortal sin is redeemed or effaced without the sacrament, which is indispensable to Catholics, there will be *more safety in living out of the Church than in it;* for no one can reckon with certitude that between the instant of the sin and that of death there will be room for perfect contrition, absolution; or the fervent desire to receive it. We render complete justice to the excellent intentions of the Abbé Frayssinous, and we ardently desire to see the day as a period of conciliation, when the Catholic Church will itself declare, by the mouth of its head or of its councils, the opinions mentioned above: if that day ever arrives, the *infallibility* will perhaps be compromised; but there will be a step in advance, in this point, that the dogma will respond better to the idea which we all form to ourselves, of the infinite love and merciful justice which are in God; and all humanity will rejoice to see it.

NOTE E.

No reason, however weak, has been omitted by Catholic writers to justify the conduct of the council and of the emperor towards John Huss. Lhomond and the Abbé Frayssinous have both sustained, that the safe-conduct of Sigismund had not been given to Huss but to protect him on the road, in order that he might arrive at Constance, but by no means to guarantee him from punishment. Both have refused to read, or have forgotten, the words so precise of the safe-conduct, and mentioned in all contemporary authors—the invitation to all to allow John Huss *to pass freely and surely, to stay; to stop, and to RETURN.*[*] The historian Maimbourg, though not less prejudiced, has not contested this fact: writing the history of that period, he could not conceal it, but he has had recourse to other arguments to weaken its consequences.[†] He allows that the emperor signed the safe-conduct a month before the arrival of John Huss at Constance, but he endeavours to prove that the latter was not as yet the bearer of it when he entered that city.[‡] He also mentions a fact stated by Dacherius and Reichental: Huss, if these authors are to be believed, finding himself disturbed at Constance, and fearing to be arrested, attempted to fly. Maimbourg considers this attempt (very insufficiently proved) as it observed) an act which justified the violation of the safe-conduct, and he draws the conclusion that it was well done to imprison him. He justifies, in the same way, his execution. "Huss," says he, "having declared that he would submit to the penalties which a heretic merits, if the council could convict him of heresy, and having failed in the article on which his safe-conduct was founded, this ought to be annulled."

It is impossible to heap up together, in fewer words, more errors and sophisms to justify an unjustifiable act. In admitting (which is false) that John Huss did not carry with him the emperor's safe-conduct, which he renewed on his way, it was not the less certain that Sigismund had granted it, and that ought to have proved sufficient to assure Huss of efficient protection. After his arrival he was frightened at the hostile dispositions which he met with, and endeavoured to fly. The event proved too well that he had judged rightly, and if his enemies supposed that they possessed a right to restrict his liberty, to oblige him to answer for his doctrine, how could they have supposed themselves afterwards freed from the engagement entered into to allow him to return freely? Huss, on his side, did not violate his word in refusing to submit to the sentence of the council; for when he had declared, two months before his departure, that he would submit to it, he had done so on the condition that he should

---

[*] See the preceding note and the decree of the Council of Constance against the Hussites, book iv. chap. iv. p. 141, and following.

[†] See the Canons of the Council of Trent and all the catechisms in use amongst Catholics.

[*] Lhomond, *Hist. de l'Eglise*, edit. 1826, Paris, p. 366—Frayssinous, *Défense du Christian.—La religion vengée du reproche de fanatisme.*

[†] *Hist. du grand Schisme d'Occident*, book v.

[‡] Maimbourg gives a proof of this assertion by the passage of a letter from Huss, in which he speaks of a safe-conduct which he did not possess in coming to Constance. The safe-conduct which he had not was that of the pope. Maimbourg omits intentionally the various passages of Huss's letters, in which it is stated that he brought with him the safe-conduct of the emperor, and that his friends informed the pope and cardinals of it immediately after his arrival.

be convicted, and convicted by the SCRIPTURE. The council refused all discussion on that basis. Huss was therefore free not to subscribe to his condemnation, and in not subscribing to it, he broke no engagement. In fine, if the safe-conduct had not been accorded, as Maimbourg says, but on the condition that Huss should submit, the document would have made mention of it, and there is not a word on the subject in it.

The adversaries of John Huss, in the council, did not stop at such wretched subterfuges; they declared simply that the safe-conduct was valueless, because no one was bound to keep faith with a heretic, and because the council could free the emperor from his word.

Thus, to justify the barbarous treatment inflicted on John Huss, it is necessary to bring forward a doctrine profoundly immoral, as his enemies formerly did; or to disguise the truth, as they do in the present day, who would not believe that the Church could subsist if they did not establish —at any price—that it cannot err!

NOTE F.

Emmanuel Chrysoloras is honourably mentioned as the chief of the Greek men of learning who brought into Italy the language of Athens, and re-opened there the sources of erudition. He was descended from one of the ancient families of Rome, who accompanied Constantine to Constantinople. His high birth, his character and rare acquirements, rendered him one of the most considerable personages of his time. He was employed by several sovereigns in important and difficult negotiations. The Greek Emperor, John Paleologus, charged him to solicit for him, against the Turks, the succour of the powers of Europe.

Chrysoloras after fixed himself in Italy; he opened a school at Florence, and afterwards at Milan, where the Duke, John Galeas, invited him to settle. The troubles which burst out in Lombardy forced him afterwards to leave it, and he came to Rome, where his pupil, Léonard Aretin, secretary to Gregory XII., invited him. It is presumable that he afterwards returned to his own country, as he was at a later period charged with a mission from the Emperor Emmanuel Paleologus to King Charles VI. at Paris. He was afterwards sent by John XXIII. to the Emperor Sigismund, and associated with Cardinal de Chalant and Zabarella, Cardinal of Florence, the pontiff's legate, to determine, in concert with the emperor, the city where the council should assemble, and the result of that negotiation was, as has been seen, the choice of Constance. He accompanied Zabarella to that city, and died there, April 15th, 1417, a short time before the decease of the cardinal. The epitaph of Chrysolorus informs us, that he was esteemed by all worthy to attain the sovereign pontificate. Here it is, such as it was to be read a few years back, and may perhaps be still, in the church of the Dominicans.

Ante aram hanc situs dominus Manuel Chrysolorus, miles Constantinopolitanus, ex vetusto genere Romanorum, qui cum Constantino imperatore migrarunt, vir doctissimus, prudentissimus, optimus, qui tempore generalis concilii *Constantiensis obiit, ea existimatione, ut ab omnibus summo inter mortales sacerdotio dignus haberetur, die 15 Apr. 1415. Conditus est apud Dominicos.*

By the side of this epitaph were inscribed, in letters of gold, verses composed by Æneas Sylvius in honour of Emmanuel Chrysolorus.

NOTE G.

In the sixth book of the *Histoire du Concile de Constance*, by Lenfant, the following dissertation is given on the subject of the *Golden Rose :* "According to Theophilus Reynaud, this custom is very ancient in the church, and it is difficult to discover the origin and author of it. Some writers assign the institution of it to the fifth century, and others to the ninth. It is certain that for a great length of time they had been in the habit of consecrating a rose on the *Lætare* Sunday, three weeks after Easter. Henry de Sponde informs us that Peter de Blois, celebrated in the twelfth century, makes mention of this custom, and assigns the mystical reason for it in some of his sermons.

"Jacques Ricart, canon of St. Victor at Paris, in his notes on the *History of England*, written by William of Newborough, about the end of the same century, gives the following extract of a letter from Alexander III. to Louis-the-Young, king of France, in sending him the golden rose. ' We follow,' says this pope, ' the custom of our predecessors, who carried in their hand a golden rose the *Lætare* Sunday; we have thought that we could not present it to any person meriting it better than your excellency, on account of your extraordinary devotedness to the church and to ourselves.' The same author speaks of a sermon which Innocent III. pronounced on a similar day, on the mystery of the golden rose, in which this pope said that the rose was composed of gold, musk, and balsam, and that the musk, united to the gold and the balsam, represented three substances found in Jesus Christ, viz. the divinity, the body, and the soul.

"No author speaks more fully on the mystical reasons of the golden rose than Guillaume Durand, who flourished in the thirteenth century. ' The day which commences mid-lent,' says he, ' the pope, in going to the church and returning, carries a golden rose, which he shows to all the people, to encourage them to support the austerities of Lent; for all that day is destined to the joy of which the rose is the emblem by its colour, odour, and savour; the colour inspires joy, the odour gives pleasure, and the savour strengthens. This rose in the hand of the pope designates the joy of the people of Israel at seeing themselves delivered from the captivity of Babylon. After having consecrated the rose, the pope makes a present of it to one of the greatest nobles who happen to be at the time at his court, &c.' "

It appears that what was at first only a religious ceremony, became at last an act of authority, by which the popes, in giving the golden rose to kings, acknowledged them for such, and the princes accepted with pleasure this kind of homage which they could have done without. Henry VIII. received with gratitude the golden rose of Pope Julius II. and of Leo X., of whom he afterwards threw off the yoke.*

NOTE H.

Two authors present at the council, the Canon Reichental and Gebhard Dacher, relate that John Huss wanted to fly before his arrest. The following is the way in which Lenfant relates this fact, according to Reichental, in his *Histoire du Concile de Constance*. "John Huss," says he, "had determined to fly in the month of March, 1415. In order to execute this design, he took a loaf and a bottle of wine, and went to hide himself early in the morning in a cart of Henry de Latzembock, which had been prepared to seek for hay in some village. When the hour of dinner came, Latzembock, to whom John Huss had been intrusted, not seeing him, demanded uselessly where he was, for no person could give any news of him. Alarmed at this absence, he ran and informed the consul, who immediately had the gates of the city shut, and ordered the archers to go in pursuit of the fugitive. When they were getting ready to pursue him, John Huss being found concealed in the cart, was placed on horseback with his chaplain, and several Bohemians, who were also on horseback, and taken by Latzembock to the pope's palace. John Huss, having heard that they were speaking of putting him in prison, got off his horse, in the hope of escaping by means of the immense crowd that had collected to see what was going on; but the soldiers suspected his design, and he was shut up under strong guard in the pontifical palace. Reichental adds, that Sigismund would have been well pleased then to set him at liberty, as well for his own honour, because he had given him a safe-conduct, as through apprehension of irritating his brother Wenceslaus and the Bohemians, but that the doctors, having informed him that it was not permitted to give a safe-conduct to a heretic, he submitted to that decision."†

Lenfant adds, that the historian Dacher relates this fact in the same manner as Reichental. *Naucler* and the Abbé Tritheme, who wrote about a century after the council, also speak of John Huss's attempt to escape; *John Cochlœus* mentions it in his *Histoire des Hussites*, on Reichental's authority; all the modern authors, in fine, *Maimbourg*, *Varillas*, and others, have taken the anecdote from the history of John Cochlœus.

After having shown all the gravity of Reichental's testimony, on which all who speak of John Huss's evasion rest their authority, Lenfant enumerates the various proofs which tend to invalidate it. The acts of the council make no mention of the fact; and had it taken place, they would without doubt have stated it as a pretext for arresting John Huss. Other contemporary authors, of whom several were present at the council, have said nothing about it either; the old *historian* of John Huss's life, *Thierry de Niem*, *Leonard Aretin*, *Jacques Piccolomini*, *Vrie*, and *Æneas Sylvius*, are silent on the point; and yet they have seized most eagerly on every thing that could throw disfavour on John Huss, or excuse his enemies. They, in fine, who have assigned a

date to the pretended evasion of John Huss, indicate March 23, 1415,* as the day. Now, all the original writers of the time attest that he was arrested at the end of November, 1414, and that he had not after that time any liberty. Reichental says, that he was shut up in the pope's palace, and Cochlœus, that he was conducted before the pope himself.† But the pope was no longer at Constance, for he had escaped on March 20. It follows, that nothing is less proved than the flight of John Huss, which, besides, would have been justified by the circumstances. This fact rests only on the testimony of Reichental and of Dacher! it is well known that these authors wrote in concert, communicating their documents to each other;‡ and it is presumable that, writing many years after the council had closed, they have given as an authentic fact, what was only an anecdote founded on some popular tradition.

NOTE I.

Cardinal de Brogni (Jean Allarmet) rose from the lowest condition to the highest rank of human greatness. He was born in 1342, of a family of poor peasants, in the village of Brogni, near Anneci, on the road to Geneva, and was a swineherd in his boyhood. He was guarding his pigs one day, when some monks, who were going to Geneva, asked him the way. Struck with his animated and intelligent physiognomy, they proposed to him to follow their design, and they would give him the means of studying. The boy accepted the proposal, and ran to buy a pair of shoes. As he wanted two pence of the price, the shoemaker gave him credit, "in the hope of being paid," he said, "when his customer was a cardinal." When he arrived at Geneva, he applied with great zeal to his studies, and made a rapid progress: he afterwards went to Avignon, where Clement VII. was residing: he there studied canon law under able professors, was received doctor, and acquired such a reputation that he was consulted from all quarters. Clement VII., hearing of his merit and his talents, confided to him the education of Humbert de Thoire, his nephew, and soon after, charmed with the progress of the young man, he loaded his tutor with benefits; he named him cardinal, gave him the bishopric of Viviers, and afterwards the archbishopric of Arles. Benedict XIII., the successor of Clement VII., appointed Jean de Brogni bishop of Ostia; and Alexander V. at last put the finishing touch to his fortune, by joining to all his dignities that of Chancellor of the Roman Church.

The new Bishop of Ostia was, however, always called Cardinal de Viviers, from the name of his first bishopric. He was as famed for his integrity as his learning, and he consecrated a great part of his revenues to acts of charity, and objects of public utility. He was seventy-two years of age at the opening of the Council of Constance, and, although his habits were simple and modest, the

---

* Lenfant, *Hist. du Concile de Constance*, book vi.
† Lenfant, ibid. book i.

* "Dominica dculi, quæ tertia est in quadragesima." (Coch. *Hist. Hussit.* p. 73.)
† "Latzembock imposuit eum equo, et adduxit in palatium ad papam." (*Idem*, p. 74.)
‡ Lenfant, *Con. de Const.* book i.

greatness of his train and the number of his attendants give an idea of the luxury and magnificence with which the prelates and cardinals lived in that age. "Jean de Brogni," says the historian Reichental, an ocular witness, "repaired to the council in a rich equipage, with an escort of eighty-three mounted attendants."[*] He constantly presided over that illustrious assembly during the vacancy of the Holy See, and evinced the greatest zeal for the extinction of the schism and of heresy. After the council had concluded, this cardinal followed Martin V. to Rome, and the pope transferred him from the archbishopric, which he still administered, to that of Geneva, the revenues of which were far inferior. Jean de Brogni, nevertheless, consented with joy to this translation, which, in his old age, brought him back to the country where he was born. His great age did not, however, permit him to take possession of his new see; he died at Rome, in 1426, but he desired to be buried at Geneva, in the chapel of the Macchabees, which he had founded.

Jean de Brogni never blushed for the obscurity of his birth; in that same chapel where his body reposes, he had himself painted, young, with naked feet, tending pigs, under an oak; and to perpetuate still more the remembrance of the adventure to which he owed his elevation, he had represented all round on the walls of the chapel, swine, acorns, and oak-leaves. He paid his debt to the shoemaker generously, by giving him the place of steward in his household, and he proved still more by his alms that he did not forget his origin. He founded the hospital of Anneci, supported manufactories in order to clothe the poor with their produce, portioned a number of young girls, and, in the latter part of his life, he supported thirty poor persons each day. He had attained the highest fortune, and yet, when he visited the village of Brogni, his birthplace, he made all the old men assemble at his table; and, in a word, by a crowd of excellent acts, and by touching conduct towards the poor, he appeared most anxious to show that he remembered having been poor like them.

Did Cardinal de Viviers show himself favourable to John Huss? The opinion that he did, has been adopted on the strength of the headings of some letters from the Bohemian martyr.[†] But it has been forgotten that these headings were not written by John Huss; they are attributed to Luther, who himself could have been led in error by a passage in the fifty-fourth letter, in which Huss speaks of a cardinal, named Jean, who wished him well. Jacques Lenfant, in his Histoire du Concile de Constance, has clearly established that he, of whom it was in question in this letter, was not Cardinal Jean de Brogni, but a doctor named Jean Cardinal, a friend of John Huss, and who acquired some celebrity after his death. Luther was, without doubt, in composing the headings of John Huss's letters, struck with this passage, and confounded Doctor Jean Cardinal with the president of the council.[‡] No solid

proof establishes that Jean de Brogni, who was distinguished amongst the most illustrious members of the clergy by his virtues and his learning, showed more respect than any of them for the sincerity of religious convictions out of his own church.

NOTE K.[*]

The ultramontanes have neglected nothing that could throw a doubt on the authenticity of the fourth and fifth sessions of the Council of Constance, and to invalidate their authority. The following is the manner in which Joseph de Maistre, the most illustrious defender of the ultramontane doctrines, expresses himself on this subject.

"Let any one fancy himself in the place of the Bishop of Constance, divided into nations, opposed in interests, worn out by delay, irritated by contradiction, separated from the cardinals, deprived of a common centre, and, to complete their misfortune, influenced by rival sovereigns. Is it then wonderful that they, pressed as they were, by an immense desire to put an end to the most deplorable schism that ever afflicted the Church, and in an age when the spread of knowledge had not yet circumscribed ideas within the logical bounds to which they are brought in our days, should have said to themselves: We cannot restore peace to the Church and reform it in its head and members, but in commanding this head himself; let us, therefore, declare that he is obliged to obey us. The assembly, therefore, first of all declared itself an œcumenical council. It was certainly very necessary to do so, to afterwards draw the conclusion that every person, of whatever condition he might be—even papal—was bound to obey the council in what regarded the faith and the extirpation of the schism.

"The fifth session was only a repetition of the fourth. An infinity of things could be said on these two sessions, on the manuscript of Schelstratus, on the objections of Arnaud and Bossuet, on the support that these writings have drawn from the precious discoveries made in the libraries of Germany, &c., &c.; but were I to plunge into these details, there would occur to me a little misfortune which I should certainly wish to avoid, if it were possible—that of not being read.

"The Catholic world was then divided into three parties or obediences, each of which recognised a different pope. Two of these obediences —those of Gregory XII. and of Benedict XIII. never received the decree of Constance, pronounced in the fourth session; and after the obediences became united, never did the council attribute to itself, independently of the pope, the right of reforming the Church in its head and in its members. But in the session of October 30, 1417, Martin V., having been elected with a

---

* Reichental, Concil. de Const. fol. 12.

† J. Hus. Hist. et Monum. vol. i. Epls. xxxviii. xxxix. xl.

‡ Hist. du Concile de Constance, vol. i. p. 343, and following.

* I have abridged this note, which, being intended wholly to clear up questions very eagerly discussed in France, possesses but a secondary interest for the readers of other countries. Its place is naturally here, yet, perhaps, it will be better to defer reading it, until after the account of the proceedings of the council. (Note of the Translator.)

unanimity without example, the council decreed that *the pope should himself reform the Church, as well in its head as in its members, according to equity and the good government of the Church.*

"The pope, on his side, in the fourteenth session, on April 22, 1418, approved of all that the council had done SYNODICALLY *in matters of faith.*

"And some days before, by a bull of March 10, he had forbidden appeals from the decrees of the Holy See, which he called the *sovereign judge.* Such was the pope's manner of *approving of the Council of Constance.*

"Never was there any thing so ridiculously null, and even so evidently ridiculous, as the fourth session of the *Council* of Constance, which Providence and the pope afterwards changed into council.

"But if certain folks persist in saying, 'We admit the fourth session,' forgetting altogether that this word *we,* in the Catholic Church, is a solecism, unless it applies to all, we shall then say on, and in place of laughing at the fourth session alone, we shall laugh at the fourth session and at those who refuse to laugh at it."

The fourth session of Constance, of which M. de Maistre speaks with so much disdain, had for object, as well as the fifth, to mark where authority resides in a Church which rests altogether itself on authority. This is, in our eyes, the capital question: the appreciation of the value of the acts which decide it is of extreme importance, and we shall give to this examination all the extent that the matter demands. In another work,[*] De Maistre has said, speaking of the declaration of 1682, founded in part on the decrees of this council : "It contains an assertion that cannot be borne out, viz.,—*That the fourth and fifth sessions of the Council of Constance were approved of by the Holy Apostolic See, and confirmed by the practice of the whole church, and of the Roman pontiffs.* I abstain from all reflection, persuaded that much is due to certain men, when even an accidental passion blinds them entirely." It is Bossuet, in particular, that M. de Maistre refers to here ; it is, therefore, Bossuet that we must be applied to. We shall quote textually a part of the objections which he brings forward,[†] and we shall give an abridgment of the answers which he makes to them.

After having quoted the decrees of the fourth and fifth sessions, Bossuet adds :[‡] "The decree o the fourth session is considerably explained by those of the fifth ; for, although the decree of the fourth session attributes to the council the sovereign power, nevertheless it could have been alleged, in cavilling on the expressions, that this power was specially attributed to the Council of Constance alone. But the fathers, having perceived that if the authority of the councils was

thus restricted, the Church could not afterwards remedy its evils, decided, in the fifth session, that the sovereign power did not belong to the Council of Constance alone, but to any other general council. These decrees were renewed at Basil by the votes of all the fathers, at a time when this council was certainly general. Then Eugene IV. was united to it, and the schism did not arise until afterwards.

"The enterprise which our adversaries had undertaken, to cast clouds over the decrees of Constance, and lessen their authority, was no small peril. They began by attacking the text, which nobody had before attempted. For every one before Emmanuel Schelstratus, doctor in theology, and librarian of the Vatican, admitted as the true production of the Council of Constance the decrees which we have just mentioned, and which are found, word for word, in the edition of the General Councils made at the Vatican. But at last, in 1683, or 250 years after the holding of the Council of Constance, this doctor appears all of a sudden to undeceive every one, presenting new acts of the Council of Constance, and he takes care to give warning, as the title-page of his work declares, that the first decree of the fourth session, of that council was falsified by the fathers of that of Basil. He speaks in that way to destroy, by a single blow, the authority of these two councils. Our adversaries also tell us that the fathers of Constance, in declaring the pope subject to the council, did not mean that this is true in all cases, but only in that of schism ; they attack, in fine, the authority itself of the decrees of Constance —and it is against this latter point that they direct their strongest batteries. We shall examine their accusations."

After having refused, with great force, the two first, which refer, one to the true text, and the other to two decrees of Constance, Bossuet considers the question the most controverted—that of the authority of the decrees—and expresses himself in these terms:

"Our adversaries do not reject the *whole Council of Constance, but simply the first sessions.* Is it then nothing to strike at the foundations which support this respectable edifice, and to act in that by their own authority, without any council or any pope having ever done any thing of the like ! If such undertakings are permitted, I am certainly ignorant what may not be attempted. But let us enter into a detail of the objections which are made to us, in order to show their weakness and frivolity.

"*First objection, and answer.*—Our adversaries pretend that there was at the Council of Constance, in the first sessions, only a third part of the Church, because there were there merely the populations and kingdoms which obeyed John XXIII. But we reply, first of all, that all the obediences had been convoked by the authority of the real pope, and consequently of a decree of the Council of Pisa. We ask, also, if it was necessary to allow the Church to perish, because some Spaniards, Scots, and a few others attached to the antipopes, opposed the union ! Who will believe that this multitude of churches which obeyed the lawful pope, were not entitled to act in the name of the whole Church,

* *Du Pape,* book i. chap. xiii.

† These are the objections made by the ultra montane doctors.

‡ Abridged by Abbé Coulon, from Bossuet's celebrated work, entitled *Défense de l'assemblée generale du Clergé de France en 1682,* second part, book v. chap. 1—3.

to appease the troubles which agitated it, or at least to lay the foundations of that great work? What destroys this objection altogether is, that when the two obediences were united to the council they declared it œcumenical, and approved of the bull of Martin V. Certainly, if they had suspected any error in the decrees, they would not have joined the council, but in rejecting expressly what would have appeared to them erroneous.

"*There was no certain pope at that period in the church,* adds Bellarmine, *and doubts concerning the faith cannot be decided without the pope.* I reply, that there was no pope recognised by every one without exception, but there was one *certain,* whom nearly the whole church recognised. For Bellarmine must allow that they who did not acknowledge him were but a handful in comparison with the others.

"*There was no pope in the council,* adds again Bellarmine, *for John XXIII., who had been present at the opening, had already withdrawn when the fourth session was held.* But does Bellarmine suppose that the disgraceful flight of that pope could have annulled the authority of the council? The pope himself did not think so, since the day after his departure he sent deputies to the emperor, with a letter of credence, by which he assured him that he would execute all that he had promised.

"*Second objection, and answer.*—The anonymous author of the doctrine of Louvain tells us, that many persons declare that all the fathers who composed the Council of Constance did not consent to the decrees of the fourth and fifth sessions; that John XXIII. did not consent to them, and never authorized them; that he even complained that after his withdrawal certain false and erroneous decrees against the authority of the Roman pontiffs had been published. . . . . As it was impossible for this author to weaken the authority of the council by bringing forward public acts, he had recourse to vague reports amongst the people. . . . . But the acts of the council demonstrate that two hundred fathers were present at the fourth session, and that after the reading of the decrees of the fifth, all the council approved of them. These very acts attest also that John XXIII. adhered to the council even after his flight, and that often afterwards he avowed, without any person pressing him to do so, that *he had fled disgracefully from Constance; that the Council of Constance, being a continuation of that of Pisa, could not err; and that he accepted, approved of, and ratified, as much as in him lay, the deposition pronounced against him.* The council was well assured that all its decrees would have been perfectly valid in spite of the pope's opposition; how then can their validity be contested when the pope approved of them?

"What matters it that John XXIII., *beset by a set of mean flatterers, who had caused his ruin,* as Cardinal d'Ailly informs us, should have complained in private of the conduct of the council in his case? All that it is of interest to know is, what he declared publicly to the council.

"*Third objection, and answer.*—Some of our adversaries pretend that the Council of Constance was not œcumenical in its first sessions, because it consented, in the fourteenth, to have a new convocation made, when the officers of Gregory XII. came to join it. But this is to take an act of pure condescension and of a truly apostolical charity, for a proceeding of necessity; for already peace had been re-established in almost the whole Church. The best heads had abandoned the two rivals, who, it was evident, were only seeking their own interests, and only a very few persons remained united to them by prejudices which they could not get rid of. . . . . The Church, full of tenderness for her children, determined therefore to admit a new convocation, made in the fourteenth sessions by Gregory XII.'s officers, but in declaring that it admitted that proceeding only in as much as it regarded the said Gregory.* . . . . When the Spaniards, who had adhered to Benedict, came to join the Council of Constance, the same condescension was evinced in their case, through a desire of peace and through consideration for the feeble.† But none of them demanded that the decrees already published should be again gone through, or at least confirmed anew, as having been made by an insufficient or doubtful authority. All the affairs commenced were continued on the same footing without any of them being begun afresh. It was no more required to revise and again take up the decrees of the fourth and of the fifth sessions, in which the superiority of the councils over the pope had been decided, than the decrees against Wycliffe and John Huss, in the sessions also held before the arrival of the Spaniards.

* * * * *

"*Fourth objection, and answer.*—Our adversaries pretend, that Martin V. did not approve of and confirm the decrees of the fourth and fifth sessions, and that what has not been approved of and confirmed by the pope cannot be considered as the decision of an œcumenical council. . . . In ecclesiastical style the word *confirm* signifies simply *consent to,* and give by that consent a new weight to the decision. Martin V., when he became pope, spoke of the first sessions as having been held by a general council. He approved of them sufficiently in communicating with those by whom the decrees had been published. He approved of them sufficiently in suffering himself to be put in the place of John XXIII., whose canonical deposition was only founded on these decrees. . . . And it is to have no knowledge of antiquity, to be ignorant in what the force of the holy canons properly consists, to fancy that a pope present at a council, and applauding its decisions, does not confirm them in the most clear and authentic manner.

"*Fifth objection, and answer.*—Bellarmine tells us, that Martin V. declared expressly that amongst the decrees concerning the faith, he should not confirm any that had not been passed (*conciliariter*) synodically, that is, after a mature deliberation, according to the use of councils. But, adds this cardinal, *it is certain that the Council of Constance published without examination the decrees of the fourth and fifth sessions.* What an absurdity! to rank decrees published in two conse-

* Book III. chap. II.   † Book III. chap. ix.

cutive sessions, drawn up with a fixed intention, laid down as fundamental principles, and finally adopted by a unanimity of votes, amongst the number of things which were treated as if *en passant*, and without examination! I say, therefore, that to call in doubt if a decree has been passed according to the rules, when it has been published by the council, after a precise and authentic decision, is to open a path to attack and overturn all canons, all decrees, all councils."

Such is in substance the celebrated dissertation of Bossuet, on the three capital questions raised as to the *authenticity*, *sense*, and *authority*, of the decrees of the fifth session of Constance. These arguments have been reproduced in modern times by an illustrious defender of the liberties of the Gallican Church, Cardinal de la Luzerne, who, in addition, proposes this dilemma to the ultramontanes. "The Councils of Pisa and Constance were œcumenical or they were not. If it is granted that they were, as we maintain, the pope must, according to the judgment of the infallible authority, be inferior to the council. If it is asserted that they were not, it must be admitted as a consequence, that Alexander V. and Martin V. were intruders, and that their successors, down to our days, are illegitimate popes."[*]

De Maistre sums up the grave consequences of this discussion, in quoting the opinion of him whom he names the greatest of Protestants, and perhaps the greatest of men in the order of the sciences. "Leibnitz," says he, "objected to Bossuet, in 1699, that *it had not yet been agreed in the Roman Church as to the seat of infallibility, some placing it in the pope, and others in the council, although, without pope, &c.*[†] Such is," remarks De Maistre, "the result of the fatal system adopted by some theologians with respect to councils, and founded principally on a unique fact, badly understood and explained, precisely because it is unique; they expose the dogma of infallibility in concealing the residence where it ought to be sought."[‡]

That is, in fact, to lay the finger on the evil—for what results from this great discussion is danger to the dogma of *infallibility*. Bossuet himself, so powerful against those who attack the authenticity, the sense, and the authority of the acts of Constance, grows weak, in his turn, when he weighs and appreciates the acts of the councils of Florence, of the Lateran, and of the popes, whose decrees, without calling into doubt in principle those of Constance, annul them in reality.[§] A strange and most awkward position is this in which the dogma of this infallibility places the Gallicans, as well as the ultramontanes, and which they all lay down as the foundation of the church, and which they grievously disturb by their discussions. This dogma condemns them, when they have established their principle to ruin the authority of the acts which lay down an opposite principle. Unity falls to the ground in this contest, and peril arises on both sides for the *infallibility*.

[*] *Sur la déclaration du clergé de France, en 1682*, third part, chap. xx.
[†] See correspondence between Leibnits and Bossuet.
[‡] *Du Pape*, vol. i. chap. xiii.
[§] See book iv. chap. v.

De Maistre comprehended this, and, therefore, avoids answering his adversaries, in order to laugh at them; but there is in this pleasantry something discordant that shocks, for it is not the joy of triumph, but the laugh of despair.

NOTE L.

RECAPITULATION OF ALL THE ARTICLES[*] ALLEGED AGAINST JOHN HUSS, AT THE COUNCIL OF CONSTANCE.[†]

Articles alleged as drawn out of the book intituled, Of the Church.

1. There is but one holy, universal, or catholic Church, which is the universal company of all the predestinate.

2. St. Paul was never any member of the devil, albeit that he committed and did certain acts, like unto the acts of the malignant church; and likewise St. Peter, who fell into a horrible sin of perjury, and denial of his master; it was by the permission of God, that he might the more firmly and steadfastly rise again and be confirmed.

3. No part or member of the church doth depart or fall away at any time from the body, for so much as the charity of predestination, which is the bond and chain of the same, doth never fall.

4. The predestinate, although he be not in the state of grace, according to present justice, yet is he always a member of the universal Church.

5. There is no degree of honour or dignity, neither any human election, or any sensible sign, that can make any man member of the universal Church.

6. A reprobate man is never a member of the holy Church.

7. Judas was never a true disciple of Jesus Christ.

8. The congregation of the predestinate, whether they be in the state of grace or no, according unto present justice, is the holy universal Church; and it is the same church which has neither wrinkle nor spot in it, but is holy and undefiled, the which the Son of God doth call his own.

9. Peter never was, nor is, the head of the holy universal Church.

10. If he who is called the vicar of Jesus Christ do follow Christ in his life, then he is his true vicar. But if he do walk in contrary paths and ways, then he is the messenger of antichrist, the enemy of our Lord Jesus Christ, and also the vicar of Judas Iscariot.

11. All such as do use simony, and priests living dissolutely, do hold an untrue opinion of the seven sacraments, as unbelieving bastards, not knowing what is the office and duty of keys or censures, rites and ceremonies, or of veneration of relics, neither of the orders constituted in the Church, neither yet of indulgences or pardons.

[*] These articles are thirty-nine in number. Several present the same meaning, and they may be all grouped under a certain number of principal heads, as we have done, book iii. chap. v. See John Huss's answers to these articles, pages 95, 96.
[†] These articles are literally quoted, as they are found in "The Acts and Monuments of the Martyrs," by John Fox.

25

R

12. The papal dignity hath his original from the Emperor of Rome.

13. No man could reasonably affirm (without revelation), either of himself or of any other, that he is the head of any particular church.

14. It ought not to be believed that the pope, whatsoever he be, may be the head of any particular church, unless he be predestinate or ordained of God.

15. The pope's power as vicar is but vain and nothing worth, if he do not conform and address his life according to Jesus Christ, and follow the manners of St. Peter.

16. The pope is most holy, not because he doth supply and hold the room and place of St. Peter, but because he hath great revenues.

17. The cardinals are not the manifest and true successors of the other apostles of Jesus Christ, if they live not according to the fashion of the apostles, keeping the commandments and ordinances of the Lord Jesus.

18. A heretic ought not to be committed to the secular powers to be put to death.

19. The nobles of the world ought to constrain and compel the ministers of the Church to observe and keep the law of Jesus Christ.

20. The ecclesiastical obedience is a kind of obedience which the priests and monks have invented without any express authority of the Holy Scriptures.

21. He that is excommunicated by the pope, if he reject and forsake the judgment of the pope and the general council, and appealeth unto Jesus Christ, after he hath made his appellation, all the excommunication and curses of the pope cannot annoy or hurt him.

22. A vicious and naughty man liveth viciously and naughtily, but a virtuous and godly man liveth virtuously and godly.

23. The minister of Christ, living according to his law, and having the knowledge and understanding of the Scriptures, and an earnest desire to edify the people, ought to preach; notwithstanding the pretended excommunication of the pope.

24. Every man which is admitted unto the ministry of the Church, receiveth also by special commandment the office of a preacher, and ought to fulfil that commandment, notwithstanding any excommunication pretended to the contrary.

25. The ecclesiastical censures are antichristian, such as the clergy have invented for their own preferment, and for the bondage and servitude of the common people.

26. There ought no interdictment to be appointed unto the people for so much as Christ the high bishop, for any injury that was done unto him, did not make any interdictment.

Articles which are said to be drawn out of the book written against Paletz.

1. If the pope, bishop, or prelate, be in deadly sin, he is then no pope, bishop, or prelate.

2. The grace of predestination is the bond whereby the body of the Church, and every part and member thereof, is firmly knit and joined unto the head.

3. If the pope be a wicked man, and specially a reprobate, then, even as Judas the apostle, he is a devil, a thief, and the son of perdition, and not the head of the holy militant Church, for so much as he is no part or member thereof.

4. An evil pope or prelate, or reprobate, is no true pastor, but a thief and a robber.

5. The pope is not, neither ought to be called, according unto his office, Most Holy.

6. If the pope live contrary unto Christ, albeit he be lawfully and canonically elect and chosen, according to human election, yet doth he ascend and come another way than by Christ.

7. The condemnation of the forty-five articles of John Wycliffe, made by the doctors, is unreasonable and wicked, and the cause by them alleged is feigned and untrue; that is to say, that none of those articles are catholic, but that every one of them be either heretical, erroneous, or offensive.

Articles alleged as drawn out of the book which Huss wrote against Stanislaus de Znoïma.

1. No man is lawfully elect or chosen, in that the doctors or the greater part of them have consented; or that he is thereby the manifest or true precursor of Christ, or vicar of St. Peter, but in that, that any man doth most abundantly work meritoriously to the profit of the Church.

2. The pope, being a reprobate, is not the head of the holy Church of God.

3. There is no spark of appearance that there ought to be one head in the spirituality, to rule the Church, the which should be always conversant with the militant Church.

4. Christ would better rule his Church by his true apostles, dispersed throughout the world, without such monstrous heads.

5. Peter was no universal pastor or shepherd of the sheep of Christ, much less is the Bishop of Rome.

6. The apostles and other faithful priests of the Lord, have stoutly ruled the Church in all things necessary unto salvation before the office of the pope was brought into the Church, and so would they very possibly do still, if there were no pope even to the latter day.

Out of these thirty-nine articles, twelve are relative to the spiritual power not recognised in priests of evil life. Huss, as has been seen (book iii. chap. v.), gave a Catholic explanation of his doctrine on this point.

According to the Catholic doctrine, every priest, however criminal his life may be, preserves the gifts of the Holy Spirit, as to the exercise of the spiritual power; the most impious always remains a canal by which the divine grace is transmitted to believers. There is, in the human heart, a natural and almost invincible tendency to protest against this opinion; and De Maistre himself has written what follows on the subject of the popes of the tenth century:—"When all-powerful courtesans, monsters of crimes and wickedness, profiting by the public disorders, had seized on the chief power and disposed of all at Rome, and carried to St. Peter's throne, by the most culpable means, either their sons or their paramours, I deny expressly that these men have been popes. He who would undertake to prove the contrary proposition, would certainly find himself in a great difficulty."*

That assertion proceeds from the heart: however, the consequences of this opinion are grave; De Maistre perceived them afterwards, and he adds in a note, that he could defend or explain this paragraph, but that he preferred giving it up.† Such is the logic of theologians.

NOTE M.

The woman of whom mention was made before the council under the name of *Agnes*, is better known by the appellation of *Pope Joan*. Ancient chroniclers have pretended that, having disguised her sex, she occupied the pontifical throne after Leo IV., in 885. This story is at present considered fabulous; but at the period of the Council of Constance, it was generally admitted as true. Had the fathers of the council entertained any doubt of it, they would have protested loudly against a supposition so insulting to the Holy See, as they did against imputations far less grave. In the writings of John Huss, and of other doctors of the period, frequent and serious allusions are found to the pretended reign of *Agnes*; yet no member of the council reproached him with having mentioned—either in his works, or his answers—this scandalous anecdote.

NOTE N.

It has been seen, in the proceedings of John Huss, how the council forced the emperor to act. The following is the manner in which writers of a grave character, and whose intentions were pure, relate the part which Sigismund had to play in this frightful drama. The following lines in the *Histoire abrégée de l'Eglise*, by Lhomond, must be read with a painful surprise. This author says, on the subject of John Huss, "*The council did not solicit this punishment; it allowed the justice of the sovereign to take its course, and it certainly can, for the good of the church, punish those who trouble civil order*.‡ The Abbé Frayssinous has said the same thing, and nearly in the same words.§

Certainly it is difficult to disguise the truth with more courage. If the best have done so, what are we to expect from the others? What does history become in, the mouth of those who consider themselves bound in duty to falsify it? The Church, in their writings, has never been wrong; and falsehood, they think, is allowable in the interest of a sacred cause. "It is not the council," say they, "it is the emperor, who smote John Huss, for it is the emperor who ordered the punishment." By this computation, it is not the Jews to whom the death of our Saviour must be imputed, for it is Pilate who pronounced the sentence.

The Abbé Frayssinous adds, for the purpose of still better justifying the assembly, "*It is not the council, but the emperor, who gave the safe-conduct!*"

* *Du Pape*, book ii. chap. vii. † *De Maistre, ibid.*
‡ Edition of [1826, published by the *Société Catholique des bons livres*, p. 367.
§ *Défense du Christian.—La religion vengée du reproche de fanatisme.*

What a lesson for princes, who become blind instruments in the hands of priests!

NOTE O.

The dissenting communions are constantly reproached with disagreeing amongst themselves on a multitude of points, whilst they all unite in a common opposition to the Roman Church. This reproach has been strongly expressed in these terms by an ancient Dominican monk, named Reiner: "The heretics," said he, "are divided amongst themselves, but they make but one against the Church: they are like Samson's foxes, which had different fronts, but were all tied together."

It is strange that this common resistance to the Roman Church could be turned into a subject of blame. It follows, as a matter of course, that the persons who adopt the principle of free examination, should agree in resisting those who condemn it in the name of the principle of authority. It is not, besides, the Roman Church alone that the former oppose so strongly; they do the same amongst all nations and churches, against every one that pretends to substitute a human authority for the revealed word interpreted by the conscience.

NOTE P.

Propositions extracted by the doctors of Paris, from the Apology for the Duke of Burgundy, by Doctor John Petit.

1. It is lawful for every subject, without any command, according to moral, natural, or divine laws, to kill, or cause to be killed, every tyrant who, through covetousness, or other improper motive, plots against the corporal safety of his king and sovereign lord, to deprive him of his most noble lordship; and not only lawful, but even honourable and meritorious; even when he is of such high power that justice cannot be well executed by the sovereign.

2. Natural, moral, and divine laws authorize each person to kill, or cause to be killed, the said tyrant.

3. It is lawful for each subject to kill, or cause to be killed, the above-mentioned tyrant, treacherous and disloyal to his king and sovereign lord, by snares; and it is lawful to dissemble and conceal the intention to do so.

4. It is sound reason and justice that every tyrant shall be disgracefully killed by snares; and it is the proper death by which disloyal tyrants ought to die, to kill them disgracefully by wiles and snares.

5. He who kills, or causes to be killed in such a way, every tyrant, is not to be blamed in any respect; and the king ought not only to be pleased at it, but ought to consider the action an agreeable one, and to authorize it as much as might be required.

6. The king ought to thank him who kills, or causes to be killed, a tyrant in the above conditions, in three ways—in affection, honour, riches, in imitation of the remunerations made to St. Michael, the archangel, for the expulsion of Lucifer from the kingdom of Paradise, and to the noble *Phineas* for the expulsion of Duke *Zambri*.

7. The king ought to love, more than before, him who kills, or causes to be killed, the above-named tyrant in the manner stated, and ought to have his faith and loyalty extolled within his kingdom and without.

8. The letter kills, but the spirit quickens; that is to say, that to always observe the literal sense in the Holy Scriptures is to kill one's soul.

9. In case of alliance, oath, promise, or confederation, made by one knight with another, in any manner whatever, should it happen that it turns to the prejudice of one of the parties concerned, or of his wife or children, he is not bound to keep it.

NOTE Q.

Profession of Faith of Boniface VIII.

I, Benedict Cajetan, &c., profess before you, St. Peter, Prince of the Apostles, &c., and before your Holy Church, of which I this day assume the government under your authority,—I promise, I say, that as long as I remain in this miserable life, I will not abandon the Church, nor renounce it, nor abdicate it in any manner, and that I will never separate from it for any cause whatever, nor through fear of any peril. That, on the contrary, I will preserve with all my strength until death, and to the shedding of my blood, the purity of the true faith of Jesus Christ, which is come to so trifling a person as I am, through you and your companion in the apostleship, the blessed St. Paul, and through your disciples and successors; both with respect to the mystery of the most holy and indivisible Trinity, which is but one God, and to the incarnation of our Lord Jesus Christ, the only Son of God, as well as of the other dogmas of the Church of God, as they are contained in general councils and constitutions of the *apostolic pontiffs* and most approved doctors of the Church; that is to say, that I will guard all that I have received from you by *tradition*, touching the purity and orthodoxy of the faith; that besides, I will maintain invariably and with the same respect, the eight œcumenical councils like that of *Nicea*, to the slightest syllable; that I will preach and teach what they have preached and determined; that I will condemn with heart and mouth all that they have condemned; that, in like manner, I will observe punctually and maintain in their vigour all the canonical decrees of our predecessors, the apostolical pontiffs, and all that they have determined and decreed in the councils (*synodaliter*); that I will all my lifetime keep inviolably the discipline and ritual as I have found them; that I will preserve the property of the Church, without diminishing, alienating, or infeoffing it in any manner whatever; promising not to diminish nor change any thing in the tradition which I have found transmitted and received by my predecessors, and not to admit any novelty; but, on the contrary, to maintain it with ardour and with all my strength, as their true disciple and minister; that if any person undertake any thing against the canonical discipline, I will correct it with the advice of *my sons*, the cardinals of the holy Roman Church, by the counsel, consent, and advice of whom I shall exercise my ministry, or I will patiently tolerate all that will not give too great a shock to the Christian religion, by your intercession, &c.

NOTE R.

Bayle has exposed perfectly the strange anomalies which the laws of the kingdom of France present in what regards ecclesiastical persons and things. After having, in his general criticism on the *Histoire du Calvinism*, mentioned several decrees of parliament, breaking the excommunications and interdicts issued by popes and generals of the different orders, against French monks; he shows, by these examples, that the jurisdiction of the kings over the religious houses extended even to *internal discipline*, and that the *exception* expressed on this head, in divers decrees of the parliament, is without sense.

"It must be allowed," adds this author, "that there is nothing more legitimate, without doubt, than the pretension of our kings, vigorously supported by our parliaments, to only depend on God in temporal matters, and to have jurisdiction over all the members of their state; but it must also be allowed that this does not always agree with the principles of their religion. For instance, it is a privilege of our monarch, that a legate *à latere* cannot exercise any of the functions of his charge in France, until after his bulls have been registered in the parliament of Paris, and the parliament never registers them but with this clause, that *the prelate cannot make use of his power but in as much as it shall be pleasing to the king;* I should like to know what would happen in case the legate performed some function before the registrations of his bull. Would the act be null? If he dispensed, for instance, of some reserved cases, would the absolution be null? That ought to be stated in the principle of the gentlemen of the parliament. Now, who will ever suppose that a pope, who confers, in the plenitude of his power, on a legate *à latere*, the power to do several things, and who establishes him his vicar, as he is himself the vicar of Jesus Christ, should have need of the concurrence of a parliament, in order that the Holy Ghost should ratify all that the legate will do by the authority of the pope? The legate will have received his full powers in due form; the Holy Ghost, by order of the pope, will rest on him, and will accompany him in his journey, in order to loose all that he shall loose, and to bind all that he shall bind, as if the pope was there in proper person; and yet should the legate, on his landing at Marseilles, exercise some of the powers which have been communicated to him by the bull of his legation, the Holy Ghost would have nothing to do to them, but would let him act alone, waiting patiently until it may have pleased the parliament of Paris to register the bull. Is there any thing in the world more absurd? And where is it found that Jesus Christ has given the apostle St. Peter a power subordinate to parliaments, and that the grace of the Holy Ghost, which the pope communicates to his legates and commissioners, when he confers on them the power to perform some ecclesiastical function, is regulated by the will of a king; so that if the legate goes in the slightest degree beyond the king's will, the grace of God goes back so much?

No matter what may be said about the affair, to that conclusion must we come; for if an ecclesiastical function, exercised before the registration of the bulls, and contrary to the king's permission, was accompanied by the blessing of God and the influence of the Holy Ghost, by which the Church is governed, as much as if it was exercised after the registration of the bulls and with the king's permission, it ought in conscience to be deemed good. But this is not the case; this function would be broken and declared completely null; therefore it must be deprived of the virtue of God on account of the non-registration of the bulls.

"I have remarked another thing connected with this. An individual, aware of a bull emanated from the pope, or of a commission pronounced *ex cathedra*, is not obliged to conform to it before the king has permitted or ordered its publication; so that to do a thing which is known to have been declared unlawful by the pope, provided it be done in the time which elapses between its being prohibited at Rome, until the king may have authorized it, is an indifferent action; but if it be done after the approbation of the bull, it would be a crime. Is not this to declare that *truths* declared at Rome do not become truths, except in consequence of the king's orders, and that the decrees of the Apostolic See are not obligatory on the consciences of those who are aware of them, except in virtue of the king's orders?

"All this conduct leads to a just suspicion that they who acknowledge with their lips the pope as the head of the church, and the vicar of the Son of God, are not persuaded of it in their souls; or, at least, this conduct shows that if they are persuaded of it in their souls, they do not act according to their belief."[a]

NOTE 8.

Confession of faith of the Taborites, such as it was presented in 1442, in the Synod of Kuttemburg.

1. As the Scripture is the word of the true and eternal God, as it has been written by the inspiration of the Holy Spirit in the books of the prophets and apostles, and confirmed by divine miracles, and as no person who has arrived at years of discretion can without it go to God, it follows that it ought to be translated into the vulgate or mother tongue, according to St. Paul's command, and ought to be followed with the greatest veneration. With respect to the doctrine of the Fathers, it must be received, when it is in conformity with the canonical books, and rejected when it is contrary to them.

2. There is but one God in three persons, as is taught in the Holy Scriptures, and in the *Nicean* and *Athanasian* creeds; we must love him with all our heart, with all our soul, and with all our strength.

3. After having been well acquainted with God, man must know himself; he must understand that before the fall of Adam, he was in innocence, but that after Adam fell by the wiles of the devil, he

became subject to sin, and was conceived from a criminal seed; that to that original fault he has added actual sins, which have engaged him in a perpetual penalty, from which he cannot escape by his own strength.

4. Man, awakened by the means of the divine word, and by the sentiment of temporal penalties, when he acknowledges his sins by the grace of the Holy Spirit, if he feels a bitter sorrow for them, if he avoids them as much as he can, if he confides in the mercy of God the Father, and in the precious merit of Jesus Christ; if, in fine, he does not resist the Holy Spirit, which, by the word, inflames and augments his faith—such a man ought to know that all his sins are pardoned him by the merit of Jesus Christ, without which no person can be saved, because he is the only propitiation between God and man, as the types of the old Testament have shown him.

5. And this salutary faith not being able to exist without works, according to St. James, justifies alone, according to St. Paul, Rom. iii. 4, 5, Gal. iii., Eph. ii., so that the believer may approach in all confidence the throne of the grace of Jesus Christ, our great pontiff, Heb. iv., and possess the tranquillity of his conscience with a firm hope of salvation, Rom. viii.

6. Although the commandments of the decalogue contain all the good works that we are obliged to perform, they are not accomplished so perfectly, on account of human infirmity, as that salvation may be hoped for by the observation of these commandments, much less by that of human ordinances. Now, the reasons for which faith ought to be accompanied with works, are: 1°, gratitude towards God; 2°, they give proof of faith; 3°, edification of one's neighbour; 4°, progress in holiness; 5°, recompense both in temporal and eternal life.

7. Wherever this doctrine is taught, the Christian church is there, of which Jesus Christ is the head; and although there are found in the midst of it dead members, whoever, however, holds this confession, and regulates his life by it, belongs to that church, and out of it there is no salvation. The apostolic succession of the ministers of the church, which undoubtedly merits much consideration and respect, is not restricted to certain persons, and to a certain place; but is founded on the purity of the saving doctrine taught in the Holy Scripture, which is confirmed by the authority of St. Jerome, St. Ambrose, *de Pœnit.* book i. chap. 6, and Tertullian in his book *de Præscript.*

8. For fear the visible church should fall into doubts and infidelity, God has given it the holy word and the sacraments, which cannot deceive. The word surpasses the sacraments in excellence, because it ought to precede them.

9. The sacraments are the visible signs of an invisible spiritual grace, and of the participation in the heavenly goods, which they signify; they are two in number,—*Baptism* and *the Supper of the Lord.*

10. *Baptism* is an outward sign of an inward washing away of sin; children can also be initiated into it; on condition, however, that when they have arrived at a more advanced age, they make a public confession of their faith.

[a] Bayle, *Critique générale de l'Histoire du Calvinisme,* by Maimbourg, letter 6.

11. The sacrament of the "Lord's supper, which consists of simple bread and simple wine, without any change, is the sign of the body and blood of Jesus Christ, abiding in heaven, which faith attributes and applies to itself; and without this faith no person can receive the things signified by the sacrament, that is to say, the spiritual and heavenly things which are the body and blood of Christ.

12. The sacrament at the communion-table is only bread and wine, which are a sign of the body and blood of Jesus Christ, who is in heaven, and who is applied to each person by faith; without this faith, no one can receive the reality of the sacrament (rem sacramenti).

13. As the sacrament is only bread and wine, one must be eaten, and the other drunk according to the institution of Jesus Christ; but it is not allowable to offer it for the living and for the dead, nor to enclose it in a shrine, as if it were a God, nor to carry it from place to place, nor to abuse it, contrary to the express prohibition of God, in the first commandment of the law.

14. Although we tolerate ornaments in churches when there is neither scandal nor superstition, and that they are matters of indifference, yet if any one were to attach to them a virtue affecting salvation, it would be necessary to retrench and prohibit them; which particularly regards images, to which, contrary to the command of God, a divine worship is paid; for if, according to Isaiah vi., it is not permitted to adore the dead, much less is it allowed to adore images, which indirectly concerns the invocation of saints.

In the 15th and last article, purgatory was ranked amongst fabulous stories.

The ministers of the church were exhorted to preach with zeal the doctrines exposed in this confession of faith; the magistrates to maintain it, and all Christians to profess it, in order to obtain eternal life, and to avoid eternal condemnation.[*]

NOTE T.

The spirit of charity, peace, and union, which distinguishes the Church of the United Brethren in its intercourse with other churches, is well exemplified in an admirable exhortation, which the venerable Commenius addressed to them about the end of the 17th century, from Holland, where he had taken refuge, and a few extracts of which we give here:—

"Your ancestors were a people penetrated with the fear of God, flying idolatry and superstition, delivered up altogether to heavenly things, and who, seated with Mary at the feet of Jesus, and attentive to his words, forgot every thing in order to listen only to him. Supporting, on account of that, contempt, outrage, and the persecutions of the world, and leaving to God alone the care of defending them, this people had determined not to separate from any member of the Christian society, not to establish or favour any sect, but rather to unite altogether all those who in all places invoke Jesus Christ with a pure heart and serve God in spirit.

"Our duty, dearly beloved, is to cherish all men, to wish good to all, and to aid all as much as lies in our power. As to those who appear to us divided by an unfortunate schism, if we cannot bring them back to union, at least we ought to live in a spirit of concord with them, after the example of our fathers, who preferred to live according to the law, to disputing concerning it. Some persons reproach us with having deviated from the footsteps of our ancestors; with being no longer those to whom Luther gave the hand in token of fraternity; we acknowledge it, and deplore it. It is not, however, as we are accused, because we refuse, like our ancestors, to persecute with hatred such persons as do not recognise the same gospel as ourselves; but it is because the zeal of piety has grown cold amongst us. . . . . . Oh! let us not depart from the example and footsteps of our fathers to such a point as to establish ourselves judges of the knowledge and conscience of others. Let us not meddle in controversies and disputes— I mean such disputes as arise amongst disciples of the gospel, for these things are useless, forbidden, and hurtful.

"Divine wisdom has placed three doors—three most Christian foundations of the Church, which are faith, hope, and charity—these three things are required for salvation and nothing more.

"True Christian philosophy is to receive the revealed word with a simple faith; true religion is to venerate it with a pure heart; piety consists in tending by it to the meditation of celestial life; the victory is to persevere in it; and supreme happiness is to conquer by its means."

Commenius pointed out the inutility and danger of disputes on questions which cannot be solved by man, relative to the person of Christ, election, predestination, and grace; and then he adds—

"For our parts, dearly beloved, let us continue to show by our example to our brethren, the disciples of the same gospel, that evangelical perfection does not consist in depth of explanations, in variety of questions, or in address in treating them; for (as St. Hilary says) it is not by subtle arguments that God calls us to the possession of his heavenly kingdom; but by that holy unity, which suffereth long and is kind; which envieth not; which vaunteth not itself, and is not puffed up with pride; doth not behave itself unseemly, is not easily provoked; thinketh no evil; which beareth all things, believeth all things, hopeth all things, endureth all things.[*]

"It is better to be humbly ignorant of certain things, than to know them vaingloriously; or to believe with timidity, than to affirm with rashness or violence, in this present life, where we only know in part, and prophesy in part.[†]

"Let us, therefore, with all our heart, follow after the things which make for peace, and things wherewith one may edify another;—with them that call on the Lord out of a pure heart.[§]

Luther himself had the confession of faith of the United Brethren, printed at Wittemberg, and in a preface which he joined to it, he accorded

---

* Lenfant, Hist. de la Guerre des Hussites et du Concile de Bâle, vol. ii. book xx.

* 1 Cor. xiii.   † Idem.   ‡ Rom. xiv. 19.
§ 2 Timothy. ii, 22.—Joh. Lusit. de Eccles. discipl. moribusque et institut. Fratr. Bohem. memorab. contin. cum admon. ad reliq. Hist. Eccles. Joh. Commenii.

them this eulogistic testimony. "As long," said he, "as I was a Papist, I felt, through religious zeal, a most violent hatred for the *Brethren.* I recognised early, in truth, that John Huss had explained the Scriptures with so much power and purity that I could not conceive, without an extreme surprise, how the pope and the Council of Constance could have condemned so great and so admirable a man. Yet, I acknowledge, through a blind deference for the pontiff and the council, I abandoned, without hesitation, the perusal of Huss's books, because I distrusted myself; but, at present I have altered my opinion with respect to these men, whom the pope condemned as heretics, and I cannot but regard and admire them as saints and martyrs of the truth. I have found amongst them this fact, extraordinary for the time, that leaving aside the traditions of men, they occupied themselves with meditating, day and night, on the law of the Lord, and that they were exceedingly well acquainted with the Holy Scriptures. Let us, therefore, rejoice with these brethren, that, after having regarded each other as heretics, we have recovered from that unjust opinion, and now find ourselves united in the same fold, under the conduct of the only Shepherd and Bishop of souls."*

* See *Hist. enc. et méd. de l'Eglise des Frères de Boh. et de Morav.* book iv. by Bost.

THE END.

MORSE'S

SCHOOL GEOGRAPHY,

ILLUSTRATED WITH

CEROGRAPHIC MAPS.

AMONG its prominent characteristics are the following:

1. The *Arrangement* is such that the Map, Questions on the Map, and description of each country, are on the same page, or on pages directly opposite, enabling the pupil to refer readily from one to the other, without the inconvenience of two books, or even the necessity of turning the leaf.

2 The *Maps* are *more numerous*, and generally on a *larger scale*, than in any other School Geography.

3. The *Exercises on the Map* are so framed as to present a *connected view* of the great features of each country.

4. The *Descriptions* are in a series of short paragraphs, written in concise style, and confined to the most interesting and characteristic matter.

5. The *correct Pronunciation* of difficult names is indicated by dividing into syllables, accenting, &c.

6. The *General and Comparative views* at the end of the volume are on the plan first introduced by the author in 1820, and since adopted in many other School Geographies. They are regarded as well fitted to exercise and strengthen the judgment

7. The *new art of Cerography* is applied for the first time to the illustration of a work of this kind, and enables the publishers to sell it at a very low price.

The whole work is the result of long and careful study, and is intended to impress upon the mind of the student such outlines of geography as will form the best foundation for farthe and extensive acquisitions.

☞ Confident of the superiority of MORSE'S SCHOOL GEOGRAPHY over every other work of the kind, the publishers respectfully inform editors, teachers, and superintendents of schools, that they may obtain *gratuitously* a copy of the work for examination from the principal booksellers throughout the United States The typography of the work, and its peculiar adaptation to teaching, together with its extreme cheapnes n hardly fail to command for it a general, if not a universal adoption in the schools of our country.

NEW-YORK: HARPER & BROTHERS, 82 CLIFF-STREET

HARPER'S FAMILY LIBRARY,

Now comprising 171 vols. 18mo, abundantly illustrated by Maps, Portraits, and Engravings. Price, neatly and uniformly bound in muslin gilt, $75 70. Each work sold
separately.

Nos. 1, 2, 3.—Milman's History of the Jews

4, 5.—Lockhart's Life of Napoleon Bonaparte.

6.—Southey's Life of Nelson.

7—William's Life of Alexander the Great.

8, 74.—Noctral History of Insects.

9.—Galt's Life of Byron.

10.—Bush's Life of Mohammed.

11.—Scott's Letters on Demonology and Witchcraft

12, 13.—Gleig's History of the Bible:

14.—Discovery and Adventure in the Polar Seas and Regions. By Leslie, Jameson, and Murray.

15.—Croly's Life of George IV.

16.—Discovery and Adventure in Africa. By Jameson, Wilson, and Murray.

17, 18, 19, 66, and 67.—Cunningham's Painters and Sculptors.

20.—James's History of Chivalry and the Crusades.

21, 22.—Bell's Life of Mary Queen of Scots.

23.—Russell's Egypt

24.—Fletcher's History of Poland.

25.—Festivals, Games, and Amusements. By Horace Smith.

26.—Brewster's Life of Sir Isaac Newton.

27.—Russell's History of Palestine.

28.—Memes's Memoirs of the Empress Josephine.

29.—The Court and Camp of Bonaparte.

30.—Lives and Voyages of Drake, Cavendish, and Dampier.

31.—Barrow's Description of Pitcairn's Island, and Account of the Mutiny of the Ship Bounty.

32, 72, 84.—Turner's Sacred History of the World.

33, 34.—Mrs. Jameson's Memoirs of Female Sovereigns.

35, 36.—The Landers' Travels in Africa, and Discovery of the Source and Termination of the Niger.

37.—Abercrombie on the Intellectual Powers.

38, 39, 40.—St. John's Lives of Celebrated Travellers.

41, 42.—Lord Dover's Life of Frederic the Great.

43, 44.—Smedley's Sketches from Venetian History.

45, 46.—Thatcher's Lives of the Indians.

47, 48, 49.—Account of British India. By Murray, Wilson, Greville, Ainslie, Rhind, Jameson, Wallace, and Dalrymple.

50.—Brewster's Letters on Natural Magic.

51, 52.—Taylor's History of Ireland.

53.—Discovery on the more Northern Coasts of America. By P. F. Tytler.

54.—Humboldt's Travels. By Macgillivray.

55, 56.—Euler's Letters on Natural Philosophy Edited by Brewster and Griscom.

7.—Mudie's Popular Guide to the Observation of Nature.

58.—Abercrombie's Philosophy of the Moral Feelings.

59.—Dick on the Improvement of Society by the Diffusion of Knowledge.

60.—James's History of Charlemagne.

61.—Russell's History of Nubia and Abyssinia.

62, 63.—Russell's Life of Oliver Cromwell.

64.—Montgomery's Lectures on Poetry, Literature, &c.

65.—Barrow's Life of Peter the Great.

66, 67.—Lives of Painters and Sculptors, Vols. IV. and V.

68, 69.—Crichton's History of Arabia.

70.—Fraser's History of Persia.

71.—Combe on the Principles of Physiology applied to the Preservation of Health, &c.

72.—Turner's Sacred History of the World, Vol. II.

73.—Russell's History of the Barbary States.

74.—Natural History of Insects, Vol. II.

75, 76.—Paulding's Life of Washington.

77.—Tickner's Philosophy of Living.

78.—Physical Condition of the Earth, and its most remarkable Phenomena. By Higgins.

79.—History of Italy: translated by Greene.

80, 81.—The Chinese. By Davis.

82.—History of the Circumnavigation of the Globe.

83.—Dick's Celestial Scenery.

84.—Turner's Sacred History of the World, Vol. III.

85.—Griscom's Animal Mechanism and Physiology.

86, 87, 88, 89, 90, 91.—Tytler's Universal History: continued by Dr. Nares.

92, 93.—Life of Franklin, by Himself; and a Selection from his Writings.

94, 95.—Pursuit of Knowledge under Difficulties—its Pleasures and Rewards.

96, 97.—Paley's Natural Theology: edited by Brougham, Bell, and Potter.

98.—Natural History of Birds.

99.—Dick's Sidereal Heavens.

100.—Upham on Imperfect and Disordered Mental Action.

101, 102.—Murray's History of British America.

103.—Lessing's History of the Fine Arts.

104.—Natural History of Quadrupeds.

105.—Life and Travels of Mungo Park.

106.—Dana's Two Years before the Mast.

107, 108.—Parry's Four Voyages for the Discovery of a Northwest Passage.

109, 110.—Life of Doctor Johnson; with a Selection from his Works.

111.—Bryant's Selection from American Poets

112, 113.—Halleck's Selection from British Poets.

114, 115, 116, 117, 118.—Keightley's History of England.

119, 120.—Hale's History of the United States

121, 122.—Irving's Life of Goldsmith, and Selection from his Writings.

123, 124.—Distinguished Men of Modern Times.

125.—Renwick's Life of De Witt Clinton.

126, 127.—Mackenzie's Life of Commodore Parry.

128.—Life and Travels of Bruce: by Sir Francis B. Head.

129.—Renwick's Lives of John Jay and Alexander Hamilton.

130.—Brewster's Lives of Galileo, Tycho Brahe, and Kepler.

131.—History of Iceland, Greenland, and the Faroe Islands.

132.—Manners and Customs of the Japanese.

133.—Dwight's History of Connecticut.

134, 135.—Ruins of Ancient Cities: by Charles Bucke.

136, 137.—History of Denmark, Norway, and Sweden; by Crichton and Wheaton.

138.—Camp on Democracy.

139.—Lanman's Michigan.

140.—Fenelon's Lives of the Ancient Philosophers.

141, 142.—Count Segur's History of Napoleon's Expedition to Russia.

143, 144.—History of Philosophy, translated, continued, and edited by Rev. Dr. Henry.

145.—Bucke's Beauties, Harmonies, and Sublimities of Nature.

146.—Lieber's Essays on Property and Labour, as connected with Natural Law and the Constitution of Society.

147.—White's Natural History of Selborne.

148.—Wrangell's Expedition to Siberia and the Polar Sea.

149, 150.—Popular Technology; or Professions and Trades. By Hazen.

151, 152, 153.—Italy and the Italian Islands. By Spalding.

154, 155.—Lewis and Clarke's Travels West of the Mississippi.

156.—Smith's History of Education.

157.—Mesopotamia and Assyria. By Fraser.

158.—Russell's History of Polynesia; or, the South Sea Islands.

159.—Perilous Adventures; or, Remarkable Instances of Courage, Perseverance, and Suffering.

160.—Constitutional Jurisprudence of the United States. By Dr. Duer.

161, 162, 163.—Belknap's American Biography; edited, with Notes, by F. M. Hubbard.

164.—Natural History of the Elephant.

165.—Potter's Hand-book for Readers and Students.

166.—Woman in America: her Moral and Intellectual Condition.

167, 168.—Border Wars of the Revolution, embracing the Life of Brant. By W. L. Stone.

169.—Vegetable Substances used for Food.

170.—Michelet's Elements of Modern History: edited by Rev. Dr. Potter.

171.—Bacon's Essays, and Locke on the Understanding.

AMERICAN LITERATURE

RECENTLY PUBLISHED BY HARPER & BROTHERS.

CLARK'S ALGEBRA. Elements of Algebra: embracing also the Theory and Application of Logarithms; together with an Appendix, containing Infinite Series, the General Theory of Equations, and the most approved Methods of resolving the higher Equations. By Rev. DAVIS W. CLARK. 8vo. $1 00.

PROUDFIT'S PLAUTUS. The Captives, a Comedy of Plautus. With English Notes, for the Use of Students. By JOHN PROUDFIT, D.D. 18mo. 38 cents.

MATHEWS' WORKS. The various Writings of Cornelius Mathews, embracing The Motley Book, Behemoth, The Politicans, Poems on Man in the Republic, Wakondah, Puffer Hopkins, Miscellanies, Selections from Arcturus, International Copyright. Complete in one volume. 8vo. $1 00.

BENNET'S BOOK-KEEPING. The American System of Practical Book-keeping: for Schools, Academies, and Counting-houses. By JAMES A. BENNET, LL.D. 8vo. $1 50.

SCHMUCKER'S PSYCHOLOGY. Psychology; or, Elements of a new System of Mental Philosophy, on the Basis of Consciousness and Common Sense. Designed for Colleges and Academies. By S. S. SCHMUCKER, D.D., S.T.P. 12mo. $1 00.

UPHAM'S MENTAL PHILOSOPHY. Elements of Mental Philosophy: embracing the two Departments of the Intellect and the Sensibilities. By Professor THOMAS C. UPHAM. 2 vols. 12mo. Sheep extra. $2 50.

UPHAM'S ABRIDGMENT. Elements of Mental Philosophy, abridged and designed as a Text-book in Academies, &c. By T. C. UPHAM 12mo. Sheep extra. $1 25.

UPHAM ON THE WILL. A Philosophical and Practical Treatise on the Will. By T. C. UPHAM. 12mo. Sheep Extra. $1 25.

UPHAM ON DISORDERED MENTAL ACTION. Outlines of Imperfect and Disordered Mental Action. By T. C. UPHAM. 18mo. 45 cents.

SUMMERFIELD'S SERMONS. Sermons and Sketches of Sermons by the Rev. JOHN SUMMERFIELD, A.M., late a Preacher in Connexion with the Methodist Episcopal Church. With an Introduction by the Rev. THOMAS E. BOND, M.D. 8vo. $1 75.

FRENCH GRAMMAR. A New System of French Grammar, containing the First Part of the celebrated Grammar of Noël and Chapsal. Arranged with Questions, and a Key in English, &c., &c. By SARAH E. SEAMAN. Revised and corrected by C. P. BORDENAVE, Professor of Languages. 12mo. 75 cents.

ENGINEERS' AND MECHANICS' POCKET-BOOK. By C. H. HASWELL, Chief-engineer U. S. Navy. 12mo.

ANTHON'S VIRGIL. The Æneïd of Virgil, with English Notes, Critical and Explanatory, a Metrical Clavis, and an Historical, Geographical, and Mythological Index. By CHARLES ANTHON, LL.D. 12mo. Portrait and many Illustrations. $2 00.

MICHELET'S MODERN HISTORY. Elements of Modern History. From the French of Michelet. With an Introduction, Notes &c., by Rev. Dr. POTTER. 45 cents.

POTTER'S HAND-BOOK. Hand-book for Readers and Students, intended to assist Private Individuals, Associations, School Districts, &c., in the selection of useful and interesting works for Reading and Investigation. By A. POTTER, D.D. 45 cents.

MALAN'S INQUIRY. Can I join the Church of Rome while my Rule of Faith is the Bible? An Inquiry presented to the Conscience of the Christian Reader. By the Rev. CÆSAR MALAN, D.D. 8vo.

RELIGION IN AMERICA; including a View of the various Religious Denominations in the United States, &c., &c. By Rev. Dr. BAIRD. 75 cents.

DEFENCE OF THE WHIGS. By a Member of the 27th Congress. 18mo. 25 cents.

STEPHENS'S TRAVELS in Yucatan.—Central America, Chiapas, and Yucatan.—Egypt, Arabia Petræa, and the Holy Land.—Greece, Turkey, Russia, and Poland. By JOHN L. STEPHENS.

THE SCHOOL AND THE SCHOOLMASTER. By A. POTTER, D.D., and by GEORGE B. EMERSON, A.M. With Engravings. 12mo.

THE LIFE OF JAMES ARMINIUS, D.D., formerly Professor of Divinity in the University of Leyden. Compiled from his Life and Writings, as published by Mr. JAMES NICHOLS. By NATHAN BANGS, D.D. 18mo. 50 cents.

SWEETHEARTS AND WIVES; or, Before and After Marriage. By T. S. ARTHUR. 18mo. 38 cents.

HISTORY OF THE CONQUEST OF MEXICO, with a Preliminary View of the Ancient Mexican Civilization, and the Life of the Conqueror, Hernando Cortés. By WILLIAM H. PRESCOTT. 3 vols. 8vo. Engravings. $6 00.

NARRATIVE OF THE TEXAN SANTA FE EXPEDITION. By GEORGE W. KENDALL. 2 vols. 12mo. With Plates.

THE HEART delineated in its State by Nature, and as renewed by Grace. By Rev. HUGH SMITH, D.D. 18mo.

☞ *In addition to the above, H. & B. have recently published several hundred volumes by American Authors —for which see their Catalogue.*

STANDARD HISTORIES

PUBLISHED BY HARPER & BROTHERS, NEW-YORK

ALISON'S HISTORY OF EUROPE.—History of Europe from the Commencement of the French Revolution in 1789 to the Present Time. By Archibald Alison, F.R.S.E. In 4 volumes 8vo. [Now publishing in sixteen numbers, at 25 cents each, at retail.]

MOSHEIM'S ECCLESIASTICAL HISTORY.—Mosheim's Institutes of Ecclesiastical History, Ancient and Modern. A new and literal Translation from the original Latin, with copious Additional Notes, original and selected. By James Murdock, D.D. 3 vols. 8vo. Sheep extra. $7 50.

GIBBON'S ROME.—Gibbon's History of the Decline and Fall of the Roman Empire. New Edition, with Notes, by Rev. H. H. Milman and M. Guizot. In 4 vols. 8vo, with Maps and Engravings. Sheep extra. $6 00.

RUSSELL'S MODERN EUROPE. —History of Modern Europe: with a View of the Progress of Society, from the Rise of the modern Kingdoms to the Peace of Paris in 1763. By William Russell, LL.D. With a Continuation of the History, by William Jones, Esq. 3 vols. 8vo. Engravings. Sheep extra. $5 00.

ROBERTSON'S WORKS. — The Historical Works of William Robertson, D.D. 3 vols. 8vo. Maps and Engravings. Sheep extra. $5 00.

ROBERTSON'S AMERICA.—History of the Discovery and Settlement of America. By William Robertson, D.D. With an Account of his Life and Writings. To which are added, Questions for the Examination of Students. By John Frost, A.M. 8vo. Portrait and Engravings. Sheep extra. $1 75.

ROBERTSON'S CHARLES V.—History of the Reign of the Emperor Charles V.; with a View of the Progress of Society in Europe, from the Subversion of the Roman Empire to the Beginning of the Sixteenth Century. By William Robertson, D.D. To which are added, Questions for the Examination of Students. By John Frost, A.M. 8vo. Engravings. Sheep extra. $1 75.

GRATTAN'S NETHERLANDS. — History of the Netherlands to the Revolution of 1830. By T. C. Grattan. 12mo. 60 cents.

SPAIN AND PORTUGAL.—History of Spain and Portugal. By S. A. Dunham, LL.D. 5 vols. 12mo. $2 50.

ROLLIN'S ANCIENT HISTORY. —The Ancient History of the Egyptians, Carthaginians, Assyrians, Babylonians, Medes and Persians, Grecians, and Macedonians; including the History of the Arts and Sciences of the Ancients. By Charles Rollin. With a Life of the Author, by James Bell. Only complete American Edition. 8vo. Maps and Engravings. Sheep extra, bound in one volume. $3 50. Bound in two volumes. $3 75.

HALLAM'S MIDDLE AGES.— View of the State of Europe during the Middle Ages. By Henry Hallam. 8vo. Sheep extra. $2 00.

HALLAM'S LITERATURE OF EUROPE.—Introduction to the Literature of Europe, during the Fifteenth, Sixteenth, and Seventeenth Centuries. By Henry Hallam. 2 vols. 8vo. Sheep extra. $3 75.

PRIDEAUX'S CONNECTION.— The Old and New Testaments connected, in the History of the Jews and neighbouring Nations, from the Declension of the Kingdoms of Judah and Israel to the Time of Christ. By Humphrey Prideaux, D.D. 2 vols. 8vo. Maps and Engravings. Sheep extra. $3 75.

MILMAN'S CHRISTIANITY.— The History of Christianity, from the Birth of Christ to the Abolition of Paganism in the Roman Empire. By the Rev. H. H. Milman. With Notes, &c., by James Murdock, D.D. 8vo. $1 90.

WADDINGTON'S CHURCH HISTORY.—A History of the Church, from the Earliest Ages to the Reformation. By Rev. George Waddington, M.A. 8vo. $1 75.

HAWKS'S PROTESTANT EPISCOPAL CHURCH IN VIRGINIA.—A Narrative of Events connected with the Rise and Progress of the Protestant Episcopal Church in Virginia. To which is added, the Journals of the Conventions in Virginia. By F. L. Hawks, D.D. 8vo. $1 75.

SCOTT'S SCOTLAND.—History of Scotland. By Sir Walter Scott. 2 vols. 12mo. $1 20.

DUNLAP'S AMERICAN THEATRE.—History of the American Theatre. By William Dunlap. 8vo. $1 75.

CROWE'S FRANCE.—History of France. By E. E. Crowe. 3 vols. 12mo. $1 75.

ROBERTSON'S SCOTLAND and INDIA.—History of Scotland, during the Reigns of Queen Mary and of King James VI. till his Accession to the Crown of England. With a Review of the Scottish History previous to that Period. Included in the same Volume is a Disquisition concerning Ancient India. By William Robertson, D.D. 8vo. Sheep extra. $1 75.

ITALIAN REPUBLICS.—History of the Italian Republics. By J. C. L. de Sismondi. 12mo. 60 cts.

MACKINTOSH'S ENGLAND.— History of England to the Seventeenth Century. By Sir James Mackintosh. 3 vols. 12mo. $1 50.

SWITZERLAND.—History of Switzerland. From the Cabinet Cyclopædia. 12mo. 60 cents.

VERPLANCK'S DISCOURSES. —Discourses and Addresses on Subjects of American History, Arts, and Antiquities. By Gulian C. Verplanck. 12mo. 60 cents.

HOWITT'S PRIESTCRAFT.— History of Priestcraft in all Ages and Countries. By William Howitt. 12mo. 50 cents.

MILLER'S GREECE.—The Condition of Greece. By Col. J. P. Miller. 12mo. 25 cents.

BULWER'S ATHENS.—Athens, its Rise and Fall. With Views of the Literature, Philosophy, and Social Life of the Athenian People. By Sir E. L. Bulwer. 2 vols. 12mo. $1 20.

THE BIBLE.—History of the Bible. By Rev. G. R. Gleig. 2 vols. 18mo. Map. [Family Library, Nos. 12 and 13.] 80 cents.

CHIVALRY.—History of Chivalry and the Crusades. By G. P. R. James, Esq. 18mo. Engravings. [Family Library, No. 20.] 45 cts.

THE JEWS.—History of the Jews. By Rev. H. H. Milman. 3 vols. 18mo. With Maps and Engravings. [Family Library, Nos. 1, 2, and 3.] $1 20.

EGYPT.—View of Ancient and Modern Egypt. By the Rev. M. Russell, LL.D. 18mo. Engravings. [Family Library, No. 23.] 45 cts.

POLAND.—History of Poland. By James Fletcher, Esq. 18mo. Portrait of Kosciusko. [Family Library, No. 24.] 45 cents.

FESTIVALS, &c.—Festivals, Games, and Amusements, Ancient and Modern. By Horatio Smith, Esq. With Additions, by Samuel Woodworth, Esq., of New-York. 18mo. Engravings. [Family Library, No. 25.] 45 cents.

PALESTINE.—Palestine, or the Holy Land. By Rev. M. Russell, LL.D. 18mo. With Engravings. [Family Library, No. 27.] 45 cts.

TURNER'S SACRED HISTORY —Sacred History of the World Attempted to be philosophically considered. By Sharon Turner. 3 vols. 18mo. [Family Library, Nos. 32, 72, and 84.] $1 35.

VENETIAN HISTORY. —Sketches from Venetian History. By Rev. Edward Smedley, M.A. 2 vols. 18mo. Engravings. [Family Library, Nos. 43 and 44.] 90 cts.

BRITISH INDIA.—Historical and Descriptive Account of British India. By Hugh Murray, James Wilson, R. K. Greville, LL.D., Whitelaw Ainslie, M.D., William Rhind, Professor Jameson, Professor Wallace, and Capt. Clarence Dalrymple. 3 vols. 18mo. Engravings. [Family Library, Nos. 47, 48, and 49.] $1 35.

IRELAND. — History of Ireland, from the Anglo-Norman Invasion to the Union of the Country with Great Britain. By W. C. Taylor. With Additions, by William Sampson, Esq. 2 vols. 18mo. [Family Library, Nos. 51 and 52.] 90 cents.

NORTHERN COASTS OF AMERICA.—Historical View of the Progress of Discovery on the more Northern Coasts of America. By P. F. Tytler, Esq. 18mo. Map, &c. [Family Library, No. 53.] 45 cents.

NUBIA AND ABYSSINIA.—Nubia and Abyssinia: comprehending their Civil History, Antiquities, Arts, Religion, Literature, and Natural History. By the Rev. Michael Russell, LL.D. 18mo. Map and Engravings. [Family Library, No. 51.] 45 cents.